IOWA—Spaces, Places, Faces
an entertaining ride through all 99 counties

Text, photos, illustrations and graphic design by
Carson Ode
Copy editing and production art by
Connie Ode
Published by
Ode Design
2009

Printed in China by
Oceanic Graphic Printing, Inc.

IOWA—spaces, places, faces

Ode Design, publisher
2706 Glenwood Drive
Des Moines, Iowa 50321 USA

Second Edition of 4,000 clothbound copies
Copyright © Carson Ode 2009

Printed in China by
Oceanic Graphic Printing, Inc.
ISBN 978-0-615-27881-0
Library of Congress Number 2009901400

This book is dedicated to the community leaders across Iowa who love their towns and work to keep them vibrant. And to the volunteers who willingly work together selflessly and with great achievement to enhance the quality of life in this beautiful state.

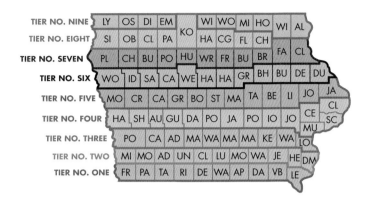

TABLE OF CONTENTS

TIER NO. ONE . . . . Page 1
Counties: Lee, Van Buren, Davis, Appanoose, Wayne, Decatur, Ringgold, Taylor, Page, Fremont

TIER NO. TWO . . . . Page 31
Counties: Mills, Montgomery, Adams, Union, Clarke, Lucas, Monroe, Wapello, Jefferson, Henry, Des Moines

TIER NO. THREE . . . . Page 65
Counties: Louisa, Washington, Keokuk, Mahaska, Marion, Warren, Madison, Adair, Cass, Pottawattamie

TIER NO. FOUR . . . . Page 103
Counties: Harrison, Shelby, Audubon, Guthrie, Dallas, Polk, Jasper, Poweshiek, Iowa, Johnson, Muscatine, Cedar, Scott, Clinton

TIER NO. FIVE . . . . Page 165
Counties: Jackson, Jones, Linn, Benton, Tama, Marshall, Story, Boone, Greene, Carroll, Crawford, Monona

TIER NO. SIX . . . . Page 215
Counties: Woodbury, Ida, Sac, Calhoun, Webster, Hamilton, Hardin, Grundy, Black Hawk, Buchanan, Delaware, Dubuque

TIER NO. SEVEN . . . . Page 273
Counties: Clayton, Fayette, Bremer, Butler, Franklin, Wright, Humboldt, Pocahontas, Buena Vista, Cherokee, Plymouth

TIER NO. EIGHT . . . . Page 321
Counties: Sioux, O'Brien, Clay, Palo Alto, Kossuth, Hancock, Cerro Gordo, Floyd, Chickasaw

TIER NO. NINE . . . . Page 361
Counties: Allamakee, Winneshiek, Howard, Mitchell, Worth, Winnebago, Emmet, Dickinson, Osceola, Lyon

Arrowheads
barn quilt

FOREWORD

I love Iowa. My wife Connie and our five children and their spouses share this sentiment. Three of our offspring live in Des Moines and all five of our grandchildren are metro residents. We have a daughter and son-in-law in Portland, Oregon, and a son and daughter-in-law in Golden, Colorado. Why do we all take pride in living in or being from Iowa? I have written this book and illustrated it with 1,400-plus photos to express my point of view. The book is admittedly positive; we made no effort to search out negatives nor did we engage in whitewashing. There was plenty of wonderful material to report.

Connie and I spent the year of 2008 visiting every county in the state. Our typical schedule was to leave Des Moines early on each Thursday morning and cover three counties over a two-day period. Thursday night we stayed at a B&B or locally owned motel/hotel in the middle county. We also ate all our meals at locally owned restaurants. We have no quarrel with franchises, but this book is about Iowa. We started in Lee County (southeast corner) in the middle of January and crisscrossed the state, visiting counties tier-by-tier, finishing in Lyon County (northwest corner) in mid-December.

In every county, we stopped at the county seat library for some early history research and at the chamber of commerce to learn of the attractions the town/county likes to promote. We also made efforts to interview people along the way. We sought out people from all walks of life and their stories are woven into the fabric of the state's history, events, natural attributes, man-made attractions and weather. It is a piece of art that I am expressing with whatever talent and experience I have. I wrote the book, took the pictures, rendered the illustrations and did the graphic design. That being said, I would not have considered taking on the project without the help of my wife Connie. Her scientific mind complements my art-oriented psyche; she is my teammate in taking on life's challenges. She made every trip with me, taking notes, navigating and providing stimulating conversation. Back home, she typed and copy edited my handwritten text, compiled the bibliography and kept track of our expenses. I love her even more than I love Iowa.

Avoiding redundancy wasn't difficult—there was something special about every county. All across the state, towns take pride in their schools and recreational facilities. New or expanded libraries are common and wellness centers with indoor pools, gyms, weight rooms and cardiovascular training machines were springing up everywhere—even in towns of only 3,000 people. When I wrote about a few of these gems, I intended it to be representative of the state's other towns. There was one area, however, where redundancy came into play. I would wrap interviews by asking for a quote on why the interviewee loved Iowa. Various versions of "It's the people," would generally be part of the answer.

The people are also part of my "I love Iowa" attitude. I find it a sane, comfortable environment with more quality things to do than I have time to pursue. I have to be careful here not to engage in boosterism—that is not the Iowa way. It is not my intention to claim superiority to other states. On the other hand, I'm not about to tolerate anyone's condescending attitude toward Iowa.

For those who are interested in statistics, we drove 15,000 miles exploring the state. We spent approximately $3,000 on lodging (33 nights) and $3,000 on food (66 days).

Enough introduction! Turn the page and begin the ride with us. There is a continuous narrative that flows from county to county with photos to help visualize the setting. You can open the book to any page and the graphics will tell you very quickly where you are in the state. I hope you enjoy the read as much as we enjoyed the trip. Iowa is a spectacularly beautiful state.

RITZ

KEOKUK PLANT

Peggy Sue's

Tier 1

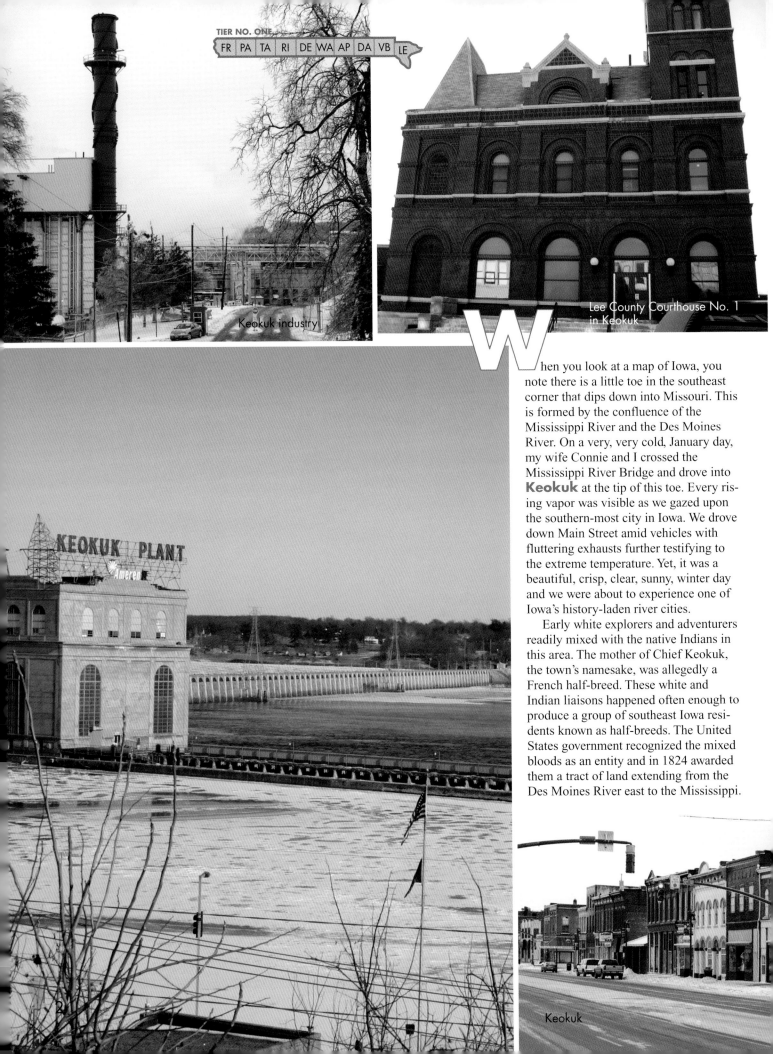

Keokuk industry

Lee County Courthouse No. 1 in Keokuk

W

hen you look at a map of Iowa, you note there is a little toe in the southeast corner that dips down into Missouri. This is formed by the confluence of the Mississippi River and the Des Moines River. On a very, very cold, January day, my wife Connie and I crossed the Mississippi River Bridge and drove into **Keokuk** at the tip of this toe. Every rising vapor was visible as we gazed upon the southern-most city in Iowa. We drove down Main Street amid vehicles with fluttering exhausts further testifying to the extreme temperature. Yet, it was a beautiful, crisp, clear, sunny, winter day and we were about to experience one of Iowa's history-laden river cities.

Early white explorers and adventurers readily mixed with the native Indians in this area. The mother of Chief Keokuk, the town's namesake, was allegedly a French half-breed. These white and Indian liaisons happened often enough to produce a group of southeast Iowa residents known as half-breeds. The United States government recognized the mixed bloods as an entity and in 1824 awarded them a tract of land extending from the Des Moines River east to the Mississippi.

KEOKUK PLANT

Ameren

Keokuk

Lee County Courthouse No. 2 in Fort Madison

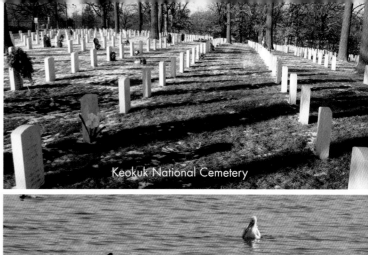
Keokuk National Cemetery

A pelican rules on the Mississippi

This, of course, became moot in 1834 when waves of whites crossed the river looking for land to settle. There was cheating and sharking by both half-breeds and whites but the whites came out the winners. They were Iowa's earliest settlers of European descent.

Keokuk scarcely grew until 1840 but by 1854 the population was approaching 5,000 and today it has more than doubled to about 12,000. The manufacturing of products from cornstarch to hog rings is the mainstay of employment for the present population.

Prior to 1910, there was a rapids in the Mississippi just above Keokuk. It was the end of the line for river traffic. The construction of U.S. Lock and Dam #19 changed that scenario. This structure, still impressive today, was completed in 1913 and, at the time, its electricity-generating plant was the largest in the world.

Keokuk played a vital role in caring for Civil War wounded. Boatloads were brought up the big river to be treated in seven military hospitals. Many soldiers died at the hospitals and were buried in what became the first national cemetery west of the Mississippi.

Samuel Clemens (Mark Twain) made his way upriver from Hannibal, Missouri, to visit his brother who had married a Keokuk girl and adopted Keokuk as his hometown. His brother offered him board and five dollars a week to encourage him to stay. Sam took him up on it and stayed for two years. His first published writings entitled "The Snodgrass Letters" were produced during this time for *The Keokuk Post*. The writing of the *1857 Keokuk City Directory* was also his early work.

Howard Hughes' grandfather, Felix Turner Hughes, was a prominent Keokuk businessman and civic leader. Howard, the son of one of his three super-achieving children, made frequent visits to his grandparents and spent enough time in the city to build a couple of houses.

The biggest stock car racing venues are in the South, but no city of any size in the country can claim more quality race-car drivers than Keokuk. They include Ernie Derry who won 12 national championships and had approximately 350 first place finishes; Don White who was USAC stock car champion in 1954, 1955 and 1958; Ramo Stott who is a former ARCA and USAC stock car champion;

and Dick Hutcherson who won the IMC driving title in 1963 and 1964 and finished runner-up to Richard Petty in nine NASCAR races.

Turn-of-the-century architecture dominates Main Street and the stately homes on Grand Avenue that overlook the river. Most of the houses have been preserved or are in the process of being restored. There seems to be a determination to maintain the city's proud heritage while living in the twenty-first century.

Amenities include the best-tasting water in Iowa, a community college, a performing arts center, golf courses and a park system with disc golf, tennis, basketball, softball and baseball. Celebrations such as the "Rollin' on the River" blues festival are great fun. And, of course, there is the river.

On the road again, we drove upriver to **Fort Madison**. On the way we looked across the wide expanse of water and saw the Mormon Temple in Nauvoo dominating a hill overlooking the river. Had the locals been more tolerant of the Mormon life-style, we might be hearing the voices of the Tabernacle Choir in the river valley today. In the past Mormons lived in **Lee**

Keokuk bridges

Fort Madison

Fort Madison Museum

St. Mary's Catholic Church and Calvary Cemetery, West Point

County and after their move to Utah, **Keokuk** was a staging area for its immigrants from Europe.

As we approached **Fort Madison**, Highway 61 made a sweeping curve so that we were traveling east when we hit the city limits. The city is located on a stretch of the Mississippi that runs east to west. This sometimes confuses waterfowl that are following the river on their migration south. When they come to the east/west stretch they can't make the adjustment and get lost.

We made the adjustment and followed the highway east to the downtown business district. **Fort Madison** is approximately the same size as Keokuk, settled at about the same time and retains the same basic river town character. It embraces the river with parallel east/west streets and cross streets that take you to the river's edge. Barges ply the river channels and, in the foreground, trains rumble by on a Burlington Northern and Santa Fe mainline. Amtrak's Southwest Chief makes a station stop after crossing the Mississippi. The crossing structure is the last remaining, double swing-span bridge (cars on top level) on the

4

Kingsley Inn and Alpha's restaurant

Fort Madison replica

Mississippi. I love these river towns.

In 1808, Lt. Alpha Kingsley and men of the First U.S. Infantry were sent upriver from St. Louis with orders to build a trading establishment near the mouth of the Des Moines River. They chose to go a little further north and by April of the following year a stockade was completed. Kingsley called his post **Fort Madison** after President James Madison. The fort didn't last long. It was subject to constant siege by the Indians. In 1813, the soldiers burned it and they returned to Fort Belle Fontaine just north of St. Louis. A replica of the fort was built on the riverfront in 1983 and it serves as an interactive museum. Across the tracks and Highway 61 is an elegant, lovingly-restored B&B named The Kingsley Inn and an adjacent restaurant named Alpha's.

Around Iowa, **Fort Madison** is a euphemism for Iowa's maximum-security prison for men. In 1839, citizens of Fort Madison donated ten acres of land to the Iowa Territory. Three years later a limestone-walled prison of 138 cells was completed. The original cell house is still in use today. It is part of a hodge-podge group of structures where Iowa's most

dangerous criminals are incarcerated. For years there has been talk in the halls of Iowa government about replacing this inadequate complex with a completely new prison. So far the will to appropriate the money has not been there.

Fort Madison is the county seat of Lee County. Keokuk is the county seat of Lee County. Neither one is centrally located geographically. It was a long buggy-ride for the early residents of western Lee County to either courthouse. But the folks in Keokuk didn't have to go to Fort Madison and vice versa. Go figure.

Fortunately, we had a comfortable car as we drove to the western reaches of the county. On the way we stopped in **West Point** to view and take photos of St. Mary's Catholic Church and Calvary Cemetery. A parsonage and school were across the street from the church. Generations of Catholics built this impressive church and complex and the present generation appears to be taking good care of it. The town of about 1,000 people was also in good repair.

The rural landscape of **Lee County** is rolling prairie farmland with patches of wooded areas. The prosperity of the

farms appeared to be mixed. During the late afternoon, school buses were pulling off gravel roads leaving dust tails behind them. Shortly thereafter, we came upon a consolidated school that is a lonely island on the prairie. If one town can't have the school, the other one can't either.

Donnellson was the last town in **Lee County** through which we passed. It is another 1,000-population town that is hanging in there. Northeast of town is the oldest Mennonite settlement west of the Great River. We will see more Amish and Mennonites as we drive west.

We were on a designated scenic highway as we entered **Van Buren County** and it soon lived up to its name as we approached the Shimek State Forest. The hilly, winding road was lined with pines and a variety of other trees including hardwoods. After a few miles, a clearing revealed a well-stocked, quarter horse ranch with a couple of young people taking a ride. These were serious horse people braving a temperature that was closing in on zero.

We continued on a few more miles before we descended into the valley of the Des Moines River. During the descent

Fort Madison

Fort Madison

SANTA FE 2913

5

Mason House Inn and Innkeepers Chuck and Joy

Mason House Inn

Tony shows Connie his arrowheads

we were greeted with a sign that welcomed us to the Villages of **Van Buren County**. The Villages are historic little towns in varying degrees of restoration.

The sun was setting as we crossed the Des Moines River and drove down **Bonaparte's** main street, a national historic riverfront district. It is home to several specialty, gift and antique stores. Also along the river there are three, large brick buildings that give testimony to a thriving industrial era in the 1800s when there was a pants factory, gristmill and a woolen mill. Antiques and a restaurant named Bonaparte's Retreat are now housed in two of the buildings. Across the street is the Bonaparte Inn—another large, brick building that has been converted to a unique B&B.

Leaving **Bonaparte** we drove a few miles upriver to **Bentonsport** and checked into the Mason House Inn for an overnight stay. In 1846, Mormon craftsmen built this structure as an inn. People have been staying at this inn for 162 years, interrupted only by an occasional, major flood. History permeates the walls and some folks say it is haunted. We found a homey, clean B&B with a queen-

Historic, one-lane, iron bridge over Des Moines River, Bentonsport

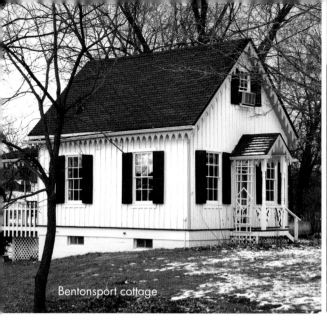
Bentonsport cottage

Bonaparte mill

size bed and modern bathroom. The floor sloped in different directions as we walked across the room reminding us of the age of the structure. I questioned the chamber pots in two corners of the room. However, I learned they were probably used as late as the 1970s because the first indoor plumbing wasn't installed until 1980. The attraction to modern man before 1980 was to experience a rustic stay at an old inn with kerosene lamps and an outdoor privy.

After freshening up we drove back to Bonaparte's Retreat for dinner. The restaurant took up the main floor of the aforementioned gristmill. The walls were exposed bricks and the ceiling was exposed beams and floor planks. The furnishings and wall decor were of a compatible rustic character. The lighting was just right. It was subdued enough to let the candles show their warmth but light enough so you could see clearly across the room. The food was good.

Back at the Inn we went to bed early and got up early. Innkeepers Chuck and Joy Hanson made a delicious soufflé for breakfast and, at our urging, regaled us with **Bentonsport** stories. We learned

it was platted in 1839 and went through several boom/bust cycles with peak population of about 1,500 to its present population of 40. It was a town of tolerance during a period of history when tolerance was not in vogue. Mormons who were rejected by some communities were welcome here. Slave owners were not welcome unless they freed their slaves. One freed slave who gave himself the name Freeman became a successful member of the community. It was a major stop on the Underground Railroad. Men fought for the Union during the Civil War and women worked in local bandage and blanket factories.

Today, it must have more artists and artisans per capita than any other town in the country. There is a stained glass artist, an artistic ironworker, a watercolor painter and a couple of potters including one who produces Queen Anne's Lace pottery. Then there is Tony Sanders, my favorite **Bentonsport** character. Tony has been collecting arrowheads since he was eight years old and I'm going to guess he is about 60 now. He displays 4,000 of them in a museum with elaborate, inlaid wood display cases and tables.

The inlaid theme continues on the paneled walls and ceiling. It is all native wood and he did all the work himself. The tops of the walls are lined with shed deer antlers he has found in the woods. He eats only what he can grow or kill with the exception of eggs and milk. A garden and fruit trees surround his house. If he sees any critters disturbing his garden, they become part of his next meal. When the **Bentonsport** community has a potluck, Tony's friends give his contribution a wary look. They are afraid to ask about ingredients. Whatever they are, Tony seasons them so that the end result has a pleasing taste.

The next stop was **Keosauqua**, the county seat of **Van Buren County** and home to the oldest Iowa courthouse that has remained in continuous use. Its location on a bend in the Des Moines River inspired its Indian name, which means "big bend." A notable landmark is the Hotel Manning, a three-story hotel with a second-story balcony completely surrounding the structure. It dates back to the short-lived steamboat days. It is presently a B&B with 16 antique-furnished rooms plus a three-bedroom suite.

Bentonsport

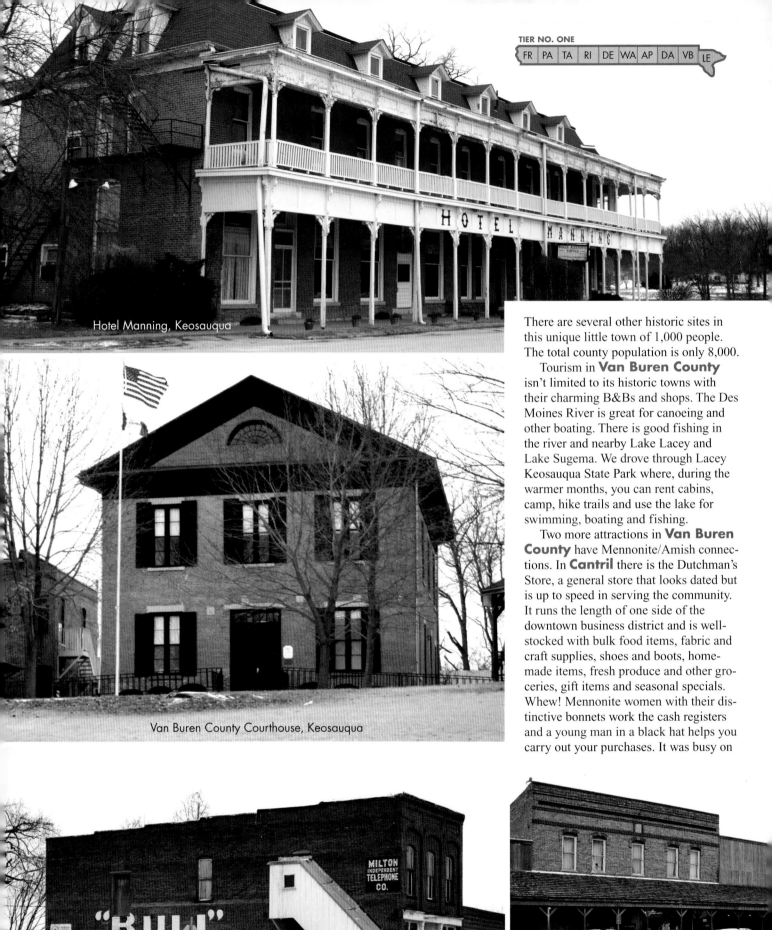

Hotel Manning, Keosauqua

Van Buren County Courthouse, Keosauqua

There are several other historic sites in this unique little town of 1,000 people. The total county population is only 8,000.

Tourism in **Van Buren County** isn't limited to its historic towns with their charming B&Bs and shops. The Des Moines River is great for canoeing and other boating. There is good fishing in the river and nearby Lake Lacey and Lake Sugema. We drove through Lacey Keosauqua State Park where, during the warmer months, you can rent cabins, camp, hike trails and use the lake for swimming, boating and fishing.

Two more attractions in **Van Buren County** have Mennonite/Amish connections. In **Cantril** there is the Dutchman's Store, a general store that looks dated but is up to speed in serving the community. It runs the length of one side of the downtown business district and is well-stocked with bulk food items, fabric and craft supplies, shoes and boots, homemade items, fresh produce and other groceries, gift items and seasonal specials. Whew! Mennonite women with their distinctive bonnets work the cash registers and a young man in a black hat helps you carry out your purchases. It was busy on

Milton

Dutchman's Store, Cantril

8

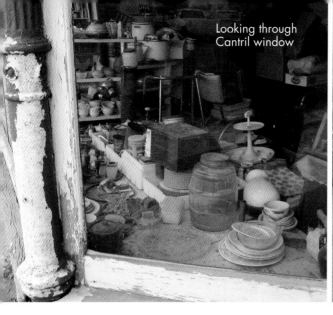
Looking through Cantril window

Dutchman's Store, Cantril

a Friday morning with its customer base of local Amish and Mennonites and tourist gawkers like us.

The second attraction is a Mennonite cheese factory known as the Milton Creamery. The products' purity begins with Amish cows grazing in season on lush pastureland where crop rotation and other traditional farming methods are used. This pure source of milk is the first step in a high-quality, cheese-making process. The brand name is Prairie Delight. It is sold on the premises and at an increasing number of specialty stores.

Immediately upon leaving **Milton**, we entered **Davis County**. It is also a sparsely populated county with 8,500 people. The terrain is hilly with the highway winding in and out of forested areas and farm fields. Iowa's famous, black topsoil doesn't reach this far south. Farming is a viable enterprise but it's on a smaller scale and not always prosperous. The reasonable land prices have attracted over 800 Amish to the county. Many of the small towns show signs of struggle. Abundant woods, a couple of man-made lakes and hundreds of ponds that are easily accessible make this southern Iowa

area an outdoor sportsman's paradise. Bass, channel cats, walleye, crappie and blue gills are caught in the lakes and ponds. In the Des Moines River you can add flathead catfish, spoonbill and sturgeon to that list. Any fish found in the Mississippi could potentially be swimming up the Des Moines River. The state's record large-mouth bass was caught in Lake Fisher.

White-tailed deer are the main attraction for hunters but there is also an abundance of pheasants, quail, turkeys, rabbits and squirrels. There is some coyote hunting and there is a known den of bobcats living in an abandoned **Davis County** limestone quarry. My guess, if you would ask around, someone could tell you of a mountain lion sighting. It would probably be true because there is ample reason for them to move into the area.

Prior to the year 1843, the land that is now **Davis County** belonged to the Ioway, Sac and Fox Indians. In 1843, a treaty was signed that gave ownership to the United States. The Indians were given three years to move beyond the Missouri River. When they were packed and ready to move, it is reported that the whole

tribe, including the bravest warriors, wept as they took a lingering farewell look at this beautiful land with its abundant game and natural resources.

There were early unofficial settlers/squatters on a ten-mile strip of land on the southern edge of **Davis County**. Both Iowa and Missouri claimed this real estate and it was known as the Hairy Nation. With whiskey providing the bribery, these folks voted in both states. They thought this was great until both states tried to tax them. Militias in each state were sent to the area but there is no indication they ever saw each other. The U.S. Supreme Court awarded the Hairy Nation to Iowa.

The first official settlement in May of 1843 was a strange land rush that was set off at night. Claims were staked in the darkness and daylight revealed much confusion. Disputes were settled by compromise and occasionally by violence. In the end 1,000 families had settled on their new purchase.

Bloomfield is a classic Iowa county seat with downtown buildings listed on the National Registry of Historic Places. Centered on the town square is an impos-

Geese find open water on Lake Sugema, Van Buren County

Drakesville

TIER NO. ONE
| FR | PA | TA | RI | DE | WA | AP | DA | VB | LE |

Basket weave jailbars,
Davis County Courthouse

Davis County Courthouse,
Bloomfield

ing, beautiful, French Renaissance-style courthouse. It was built in 1877 for $50,000. The jail in the basement housed city and county offenders until 1973. You can still see basket weave, iron cell partitions in the county assessor's office.

There are many historical sights of interest in **Bloomfield** and **Davis County** and P. Buckley Moss has painted most of them. She has taken a personal interest in the community by creating a fund for disadvantaged and handicapped children in the area.

The character of **Bloomfield** has inspired many more people. The town can claim two governors, two U.S. senators, seven U.S. representatives, one academy award winner, two successful music composers, one Olympian, two major league baseball players and two editors of major newspapers. This must be a record for a town of 2,700 people.

A special event held in September at the fairgrounds is the Davis County Country and Old Time Music Festival. Participants and their fans line up their campers and RVs on Sunday prior to the weekend show in order to be the first ones in when they open the gates on

Davis County

Bloomfield

Monday. I visualize a stampede of bulky RVs and campers trying to squeeze each other out at the gate and racing to stake their camping spot. However, I'm sure it is more orderly than that. Music emanates from these campgrounds all week and, on the weekend, spectators are treated to stage shows, band jambles, a kids' show and a Sunday morning gospel sing. This festival has its roots in the Drakesville Old Time Bluegrass Festival. We visited **Drakesville** and I imagined these pickers and fiddle players playing in their rustic park. We regret that we've never had a chance to experience it. Drakesville still hosts the Old Soldiers and Settlers Reunion.

While we were doing some research at the Bloomfield Library, we made an acquaintance with Stephen Tews, a retired union man who was well versed on the area and a good storyteller. We asked about a town character and, with no hesitation, he chose a sign painter named Lowell Loper. Lowell had trouble painting signs without adding goofy touches such as putting eyeballs in words with double letter 'o' (oo). Painting an LP tank to look like Thomas the Train was anoth-

er example. A storeowner who needed some paper signs to promote a sale informed Lowell he wanted a straight job with no funny stuff. When Lowell delivered the signs, the storeowner was upset that they were done in a silly style but he calmed down when he looked on the other side and saw the straightforward signs he requested. On another job he was asked to paint a sign on the side of a truck door and, again, he was told, "no funny stuff." He followed instructions and painted a nice sign. The window was down on a warm summer day when the owner picked up the truck. When he got home and rolled up the window, there was another sign in removable paint that read, "Don't fart in the cab!"

With a smile on our faces we left the library and got into our fresh-smelling car and motored out of **Bloomfield** heading west. The hilly, patchy woods of **Davis County** became more heavily wooded with steeper hills as we entered **Appanoose County**. On our left we noticed an unmapped, man-made lake inserting itself into this southern Iowa wilderness. We learned later that this is a private development named Lake

Sundown. It is a very attractive setting and the lots should sell.

We continued our drive over huge deposits of coal that were heavily mined in the early 1900s. The industry played itself out when concerns with air pollution became more prevalent. The problem with Iowa coal is its high sulfur content, which causes it to burn dirtier than harder coal found in Appalachia and Wyoming. However, for most of the first half of the twentieth century, southern Iowa was a booming mining area. **Appanoose County** was at the heart of this boom/bust period of history.

Many towns owe their start to coal mining. It is not uncommon for an **Appanoose County** town with present population of about 100 to have a past of robust growth with peak populations of about 1,500 people. Then there is Coal City. This town, referred to as "The Patch" because of the arrangement of the houses, grew up amongst ten coalmines. It was also referred to as "Little Chicago" because of the behavior of its residents. It thrived from 1905 to about 1930. Today, nothing remains of Coal City. It has reverted back to farmland.

Appanoose County

11

TIER NO. ONE
FR PA TA RI DE WA AP DA VB LE

Blue Bird Cafe, Centerville

LITTLE FLOCK CHAPEL

Centerville theater

RITZ

POPCORN 10¢

Centerville, the county seat of **Appanoose County**, is a surviving coalmining city of 6,000 people. Business on the square that serves area residents and tourists appears to be doing well. We ate lunch at a delightful down-town café named the Blue Bird. It had a whimsical look with colorful mobiles, neon-trimmed wall art, running lights on one of the counters and a nightscape mural on the back wall that featured the "Man in the Moon." Their chili special hit the spot on this winter day.

Croatians, Italians and Swedes were brought in to work in the mines. Their descendants provide the basic fabric of today's residents. It is a community of warm, can-do people who have worked together to bring in manufacturing to replace coalmining as a source of employment. In recent years there has been an emphasis on the arts, culture and projects to beautify and preserve the historical character of the city.

We had the opportunity to visit with Bill Benz, a retiree who is an active community volunteer. In Bill's view, a load of credit for **Centerville's** success goes to Robert Beck, a former owner and

Honey Creek Resort Lodge

Bill Benz

Appanoose County Courthouse, Centerville

editor of the **Centerville** newspaper, *The Iowegian*. He was a wonderful writer who kept the town pumped up as he wrote about the present good and future possibilities. He was always promoting cooperation. Bill also mentioned another good man named Boyd O'Briant who served as the chamber of commerce director. Boyd was a Studebaker dealer who unfortunately did not keep any of those rare, classic models that are worth big money to today's collectors.

An Italian descendant named Tony Caraccio was another good man who lived a colorful lifestyle. He owned the Smoke Shop Tavern, a popular gathering spot. He drove big cars and loved to play cards and gamble. He always had money that he readily lent to his patrons. He employed an African American named Charlie Bandy who was quite colorful in his own right. Charlie ran errands and sometimes tended bar. On an errand run, he would walk into a bank and whistle at the girls and indulge in give-and-take with the customers. This scene of give-and-take was his trademark as he greeted the townspeople on his runs.

The trademark of another African

American from **Centerville** is a world-class baritone voice. I am, of course, referring to Simon Estes, the great Metropolitan Opera singer. This elegant man is a 1956 graduate of Centerville High School. He is a man of immense talent and accomplishment and a good man who respects his roots. He returns to Iowa frequently to visit his mother who lives in Des Moines and to give concerts that are often charity benefits.

For 50 years the business people of **Centerville** have been showing their appreciation for the patronage of people from surrounding farms and small towns by inviting them to Pancake Days. The guests are treated to a parade, a beauty queen contest, free entertainment and free pancakes. An estimated 20,000 to 25,000 people attended the last event.

The Croatian Fest is another fun **Centerville** celebration. Their heritage is honored with colorful ethnic costumes, home-cooked ethnic food, music and dancing. A polka Mass at St. Mary's Catholic Church fits the occasion.

Rathbun Lake, Iowa's largest man-made lake, was completed in 1969 and estimates are that it has already prevented

over $142 million in flood damages. The cost of construction was $26 million. Its other value is that it is worth millions as a source of recreation. This is an asset in **Appanoose County** that is just beginning to be tapped. The state is developing a vacation destination named Honey Creek Resort. It is presently under construction. It will include a 108-room lodge, 28 cabins, a restaurant/lounge, an indoor water park, an 18-hole golf course and other amenities that guarantee fun for guests. We drove through some villages located close to the lake that have abandoned downtowns with surviving brick and stone buildings. We hope there are some hard-working entrepreneurs who will bring these buildings back to life to take advantage of the growing tourism.

As we left **Appanoose County** and the big-time Rathbun Lake project, we experienced the opposite at the Little Flock Chapel. This diminutive chapel marks the spot where two Baptist churches once stood. A decline in church membership brought on the decision to raze the last one and use remaining monies to build the Little Flock Chapel.

Snow flurries that had been swirling

Rathbun Lake Marina

Inn of the Six-Toed Cat, Allerton

Allerton

Corydon

WAYNE COUNTY COURTHOUSE

Inn of the Six-Toed Cat

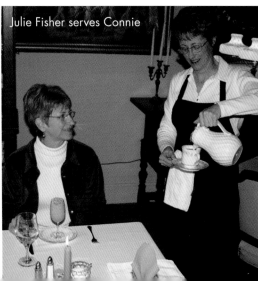

Julie Fisher serves Connie

around us most of the day evolved into flakes and became more frequent. We decided it would be wise to make our overnight stay the next stop. So far on this trip we have had sunny, cold, crisp days; overcast days; snowy days; and thawing days. To me each day was beautiful. I like all the seasons, including winter. The hardest part of winter for me is listening to people complain about it. Ice storms are an exception to this attitude. There is some beauty in the sun glistening off the prism-like, ice-covered trees but broken branches, downed power lines, cars in the ditch and broken bones negate the pleasure.

The Inn of the Six-Toed Cat in **Allerton** is a B&B that was built as a hotel in 1909. The interior with its open staircase and wide, upstairs hall looks like a western movie set. Classic wall art of nudes and nymphs in many poses and settings add to this theme. I expected Miss Kitty of Dodge to greet us.

It was Julie Fisher who greeted us and she proved to be the gracious hostess to which Miss Kitty could only aspire. There was a kitty on the premises—a black, furry critter with night eyes that

14

Allerton

Corydon

glowed in the dark. It had only five toes, however. The six-toed cat that inspired the name was a stray that hung around the workers as they were renovating the Inn.

At Julie's recommendation we backtracked a few miles to **Corydon** for dinner at Ludlow's Steak House. It was perfect. There were red walls and black, upholstered chairs. Hawkeye photos and other memorabilia adorned the walls. Cheerful, pretty, country girls waited tables and a tall, wiry, young boy with a seed corn cap was the busboy. Country music played in the background as we dined on delicious sandwiches and crisp, tasty french fries. The only deviation from perfection was the portion size; the sandwiches were huge and the french fries were piled high. Burp!

Arriving back in **Allerton**, we stopped at the South Forty Tavern and joined a few patrons wiling away a quiet Thursday evening. Connie ordered an after-dinner beer and I requested bourbon on the rocks to cut the grease.

We awoke the next morning to a hazy sunrise showing through the leafless trees. Later in the morning the sky cleared and the sun's rays caused the

newly fallen snow to sparkle. The pleasure of the day's weather would continue with an afternoon thaw.

After gazing at the sunrise, we found a table in the dining room that was elegantly set for us. We dined on almond French toast and link sausage. It's Julie's signature breakfast and it was delicious.

Following breakfast Julie poured herself a cup of coffee and sat down to visit with us. She described how she and her husband Scott were warmly welcomed to the community after they bought the Inn. It had been vacant for a couple of years and the community was appreciative of the Fisher's efforts to bring it back. Most of the interior with antiques, oriental rugs and classic art on the walls came with the purchase. Mechanical and structural problems also came with the purchase and the Fishers addressed them. They did what they could themselves and hired local craftsmen where they needed help. Generous neighbors bringing gifts of fresh produce and other food continually interrupted their workdays.

A plugged sewer line was one of the problems that needed attention. They called in a backhoe operator and a

plumber to deal with it. The sound of the backhoe served as a call to all the retired, old men of the community to come and see what was happening. They lined the perimeter of the ditch in a manner that the plumber must have thought he was performing in a theater-in-the-round. When the plumber had completed his work, he asked the Fishers to turn all the water on and flush the toilets to test it. One of the bystanders said there was no need for that. He could get a fire truck with a hose that would really test it.

I love small towns.

Our drive along the southern tier of counties basically follows the Mormon Trail. When the Mormons came through in 1846, these counties were truly on the frontier. The trail opened the way and rapid settling followed. **Wayne County** was officially organized in 1851. By 1855 practically the entire county was settled and, by 1860, the population was 6,400. It peaked in 1900 at 17,500. Today's population is 6,700.

In the late 1800s, every small town's settlers envisioned a great and thriving city. These settlements had the basics—a post office, a store and a blacksmith

Wayne County

15

Founders Park, Leon

Prairie Trails Museum, Corydon

shop. The coming of railroads, telephones and rural free delivery consolidated the services and doomed all but a few towns. Farmers still uncover articles from an early store or blacksmith shop.

Corydon, the county seat of **Wayne County**, is one of the survivors. Its 1,600 residents have worked together to keep it vital. Bill Gode is one of those community-minded people. He owned Keller's Floral Shop and a hound named Ludlow. The dog was good for business because kids were always urging their parents to take them to Keller's so they could pet the dog. The floral shop is now Ludlow's Steak House.

One of Bill's special contributions to the town was his management and promotion of an impressive Fourth of July parade. His contacts and follow-ups to encourage participation were valuable skills. He is in his mid-80s and has decided to retire from this endeavor. He had no apprentice working for him; someone else will have to learn from trial and error in the same manner he did.

Corydon is another town with businesses on a square. However, there is a twist in that the Wayne County Court-

JCT
S22
COUNTY

16

Wayne County

Davis City

Decatur County Courthouse, Leon

house is a new structure with contemporary style architecture. Another contrast to old, traditional storefronts is a brightly colored, art deco, movie theater.

Wayne County has a passion for sports going back to the pioneers and the great Shane Hill Baseball Club. From 1875 to the early 1900s, they toured Iowa, Missouri and Kansas. Their best pitcher, Burl Maytum, developed a curveball that was almost impossible to hit. Their only losses were to teams that loaded up with professionals and they often beat them. **Corydon's** George Saling won the Gold Medal in the 110-meter high hurdles at the 1932 Olympics. In the 1940s, the Seymour Warriorettes were a dominant, girls' basketball powerhouse. They went to state nine years in a row and won it all in 1947.

In addition to hunting and fishing as a draw for visitors, there is the Prairie Trails Museum of **Wayne County**. It is located on Highway 2 on the eastern side of **Corydon**. It features a 21,000-square-foot brick building that houses 25,000, historic artifacts and there is a large barn filled with farm antiques.

The rolling terrain continued with wooded areas increasing in size as we drove into eastern **Decatur County**. Our first stop was **Leon**, the county seat. This town is similar in size and character to **Corydon** except that we are back to the traditional, 1900s-style courthouse centered in the town square. **Leon** is located near the Little River Lake recreation area and, within **Decatur County**, you will find Nine Eagles State Park, bike trails and a canoeing river. A top-notch, IRAC sanctioned, award-winning rodeo is another attraction. It is held in **Leon** on the Fourth of July weekend.

Almost immediately upon leaving **Leon** via Highway 69, we entered some very hilly, forested terrain. This continued for about seven miles until we crossed the Thompson Fork of the Grand River. **Davis City** sits on a hill on the other side. It is another one of those southern Iowa towns that has an abandoned look to it. However, it appeared someone was working on some downtown restoration. We wish them the best.

A few more miles down the road, we crossed over Interstate 35 and entered the outskirts of **Lamoni**. The first thing to catch our eye was a large, livestock auc-

tion barn. There were some livestock trailers hooked up with pickups in the parking lot and an 18-wheel semi at the loading dock. There was also an Amish horse and buggy tied to a tree.

On the other side of **Lamoni** is a beautiful little college that shares an interesting history with the town. Their roots reach into the early days of the Latter Day Saints religion.

The church splintered into different groups after Joseph Smith II (the founder of the Latter Day Saints movement) was killed. His son, Joseph Smith III, rose to become leader of a group known as the Reorganized Church of Jesus Christ of Latter Day Saints (RLDS). Wealthy leaders of the group bought 2,500 acres in Fayette Township in **Decatur County** for a church settlement. It was named **Lamoni** in honor of the king of the Lamanites in the Book of Mormon. In 1879, **Lamoni** was selected as the RLDS church headquarters with Joseph Smith III as its president.

The church's headquarters was later moved to Independence, Missouri, where it remains today. RLDS is no longer the religion's name. It is now known as the

Decatur County

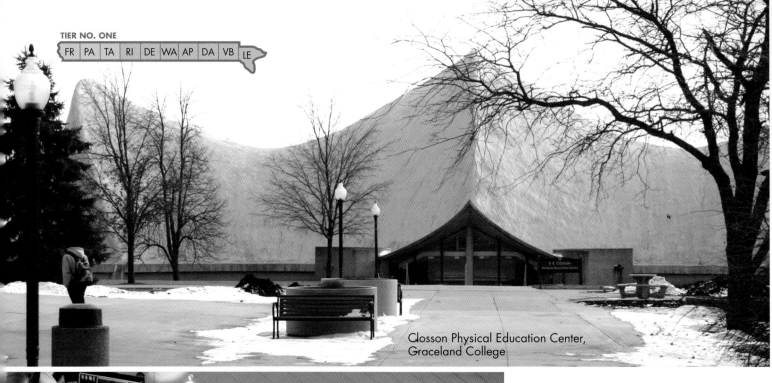

Closson Physical Education Center,
Graceland College

Closson Physical
Education Center

Community of Christ and a lady from admissions at Graceland University informed us that there is a big difference between it and the Mormon faith.

There was originally some disagreement on where to locate the church's first institution of higher learning. Some felt everything should be centrally located in Independence and others thought the wholesome character of **Lamoni** would better serve the students. Wholesomeness won out, but it was probably the generous offers of land in **Lamoni** that tipped the scales. At the time Graceland opened in 1895, **Lamoni's** population was 1,475. If you subtract the student body's 1,000 students, its population would be about the same today.

The wholesome image continues as *America's Promise* named **Lamoni** to a list of "The 100 Best Cities for Young People" in the nation. Among the reasons the town was chosen is their Across Ages mentoring program that matches at-risk, middle school students with senior citizens in the community.

We took a self-guided tour of Graceland University with well-designed signage identifying each building and

Higdon Administration Building,
Graceland College

Ringgold County

18

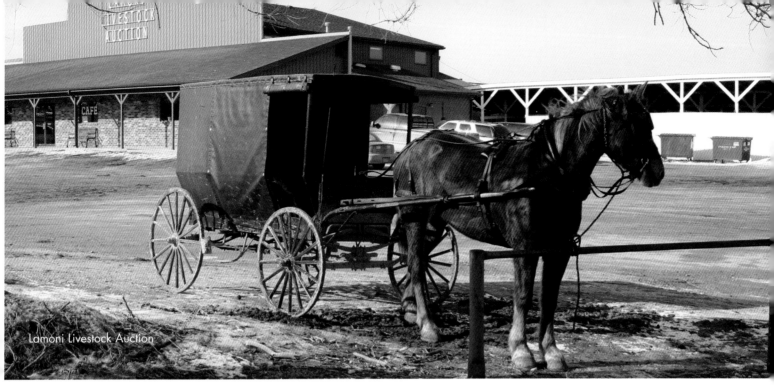

Lamoni Livestock Auction

giving directions to other buildings. Its graceful, undulating landscape was the inspiration for the name. Our first stop was at the admissions office in the 110-year-old administrative building that was the first, permanent building on campus. It is a beautiful, old building that obviously has had a lot of love. The admissions' staff was outgoing and eager to please; we received plenty of material on which to base our campus report.

The administration building stands out among the contemporary-designed buildings that house other functions on campus. There appears to be an equal emphasis on academics and student activities.

The Bruce Jenner Sports Complex includes a football and track field, tennis courts, soccer field, intramural fields and sand volleyball courts. Bruce Jenner came to Graceland with a partial scholarship to play football. A knee injury in football led to giving up the sport and turning his efforts toward basketball and track. He competed in the decathlon for the first time in 1969 and won the NAIA National Championship in 1971. He went on to compete in two Olympics, winning the gold in 1976. He is not the only ath-

lete to excel at Graceland. Browsing through the school's brochures, I became aware of an outstanding tradition of athletic accomplishment for a student body of 1,000 students.

Indoor sports take place in the Closson Physical Education Center, the most unusual building on campus. The exterior looks like the top of a covered wagon. It shelters volleyball and tennis courts, as well as five basketball courts. A 200-meter track circles the perimeter. Movable bleachers provide 2,000 seats for intercollegiate competition.

Looking at the other activities offered in music, theatre and art, it became apparent that virtually every one of the 1,000 students must be involved in an activity beyond class work. And, of course, its close affiliation with the Community of Christ Church provides spiritual direction.

Entering **Ringgold County** we encountered nine deer frolicking in a snowy meadow. There was potential for a great photo so we reversed our direction and returned to the scene. As soon as they saw us stop, they turned up their white tails and ran in their graceful style, leapt

a fence and disappeared into the woods. I didn't get the photo but it was a beautiful sight to see. It turned out to be the day of the deer. There were four more sightings of them playing their games. It was also the day of the skunk. We saw two dead ones in the road and that evening we contributed to the carnage by hitting one of our own. Its sprayer went off quickly enough to give the under-carriage of our car that distinctive smell. It took two more days of driving to air it out.

An abundance of wild game has long been an enticement for camps and settlements in southern Iowa. Deer, turkeys, prairie chickens, quail, pheasants, rabbits, squirrels, ducks and geese sustained the Indians and early settlers. These species still populate the area in large enough numbers for excellent hunting.

The only signs of human life for early settlers of **Ringgold County** were the Mormon Trail and the Dragoon Trace. The Dragoon Trace was a buffalo and Indian trail used by soldiers traveling between Fort Leavenworth, Kansas, and Fort Des Moines. These trails were easily seen as they broke down the luxurious growth of prairie grasses.

Ringgold County

Ellston

The first white settlers of record in the county arrived in 1844. They were a bit lonely for two years before the next family arrived. This pace of settlement continued for a few more years. Following a survey of the county in 1854, a commission was organized and authorized to pick a site near the geographical center of the county for a county seat. Towns on the frontier owe their locations to many factors such as a river, a trade route, a retail center or mineral deposits. Not **Mount Ayr**. It was developed to be the county seat of a county that was just beginning to be settled.

The first courthouse was a 14- by 14-foot, log building built in 1856. A new frame building replaced it in 1859; in 1884, a beautiful brick building, inspired by French architecture, was erected. Unfortunately, shoddy construction caused the building to crack badly; it was condemned in 1921. The replacement, that is in use today, is constructed of reinforced concrete with brick facing. The contemporary style of the 1920s isn't as charming as its predecessor, but it won't be condemned anytime soon.

The most recent settlers in **Ringgold**

Mount Ayr

20 Mount Ayr

Ellston

Lenox

Ringgold County Courthouse, Mount Ayr

County are building beautiful homes around Sun Valley Lake. It is a private, man-made lake with springs as its water source. Its water quality is excellent and amenities include a full-service marina, tennis and basketball courts and a nine-hole golf course. The lake is stocked with bass, channel cat, bullhead, walleye and crappies. The Sun Valley Bar and Grille features family-style cuisine.

We drove on to **Ellston** where we got caught in a small-town traffic jam. There was a parked John Deere tractor hooked up to a trailer loaded with ten, large, round bales. It looked like a hay train. On the other side of the street, a pickup was attempting to back out of his space but was being held up by two pickups in the street whose occupants were conversing with each other. When the driver saw who it was, he pulled back in and went out and joined the conversation. We started looking for side streets so we could detour around this scene.

Mount Ayr, the town that was designated to be a county seat before it was platted, would, of course, have a town square with a courthouse in the center and brick streets to add to the charm.

Adding to the charm of the International Space Station, which the United States shares with Russia, is **Mount Ayr's** own Peggy A. Whitson. She is the Expedition 16 commander, the first woman commander in space history. The *Mount Ayr Record News*, an excellent weekly newspaper, is printing a running commentary of her experience.

After stopping at the post office to look at a neat mural of King Corn painted in 1941 by Orr C. Fisher as a New Deal project, we ate lunch at Peggy Sue's. The restaurant's exterior features a '50s Chevy that was sliced in half length-wise and mounted to the wall above the windows. The interior was well-done nostalgia including all the class photos of **Mount Ayr's** '50s graduates. Chili cheese dogs and homemade potato chips were a tasty complement to the theme.

After lunch we drove into **Taylor County** and pointed our car northeast to the town of **Lenox**. In the '70s when **Taylor County** lost 19 percent of its population, Lenox grew by 10 percent. A progressive attitude in this community of 1,400 is responsible for the trend-breaking success. A new bank building,

new high school/gymnasium, new tennis courts, new ambulance and new fire equipment instilled a pride that continues today. We noticed that some of the businesses were clever with their names. The Nowhere Tavern, that is housed in a rustic, freestanding building, comes to mind.

On our drive between **Lenox** and **Bedford**, we stopped to take a look at the Lake of Three Fires State Park. In 1935, WPA workers cleared timber from the site and CCC workers made roads, parking areas, campsites, dams, cabins and shelter houses. You see good work by these crews in parks in Iowa and across the country. The 85-acre lake provides good fishing and there are 700 acres of woods with marked trails for hikers, bicyclists and horse riders. The cabins and campgrounds have been updated.

Bedford, the county seat of **Taylor County**, is steeped in history. The courthouse, a magnificent structure, was completed in 1893 and is in excellent shape today. The clock in the white crown is a Seth Thomas. Only 82 of this model were built. **Bedford's** early entrepreneurs from the British Isles and northern Europe must have prospered and had

Lake of Three Fires

Bedford Main Street with Garland Hotel on the left

Taylor County Historical Museum

good taste. They built a striking down-town that is on the National Registry of Historic Places.

The Garland Hotel on the east end of Main Street was built in 1857 with the main front added on in 1877. It was a stagecoach depot until the arrival of the railroad in 1872. Nearly all of the fixtures in the hotel are original. The Taylor County Historical Museum located just west of **Bedford** on Highway 2 rounds out the historical experience. Features include a restored round barn, an 1800s' cabin, a one-room schoolhouse, a train station with a caboose, a machine shed full of old machinery and a genealogy information center.

The town of 1,600 people takes on an ambitious slate of festivals and events. Flower farming in the area prompts Bloomfest in May and Daylily Daze in July. There is harness racing in June. It is one of 12 harness racing tracks in Iowa and the only one in southwest Iowa. Vintage, customized cars make their appearance at an August car show. And, their most unique event, Main Street Alive, is held in June. Once a year the townspeople perform skits on Main

Taylor County

Clearfield

Taylor County Courthouse, Bedford

Street depicting people of the past who have lived in or visited **Bedford**. Last summer, William Jennings Bryant, Carrie Nation and Billy Sunday were among those selected to be recognized.

You meet the nicest people in libraries. At the Bedford Carnegie Library (also on the National Registry of Historic Places) we made the acquaintance of librarian Sandy Kennedy and Pastor Randy Allman of the United Christian Presbyterian Church. We had a pleasant chat as we talked about Iowa and **Bedford**. They confirmed our favorable, first impression as they told us about good people who make this community work. I'm going to single out one of them—a 93-year-old lady named Ellen Lemke.

Ellen is one of those people who keeps the juices flowing by staying active both mentally and physically. She is a member of Pastor Allman's church and is well-versed in the Bible. She has written eight books of poetry. She reads stories to nursing home residents and uses her sense of humor to brighten their day. She enjoys working with kids. She is nimble enough to jump rope if they spin it for her. She performs very funny skits as the "panty-

hose lady." Recently she was asked if she wanted to take the elevator or the stairs. She clicked her heels and said, "I'll take the stairs!" Well, you get the idea. Here is one of her poems:

SMALL TOWN

You can talk about your cities,
With people by the score,
Of public transportation
That goes right by your door.
You can talk about tall buildings,
Reaching towards the sky,
Cathedrals and museums
And crowds a rushing by.
I prefer a small town
Where I know my neighbors well,
If you have a lot of time,
All its virtues I can tell.

At our next overnight, we bedded down at Iowa Country Cabins located about five miles east of **Clarinda** in **Page County**. Denise and Arlan Hoskins built a nice, two-room cabin on their farmstead. A front porch with a swing faces east overlooking a pleasant landscape of rolling farmland and wooded areas. The interior of our room was

knotty pine with bear motif accents.

We took our hosts' recommendation for a Valentine Day's dinner at J. Bruner's Steakhouse in **Clarinda**. The temperature was below freezing with a 15-20 mph wind when we arrived at the steakhouse. There was about a half-hour wait so we went to the lounge for a beer. At first glance we noticed there was a fireplace. Yes! At second glance we saw there was no fire. No! The cold beer was good but a warm fire would have been nice.

The dining room was comfortable enough but nothing special décor-wise. I ordered a small filet and Connie chose an Iowa pork loin. We told the waitress we would like to split a bottle of wine and asked to see the wine list. She responded, "We don't have a list. Do you want red or white?" Our reply, "Red!" After all, it was Valentine's Day. My steak was cooked and seasoned perfectly and Connie experienced the same with her pork loin. However, it was the side of snow peas (rather than the usual litany of potato offerings) that pleased her.

After a good night's sleep we arose to a beautiful sunrise that tempted me to go out and sit on the porch swing even

Sunrise at Iowa Country Cabins

23

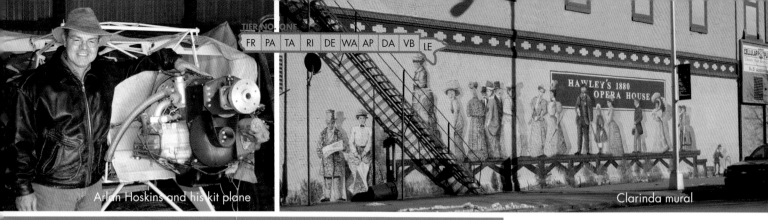

Arlan Hoskins and his kit plane

Clarinda mural

Page County Courthouse, Clarinda

though the temperature was zero degrees. I thought better of it and joined Connie walking over to the house for breakfast. Arlan served us an egg dish with stewed fruit, juice, coffee and coffee cake. Denise had done the cooking that morning before she left for her teaching job at **College Springs**.

In talking to Arlan after breakfast, we learned that he was a flying farmer. He has a four-passenger Cessna he keeps at the Clarinda Airport. However, he would rather talk about the Avid kit plane he is building. If he ever finishes it (his son has graduated from high school and college since he started) it will seat two people and fly at a speed of 100 mph. He is also developing a runway on his farm that follows the undulating landscape and curves slightly. I'll have to check back in a couple of years for a report.

When we visited with Pastor Allman in **Bedford**, he had mentioned a group of performers known as "Country Church." Arlan Hoskins provided us with more details and we gleaned additional information on their website. They are a Clarinda-based group who bring a biblical message and cowboy-style songs to

Judge Wendell Leonard in
Glenn Miller Birthplace Home Museum

24

Clarinda

county fairs, prisons and other gatherings in a three-state area. They started their show in **Braddyville** near the Missouri border and it remains their home base for performances.

Scott Davison, a singer and banjo player, is the organizer and leader of the group. His daughter Sarah, a professional singer and piano player in Nashville, joins the group when she is in town. Other members are Charles Johnson (vocals/guitar), Brooke Turner (vocals/guitar), Rande Montgomery (vocals/guitar), John Marriot (vocals/bass guitar) and Janice Hardel (vocal/piano). Preachers Gary Jaeckle or Cole Edwards deliver the biblical message. Typically there is about an hour of gospel music and a 10-15 minute message. We bought their CD and played it as we drove along those southern Iowa highways. I love country gospel and the "Country Church" musicians are good.

I also love jazz and **Clarinda** lays claim to one of the greatest, if not the greatest, big band leader of all time. Alton Glen Miller was born March 1, 1904, in a small frame house on South 16th Street (now Glenn Miller Avenue).

He was called by his middle name from the beginning and while in high school he added a second 'n' to Glen. Glenn was between two and three years old when his family left **Clarinda** to homestead in the sandhills of Nebraska. Although he lived in **Clarinda** only a couple of years, his family's roots run deep. His grandfather, "Pop Corn Bob," who served in the Union Army, was one of the early settlers. There is a photo of him standing by his popcorn cart at the Birthplace Home Museum. Glenn's father, Elmer, was a carpenter; his mother, Mattie Lou, was his early music influence. She played the pump organ and is credited with the primary music training of the children.

Judge Wendell Leonard, a colorful magistrate in **Clarinda**, is a Glenn Miller historian. He gave us a personal tour of the Birthplace Home Museum. He asked if we wanted the basic or super-duper tour. We said basic, but I think we got the full load anyway. I'm glad we did. It's a great story. We complimented him on his knowledge and presentation. He said that he talks about things he doesn't even know. We learned that Glenn flunked a music harmony class at the

University of Colorado; his best grade was in trigonometry; he was featured in several films; Jimmy Stewart played him in his life story; and he was the first recording artist to sell one million records ("Chatanooga Choo Choo"). We recommend you visit this little house that is full of memorabilia, including the piano Glenn used for composing and one of the two trombones he played. If you are lucky, Judge Wendell will be there to give you the super-duper tour.

Each year, the Glenn Miller Festival in **Clarinda** features the best big bands in the country and many more attractions.

There were some settlers who preceded Glenn Miller's grandfather. The earliest pioneers in **Page County** arrived in the early 1840s. They didn't have a lot of material possessions, but what they had, they readily shared. The county's few dwellings were often crowded with pioneer guests who were passing through on their way west. They were offered shelter without question.

In 1853, **Clarinda** was platted in a checkerboard pattern over 160 acres. The first building to sit on one of the squares was a shanty that was dragged by oxen

Glenn Miller Birthplace
Home Museum

25

Clarinda Academy, Mental Health Complex

United Methodist Church, Shenandoah

from a farm. The first sermon preached and the first kids taught in Clarinda happened in this lonely, little shack.

The following are other interesting historical tidbits on **Clarinda** and **Page County**: A rural schoolteacher, Jessie Field Shambaugh, founded the 4-H movement as she taught practical skills, as well as the three 'r's. In 1943, during World War II, a prisoner of war camp was established here where 3,000 German prisoners were interred. A Chautauqua, the second one in the United States, was held at the fairgrounds in 1897. The Ray Schenek Airport was named after a pioneer **Clarinda** flyer whose license was signed by Orville Wright in 1928.

On the evening news during state wrestling tournament week, there was a human-interest feature about a young man who had been living a misguided life of drugs and wasted opportunities. He was sent to the Clarinda Academy in hopes he would get his act together. It worked and he and his father spoke glowingly of the academy. He was the picture of health as he wrestled match by match in pursuit of a state championship. That young man is not the only success story

Shenandoah

Pella manufacturing plant

coming out of Clarinda Academy, a duly accredited school for at-risk boys and girls—ages 14 to 18.

The Academy is part of a large complex of buildings that was formerly a state hospital for the mentally ill. Mental health is still treated there on a smaller scale. It also houses support services for a new, nearby, medium security prison.

Clarinda is a progressive town of about 6,000 people, that thrives with a good manufacturing base. It is the retail center of a trade area of about 30,000 people. The schools and recreational facilities are excellent.

As we drove west, we continued to enjoy the snowy, rolling hills—a landscape with variegated coloring of yellow-ochre grassy areas, the warm, dark grays of leafless trees and the muted greens of the pines. The farmsteads and both domestic and wild animals provided the accents. This pleasant drive led us to **Shenandoah** in the Nishnabotna River valley. The vibrant little town owes its name to soldiers returning from the Civil War. They saw a striking resemblance to the Shenandoah Valley of Virginia. Our first stop was at the

Chamber of Commerce where we met executive vice-president Gregg Connell and marketing director Shelly Smith. These articulate, enthusiastic people are representative of a special community. We had an interesting, enjoyable dialogue with them. It was informative without excessive boosterism—very Iowan.

Shenandoah is not located on a major river or interstate. There is no college or casino. It is not a county seat; in fact, it is not even sure what county it is in as it straddles the line. Gregg stressed, "**Shenandoah** thrives for two reasons—great entrepreneurs and a willingness to redefine itself."

Shenandoah's existence dates back to the 1870s when the Chicago, Burlington and Quincy Railroad was completed. Travelers who liked what they saw decided to stay and call it their home. Early entrepreneurs of note were in the nursery industry. Henry Fields sold his first packet of seeds when he was six years old. Fifteen years later, he was growing, harvesting and selling his seeds locally. By the time he passed away in 1949, the Henry Field Company was one of the largest of its kind in the United

States. Earl May, a Nebraska man, sold seeds to pay his way through college. May moved to **Shenandoah** in 1915, and three years later, he founded the company that bears his name.

Marketing is a large part of building a successful company; Fields and May were strong in that area. In 1924, Fields launched radio station KFNF and in 1925, May launched a competitor with KMA. Live broadcasts of music, news and information drew entertainers trying to further their careers. It was the draw that enticed the musical Everly family to move from Kentucky to **Shenandoah** in 1945. The Everly Brothers, Don and Phil, went on to rock-and-roll fame.

A talented labor pool and an environment conducive to family living have attracted solid manufacturing companies to **Shenandoah**. Pella Corporation employs 600 people in a plant that makes specialty windows. Eaton Corporation produces heavy-duty transmissions for trucks. Green Plains Renewable Energy (GPRE) recently built an ethanol plant that produces 50 million gallons a year. Smaller industries and retail businesses also thrive in this progressive town.

Gregg Connell and
Shelly Smith

Everly Brothers shrine in
The Depot restaurant

Rodeo grounds, Sidney

PASS GATE | YOU MUST SHOW PASS

ENTRANCE
SECTION 7 & BOXS & GEN ADM

Rodeo grounds

The arts flourish with Iowa's longest, continuous running theatre group leading the way. The Southwest Iowa Theater Group has performed quality plays and musicals for over 50 years. Each summer, 160 budding artists attend the Wabash Arts Camp. Festivals abound with weekly and yearly events and there are unlimited recreational opportunities, including the inviting 63-mile Wabash Trace Nature Trail for bicyclists, joggers, walkers and cross-country skiers.

It was too cold to bike so we again settled into our warm car and drove further west. We entered **Fremont County** where we said "goodbye" to the rolling, southern Iowa hills and "hello" to the Loess Hills. **Sidney**, the county seat, sits on the eastern edge of this unique piece of geology.

The strip of terrain, known as the Loess Hills, stretches 200 miles along the eastern side of the Missouri River valley. It is about 15 miles wide at its widest point. Wind deposits of soils, that had been ground as fine as flour by glaciers, are piled higher here than any other place in the world except China where there are some similar formations.

St. Patrick's Catholic Church, Imogene

Erskine Powles

Loess Hills, Fremont County

Fremont County's western border is the Missouri River. French explorers found their way up the Missouri as early as 1750 and were the first whites to set foot in **Fremont County**. Lewis and Clark passed by, but did not stop, in 1804. By 1836, there were a few white people living in the Hamburg area where a ferry crossed the "Big Muddy."

The county was formally organized in 1849 and **Sidney** was selected as the county seat. Early county business was conducted in a store/residence. There was no pomp at the meetings and the commissioners sat on nail kegs, boxes or upon the counter of the store. The first courthouse was built in 1852 using cottonwood from Civil Bend. This structure was outgrown and replaced by a brick one in 1859. Courthouse history from that point to today includes: an attempt to blow it up; an arson fire; a lightning strike; painting the bricks, then later sandblasting the paint off; and a new addition added in 1960. Today, it sits proudly on the square serving its people with honor.

Sidney's main claim to fame is the nationally known Professional Rodeo Cowboys' Association rodeo held in

August. It started in 1923 with an arena formed by a circle of cars. The handlers blindfolded the bucking horse and twisted his ear to keep him calm until the cowboy was mounted. When they pulled the blindfold off and let go of the ear, all hell broke loose and the cowboy's skills were thoroughly tested. Today, there is a well-equipped grounds with seating for 7,000 people. The town provides a festival atmosphere to accompany the event.

While in the Sidney Public Library doing some research, we noticed an elderly gentleman approach the checkout desk. He had a bag with several books to return and, there waiting for him, were more books to check out. The library staff greeted him warmly and offered assistance and recommended a book they thought he might like. There obviously was a lot of love flowing in both directions. We asked if we could interview him and he graciously accepted.

The first thing we learned was that this healthy, alert man with good posture was 91 years old. His mind was sharp as he recalled some interesting times during his 91 years as a **Fremont County** resident. The following is some reminisc-

ing by our new acquaintance, Erskine Powles. He grew up on a farm near **Thurman** and is a 1924 graduate of Thurman High School. As a kid during Prohibition, he has vivid memories of the illegal activities in and around **Thurman**. At its peak there were 15 bootleggers in **Thurman**. This included the free-lancers. The most popular fellow at Saturday night dances was a young man in a big overcoat. His custom-designed coat had multiple pockets on the inside that fit nicely around whiskey bottles. He must have been stoop-shouldered with all that weight. Erskine's dad said that if he ever fell over, he would bleed to death. The road going by Erskine's house was one of the back roads used by organized crime bootleggers transporting liquor from Kansas City to Omaha. They drove big cars (such as a Stutz Bearcat) with cutout mufflers that would roar by on a regular basis. You stayed out of their way. Today, you can still find pieces of chopped up copper pipe that is evidence of a still that was raided and destroyed.

Erskine is an avid reader. He has read every Louis L'Amour book. He says they are fiction, but emphasized that there is

Fremont County Courthouse, Sidney

29

Hamburg, borders Loess Hills and Missouri River valley

Hamburg

history in them, too. With encouragement from friends and relatives, he has begun writing some memoirs. We encouraged him to continue recording history as he sees it. What a delightful man!

Hamburg, a town of about 1,200 in the southwestern tip of the county, has the appearance of an agricultural center. As we drove amongst the skyscraper elevators, rows of grain bins and implement dealers, we saw many brand names such as ConAgra, Cargill, Bartlett and Co., John Deere and IH Case. It is home to the Vogel Popcorn factory that produces Act II and Orville Redenbacher popcorn. Popcorn Days is a **Hamburg** festival that celebrates this industry.

We returned to **Sidney** and took Highway 2 into the Loess Hills where we descended through a wooded area to the wide expanse of the Missouri River valley floor. Motoring on for about five more miles, we crossed flat bottomland that is probably the richest soil in a state known for its rich soil. When we came to the Missouri River bridge, a non-descript structure, we turned around and drove back to the Loess Hills and followed a scenic byway north.

Hamburg

The Davies Amphitheater, Glenwood

Glenwood Resource Center

MILLS COUNTY SHERIFF

ADMINISTRATIVE OFFICES AND JAIL

SHERIFF
MILLS COUNTY

Mills County sheriff's office

Jim Thomas

From Fremont County we drove north through the Loess Hills to **Mills County**. As we enjoyed the special landscape, we gave some thought to its earliest human residents. There is archaeological evidence of Earth Lodge Indians living on the summits and slopes of these hills as early as 900 A.D. They resided in earth-covered pit houses. They would dig a pit about 20 feet wide, 40 to 60 feet long and 3 to 6 feet deep (not that difficult in the soft, loess soil.) The pit was lined with saplings that were bent to form an arched roof. Support poles were inserted down the interior center and the roof was covered with mud and grass.

Evidence of this culture keeps popping up whenever soil of the Loess Hills is disturbed. It is not uncommon for people who build houses in the hills to uncover artifacts and human remains. The state of Iowa and the Smithsonian have conducted official archaeological digs. The earth lodges lasted only about ten years and the tribes who built them had moved on before tribes of Ioways moved in. One tribe, the Pottawattamies, was well settled in this land when they were ordered by the federal government to

View of Nishnabotna River valley from the Loess Hills

relocate in Kansas. A tall, distinguished, well-built chief named Waubonsie refused to leave. He remained on the land he owned until his death. He has been honored; a state park was named after him and his image was hand-carved on the frieze across the front of the Mills County Historical Building.

I noted while traveling the southern tier of counties that we were following the Mormon Trail. That trail splinters when it reaches the Missouri River. The Mormons' 1846 winter quarters on the Nebraska side of the river housed only 4,000 of 12,000 to 15,000 followers. It was not feasible to ferry 8,000 to 11,000 people and their belongings across the river before winter so they developed settlements up and down the Iowa side. When weather permitted these settlers to move on to the Salt Lake community, new immigrants would take their place in the settlements. For the next six years, the majority of the Church's membership lived in western Iowa.

Glenwood, the county seat of Mills County, got its start as one of those Mormon settlements in 1848. Its original name, Coonsville, honors Mormon leader L. T. Coons, who lived in southwest Iowa for about 19 years before moving to the Salt Lake community. In 1852, the settlement was renamed **Glenwood** after the bulk of Mormons left for Utah.

As we drove east, we crested the last hill before the Keg Creek valley where **Glenwood** is located. It must be one of the high points in the Loess Hills. A beautiful, panoramic view of the valley unfolded before our eyes. We drove into this scene where the neat little town of about 5,500 people, graces the landscape.

Towns like **Glenwood** thrive because they have leaders and residents who care deeply about their community. We had the opportunity to visit with Jim Thomas, an attorney, whose roots run deep in **Glenwood**. He told us, "Every time I talk to my law school friends from around the country, I return to **Glenwood** thinking they don't know what they are missing." His enthusiasm was infectious as we talked about the town and the people who live in it.

Agriculture plays a major role in **Glenwood's** economy, but it wasn't always centered on corn, soybeans, hogs and beef. In the nineteenth century, it was a center of fruit production. At one time there were more apples produced in **Mills County** than any other county in the United States. Today with readily accessible railroad and in-state transportation, the county is becoming attractive to commercial and industrial expansions. Added enticements are amenities such as excellent schools, a beautiful park with a really cool amphitheater, an indoor activity/sports complex and numerous, outdoor recreation venues which include ballparks, golf courses, lakes and the Wabash Trace trail.

At the end of the Civil War, a home for the orphans of Iowa Veterans was established just outside of **Glenwood**. In 1876, it evolved into the Iowa Asylum for Feeble-Minded Children. The facility expanded with the treatment of mental retardation and acceptance of eugenics. The name was modified by changing the word "asylum" to "institution." By 1925, the Glenwood IIFMC was home to 1,555 patients. The IIFMC became the Glenwood State Hospital School in 1941 and the patient population grew to about 2,000. In the 1970s, there was transformation from traditional ward buildings

Mills County Courthouse, Glenwood

Glenwood State Bank

33

Clint Howard (owner)
Mineola Steak House

Silver City

into group-home cottages. The present name of the facility is the Glenwood Resource Center and it continues to operate near capacity. The people of **Glenwood** welcome its presence and treat the clients with respect.

Mills County is the "Garden of Eden" according to **Glenwood** banker John Dean. No, he is not the John Dean of Watergate fame although he happened to be in Washington, D.C. during the scandal and when he signed in at the Watergate Hotel, he got a disbelieving look from the desk clerk. It's not the first time he has seen this look. John is an intelligent, distinguished, excellent businessman who likes to freelance as a colorful cowboy who plays practical jokes on people. When federal regulators came to examine his recently acquired Mineola State Bank, he posted a sign in the bathroom that said the septic tank would allow only one flush a day. (I don't know if they worked that day with a pungent aroma or if they went out behind the bank.) A Glenwood State Bank senior club enjoys getting together for social events and travel excursions. Occasionally, they go on trips where destinations

Montgomery County Courthouse, Red Oak

Heritage Hill, Red Oak

Red Oak square

are unannounced. On one of the trips, John asked the bus driver to stop briefly at an adult bookstore that had recently opened on the interstate. The people of **Glenwood** were not happy about the enterprise. John could only imagine the reaction as he got off the bus and faked a walk to the store. The report is that there was an initial gasp followed by laughter when they realized it was a joke.

When John dons his cowboy hat, he is not being phony; he owns a ranch in Nebraska where he rides horses and raises cattle. He is also a self-reliant lawyer, businessman, rural economic developer and community philanthropist. In business, he operates in a straightforward manner with no games. During the agricultural crisis in the 1980s, Glenwood State Bank was ranked by an investment research firm as the nation's 11th strongest among institutions with assets of more than $25 million.

We drove north out of **Glenwood** and the town seemed to be following us as we drove by a string of houses on large lots and acreages that continued for miles. When we finally escaped the town's grasp, we were within a few miles

of **Mineola**, where we stopped for lunch. It was "Taco Thursday" at the Mineola Steak House, the only viable business on Main Street in this once thriving German community. It was quiet at the restaurant on this winter day, but "Taco Thursday" during the summer is another story. It has become a tradition for hoards of bicyclists from the Council Bluffs/Omaha area to ride ten miles down the Wabash Trace Trail to Mineola for tacos and beer. Behind the bar there was a shelf that held 30 pitchers or more—evidence that the owners, Clint and Rebecca Howard, were prepared. Slick, the bartender, told us, "There are always more bike accidents in the rush to get to the bar than on the leisurely ride home."

Fueled by a sinful, breaded pork tenderloin, topped with fried onions, bacon and cheese, I drove us to **Red Oak**, the county seat of **Montgomery County**. As penance for that sandwich, I won't be able to order a bacon-cheese-burger or pork tenderloin for at least another six months.

In **Red Oak** we drove past the towering Montgomery courthouse that was built in 1901. A block beyond the court-

house is the main square of downtown. A park in the middle of the square is the setting for war memorials of World War I, World War II, the Korean War and the Vietnam War. Starting with the Civil War, **Red Oak** has paid an extraordinary price in the loss of its sons. The town provided more Union troops per capita than any other in the state. Early World War II battles claimed a disproportionate number of casualties from **Red Oak**. On March 6, 1943, more than 100 telegrams arrived bearing news of **Red Oak** soldiers missing in action. In 1944, the recognition and gratitude of the nation was expressed with the U.S. Navy christening a cargo and ammunition ship, "Red Oak Victory." This ship is presently part of the Richmond Museum in Richmond, California.

We drove through downtown into a residential district known as Heritage Hill. On this hill there is a plethora of grand houses built during **Red Oak's** heydays between 1870 and 1916. These impressive structures embody the Victorian, Queen Anne, Georgian, Italianate, English Tudor and Prairie styles of architecture. Most of them are

Heritage Hill

Heritage Hill

Jerry Dietz, KCSI radio

well-maintained or have been restored.

After research at the library, we drove to the Cabin on the Creek B&B where we were to bunk down for the night. A sign over the entrance read, "Come as a guest and leave as family." The family feeling began immediately as we entered the large, modern-day, log home. There was no lobby or sign-in. The entrance opened to a spacious, vaulted-ceiling living room with log crossbeams and a stone fireplace. Ron and Carol Keast warmly greeted us at the door. They showed us our room off a loft area on the second floor. We shared a bathroom with another couple—just like family.

That evening we dined at Johnny's Steakhouse in **Red Oak**. The exterior had a worn, uninviting look but Ron and Carol assured us the food was good. We opened the unfinished, plywood entrance door and entered a bar and adjoining dining room. It was clean and pleasant enough. The walls were partially covered with sheet paneling. Wall art consisted of Budweiser displays and "No Smoking" signs. We were seated at a table with stack chairs below a Budweiser display of historic Bud labels. The food was good;

Stanton white house

36

Stanton

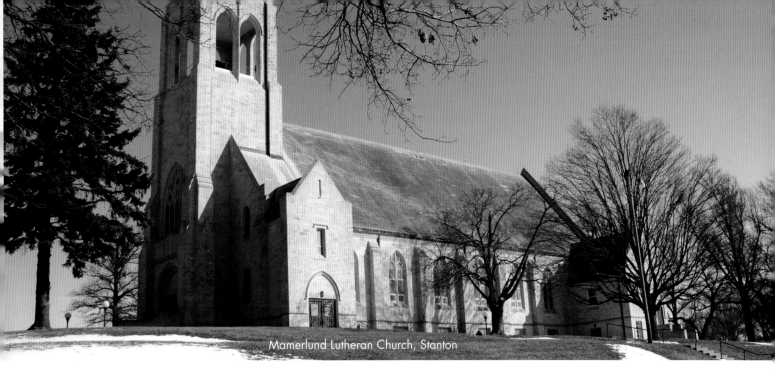
Mamerlund Lutheran Church, Stanton

we each enjoyed a jumbo shrimp dinner.

After a good night's rest, we joined the Keasts for breakfast. Ron and Carol began their relationship as the only two kids in third grade in a country school. They grew up as buddies playing games and enjoying the amenities of farm life, such as building a community of rooms and tunnels out of square hay bales in the barn. When they got older, they split and went to different schools. They eventually married other people. A few years after their spouses passed away, they reunited and the buddy relationship became a love relationship. They have been happily married for eight years.

Country Sunshine Radio Station (KCSI) beams out across **Montgomery County** with local and national news, music, swap meets, school menus, church services and any information that the people of the county need to know. The advertisers who support this station get their money's worth. Promotions generate large flows of customers. Items sell quickly on the swap meet and the other, aforementioned services are greatly appreciated. And it's always fun to listen to some country

music during the week and gospel on Sunday. Jerry Dietz and his wife Marilyn are the delightful personalities who make this station a valuable asset to **Red Oak** and surrounding towns.

We stopped to take a photo of Jerry at work behind the mike. Marilyn told us he would be done with an interview in a few minutes and would be happy to pose for a picture. He finished the interview; I took the picture and was about to leave when he asked if he could talk to me for a couple of minutes. Not knowing what he had in mind, I said, "Sure." As soon as I sat down, a microphone appeared and Jerry started asking questions. My plans for this book went out on the airwaves in **Montgomery County**.

Every June, planes of many designs and vintages fly through the air with the Red Oak Airport as their destination. A large breakfast awaits the pilots. After partaking in this delicious feed, they look at each other's aircraft and compare notes. Curious area residents are also drawn to the unique display of aircraft.

Many of **Red Oak's** 6,200 residents work in manufacturing plants that produce military batteries, hydraulic hoses,

plastic bottle covers and flour tortillas. They can work out in a new, state-of-the-art YMCA. Other recreational facilities are typical of Iowa towns of this size.

Down the road is a special little community of ethnic Swedes named **Stanton**. It is the hometown of actress Virginia Christine who played Mrs. Olson in Folgers coffee commercials. Consequently, the town's two water towers have added handles to make them look like coffee cups. They are painted in a bright, Swedish rosemalling pattern. To set them off, all the houses in town are painted white. Well, almost all of them are; we noticed one that was yellow. The owner of that house is probably a Norwegian who is confused about his colors.

Further down the road is a pretty little town of about 1,300 people who had to live down the most notorious unsolved murder in Iowa history. On June 10, 1912, an unknown assailant with an ax killed six members of the Moore family and two young houseguests. The town of **Villisca** first tried to make the memory of this tragedy go away. That, of course, failed so presently the house is identified with a sign in front. Strange things have

Cabin by the Creek Inn

Carol and Ron Keast

37

Johnny Carson's birthplace, Corning

Ax murder house, Villisca

happened in the house since the murders and many people are convinced it is haunted. A paranormal investigation provided audio, video and photographic proof of paranormal activity. I haven't seen this proof, but I doubt there is a better setting for such activity.

As we continued east, we stopped to look at Viking State Park. It's a nice interlude in farm country. Cedar trees accent the hilly wooded terrain. The centerpiece is beautiful Viking Lake.

The southern Iowa countryside continued its rolling prairie character as we moved on to **Adams County**. Maybe rolling doesn't accurately describe it as it's becoming more rugged with hills becoming sharper and valleys deeper.

Early pioneer reports in the **Adams County** area tell of vicious wild animals. Cougars, bobcats and wolves continuously harassed the settlers. It was a challenge to farm and protect livestock.

The county's first settler, Elijah Walters, was up to the challenge. He was a well-muscled, 6-foot-4-inch Kentuckian who immigrated to Missouri and then to Iowa in 1846. He brought his wife Nancy, son Isaac, daughter Mariah and a supply

Adams County Courthouse, Corning

Juke Box Cafe, Corning

Adams County House of History, Corning

Adams County Speedway, Corning

of corn meal. This staple was supplemented with game, nuts and acorns. In their habitat, Walters found evidence of earlier Indian occupants. Occasionally an Indian would return to look over the deserted camps and graves and silently leave. At a later brush with Indians, his corn crop was burned and the family nearly starved to death. They survived by selling furs and skins to secure food. In 1849, he moved his family to a site that is present day Carbon and built a gristmill. Most of **Adams County's** subsequent settlers came through Missouri.

An exception to the Missouri scenario was the 1852 immigration of French Icarians. They were a group led by Frenchman Etienne Cabet who was convinced men could share labor and profits and that capital should be owned by all and all should work for the common good. Their motto was, "All for each and each for all." They made a gallant effort at Utopia by setting up a community of various tradesmen and well-educated people. Among the possessions toted to the new land was a 2,000-volume library. They taught language, music, painting and dramatic art to their own people and

others in the county. Alas, there was no Utopia in the new land. After a time, dissatisfaction arose and the people could not agree on how to conduct affairs. In 1876, a division was made and, in 1895, the end of the colony was declared.

Adams County was established in 1851. Historians are unclear if it was named after John Adams (second president) or his son John Quincy Adams (sixth president). The first county seat was Quincy (I don't know if the sixth president's middle name figures in this). At any rate, Quincy was abandoned when the seat was moved to **Corning**. Quincy is no longer part of the landscape. After a couple of short-lived frame structures, a brick, Queen Anne-style courthouse was built in 1890. It began to deteriorate in the '40s so it was razed in 1955. The new, contemporary building that replaced it was praised by *The Des Moines Register* in 1955. Years later, the *Register's* Iowa Boy, Chuck Offenburger, called the coral and turquoise structure "the ugliest courthouse in the state." Today, it is gleaming white and looks pretty good.

Corning's main business street rises in elevation to meet the courthouse at the

top of the hill. Stores on both sides of the street step up the incline. Brick streets stretch out into the residential areas. Behind one storefront is an art gallery and behind another is a large antique/consignment shop named Antiques on Main. One corner of the shop has been converted to a small, '50s-style snack eatery named Jukebox Café. My lunch here was a healthy contrast to that Mineola tenderloin. I'm on the road to recovery.

Famed, talk show host Johnny Carson began life in **Corning**. His birthplace is being developed into a museum. He has acknowledged his roots by generously donating money to community projects.

A county museum is housed in an old, stone jailhouse. The bars are still on the windows. It served as a county jail and sheriff's quarters from 1877 to 1955.

When it is playtime, you can go boating, skiing, fishing or swimming at nearby lakes. Camping sites and log guest cabins are available at Lake Icaria. Auto racing at the Adams County Speedway in **Corning** features the Whelen All-American Series with late models, modifieds, pro streets and hobby stocks. And you can celebrate the good life at the

Corning Activity Center

Corning

Lake Icaria, Adams County

Creston Coffee Club—Marshel, Roger, Dennis, Bernard, and Ron

annual Main Street Fiesta. Youth games in the park, Texas Hold'em in the legion and music in the beer garden are some of the favorite attractions.

Corning and **Adams County** are fortunate to have selfless business leaders who put the community first. The late Austin Turner was often mentioned as a "mover and shaker." Clothing was his business and promoting **Corning** and **Adams County** was his passion. He also served the state as chairman of the DOT and as a Blue Cross/Blue Shield board member. He was the founder and first president of the Southwest Iowa Coalition and was the first president of the Adams Community Economic Development Corporation. ACED was instrumental in raising $1 million for the purchase of land and for the construction of a speculative building in an effort to lure industry. It worked—the industrial park now has four buildings and three industries. Mike Grundman, the current president of ACED, says, "Everyone in this organization is the same height. We work together and at our coffee sessions; we keep each other humble. It's a constant struggle, but it is a labor of love."

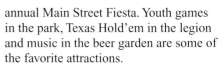

Kelly's, Creston

Creston Depot

Creston Depot

This winter has been one of the snowiest and coldest on record and the first thawing days in March were a welcome relief. However, it was just a teaser as we were again hit with a cold blast as we entered **Union County**. My positive attitude of enjoying all the seasons is tested when winter drags on into March.

In the **Union County** seat of **Creston**, there is no downtown square—it is a railroad town. It was platted with the tracks as the central focal point. The business district sprouted on the north side and the early wealth was concentrated in that area. The Burlington and Missouri River Railroad chose the town site in 1878 because it was level and the crest point between the two great rivers. The name **Creston** was derived from this geological fact.

The railroad made **Creston** a division point for all trains crossing Iowa, thereby building a major locomotive repair shop and round house (largest west of Chicago) among other railroad service facilities. The resulting boom made the town more like Chicago in character than the typical agriculture-based communities of Iowa. Early residents came from

Ohio, Illinois, Pennsylvania and New York. Immigrants from Ireland, Germany, Sweden and Bohemia added to the mix to make **Creston** a very interesting city.

This interesting mix didn't always get along real well. The early days were depicted as rough and ready. English novelist Robert Louis Stevenson's reaction to **Creston**, as he traveled by rail around the U.S., was that it was "where the West begins." Writing in 1879, he noted it was where he encountered the first open display of handguns and experienced seeing a passenger without a ticket bodily thrown from a moving train.

Railroading is still a major part of **Creston's** psyche today. Its passenger service continues with one of Iowa's few Amtrak stops and there are 30 freight stops daily. A magnificent, three-story railroad depot built in 1899, still dominates the central part of the city. It originally serviced countless travelers ranging from presidents to circus troupes. The second floor housed the **Creston** division headquarters on the Burlington line.

Today, **Creston's** senior citizens enjoy meals and cards in a first floor senior center. There is a doll collection of

first ladies in a wide hallway and a large, model train display occupies the original waiting room. Municipal offices are located on the second floor.

Another gathering place for seniors is the genealogy room in the Creston City Library. Six to eight "old guys" meet at 9 a.m. and another six to eight meet at 10 a.m. Monday through Friday. They rest on Saturday and Sunday. We sat in with the 10 a.m. gathering of Marshel Fredrickson, Roger Nurnberg, Dennis Kirkland, Bernard Shea and Ron Cook. They are diverse in their former occupations—from Marine to carpet-layer to police chief. Roger is not quite retired yet, so he is called the apprentice. The first thing on the agenda is to make the coffee and then let the enlightened conversation flow. At the urging of the rest of the group, Bernard bought a computer to aid in his genealogy pursuits. In his first effort, he bought a word processor, which wasn't of much use since he didn't type. He then ordered a computer by phone from Dell, and in another order, they sent him two of the same model. To date, this plunge into the computer age has resulted in purchasing six computers. I was afraid

Creston grain elevator

41

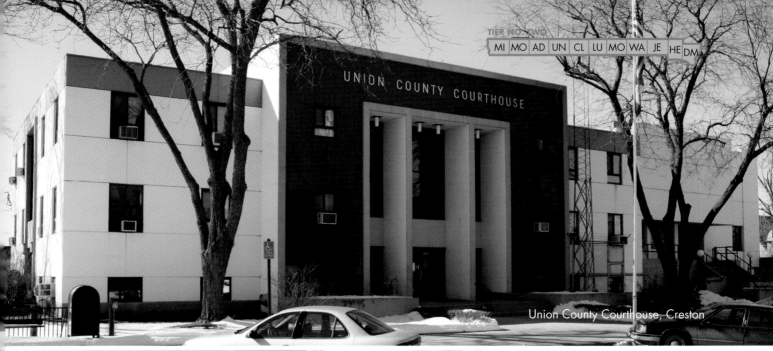

Union County Courthouse, Creston

Creston Red Hat Society

to ask how they were working for him. When asked why they live in **Creston**, Roger said, "Can't beat the green grass and trees." Ron said, "It's the fresh air." Bernard said, "Not enough money to get out." He lives in the same house he was born in. Roger says that it's falling in. Bernard responds, "Just the ceiling!"

We decided it was time to get serious so we called on Ellen Gerharz, director of the Creston Chamber of Commerce. Ellen is an Iowa native who lived in Billings, Montana, for 14 years. She is a University of Iowa graduate and, when her two daughters also chose to be Hawkeyes, she decided it might be a good idea to move back to Iowa and pay in-state tuition. While she likes Iowa and does a wonderful job of promoting **Creston**, she doesn't mask her love of the Rocky Mountains. We learned a lot about her other love—present day **Creston**—in our visit.

The downtown area is referred to as "uptown" in **Creston's** promotions to emphasize its progressive, "can-do" attitude. Ninety-six percent of its stores are occupied. No apologies are made for a large Wal-Mart on the edge of town. They

42
One of the first Phillips stations, Creston

Ellen Gerharz

"Uptown" Creston

pay taxes, employ workers and draw people from their trade base of 40,000 people. But, uptown is the heart of the community and it is imperative to keep it healthy. **Creston's** leaders aggressively pursue agriculture and industrial development. Sixteen industries employ about 1,600 workers. A couple of names you might recognize are Bunn-O-Matic coffee makers and GummiBears. Festivals include Hot Air Balloon Days in September and an impressive Fourth of July celebration with a parade and fireworks. Roger, from the library coffee group, plays a major role in the success of the fireworks display.

We ate lunch at Kelly's Flower and Gift Shop in **Creston**. The restaurant has a small, central dining area and additional tables set among the floral and gift displays. The ceiling is corrugated steel and the walls are knotty pine. It all works and the sandwiches were tasty. Back in a corner behind the floral and gift displays was a gathering of Creston's Red Hat Society. Their resplendent appearance with red hats and purple dresses begged to be photographed. I obliged.

On to **Afton**, a town of 900-plus, that was the first **Union County** seat. It has a square where a courthouse stood and was operational from 1857 to 1890. Meanwhile, **Creston** built a spec building that had all the earmarks of a courthouse. An election was held and the voters okayed a move of the county seat to **Creston** where the aforementioned building was leased to the county for 99 years for one dollar. The rejected **Afton** building was used for many purposes, including a college, before it was demolished in 1946. A contemporary-style building in **Creston** presently serves the needs of **Union County**.

A couple of miles north of **Afton**, there is an 80-acre piece of land that has been in Doug Seeley's family for four generations. Doug, who retired from a job as the vice-president of accounting for Wells Fargo Financial in Des Moines, built a nice house on a wooded hill where he resides with his wife Joy and three yellow labs. He likes the quiet atmosphere and easy access to outdoor sports of hunting and golf. Twelve Mile Lake is less than a mile away. He finds taking in the Union County Fair in Afton refreshing. He says, "You're around a great bunch of

kids who exhibit and there is a great deal of parental involvement."

The Mormon influence on Iowa history once again rises out of the rolling prairie. Mt. Pisgah in eastern **Union County** is where several thousand Mormons settled before they pushed on westward to Utah. A memorial is all that remains at the site. A marker bears the names of 65 Mormons who died there; there are no individual graves.

Because the site was only a few miles off our route, we decided to motor on over. We followed the signs to an unpaved road where an arrow pointed two miles to Mt. Pisgah. Unpaved did not describe the condition it was in. As we started down a hill, the road became softer and the ruts deeper. We realized we had made a mistake. Looking for a place to turn around replaced our quest to see Mt. Pisgah. Turn around we did, and we slowly returned to pavement with our undercarriage scraping mud.

Back on solid surface with mud flying, we crossed the **Clarke County** line heading for **Osceola**. Osceola is another county seat with a courthouse planted in a town square. In the early

Doug Seeley

United Methodist Church, Osceola

43

Mary Ellen and Jim Kimball

Chief Osceola

TIER NO. TWO
MI MO AD UN CL LU MO WA JE HE DM

OSCEOLA

days, before a courthouse was built, the town square park was rented to a farmer who pastured some of his Jersey cows there. A water tank and a windmill provided the ornamentation. Today, a contemporary-style courthouse with a need of ornamentation sits on the real estate.

The businesses around the square looked interesting so we decided to take inventory. This is what we saw: fashion and bridal shop, vision center, women's exercise facility, bank, clothing store, hardware store, restaurant, art gallery, boutique, salon, consignment shop, tax service, inspirational gift store, Chinese buffet, flower shop, card shop, vacancy, accounting firm, court services, post office, eye care center, office, theater, salon, plumbing/heating firm, gift shop, tavern, vacancy, ISU extension, dentist, medical supply store, coffee parlor, American Legion, public health, shoe and clothing store, appliance store, law office, video store and law office. These are businesses that keep a downtown vital. We tip our hats to them.

We stopped in Whites' Woodworking and Art Gallery on the square. It is a very nice, professional business that special-

OSCEOLA

AmTrack Station

OSCEOLA
PUBLIC LIBRARY

Kim White

Clarke County Courthouse

izes in signed prints of paintings and photos. Downstairs, they have oak furniture for sale and, in the back of the store, there is a room for ordering frames. A selection of frame samples covers one long wall and samples of their framing were on another wall. Kim and her husband Don started out as hog farmers, but tough economic times forced them to look elsewhere for their livelihood. They hit upon an idea of making frames from their farm's native oak and walnut. After making personal calls and explaining the process, they secured a contract with Pheasants Forever. This proved to be the springboard to a successful framing and gallery business. Kim is an active leader in the community. She was instrumental in getting two downtown organizations, Main Street and the Chamber of Commerce, to merge into one strong force. In visiting with her, we could feel the strength of her character and her love of the Osceola community.

Another capable lady who cares very much about Osceola is Mary Ellen Kimball. She and her husband, Dr. Jim Kimball, have served and continue to serve on many boards and committees

and, at present, Jim is a city councilman. Mary Ellen, who heads a PR firm (Kimball and Associates), was instrumental in convincing a riverboat gambling company they should locate in Osceola after they were turned down by Des Moines. She felt that the city reservoir, West Lake, would be a perfect location. Not everyone agreed. Opponents brought up the specter of a drunken gambler urinating off the side of the boat, trash everywhere and unsavory types moving to town. As it turns out, the only people urinating in the lake are fishermen; the trash and unsavory types never materialized. There are documented negatives with casino gambling and there are positive contributions to the communities. We heard the positive side from the Kimballs and others we talked to. Terrible's Lakeside Casino and Resort is well managed; brings in name entertainment; provides an excellent restaurant, meeting and banquet rooms; and is a generous contributor to Osceola's public works.

Other companies that make the economy hum are Hormel (processing plant), Simco (drilling machines), Moeller (stainless steel tanks) and Boyt (luggage

and sportsmen's clothing). Hispanics who work at some of these companies have added to the diversity of the community.

Osceola's namesake is not a local Indian chief; in fact, it is likely that Indian blood played a minor role in his ethnic makeup. His real name was Billy Powell and he was mostly white. He lived with runaway slaves, Seminoles and Caucasians in a Florida community that had no social structure. None of the Seminoles would admit to being chief. When President Jackson ordered the move of all Indians to territories west of the Mississippi, Billy Powell/Osceola took up the leadership mantle and refused to go. He and his 1,500 followers fought the move. Osceola was captured and imprisoned. While he was being held captive, New York artist, George Katlan, painted Osceola's portrait. Osceola died before the Civil War and became a folk hero. An Iowa settlement in its infancy adopted the hero's name.

After an afternoon of exploring the town and talking to the natives, we checked into the Evergreen Motel, a pre-franchise Route 66-type of facility. Owners Joe and Mary Erickson com-

Osceola

John L. Lewis Mining/Labor Museum, Lucas

Evergreen Motel in foreground and owner's house in background

pletely refurbished the '40s classic with new siding, new fixtures, new carpet and tile and fresh paint.

We signed in and were given a key on a plastic holder with the room number. We parked the car on the numbered slot in front of our room. There was an economy of space in the room, with a queen-size bed, new TV and small table and chairs. It also was an economy of price; it was a very good value.

After we unloaded our luggage and splashed some water on our faces, we went out for dinner at Redman's Pizza and Steak House and then it was on to Terrible's Lakeside Casino.

Casino gambling is not my thing. In games of pure chance, I have a history of bad luck. When I was in college and matched coins with buddies to see who bought the next round, I lost at least two-thirds of the time. It got so bad that my friends would ask, "Should we match coins or do you want to just go ahead and buy?" I was, however, lucky in love and my lovely wife does not share my attitude on gambling. Gambling is a significant part of the Iowa landscape these days so we hit upon a plan for reporting it. At

HARNESS

103
FRONT STREET
ANTIQUES

THE
COAL PONY
GRILL

46

Lucas

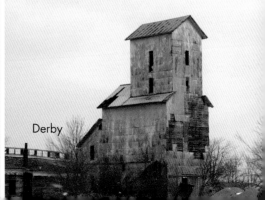

Derby

Amish wash day, Lucas County

each casino, Connie takes $10 out of my billfold and plays the slots. She plays until she loses it or wins $100 or to a time limit of 30 minutes. We are going to find out who has the loosest slots.

At Terrible's, I went to the cashier and asked for $10 worth of quarters. She informed me they don't use quarters in the machines—only dollar bills. I asked, "Are all the machines a dollar or more?" "No," she said, "You can play 25 cents, 50 cents or whatever you choose by . . ." She stopped when she saw the bewildered look on my face and asked one of the floor employees to give us slot machine instructions. At the end of the instructions, Connie was told to push a button to complete the play. She said she used to like it better when there was a lever to pull. He said to look to the right of the machine where there is a lever for people like you. Connie alternately worked the button and lever for 30 minutes and ended up even. We then added a new rule that you can't quit when you're even. She put one more dollar in and won $19. Yes!

The next morning we awoke to bitter cold with the wind blowing snow flurries around. On TV there was a report that it

was snowing even harder in Texas. We drove into **Lucas County** without much hope for a warmer day.

After proceeding for a few miles, we came to John L. Lewis' hometown of **Lucas**. Lucas started modestly as a shipping point for the railroad. It was first known as Lucas Station. Station was dropped in 1863 when the town applied for a post office. Coal was discovered in 1873 and the town was off to "boomsville." It, along with environs Cleveland and East Cleveland, reached a population of about 5,000 before the decline began.

Seven years after they began digging the **Lucas** area mines, a pioneer in the labor movement was born to Welsh immigrants. Early in life, he married Myrta Bell, a doctor's daughter, who had become a schoolteacher. She taught him the art of language and accounting. This man with the dark, bushy eyebrows and distinctive carriage rose to become president of the United Mine Workers of America. John L. Lewis is the most recognized and beloved labor leader of all time. In dedicating her book on **Lucas**, Betty Jane Spoon said this about John L. Lewis, "He is a man who does not let

others make the decisions he feels he should make. He is very humble, yet very proud. No man is too little for him to shake hands with, and no man has gotten too big for him to tell, 'no'."

Lucas has shrunk to about 300 people and shows the scars of decline. There are a few businesses still active on Main Street and there is a John L. Lewis Mining and Labor Museum that is worth a visit. The museum also pays tribute to another former **Lucas** resident, George Bernard, who wrote my favorite hymn, "The Old Rugged Cross."

About a mile west and south of **Lucas** is Stephens State Forest where you will find camping sites, picnic areas, hiking and biking trails, horseback riding areas, hunting and fishing.

Chariton, the **Lucas County** seat, is another one of those southern Iowa towns of 4,000 to 5,000 that lives big. An impressive, stone, Romanesque-style courthouse perched in the square is a focal point of a charming, downtown business district. Hy-Vee and Johnson Machine Works are two high profile companies that are the largest employers.

Charles Hyde and David Vredenberg

Lucas

Pin Oak Marsh, Lucas County

Lucas County Courthouse, Chariton

first established a grocery store in **Chariton** in 1936. This was the seed that sprouted into a major, Midwest chain of supermarkets with the brand name, Hy-Vee. The headquarters has since moved to Des Moines, but large and very sophisticated distribution centers remain in **Chariton**. Thirteen hundred employees work in these centers that serve a seven-state area. There is also a truck department that makes deliveries day and night, seven days a week. Another department is a carpentry shop where they build checkout lanes, shelving, courtesy counters, video displays and produce tables for the stores. As we were entering **Chariton** from the west, we took a left on Hy-Vee Drive and got caught up in the traffic of Hy-Vee trucks entering and leaving two huge complexes. One was the Hy-Vee dry goods distribution center and the other was the refrigeration distribution center.

Across the street from the distribution centers are two major production facilities of the other aforementioned high-profile company. In 1907, a Swede by the name of David Johnson started a shop for blacksmithing and repairing farm

48   Johnson Machine Works, Chariton

Ruth Comer

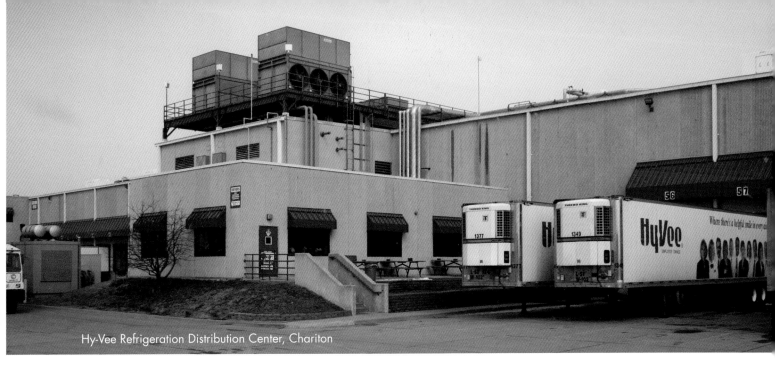
Hy-Vee Refrigeration Distribution Center, Chariton

machinery. This business evolved into fabricating steel, along with the typical machine shop work. In 1923, David died abruptly and the business was turned over to his 18-year-old son, Russell, who was a senior in high school. With permission from the school superintendent, he was given time off to run the business. As it happened, his company was erecting the steel for the town's new high school. Russell said that was probably the reason he got his diploma after missing so much school. Russell, a self-taught man, started the company on the road to taking on increasingly complicated projects. Today, its team of 100 employees works on commissions such as structural steel for all types and sizes of buildings and bridges. They have created large, elevated water tanks, and fabricated gates for locks and dams. Its sewage treatment equipment operates on every continent of the world, except Australia. Johnson Machine Works is still family-owned with Jeff Johnson as its leader. Old-fashioned, small town values and work ethics are applied to complicated projects with great success. There is no plan to change the formula.

To glean some more gems about

Chariton and **Lucas County**, we talked to Chariton Chamber Director, Ruth Comer. We learned that after the Mormons passed through, settlers slowly streamed in until the railroad came through in 1867. The flow increased when immigrants from Germany, Ireland and East European countries came to work in the coalmines. Recent migrations to the area are old order Amish and Ukrainians who came by way of Washington state. The Ukrainians chose Iowa because the weather and terrain are similar to their home country.

John Pierce, a county historian and owner of a pumpkin farm, believes there is a Civil War cannon buried beneath the courthouse. He secured the services of metal detection experts from Iowa State University to locate it. With IPTV watching, they started digging at a designated spot. They dug and dug, but there was no cannon. John is still convinced it is somewhere below the town square's surface. He might have trouble, however, convincing the supervisors to break up the basement floor of the courthouse in search of the elusive cannon.

John's Pumpkin Patch has been in

operation for 27 years. It is open daily from the last weekend in September through October. An annual festival features craft booths, caramel apples, antique tractors, oats threshing, a hay bale maze, a delicious fall-fare lunch and more. There is no admission charge.

We drove into **Monroe County** with the temperature rising to a spring-like day. The countryside had a Holstein appearance with large patches of white snow against a dark background. We met a convoy led by a pickup bearing a sign that read "over-sized load." Three, stretched-out trucks were each hauling a blade for a large wind turbine. Iowa is one of the nation's top three leaders in wind power generation.

The first white settlers in **Monroe County** came from mountainous regions in Pennsylvania, North Carolina and Virginia. They shunned the tall grass prairie in favor of clearing wooded areas as they did in the mountains back east. Settlers who came later took on the task of cutting into the sod of the prairie with a break plow that was designed specifically for that task. Two or three oxen provided the power to turn up the black dirt.

Red Haw State Park and Lake, Lucas County

Historic A. J. Stephens House, Chariton

St. Patrick's Catholic Church, Georgetown

Tim Holmes

Monroe County Courthouse, Albia

Large groups of Irish immigrants settled around **Georgetown** and **Melrose**. The best known of the country churches is St. Patrick's Catholic Church in **Georgetown**. Called the "Cathedral of the Prairie," it was built by Irish immigrants using locally quarried limestone. Today, it stands almost exactly as it did 140 years ago. **Monroe County** still has the largest percentage of Irish descendants in the state.

The heart of the southern Iowa coalfields is centered in **Monroe County** and the most compelling story of the rise and fall of the coalmining industry took place in its northeast corner. Ben Buxton, a Chicago and Northwestern Railway Company agent, was sent by the railroad to look over its interests in Iowa coal. Black laborers were brought from Kentucky and Tennessee to work in the mines alongside European immigrants. When mines north of the county ceased being profitable, tracks were extended south over the county line. Ben Buxton moved his laborers, both white and black, to a spot 12 miles north of **Albia** and founded the town of **Buxton**.

At the turn of the century, **Buxton**

Monroe County Courthouse

David A. Johnson

Monroe County Museum, Albia

quickly became one of the largest coalmining towns west of the Mississippi. At its peak there were 5,000 residents, half white and half black, working the mines and providing services. Blacks were as prominent as whites in the businesses and professions.

Buxton was probably the largest unincorporated town in the United States. There was no city government and no police force. Maintaining some semblance of order was the responsibility of county officers. Rowdiness and violence were prevalent but the town wasn't all bad. There were black Methodist and Baptist churches and a Swedish Lutheran church. There were schools for both races and, typically, they were integrated. Neither race could be blamed for all the evil influences nor could either race take credit for all the good.

In 1906, the Buxton area mines produced 1,183,143 tons of coal, which made Monroe County the most productive in Iowa. The peak of Iowa coal production was reached in 1917 when over nine million tons were mined—nearly one-fourth in Monroe County. Increased competition, the Great

Depression and other factors turned the boom into a bust and weeds started taking over abandoned buildings. Mine shafts were dynamited and Buxton became a ghost town. All that remains today is a cemetery.

A descendant of one of Buxton's Swedish miners is David A. Johnson, president of the Albia Industrial Corporation. We enjoyed a visit with him discussing past and present Albia. Present day Albia has the most beautifully preserved and restored downtown square that I have ever seen. David told us it wasn't always that way. It was an established town when the coalmining industry hit Iowa and benefited from the ensuing wealth. Impressive, Victorian-style business buildings were erected around the square. When the mines shut down, so did Albia's economy and it became a dirty, poor town. The buildings, however, withstood the decline to live again in splendor.

In the 1960s, Robert T. Bates, an interior designer in California, returned to his hometown and spearheaded a move called Operation Facelift. An architect was hired to provide a plan to refurbish

and paint 110 buildings. The funds were raised and the plan was executed to perfection. When Bates died, he left the city two and a quarter million dollars in the Robert T. Bates Foundation for future needs to maintain the square. His leadership prompted others to make contributions for community-enhancing projects. Albia's example has also been an inspiration for Iowa towns with similar challenges. I love these efforts and express my appreciation to those who work to keep small-town Iowa vital.

One of the projects the town took on was developing an elegant, first-class restaurant on the square. After mixed success in previous efforts, David said they have a new owner who appears to be doing quite well. We decided to see for ourselves. The Skean Block was the elegant, traditionally-decorated restaurant envisioned by the town's leaders. The soup and sandwiches we ordered lived up to expectations. When the owner entered the dining area, I recognized him as the same person who had developed an excellent, neighborhood restaurant in Des Moines. I can assure David that owner Tim Holmes is a good restaurateur.

Albia

Cargill ethanol/ag products complex, Eddyvillle

Wapello County Courthouse, Ottumwa

52

St. Mary's Catholic Church, Ottumwa

The effort to make **Albia** more attractive has paid off in drawing industry. One of the first companies that chose to locate there gave this reason for their decision, "**Albia** looks like a town that will be here 50 years from now." There have been a variety of companies setting up shop, providing stable employment.

We took a pleasant walk around the square and through the courthouse where we found a waiting room right out of the '30s with red, white and blue bunting over an exterior door. The sunny, 60-degree weather and picturesque town made us feel like we were on vacation.

As the day warmed up, more snow melted and the countryside took on the March blahs—dung-colored landscape, with mud everywhere; it was a "darkest before the dawn" scenario. It was not a feast for the eyes, but the weather was warmer and the blossoming of spring growth was imminent.

Common sights in Iowa these days, competing with grain elevators, are plumes of smoke/steam from ethanol plants. One of the largest is in Cargill's ag products processing complex in **Eddyville**, a town that straddles three

Joseph Helfenberger

Angry Des Moines River at Ottumwa dam

Ottumwa skateboarders

county lines. Cargill's operation also produces gluten and high fructose corn syrup among other products. They employ between 1,200 and 1,400 workers. **Eddyville** is also home to some great drag-racing at Eddyville Raceway Park with a full slate of events May through October.

Although this is the least attractive time of the year to view the Iowa landscape, we found the drive down the Des Moines River valley from **Eddyville** to **Ottumwa** pleasing. It is easy to understand why three Indian villages were established in the valley and surrounding hills of present-day **Ottumwa**. The Indians called it Ottumwanoc and this location was perfect for their lifestyle. A wide, crystal-clear river (as were all Iowa rivers before the plow) brimming with fish, turtles and clams complemented the woods full of game and fowl. Indian women with primitive tools easily cultivated clearings of fertile soil. The early white traders mixed with the Indians and provided them with blankets, traps, guns and ammunition on a credit basis. They knew they could collect with payments of furs and land. The bottom line is that

Ottumwa was a bustling community before Iowa became a state.

Chief Wapello, a powerful Indian ruler, pitched his tepee in the middle of present day **Ottumwa**, the county seat of **Wapello County**. The chief of Fox and Sac tribes was friendly to the whites. When he died in 1842, he was buried, at his request, by the side of his friend General Joseph M. Street, the first Indian agent in this territory. There are markers for their graves near **Agency** where the old Indian agency was located. This is also near the site of the signing of the treaty for purchasing Iowa from the Sac and Fox Indian tribes.

Steamboats plied their way to **Ottumwa** via the Des Moines River as early as 1843. The town was incorporated in 1851 and, by 1855, it was a thriving village of 1,000 with most of the requisite enterprises to serve the populous. The river with transportation and power potential in an area of untapped agricultural wealth drew the railroad and highways. Industry followed and continues to be a mainstay in **Ottumwa's** economy.

Cargill Excel Meat Solutions (2,250 employees) and John Deere Ottumwa

Works (950 employees) lead the way in food processing and manufacturing. John Morrell started a meat packing plant in the 1850s and John Deere has been making quality farm equipment since 1910. This is **Ottumwa's** character—quality manufacturing and processing.

Joseph Helfenberger, city administrator, can expound on **Ottumwa's** plusses from a fresh perspective as a resident of only three weeks. Iowa's friendliness is an overworked compliment in our state but Joe says, "Ottumwans are exceptionally friendly, even by Iowa standards." The only thing Joe knew about Iowa before looking into his present job was that someone in Green Bay, Wisconsin, told him it was a good place to hunt. A Wisconsinite coming to Iowa to hunt? I like that! Yes, it is a good place to hunt, especially in the unglacierized region of southern Iowa. Joe agrees, but says there are many more amenities that make **Ottumwa** a great place to live. Beautiful, old and new buildings sit in their groupings amid open space and hundreds of acres of parks. The Bridge View Center, that opened in 2007, provides 50,000 square feet of meeting,

Agency burial site

American Gothic
House Visitor
Center, Eldon

Bridge View Center, Ottumwa

Hotel Ottumwa

exhibition and banquet space, as well as a state-of-the-art theater for music and performing arts. It also has some neat architectural touches such as retaining part of the façade of the old armory building and commissioning an inlaid, marble mural as a focal point in the lobby floor. There is also a fine museum, an outdoor water park, a full-service YMCA, a junior college, good shopping and more. Festivals include Pro-Balloon Races in June, Sand in the City (sand sculpture competition) and Oktoberfest (brats, beer and entertainment). Then there is the joy of watching bald eagles soar along the river where they have a major nesting area.

For our overnight, we booked a room at the Hotel Ottumwa in the heart of downtown. This is a very nice, refurbished, 1917 hotel with a bar, restaurant, salon and banquet meeting rooms. Our room was spacious, well-appointed and had a welcoming king-size bed.

Before we could rest our bodies on that bed, we had some nourishment needs to take care of. The "luck o' the Irish" was with us when we discovered Nick & Joie's Ristorante Italiano and Irish Pub. It had the feel of a nineteenth century pub

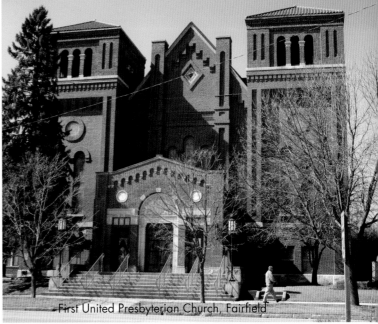

Nick & Joie's Risorante Italiano and Irish Pub, Ottumwa

First United Presbyterian Church, Fairfield

with a bar taken from an old New York hotel and mirrors with hand-carved, English oak frames. Marble columns, a majestic lion and gargoyle heads added to the charm. It was beautiful and the concept of serving Italian food with Irish drinks is brilliant. We each ordered a Smithwicks draft to go with our lasagnas. It doesn't get any better!

After a good night's sleep, we drove southeast with **Eldon** as our destination. On the way, we stopped to pay our respects to Chief Wapello and General Street at their gravesites near Agency. The house depicted in Grant Wood's famous *American Gothic* painting was an **Eldon** residence. It appeared to be freshly painted (the masking was still on the windows). A new interpretation center, with professionally arranged displays and photos including an entertaining collection of parodies, is located across the street. You can also view a video of Grant Wood and his work, as well as purchase a memento, T-shirt or book in the gift shop.

As we continued our trip, fields were revealing themselves from under the snow, exposing corn stover mixed with black dirt—a result of fall plowing or disking. We observed a farmer or two out taking notice of conditions. I'm sure they were anxious for the ground to dry enough for spring planting.

Today's farmers rework terrain that was once wild prairie with grasses reaching the height of six to eight feet. Breaking this sod would be formidable with the equipment available to a modern day farmer. Can you imagine walking behind a pioneer break plow pulled by oxen? Early **Jefferson County** settler John Rush Parsons grew tired of making the difficult, six-mile trip from his farm to **Fairfield**. He decided to open things up a bit by hitching a four-yoke team of eight oxen to an enormous, sod-breaking plow. He drove them as straight as he could through the tall grass with the lead oxen disappearing as the grass folded back around them. It took him two days to reach **Fairfield**, but the resulting trail made the trip easier in the future. We were about six miles from **Fairfield** as we breezed along Highway 34. We arrived six minutes later.

The roots of the highly-acclaimed Iowa State Fair reach from Des Moines to **Fairfield**. In the fall of 1852, E. S. Gage, a **Fairfield** storekeeper, made his barn and barnyard available for a small exhibition of livestock and new farming equipment. It was not very successful, but they tried again the next year. Things improved the second time around with added exhibits and prizes. In 1854, a fairgrounds was built and Iowa's first State Fair was held in **Fairfield**.

The State Fair has since moved to Des Moines, but **Fairfield** has continued to thrive. Forty-three manufacturing plants employ 1,710 people. They include: Dexter (commercial laundry products); Fairfield Aluminum Castings; Nelson Company (machine castings); Agri-Industrial Plastics (blow molded plastics); and Creative Edge (inlaid marble designs). The latter has a brochure of impressive examples of their work done across the country.

After driving around **Fairfield's** square and checking out the imposing, Romanesque-style Jefferson County Courthouse, we stopped at the Entrée Café for an organic lunch. I ordered a sandwich and asked the waitress for milk. She proceeded to pour me a cupful out of a plastic jug. I noticed there were some

Ottumwa

Iowa field in March

55

Fairfield Community Theatre

Jefferson County Courthouse, Fairfield

curd-like objects floating in the milk and pointed them out to the waitress. She said that was because it was organic. I spent some time on a farm during my youth and saw milk come directly from a cow's teat and there were no curds popping out. Those cows ate grain and hay. I wonder what organic feed consists of today.

The latest waves of immigrants to **Fairfield** are Transcendental Meditators, followers of Maharishi Mahesh Yogi. The migration began in 1974 when the leaders of Maharishi International University abandoned their pricey Santa Barbara, California, location in favor of a recently purchased college campus in **Fairfield**. They paid $2.5 million to creditors of the abandoned campus of bankrupt Parsons College.

The followers of Maharishi's TM movement (it is not a religion) were not an immediate hit with the natives. They did not raid each other's camps, but the very diverse cultures took time to adjust to each other. Generally, the adjustment has been made to **Fairfield's** benefit.

The school is presently known as Maharishi University of Management to reflect its emphasis on business. There is,

Golden Dome, Maharishi
University of Management

ICON Art Gallery, Fairfield

Americus Gallery, Fairfield

however, no de-emphasis on science and the arts. It is accredited by the Commission on Institutions of Higher Education of the North Central Association of Colleges. Doctorate, master's and bachelor's degree programs are taught by internationally recognized scholars and researchers. It is the only accredited university in the world that adds TM to traditional education. Students round out their educational experience by participating in clubs, sports and recreational events.

Film maker David Lynch (*Elephant Man, Blue Velvet, Straight Story* and *Mulholland Drive*) donated $1 million to fund scholarships for students who want to learn meditation techniques taught at Maharishi University of Management. He said, "America needs at least one university to teach the sciences of peace and to actually promote peace in the world."

Achievers interested in TM can get a head start at Maharishi School. It is a private school for grades K-12 with grades 7-12 accredited as a college preparatory school. A marquee in front of the school claims state championships in drama, golf, history, math, photography/art, poet-

ry writing, science, spelling bee, academic decathlon, tennis, track, National Merit Scholars and Odyssey of the Mind.

It should be pointed out that the TM aspects of **Fairfield** are getting a little extra ink because it is a unique situation. They are being assimilated—while maintaining their character—by a progressive Iowa town that has a special character of its own. This makes Fairfield a very interesting place with a great future.

The arts community is getting a head start on that great future. There are so many things happening that I can only hit the highlights. To help us in that regard, we talked to Cathy Wadsworth and Kemlyn Tan Bappe. These are two, international ladies who love **Fairfield**. Cathy, the executive director of Art Walk, was born in England and grew up in Fiji. Since September 2007, Cathy has been the first, full-time, paid employee of Art Walk, a tradition dating back five years. On the first Friday of every month, all of **Fairfield's** art venues open up for an evening celebration of the arts with a different theme each month. There are 19-plus galleries, as well as many stores that include art and crafts in their inventory.

Three hundred local artists create a wide range of art pieces. In February, the theme was film; in March, it was dance (18 groups); and in April, dolls and toys. Art Walk is a big draw for **Fairfield**.

Kem Bappe, who was born in Singapore, is an international traveler and an agent for 18 artists. She is an artist in her own right; her current work is done in batik style with liquid resist and silk dyes on rice paper. She finds **Fairfield** very welcoming. She says, "If you ask directions, people often escort you to your destination. You have space to create and Art Walk is a dialogue platform."

Kem took us to Iowa Contemporary Art (ICON) gallery where Steven Erickson's profound oil paintings were on display. In the rear of the gallery is a studio/ classroom where ICON artistic director, Bill Teeple, teaches. She then took us to Revelations Bookstore/Café where we met John and Cindy Preston. Cindy's special craft is textiles. She has taken wool from sheep she raised and used Kool-Aid to make dyes for the yarn in making sweaters and afghans. She is also a writer and editor.

When John came to Iowa from

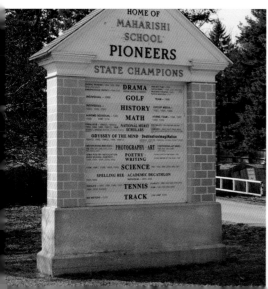

Connie takes notes as we visit with
Cathy Wadsworth and Kemlyn Tan Bappe

57

Vedic City

John and Cindy Preston

Oakland Mills dam

58

Maryland, he fell in love with the Iowa landscape and has been painting it ever since. He has a home and studio on a rural acreage situated in that beloved landscape. He captures every aspect of the Iowa scene—the light, the weather, changing seasons, the crops, the undeveloped and the developed. And it is done in a beautiful style that is not mundane.

There is also some serious theatre work taking place in **Fairfield**. They have a beautiful, new building with the latest theatre technology. Besides community theatre, there are off-Broadway (entitled Way-Off Broadway), professional, experimental theatre performances.

I wanted to explore this renaissance story further, but we had to move on to Maharishi **Vedic City**. Located north of Fairfield, the city was incorporated in 2001. Vedic is taken from the Sanskrit word, "Veda," which means knowledge. It is the world's first city built according to Vedic architecture in harmony with Natural Law. In its present form, there are a few public buildings and residential developments scattered around the incorporated area. They all face east and are crowned with a kalash that caps the

Krista Watts

Brahma-Sthan (a central atrium or open space). The current population of 420 is expected to be 1,200 by the year 2010.

Shortly after leaving brand-new, Maharishi **Vedic City**, we crossed the **Henry County** line and arrived at the almost-new city of **Westwood**. Established in 1982, it was a more typical Iowa scene consisting of traditional and ranch style homes. The setting was wooded hills bordering the Skunk River with a pond as the focal point. It was a pleasant residential development within a short drive to **Mount Pleasant**.

We returned to Highway 34 and drove a few more miles until we saw a sign pointing to Oakland Mills, a park and nature center. We took a right and after about two miles, we crossed the Skunk River and entered a park located adjacent to a dam. There was a rusty, old, double-span bridge a couple hundred yards upriver from the dam. It was built for horse and buggies and early autos; it is now a walking bridge. A campground with picnic tables, grills and hookups looked inviting—even in the winter.

The original dam, built in 1839, was the first on the Skunk River. The adjacent gristmill was milling grain before Iowa became a state. Oakland Mills consequently became a retail center and was promoted as a location of the **Henry County** seat but lost out to more centrally-located **Mount Pleasant**. A sawmill and a woolen mill were added to the industrial base. I could feel the history of pioneers harnessing the forces of nature as I walked around the deserted park on a mid-March day.

Other than central location, **Mount Pleasant** had another quality that made it attractive—the spirit of cooperation. Deeply religious settlers put others before themselves. Before the government survey was made, they began making claims on land in 1835, using their own system. In 1838, after the government survey, they developed a "pro-tem" law stating that the first person settling a piece of land had first chance to bid on his land when it came on the market. The land grab and resulting disputes did not happen. That spirit is prevalent today in this beautiful town with the pleasant name.

Our first stop in **Mount Pleasant** was at the library located in a refurbished, former high school building. The art deco building also housed the original gym and auditorium, which are now used for community events. It is a very well-done conversion—a great idea.

At the Area Chamber Alliance, we met executive vice president Jennifer Daly and administrative coordinator Krista Watts. These lively ladies gave us a run-down on how the spirit of cooperation still benefits the town. This is manifested in the successful celebrations and festivals held throughout the year. A Wal-Mart on the outskirts of town lives in harmony with a vibrant downtown that has no store vacancies. A 900-employee Wal-Mart Distribution Center gives them additional affection in the community.

The Midwest Old Threshers Reunion is a high profile festival that dates back to 1950. It is a nostalgic look back to our Midwest agricultural heritage. The five-day festival takes place during Labor Day weekend and draws tens of thousands of people from across the Midwest and country. Live action displays center on restored mechanical equipment such as steam engines, farm tractors, stationary gas engines and popular, narrow-gauge trains and electric trolleys. The Midwest

Oakland Mills campground

Mount Pleasant

Old Main, Iowa Wesleyan College

Henry County Courthouse, Mount Pleasant

Old Threshers Heritage Museums located on the exhibition grounds are open daily from Memorial Day to Labor Day. The museums' buildings are stocked with displays of virtually every aspect of turn-of-the-century, Iowa farm life.

One of the Old Threshers Reunion's most popular activities is a ride on the Midwest Central Railroad (MCRR). For 40 years, a non-profit, all-volunteer organization has dedicated itself to preserving steam-powered trains. They put in thousands of hours each year to keep the steam engines working and the tracks repaired. In October, you can ride with ghosts and goblins on the Haunted Rails, and on the first weekend in December, you can take a trip to the North Pole on the Polar Express. Santa will be in the caboose awaiting your request for Christmas presents. The train is also used for special occasions.

One more item for which the Old Threshers Reunion takes responsibility is the Theatre Museum of Repertoire America. It houses a unique collection of memorabilia from early American popular entertainment. This includes stage drops, quaint artifacts and a massive,

Salem

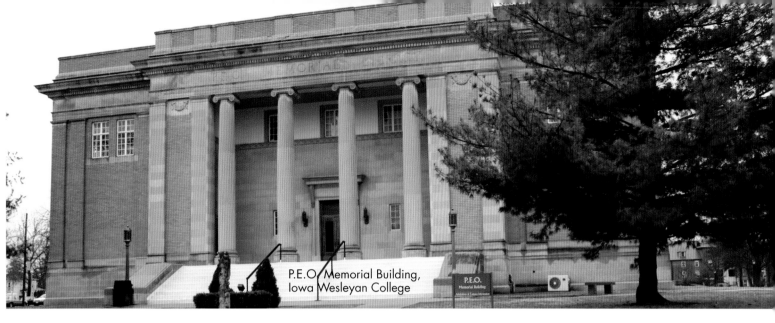

P.E.O. Memorial Building,
Iowa Wesleyan College

computer-catalogued library of scripts and music scores dating from 1850.

It isn't all play in **Mount Pleasant**. A diverse commerce base of 18 industries plus many local and national businesses provide livelihoods for its 8,700 residents. Hearth and Home (Heatilator fireplaces), Pioneer (seed corn), CECO Building systems (steel buildings) and West Liberty Food Processing are examples. A medium security prison and a mental health institute also provide jobs.

Iowa Wesleyan, a college affiliated with the United Methodist Church, is located in the heart of the city. This liberal arts college of 700 students dates back to 1846. It is rooted in the religious, educational and cultural aspirations of the early settlers. Coeducation was practiced almost from the beginning with Lucy Webster Killpatrick's graduation in 1859. Belle Babb Mansfield, who graduated in 1866, was the first woman admitted to the bar in the United States. In 1885, Susan Mosely Grandison was the first female black graduate. A more recent, woman graduate, Peggy A. Whitson, a Mount Ayr native was the first woman to command a space expedition.

In 1869, seven young philanthropists founded the P.E.O. Sisterhood on Iowa Wesleyan's campus. In 1927, the P.E.O. Sisterhood erected a library building on campus to honor those seven ladies. The building is now home to administrative offices of the college.

It is not only women from **Mount Pleasant** who went on to fame. James Van Allen, America's foremost space scientist, was born in Mount Pleasant and graduated as valedictorian from Mount Pleasant High School.

After our rainy tour of the town, we took refuge at the Bamboo House for lunch. They were serving a buffet of Asian dishes with Thai specialties—thoroughly enjoyable fare.

After lunch we drove to **Salem**, a Quaker settlement with a history of justice. With at least six homes used to hide runaway slaves, the town became known as the ticket office for the Underground Railroad. The Lewelling House, now a museum, had secret closets and trap doors to hide the runaways. In 1848, an angry mob of Missourians arrived in **Salem** toting a small cannon and threatening to blow holes in the house if nine

slaves weren't returned. The Quakers ended up making a pragmatic deal that returned a few slaves to their owners so the others could escape.

Leaving **Salem**, we drove in and out of the Skunk River valley. Why did they name the river the Skunk? It doesn't sound right when you are describing a beautiful part of Iowa. I suppose it is better than the Opossum River, but really!

We stopped at Geode State Park in the southeast corner of **Henry County**. It is a hilly, wooded getaway with a manmade lake and the usual camping facilities. The water on the lake was open—no ice. Is spring really here?

Arriving in **Burlington** on Highway 34, we were further into the city than I realized. We came over a hill and there was the big river immediately in front of us with its new bridge looking like a huge sailboat. I applied the brakes, fearing I was going to drive right into the river. When I realized it was a bridge, I feared there would be no more exits and we'd be in Illinois before we could turn around. At that moment I saw an exit for Main Street, flipped my turn signal and drove safely into downtown **Burlington**.

Geode State Park, Henry County

61

Mississippi River, Burlington

Des Moines County Courthouse, Burlington

It was late afternoon on a gloomy, rainy day as we wandered around the central business district and nearby residential areas. The character of the city gave our spirits a lift as we viewed vintage, well-maintained buildings situated on bluffs overlooking the river. Trains and barges added to the atmosphere. Overcast weather gave it a moody quality but did not detract from the ambiance.

After a research stop at the beautiful, new library, we checked into the Mississippi Manor, an elegant B&B near the business district. We parked our bags in the Tom Sawyer room and freshened up for a modest night out.

First on the agenda was dinner at the Drake restaurant on the riverfront. Drake Hardware was incorporated in 1899 and built this building in 1906. During its heyday, it was one of the top hardware distributors in the Midwest serving customers from Appalachia to the Rockies. Today, it is a top restaurant that knows how to prepare barbecue ribs. They were smoked to perfection before the sauce was added. Connie and I each ordered this entree and enjoyed every bite.

Thirty plus years ago at a social gath-

Burlington

Florence Patero and Connie

Burlington

ering, I met a person who worked in Des Moines but was not a native of Iowa. He said to me, "You know what Iowa should do? They should legalize gambling. It would make the state a lot more interesting." I kind of laughed and said, "Yeah, I suppose it would, but we don't need that and it will never happen." A few years later, Iowa became the third state to legalize gambling and the first state to have riverboat gambling. The idea was to pump some economic stimulus into its river cities. The law at the time had betting limits and the boats were required to cruise from time to time. Then Illinois decided to copy the idea, but they removed the betting limits. Soon thereafter, Iowa had to do the same to compete. Other gambling venues—horse racing and dog racing—were allowed in some additional cities. These operations lost money. To rectify this, new gambling laws allowed racetracks to install slot machines. Today, gambling establishments no longer have to be riverboats. Most types of casino gambling—from poker to slots—are legal. Many cities have large casinos and many more want in on the action. The person I talked to at

the party has seen his vision come true. **Burlington** was one of those river towns granted a riverboat casino at the beginning of the Iowa gambling saga. They named it Catfish Bend. This little riverboat has been dry-docked big time. Catfish Bend Casino is now a new, large complex located several miles from the river on the west side of the city.

Connie and I made our obligatory trip to the casino to see how loose their slots were. As it turned out, they were pretty tight. Connie lost the allotted $10 in 20 minutes. With two casinos in the bag, the running score is $9 ahead.

After a good night's sleep in Tom's room, we awoke to a bright, sunny day. Our breakfast was served at a table set in a window bay with a delightful view of the neighborhood. The interior view was also pleasant with eclectic furnishings, rugs and wall coverings complementing each other. After breakfast, innkeeper Florence Patero sat down with a cup of coffee and we were off on a very enjoyable discourse on **Burlington**.

Although the natural setting of this area has always been gorgeous, the first settlement was not. There was a lot of

sickness, rattlesnakes were prevalent and there were some rough types; murder was not uncommon. Suicide was rare because people died off fast enough without killing themselves. It was derisively labeled Catfish Bend—not a compliment. In 1834, a pioneer from Burlington, Vermont, settled in Catfish Bend and eventually persuaded the townsfolk that the community should be renamed **Burlington** after his hometown. Another name that has its roots in Burlington is Hawkeye. It was the early, and is the present, name of Burlington's newspaper, and in 1840, editor James G. Edwards successfully promoted it as the nickname of Iowa. More settlers poured in from the east. Many were professionals who brought culture and refinement and the groundwork was laid for a classy town that experienced rapid growth.

Burlington was a bustling port during the steamboat era and was well connected to rail transportation. The only steam style riverboats to dock in present-day **Burlington** are excursion boats. There is, however, serious port activity with commodity-hauling barges. The Burlington Northern Santa Fe, a major

Mississippi overlook, Burlington

Aldo Leopold display, Iowa Welcome Center

Snake Alley, Burlington

Burlington

U.S. railroad, crosses the Mississippi at **Burlington** and there is an Amtrak depot for passenger service. Commerce is alive and well with an array of industries.

In 1894, **Burlington's** famous Snake Alley was constructed as an experimental street design. The "crookedest street in the world" consists of five half-curves and two quarter-curves over a distance of 275 feet. It rises 58 feet from Washington Street to Columbia Street. The Snake Alley Criterium is one of the most physically challenging bike races in the Midwest. The centerpiece of this street race is a climb up Snake Alley.

Fun events and festivals include a duck-calling contest, bluegrass festival, foot races, farmers' market, blues festival, jazz festival, Steamboat Days and more.

Innkeeper Florence told us of a delightful man, Lloyd Maffitt, who lived on her street. He was a colorfully-dressed journalist who wrote for the *Burlington Hawk Eye*. He never owned a car or computer, walked everywhere and lived to be 92 years old. He was always an upbeat, "life is wonderful," kind of guy. If he passed her B&B and caught her eye, he would greet her with, "Good morning;

it's a great morning! I'll see you subsequently." He belonged to the symphony guild and was very involved in the arts. There is a piece of art at Diggers Rest Coffeehouse with his likeness and his name patterned after a familiar, impressionist art poster. Diggers was a favorite haunt of this unsung hero.

A "sung" hero, Aldo Leopold, was born and raised in **Burlington**; it was here he developed his love for hunting, exploring natural areas, writing and reading books about natural history. Armed with a Yale master's degree in forestry, Aldo was a pioneer in developing a concept of land ethics. He taught and wrote about stewardship as a way of using natural resources in a sustainable way, while maintaining an ecological balance among natural systems. In *A Sand County Almanac*, he wrote, "A thing is right when it tends to preserve the integrity, stability, and beauty of the biotic community. It is wrong when it tends otherwise."

We abandoned the city streets and drove north to **Mediapolis**. I associate the name with girls' basketball. As I recall, the Bullettes had a period of very good teams competing at the state level.

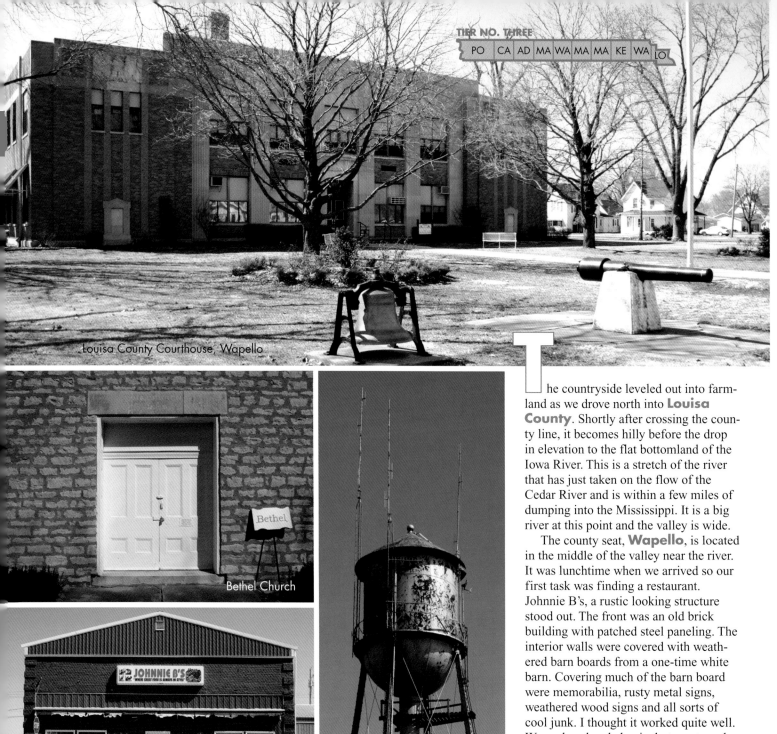

Louisa County Courthouse, Wapello

The countryside leveled out into farmland as we drove north into **Louisa County**. Shortly after crossing the county line, it becomes hilly before the drop in elevation to the flat bottomland of the Iowa River. This is a stretch of the river that has just taken on the flow of the Cedar River and is within a few miles of dumping into the Mississippi. It is a big river at this point and the valley is wide.

The county seat, **Wapello**, is located in the middle of the valley near the river. It was lunchtime when we arrived so our first task was finding a restaurant. Johnnie B's, a rustic looking structure stood out. The front was an old brick building with patched steel paneling. The interior walls were covered with weathered barn boards from a one-time white barn. Covering much of the barn board were memorabilia, rusty metal signs, weathered wood signs and all sorts of cool junk. I thought it worked quite well. We each ordered classic, hot meat sandwiches. For the uninformed, this is meat on white bread alongside mashed potatoes with the whole ensemble covered with gravy. Connie's meat choice was turkey and mine was meatloaf.

Bethel Church

JOHNNIE B'S

HAT CREEK CATTLE CO.
Lonesome Dove, Tx
We Don't Rent Pigs

RMERS HYBRID HOGS

66

Johnnie B's, Wapello

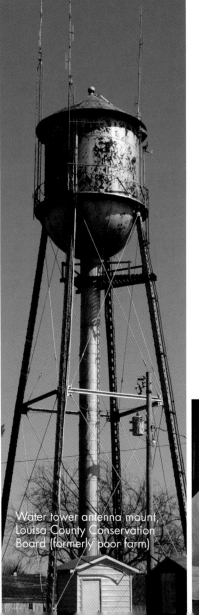

Water tower antenna mount, Louisa County Conservation Board (formerly poor farm)

Dale and Esther Rickert

Bethel Church, Louisa County

In the genealogy section of Wapello's library, we happened onto a distinguished, elderly couple doing a little family research. We struck up a conversation with Esther Jamison Rickert and her husband Dale and learned that Esther's Scotch-Irish ancestors were among the first **Louisa County** settlers in 1840. Esther and Dale have lived on a farm for 51 years that is across the road from where Esther grew up. The Farmers Elevator and Exchange in Wapello, a sprawling complex of storage and processing units, was started by Esther's grandfather in 1917. Dale served a term in the Iowa House of Representatives in 1965. They have two children who live Tampa, Florida, and one in Burlington. They love to come back to the freedom and comfort of the farm and Esther and Dale have no desire to leave it.

At Esther's request, we drove a few miles south of **Wapello** to look at Bethel Church. We turned off the highway onto a little gravel lane that took us a quarter of a mile into the woods. At the end of the lane is a small, limestone church that was built in 1855. It had a restored, well-maintained appearance and

was surrounded by a manicured graveyard. Many of the gravestones were inscribed with the surname Jamison. The surrounding wrought iron fence looked new. Walking the grounds with Connie on this sunny, March day and listening to the sounds of spring was spiritually moving.

This church was built on land donated by Esther's ancestors. It has not been in weekly use since the '30s but still serves as a place for meditation and picnics. The Rickerts have dedicated themselves to maintaining the church and the grounds.

The first white men to step on **Louisa County** soil were Joliet and Marquette. They had traveled to the new territory from a Jesuit mission on the Straits of Mackinac using the Wisconsin River as the last leg of their journey to the Mississippi. They continued down the Mississippi until they came to the mouth of the Iowa River. It was 1673 when they made their first Indian contact and, to their surprise, the natives were friendly.

A friendly Indian from the other side of the river was Chief Wapello who moved his tribe of Fox from a village on the Rock River to a village on the Iowa River. The year was 1829 and the village

is now the town of **Wapello**. As other Indians were being forced to move west of the Mississippi, many chose **Louisa County** because there was an abundance of game, fish and fowl inhabiting the woods, lakes and rivers.

From 1841 to 1870, light draft steamboats, stern- and side-wheelers plied the Iowa River. **Louisa County** towns of **Wapello** and Columbus City (Columbus Junction) were stops as the boats traveled to Iowa City and back to the Mississippi. In 1846 small barges that were powered by oarsmen were developed to haul grain downriver and manufactured goods and other merchandise upriver. Due to the arduous task of poling upstream, this system was short-lived.

Much of what the Indians like about **Louisa County** has been preserved for today's outdoorsman. Twelve public hunting areas are excellent habitats for all types of Iowa game. The 6,600-acre Port Louisa National Wildlife Refuge is the county's premier wetland area. It is a stopover for thousands of migrating waterfowl and a beautiful place to enjoy fishing, hiking and wildlife observation. If you like to explore nature with a

Farmers Elevator and Exchange, Wapello

Columbus Junction

Tyson Foods plant, Columbus Junction

Washington County

Washington County

paddle in your hand, you'll love the Odessa Water Trail that takes you through a series of ponds, chutes and waterways, including the Mississippi.

While touring around the county, we found ourselves in **Morning Sun** and weren't quite sure of the highway location to **Columbus Junction**, our next destination. We flagged down a lady who was about to cross the street and asked about the highway. Marjorie Walker Kimble leaned her head in the passenger side window and said, "I don't drive, but I can tell you how to get there." After giving directions, she proceeded to ask who we were looking for and commented that Connie looked familiar. She continued the probe and learned about our book research that she thought was super. She said she would like to write a book on how her family wandered around the country before settling in Iowa. I love these outgoing Iowans.

Columbus Junction is located at the confluence of the Iowa and Cedar Rivers. It is a colorful town of about 1,900 people with downtown buildings that date back 100 years or more. They house unique shops, restaurants and pubs.

Marjorie Walker Kimble

Amish school near Kalona

A large, Tyson Foods processing plant is located on the north side. Hispanics who have moved in to work at this plant have added to the flavor of the community.

It was the first of April as we entered **Washington County**. The thawed countryside still had the beige look; however, April showers had begun and I think I saw some greenish areas.

We were in Amish country. Driving around the back roads, you can smell the horses—a pleasant smell for a country boy at heart. Amish settlements interspersed with conventional farms are readily distinguishable by a buggy rather than a John Deere in the yard. Buggies, black with the bright orange triangles mounted on the back, outnumber mechanical vehicles in this area. Time stands still.

The Amish were among the earliest settlers in **Washington County**. They arrived in 1846, settled in and prospered, as they became an accepted part of the overall community where their differences were respected. Their ancestors in Europe did not receive this respect. Both the Amish and Mennonites share an Anabaptist heritage dating to the Swiss Brethren movement that evolved from the

sixteenth century Protestant Reformation. Both sects were persecuted for their beliefs. In 1693 the Amish, who have resisted change to this day, dissented from the Mennonites who were accepting some changes. The Amish spread across Europe looking for havens until 1729. Then at the invitation of Quaker William Penn, they immigrated to America. Today, the **Kalona** area is home to the largest Amish-Mennonite settlement west of the Mississippi River.

Given the need of horsepower in the flesh for the Amish, it follows that the Kalona Sales Barn would have a semi-annual, draft horse sale. These sales in April and October draw 400 to 500 draft horses from across the country. Tack, horse-drawn equipment, carriages and buggies are also put on the block. And for the fun of it, draft horse pulls are held.

Another big **Kalona** event that has its base in the Amish community is the annual Kalona Quilt Show and Sale. This year 350 quilts are expected to be displayed for an anticipated crowd of 1,500 people. About a third of the quilts on display will be antiques. The remaining quilts are made by artisans from across

the state and local communities—mostly Amish and Mennonite.

From **Kalona** we moved on to the Riverside Casino and Golf Resort—probably the ultimate contrast on our trip. We had to follow through on our mission of slot machine testing. Starting with $10 and a 30-minute time limit, Connie walked out of the casino with $17.50 in winnings. The running score (after three casinos) is $26.50 ahead.

The adjacent town of **Riverside** got its start when the railroad came through the north side of the English River where Jesse Boyd had a mill. He also owned the land where the new town of Riverside was platted in 1872. Jesse wasn't out to make big bucks. He encouraged immigration by selling low and giving away lots. Forty buildings occupied the town in 1874 and 100 more were built that year. The depot was a boxcar, but large amounts of wheat, oats, rye, produce, hogs and cattle were shipped from **Riverside**. Those early days were wild. In 1877, a writer complained of Riverside saloons, "No matter how drunk a man was, he could always get more at any of them." The Wild West character of

Riverside

St. Mary's Catholic Church, Riverside

Lorraine Williams in her Dodici's Cafe, Washington

the town caused a frequent turnover of editors at the *Riverside News*.

So much for the past. In the future, Captain James T. Kirk (played by William Shatner) of Star Trek will be born in **Riverside**, Iowa. The town holds an annual Riverside Trek Fest that includes a parade, carnival rides and fireworks. Minor Star Trek celebrities have attended some of the past events.

Washington County started its frontier life in the 1840s. Land speculators were very active in the 1850s, and by most accounts, they were decent people who provided a service without excessive profits. They took about 35,000 acres of the original entry land in **Washington County** and were of professional help to the settlers. This was not always the story in frontier dealing. Joseph Quincy Adams and his family were the first residents in the town of **Washington**. Their timing was not great as they arrived on October 17, 1839, just as winter was about to set in. Building a cabin as the freeze began was a daunting task. Joseph had to dig through the frozen ground to get soft earth to use for chinking mortar. It froze as fast as it was applied but stuck until

Washington

Suzanne Ackermann

Washington County

Washington County Courthouse, Washington

the spring thaw. It must not have stuck in all the cracks because he reported the snow was ten inches deep on the family's bed one morning following a blizzard.

The weather was a little better in the spring of 1840 when Amos Embree came to **Washington**. He attached a shed to his house and began selling whiskey; the shed became the town's first liquor store. In order to make more money and at the same time make his product "less dangerous," he watered his liquors so much that they would occasionally freeze.

Lorraine Williams does not water the drinks in her restaurant, Café Dodici. This elegant Italian restaurant was born out of a desire to do something for her hometown. At the age of 19, she visited Italy, married an Italian, became an Italian citizen and stayed there for 25 years. A few years ago, she and her husband returned to **Washington** to care for her father. She was disappointed with the deterioration of the buildings on **Washington's** beautiful town square and decided to do something. She bought one that was in the worst condition and reworked it into a beautiful restaurant. She had a vision and never considered

failure. The Café Dodici opened in December of 2004 and has drawn customers from all over. Lorraine says, "After living in Europe and having been gone 30 years, I enjoy being five minutes from work and I enjoy viewing the sunset and farmland behind my home. In this community, you can make a difference and feel that you are doing your part to change the world." Her Italian husband tells her he's proving his love by following her to Iowa, but he admits he also enjoys the aforementioned amenities.

Dodici's Shop, located next door, was born because people were buying things off the tables in the restaurant. The smart exterior of these two establishments caught our attention as we drove around the square so we stopped for lunch at the Shop. We each chose a chicken wrap and Tuscan tomato soup to satisfy our appetites. We sat at a table in a small dining area amid the specialty shop's pleasing merchandise displays.

Suzanne Ackermann, the shop's manager, came to town three years ago for a three-week project—the ministry in international hospitality at the Shiloh Conference of the Living Word. After the camp

was over, she stayed for evaluations and was encouraged to make a permanent home in **Washington**. This Indiana native has had an interesting life that includes growing up in a well-to-do family that encouraged stretching your abilities. Performing as a professional dancer is also in her past. She feels that God has placed her in **Washington** and she is doing her part to enhance the quality of life there. She says she was just a bridge, a facilitator, for a group of 200 who came together in 2005 without organization. There were no votes; they operated by consensus. They used Iowa's Main Street program that provides free-of-charge, professional designers who make plans and recommendations for restorations and renovations of downtowns. "When different cultures move in," Suzanne says, "we want to acclimate to them where we create a climate for them to acclimate to us." It all seems to be working well. **Washington** is a very attractive town.

The early April showers continued as we entered **Keokuk County** on our way to **Sigourney**. BB-size hail accompanied the rain from time to time.

As settlers moved west across Iowa,

Washington

Keokuk County Courthouse, Sigourney

John Clubb

some on the leading edge had previously settled in eastern Iowa. These pioneers realized they had made a mistake in choosing river or timber locations over the open prairie. They sold out to their neighbors or later arrivals at a reasonable profit and moved to the front of the westward expansion. They learned from experience and made better choices in land selection and were prepared to develop it. Some of **Keokuk County's** first settlers fell into this category.

The county seat of Keokuk County, **Sigourney**, was incorporated in 1858 and experienced modest growth with the requisite services of an early trade center. During the Civil War there was no growth, but after the war there was a new vitality. They began to tear down old buildings and replace them with durable structures. The railroad came and, with it, a more sophisticated character in keeping with its elegant name.

Mrs. Lydia Huntley Sigourney was a Connecticut lady of considerable artistic talent. Her husband, Charles Sigourney, was a wealthy merchant who, after years of prosperity, experienced heavy losses. Thus they were forced to move to a lower

Keokuk County Courthouse

Keokuk County Courthouse

Sigourney

Marilyn Adams and Mickey Jung

Cat n' Fiddle B&B, Sigourney

class neighborhood. During the last seven years of Mrs. Sigourney's life, she wrote columns for the *New York Ledger*. She loved to write about the developing west-especially Iowa—which is the setting of one of her most touching poems entitled "The Indian Girl's Burial." It was about an Indian girl who died of consumption. In the Connecticut lady's honor, the county seat was named Sigourney. She showed her appreciation of the distinction by donating trees for the courthouse yard.

The present Keokuk County Courthouse is a neoclassical building built in 1910. In the central tower, there is a stained glass window at the top. On the four walls of the upper dome are murals of early Iowa painted by Chicago artist, C.E. Rang. Rang also painted portraits of Chief Keokuk and Mrs. Sigourney that hang in the stair hall. On the first floor there is a collection of arrowheads arranged cleverly in the shapes of Indian figures. It is worth a visit.

Keokuk County has two fairs. **What Cheer** lost the battle for the county seat but refused to give up the county fair. The livestock portion of the fair is named the Keokuk County Expo,

which is held in Sigourney.

While in **Sigourney**, we visited with John Clubb, who has lived there all his life. He says, "It's small town Iowa. You know everybody. It only takes a couple of minutes to go anywhere. It's quiet, except for today, when a mad bull got loose and they had to lock down the school." I love small town problems.

Deborah Clubb, the wife of John's cousin, runs a restaurant named the Clubb House. This building has quite a history, including a period when John's brother and sister-in-law, Donnie and Donna, ran it as a furniture store. In earlier days, it was a furniture store and funeral home. During this period a circus came to town and one of its gorillas passed away before they packed up to move. Legend has it that the gorilla was brought to the funeral parlor to be embalmed!

John likes to work on cars and fish during his time off. Fishing is good at nearby Lake Belva Deer and the Skunk River. He told us of a 90-year-old sportsman who recently pulled a 40-pound catfish out of the river.

Our overnight was at the Cat n' Fiddle B&B in **Sigourney**. It is a large, old

Victorian house well-stocked with antiques. Innkeeper Mickey Jung loves the hunt for these old treasures and he attends multiple sales and auctions. He is going to have to start a chain of B&Bs to display all his finds.

We put the gorilla out of our minds and had dinner at the Clubb House restaurant. The décor was patriotic with several American flags on display along with other America motifs. Owner Deborah Clubb is a lifetime member of the VFW service organization.

When we returned to the B&B, Mickey and his companion, Marilyn Adams, had some freshly baked rhubarb cake awaiting us. The conversation came easy; I'm sure it could have gone into the night but we had to get some sleep. Christopher Dodd stayed there while campaigning for the Democratic nomination for president. Mickey said he sipped wine with him until 1:00 a.m.

A tornado went through **Delta** in 1983 and the town never completely recovered. But, thanks to Dixie Shipley, they are still working on it. Dixie, who has lived within a five-mile radius of **Delta** all her life, was in the last gradua-

Deborah Clubb

Clubb House Restaurant

73

What Cheer Opera House

What Cheer Opera House

What Cheer Opera House

Dixie Shipley

tion class in 1961. She used to work at an **Oskaloosa** overall factory but her husband didn't want her to make that 20-mile commute so he bought her a grocery store in **Delta**. She has owned and operated that store for 46 years. The building has a worn look and there is stuff piled everywhere, but you can find what you need and you have the pleasure of dealing with Dixie or her aunt, Bette Dilley. When we stopped in, Bette was in charge, and her husband Ernie was sitting in a chair in the conversation area where there were three more available chairs. Dixie was subbing for the postmaster at the post office down the street. Bette and Ernie are from **Oskaloosa** where they used to own two grocery stores on the same block. Bette was quick-witted and easy to talk to. Ernie's contribution to the conversation was, "You're a lot older than your wife, aren't you?" For the record, I'm only four and a half years older.

We walked down the street to visit Dixie at the post office. We met a charming, personable lady with a perpetual smile on her face. She listed activities that happen in **Delta** and projects they are working on such as building a replica

Mike Walker

Bette Dilley and Connie

Delta Grocery

of a covered bridge that was destroyed by arson. The old high school gym is used as a community center for senior activities and roller hockey. I'm guessing the hockey is for younger folks. I'm also guessing that everyone loves Dixie.

After our enjoyable session with the **Delta** folks, we went to the car and I reached for my keys and, you guessed it, there were no keys in my pocket. They were in the car. Connie, assuming I had the keys, had locked the doors from the inside. We were in a very small town in a sparsely populated county and I was planning on being stranded there for at least two hours or all day or into the next day. Never underestimate the resourcefulness of people who live in these communities. After standing there and feeling stupid for a few minutes, we decided we had to deal with it. Sheepishly we walked back into the Country Store and Bette smiled and said, "I'll call Dixie." When I heard the name Dixie, my hopes lifted. Dixie called the sheriff and within 15 minutes, an officer was prying the door open a crack, slipping a probe in and hitting the button on my keychain. Valuable time lost—about a half an hour. If I

weren't a shy Norwegian, I would have kissed Dixie. I did thank her profusely.

We drove to **What Cheer** to see their well-known opera house. When we arrived, the first thing I did was check the door to see if it was open. It was locked so I started across the street with the intention of going into a business to see if anyone had a key. At that moment, a man in messy clothes asked me if I was supposed to meet someone at the Opera House. I said, "No," and explained who I was and what we were doing. As it turned out, he had a key because he was involved in some interior restoration work. He proved to be quite interesting in his own right. His name is Mike Walker and his life's experiences include riding horses as a cowboy and then riding the waves as a surfer for 15 years in Hawaii. He returned to **What Cheer** to help his folks and has been working on painting and restoration projects.

Built in 1893, the Opera House has been in use for over 100 years starting when **What Cheer** was a coalmining town of 8,000 to the present town of 800. Mike's mother ran the shows for ten years serving as emcee and singer. Many name

performers, in addition to local talents, have made appearances on its stage.

Incidentally, the name **What Cheer** did not come from one of the pioneers riding over the hill and exclaiming, "What's here?" or "What Cheer!" as he viewed the future town site. English settlers brought the English greeting, "What Cheer," to New England and Joseph Andrews, a native of Providence, Rhode Island, brought it to Iowa and offered the name for a post office in a town named Petersburg. Petersburg was renamed **What Cheer** in 1879.

On our way to **Oskaloosa**, the county seat of **Mahaska County**, we stopped to tour Lake Keomah State Park. Dedicated in 1934, the park was built by the Depression-fighting Civilian Conservation Corps (CCC). The accomplished stonework of these hard-working individuals is still prominent in the park. An 83-acre lake and 366 acres of woods make a great environment for camping, picnicking, fishing, swimming, hiking and winter snowmobiling.

A few more miles down the road, Highway 92 becomes Avenue A, a street that bisects the town of Oskaloosa. Upon

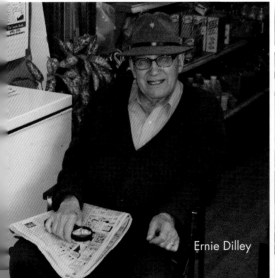
Ernie Dilley

Keokuk County Sheriff fishing for our keys

75

Lake Keomah State Park, Mahaska County

Oskaloosa town square and Mahaska County Courthouse

entering the business district we searched out the library for our early history research. So far on this trip, we have stopped at every county seat library and plan to continue the practice in the remaining counties. We are finding many original Carnegie libraries that are still in use—some are refurbished and some are not. In some towns the Carnegie library has been put to another use and a sparkling new library was built. Another town converted part of an abandoned, traditional-style high school into a library. In **Oskaloosa**, their beautiful Carnegie library has a well-done, compatible addition that doubles its size. All of these libraries match or exceed the needs of their respective communities with books and high tech information centers. Iowans have their priorities.

After our research session, we moseyed on down the street to Big Ed's Barbecue for lunch. Ed Dowd and his German-born wife Hanna own and operate the quintessential barbecue restaurant with pine paneling and checkered tablecloths. A special touch is the hot German potato salad Hanna makes using her mother's recipe. It complemented the best

Smokey Row Coffeehouse, Oskaloosa

Mary Barnard

76

Hanna and Big Ed Dowd

Sue Sheehy

barbecue pork sandwich I have ever eaten—Ed's specialty.

VOOM Portraits, the most elaborate touring art exhibition ever set up in an Iowa art museum, recently came to the University of Iowa Museum of Art. At a cost of $200,000, the curatorial staff worked for two months removing the permanent collection, building walls, covering windows and installing wiring for the art. The art was created by Robert Wilson, an avant-garde artist of international fame. **New Sharon** native and present **Oskaloosa** resident, Sue Sheehy, and Robert Wilson go way back. While in town, we visited Sue.

Sue Sheehy is her own person and says what's on her mind. She does not cull thoughts that might offend. After high school she worked in jobs at various locations around Iowa and Minnesota. She was working as a waitress in Iowa City when a customer asked her if she wanted to be in a play. That customer was Robert Wilson and the play was a seven-hour "silent opera," entitled *Deafman Glance*. The play was Wilson's ticket into the international spotlight of experimental theater. Sue went along on the ride.

After the play had its run, she stayed in New York and took a job as a word processor for the New York Council of Boy Scouts of America. Thirty-seven years later, she returned to **Oskaloosa** to be near family. She had a reunion with Wilson when he returned to Iowa City with his VOOM art show.

Another international show that engulfs Iowa every four years is the first-in-the-nation presidential caucus. Mary Barnard, administrative assistant to the **Oskaloosa** chief of police, gives this as one of reasons she likes living in Iowa. The Hawkeye fan, who likes small town living and the closeness to large cities, is a cantor for St. Mary's, the only Catholic church left in **Mahaska County**.

Following a photo shoot around the square, I stopped at the Area Chamber and Development Group and Main Street Oskaloosa office to pick up some brochures. The executive director, Jon Sullivan, was in and he took the time to talk about what makes **Oskaloosa** and **Mahaska County** a great place to live and work. The next few paragraphs encapsulate the Oskaloosa/Mahaska County story gleaned from Jon, the

brochures and other research.

Chief Mahaska was a physically well-built, six-foot-two Indian who loved peace but knew how to fight, if necessary. He was a leader of the Ioway tribe that settled in the area. Legend has it that when these Indians first set eyes on our state, from a Mississippi bluff, they exclaimed, "Ioway, Ioway," meaning "beautiful, beautiful." They called the river they were looking at "the Iowa" and the state later took the Iowa name. I wish the white men hadn't translated an Indian word when they named another river. The Indians called the stream Che-qua-que, their word for smelly. Wild onions that gave off an odious smell grew on the river's banks. The white man's translation? Skunk! A few counties back, I expressed my thoughts on that name.

Mahaska County was established in 1843; it's been self-governing since 1844. It was the first county in Iowa to have a sheriff and justice of the peace.

Oskaloosa was named for a Creek Indian princess named Ouscaloosa. She was married to another Iowa town namesake, Seminole chief Osceola. The first white settlers were a group of Quakers

New streetscape for Oskaloosa

77

Spring training at William Penn University

William Penn University

who chose this rise of land midway between the Des Moines and Skunk Rivers. In the 1850s and 1860s, the Western Stage Company maintained barns in **Oskaloosa**. **Mahaska County** and Oskaloosa took part in the coal boom and bust.

Today, Osky (as the natives call it) is a progressive, thriving community of 11,000. MUSCO sports lighting is a high profile company that calls Osky home. If you are a sports fan, you have seen these folks at work providing temporary and permanent lighting at major athletic events across the country. They also provided lighting at New York's Ground Zero so clean up crews could work into the night. Other industry thrives producing valves and hydrants, septic tanks, power tools, gearboxes, molding and cabinets, feed conveyor systems and more.

The arts are alive and well with community theater, a municipal band and a symphony orchestra. The George Daily Auditorium has been the venue for the performing arts since 1997. A first-class, 700-seat facility—it serves the high school, William Penn University and traveling professional acts that stop in

Tassel Ridge Winery, Leighton

Oskaloosa High School and George Daily Auditorium

Oskaloosa. The Oskaloosa Arts Fellowship promotes visual arts as well as the performing arts.

Major events include Art on the Square, Thursday evening band concerts, Sweet Corn Serenade (4,000 ears of sweet corn and pork burgers), the Southern Iowa Fair and a lighted Christmas parade.

In 1873, the Quaker settlement founded William Penn College. Now a university with a graduate level program in business leadership, William Penn continues to grow—serving its students with a liberal arts education. The Penn Activity Center (PAC), a 150,000-square-foot, three-story facility, is nearing completion. This impressive building will be comprised of three basketball courts, 50 yards of artificial turf and an elevated running track. It will also have locker rooms, training facilities, classrooms and offices. North of the PAC is the MUSCO Technology Center. The south wing is the home of industrial technology programs and the north wing is for programs in communications technology. The emphasis at William Penn is leadership development. Contributing to this is a full slate of

intercollegiate athletic competition for men and women. They compete in the Midwest Collegiate Conference that is affiliated with the National Association of Intercollegiate Athletics, Division II.

In mid-April the grassy areas of the countryside showed their spring green color. The fields still had a neutral hue and buds had yet to appear on the trees, but the spring season was definitely here.

In about three weeks the tulips of **Pella**, our next stop, would be blooming with bright primary colors. And the good folks in **Pella** would put on a spring celebration like no other in Iowa—the renowned Pella Tulip Festival.

The site of present day **Pella** was first settled by pioneers from the British Isles and eastern United States, much like the counties we had covered so far. In 1843, Levi and Wellington Nossaman, their wives and babies staked a claim for a home of their own in the **Pella** area. Other pioneers followed and a small community formed. Four years later, a group of 800 Hollanders, under the leadership of Dominie Hendrik Peter Scholte, left the Netherlands in search of a place where they would have freedom of wor-

ship and could educate their children as they pleased. They could not go land hunting with 800 people so Scholte and five other men went looking for a place to settle. On a high ridge between two rivers, they were led to Nossaman's cabin where they made their headquarters while they bought claims and available government land. They accumulated 18,000 acres where the colony of 800 quickly built dugouts with roofs of branches and slough grass. It was known as Strawtown. The original pioneer settlers helped the inexperienced Hollanders adjust to life on the frontier. By working together, they surveyed the land, laid out the streets and built more permanent structures. The roots of **Pella** were in place.

In 1850, a Scotsman named Nicholas Earp brought his family to **Pella**. They came by way of Virginia where their ancestors first settled in the early 1700s. They also came for religious freedom. A two-year-old member of Nicholas Earp's family was named Wyatt Berry Stapp Earp. During his early childhood and teenage years, he was one of the kids growing up in Pella. That changed in 1864 when his father organized a wagon

Abandoned, coal strip mine, Mahaska County

Farmhouse (mansion), Mahaska County

79

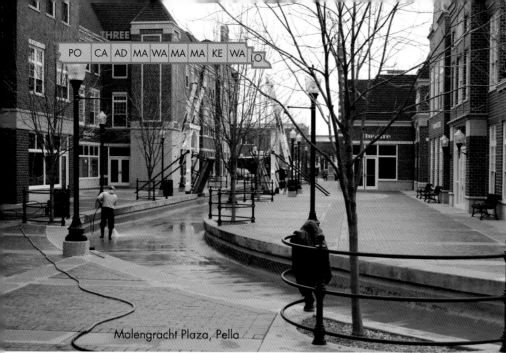

Molengracht Plaza, Pella

Loren and Alma Witzenburg

Pella Corporation headquarters

train of 40 families for a move to California. Wyatt was given his first firearm for the trip; dealing with dangers as they crossed the West made a man out of him. Wyatt went on to become a legendary gunslinger serving some time as an outlaw before becoming a U.S. Marshal. He was the only participant in the gunfight at O.K. Corral to escape being killed or wounded. He lived to be 80 years old, no small feat for a Western gunman. Perhaps there was a touch of Irish in that Scotch ancestry.

There is no touch of Dutch in **Pella**; it completely overwhelms the community. The early settlers were talented, industrious and hard workers and they passed on those skills to their descendants. The clean, well-maintained buildings and streets are testimony to the spirit of the community. Dutch motifs are everywhere including franchises like McDonalds and Papa Murphy's. The downtown square would not look out of place in the Netherlands. An authentic, 135-foot-tall, 1850 Dutch windmill (from Holland) is located just off the square. Flour for Jaarsma's Bakery is ground at this mill. The Molengracht Plaza is a newly con-

Dutch windmill and Opera House, Pella

Henry Schutte and customer

Historic houses, Pella

structed replica of a Dutch street scene complete with a canal and drawbridge.

On a recent trip to Israel and Jordan, we met **Pella** natives Alma and Loren Witzenburg. We decided to pay them a visit. They graciously welcomed us to their home and served us coffee, tea and Dutch pastries as they gave us some insights to life in Tulipland. A custom of Sunday night scooping the loop on the downtown square started about the time automobiles became popular. It is where Alma (who went to Christian school) and Loren (who went to public school) first met as they rode with their friends. For many years it was an enjoyable gathering of young people checking each other out. Unfortunately, it was stopped three years ago because the rowdies took over.

Alma and Loren told us some of the background on the success of **Pella's** activities and festivals. For starters, **Pella's** companies put a lot back into the community. This is complemented by talented volunteers; committees work year around to bring off the Tulip Festival. This is no small time celebration. They have afternoon parades and evening parades for three days and it builds from

there. The festival spirit of cooperation prevails in other projects.

We recommend a visit to **Pella** anytime of the year. If you are lucky, you may run into Henry Schutte, a true Dutchman, who emigrated from Holland after World War II. He knew some of the workers who came from Holland to reassemble the 1850s windmill. I could describe him to you but he has a different look when he dons a curly-haired wig. I had the pleasure of stepping into his barbershop to take his picture. It was perfect—a lot of stuff on the walls and the sweet smell of a cigar.

Manufacturing jobs are plentiful for **Pella's** 10,000 inhabitants. It is home to Pella Corporation, a national leader in window and door products. Vermeer (Pella's other major corporation), got its start when Gary Vermeer designed a simple wagon hoist to make unloading grain easier. Simple is not the word you use to describe today's products. Invention and innovation continue to propel Vermeer as they have become a world leader in manufacturing round hay balers, wood chippers and all types of digging machines. Other manufacturers of note are Van

Gorp and Precision Pulley who make industrial pulleys. Precision Pulley is employee-owned.

Central College, a liberal arts college of 1,600 students, makes a substantial contribution to the economic and cultural health of **Pella**. The Dutch settlers founded it as a Baptist institution in 1853. Fires, three wars and the Great Depression took their toll but the faith and dedication of early faculty members (some of whom accepted farm produce as payment) kept it solvent. In 1916, Central transferred its affiliation from Baptist to the Reformed Church in America.

Today, Central is a vibrant college that excels in the arts and athletics, as well as academics. There are over 80 clubs and organizations for the participation of students. The art department offers classes from ceramics to glass blowing and off-campus opportunities. Music choices range from jazz to choir to classical ensembles. In theatre productions, students not only act but also are involved in designing the lighting, sound, costumes and sets. The athletic teams have won 11 NCAA national team championships— more than any other Division III college

Central College

Central College

PO | CA | AD | MA | WA | MA | MA | KE | WA | LO

Red Rock Dam, Marion County

Marion County Courthouse, Knoxville

in Iowa. And faith matters with many venues to express the students' spiritual side such as chapel, campus ministries, Fellowship of Christian Athletes, ACTION and mission trips.

On to Pella's rival, **Knoxville**, the county seat of **Marion County**. This 15-mile trip took us across the dam for Red Rock Lake, an amenity shared by both communities. Iowa's largest man-made lake provides recreational fun with boating, sailing, swimming, fishing and shore-based activities such as camping, disc golf, archery, bird watching and a beautiful biking/hiking trail.

In 1843, the Red Rock Line, another boundary that separated Indian-owned lands from lands available for white settlement, divided **Marion County**. The boundary, of course, moved west and western **Marion County** was opened up to settlement in 1845. In the vicinity of **Knoxville**, on the extreme western border of the government lands, Lysander W. Babbitt settled in. He spent the winter of 1842–1843 trapping and hunting. This ambitious frontiersman went on to become the first clerk of the board of county commissioners, the first postmas-

North stands and Sprint Car Hall of Fame building

Ralph Capitani

Sprint Car Hall of Fame Museum, Knoxville

ter of **Knoxville**, a member of the state legislature and registrar of the land office at Council Bluffs.

The beginning of **Knoxville** is rooted in an 1845 report by the territorial legislature that named the settlement a seat of justice of **Marion County**. The first survey was made in 1847 and it was platted into 23 blocks. The population increased rapidly from 1854 to 1875 when it was first bypassed by the railroad. In 1875, a railroad line finally found its way into town and growth accelerated once again.

Acceleration of a different type defines **Knoxville** today. I'm speaking of sprint car racing—little cars with 800 horsepower engines and wings to keep them on the ground as they tear around a half-mile, dirt track, accelerating to 130 mph on the short straightaway and braking as they slide around the corners. To me, it is the most spectacular racing anywhere and you have to be there to appreciate it. Television doesn't do it justice.

In 1914, the first auto race was staged at the Marion County Fairgrounds. This preceded the grandstand that was built in 1917. In 1954, the track was banked, new fencing was put in place and lights were added for weekly racing of stock cars. Marion Robinson was hired in 1956 to promote racing and he served in that capacity until the mid-seventies. During that period, stock cars evolved into modifieds (not true stocks); then to super modifieds (car bodies cut down); then sheet metal completely replaced channeled car bodies; then the car frames were replaced with tubing; then roll cages were added and the sprint car was born. Robinson is credited with conceiving the idea of the Knoxville Nationals in 1961. It was two days of racing with time trials on Friday and racing on Saturday. The 2007 Nationals were four days of racing with the finals on Saturday night drawing a crowd of 24,000. The payout was $910,000 with the winner taking home $150,000. The National Sprint Car Hall of Fame Museum, adjacent to the track, illustrates the **Knoxville** story with displays and vintage cars.

Ralph Capitani, a Knoxville High School football coach (during his tenure, they never lost to Pella) took a summer job managing the raceway office. When Robinson stepped down and P. Ray Grimes finished a one-year stint as promoter, Capitani was hired as race director. He is well respected in the racing community and has presided over the impressive growth of the raceway and the Nationals for the last 40 years. We had the pleasurable experience of visiting with Mr. Capitani.

Ralph, the son of a coal miner, had no interest in auto racing before he took the summer job. Over the years he learned to like and respect the racing crowd. He says, "During the 40 years I've been on the job, I've only dealt with two or three people who I would not consider a friend. Racing draws people from all walks of life—white and blue collar. The board has been good to me." Then, of course, there are the racing stories such as the time he black-flagged hard-driving Doug Wolfgang. Later, the car owner, a man from Lincoln, Nebraska, came into his office and jumped all over him. Ralph normally keeps his cool, but this time he told the owner to take that piece of junk back to Nebraska and not to come back. Doug, a 19-year-old kid at the time, had the integrity to admit Ralph was right. He was welcomed back and became a

South stands, Knoxville Raceway

Card game at Pine Knolls Country Club, Knoxville

Sally and Leland Vander Linden

Calvin Roose and Krista Bennett inspect coffee beans

favorite Knoxville regular and a Nationals' winner.

Knoxville and Pella have put their rivalry on the back burner and combined their resources to enhance life in **Marion County**. Each town's 48-page brochure of 2008 features their respective town on the cover and, on the inside, promotes both towns. They realize that the amenities I've written about are exceptional and interchangeable in the pursuit of the good life.

We moved on to another **Marion County** town named **Pleasantville**. Here we found good examples of the kind of people who keep small towns percolating. One couple has made their mark and another couple has the marker in hand. The former, Leland Vander Linden, (a Dutchman) grew up in **Pleasantville** and his wife Sally grew up in New Sharon. After serving in the US Army and studying architectural engineering at Iowa State University, Leland started work in the construction business. His brother Jack had taken a similar road and, in 1958, they joined forces and formed Vander Linden Construction, Inc. They proved to be a good team and were very

84

Esther Kauffeld-Hoffa

successful securing work and investing in properties—both commercial and residential. He and Sally have continually given back to the community with their time and generosity. One example is a 20-foot, chimney swift tower and shelter in the Gladys Black Memorial Garden. Sally had befriended the eccentric Gladys Black, who lived alone in a small house with birds flying around the interior. These were no canaries or parakeets. They were large birds that were fed dead mice that Gladys secured from Drake University labs. She drove a Nash Rambler that fortunately had a distinctive look so people could avoid her when she came down the road. When she saw a bird of interest, she would jerk the Rambler in any direction without warning. It was an adventure to enter her house with birds flying freely and well cared for—unlike the rest of the house. She once said, "When I go, they'll bulldoze my house down." That proved to be prophetic. She was Iowa's "Bird Lady"—an award winner and author who had an uncanny way with birds.

Monte and Krista Bennett, a younger entrepreneurial couple, are using their talents to make a mark in the coffee house business. They started with a flower shop and later added coffee to the fare. Two buildings in the downtown business district came up for sale and the price was right so they bought and rehabbed them. They converted one into a coffee shop/soda fountain and the other to a gift shop. They have since opened coffee houses in Pella and Oskaloosa and are in the planning stages of opening one in the Sherman Hill district of Des Moines. To serve this expansion, they bought a couple more buildings adjacent to the coffee shop/soda fountain to house offices and a coffee roaster. Among other duties, Calvin Roose, their right hand man, is in charge of roasting their special blends for the coffee houses and retail.

The name of this enterprise is Smokey Row. The **Pleasantville** street where they are located had an early history of fires so the residents began calling it "smokey row." The three, operational, Smokey Row coffee houses are very well done and we are looking forward to a Des Moines' opening.

We drove further west and entered **Warren County** where early settlements were a continuation of claims made west of the Red Rock Line in 1845. The initial settlers were of the Methodist faith. They were followed by the more typical array of newcomers from eastern states and southern states. Catholic immigrants of Irish and German descent added to the ethnic mix.

When we arrived in **Indianola**, we took a left on Jefferson Way and located our lodging for the night—the Garden and Galley B&B. This 1950s-style ranch with a two-story addition takes its name from a picture window view over the South River valley with gardens in the foreground and innkeeper Esther Kauffeld-Hoffa using her large kitchen to teach cooking classes. The '50s theme is carried out with accessories of the era. Our room had so many little knick-knacks that I was afraid I might accidentally pack one when we left. When I mentioned this to Esther, she said, "I probably wouldn't know it was gone."

Cal's Fine Food and Spirits on the north side of town was our choice for dinner. It was a comfortable place, with red leather booths and gray barn board paneling, that served comfort food. Proud

Indianola

Indianola

85

National Balloon Museum

Warren County Courthouse, Indianola

grandparents sat in the next booth and they spoke loudly enough in their enthusiasm that we weren't eavesdropping to hear them. It started with two women, and then three, and shortly thereafter, their husbands came. We learned that a new grandson was named Hayden after Hayden Fry, a former Iowa football coach, and that one of them had waited in line to get Hayden's autograph. Then there was a lot of talk about Arizona.

After a good night's sleep in our '50s bed with indirect lighting in the headboard, we awoke to our first foggy day. As we gazed out the picture window during breakfast, we observed that the fog was showing no signs of lifting—no panoramic photo shots today. As it turned out, it did lift later as it started to rain and continued to rain in varying degrees of intensity the rest of the day.

Esther served us a gourmet breakfast that featured shirred eggs with a combination of seasonings that included Parmesan and pesto. It was delicious. Following breakfast, Esther enlightened us with a few **Indianola** stories starting with how the town was named. The city fathers were considering name possi-

Blank Theatre for the Performing Arts, Simpson College

National Balloon Museum, Indianola

bilities when one of them glanced at a newspaper lying on the floor by his foot. He noticed a paragraph about a shipload of camels that had been unloaded at Indianola, Texas. The fathers all thought Indianola had a good ring to it. She also told us about a facility that takes care of veterans who have some issues. The townspeople are good to them. One of them gave a restaurant employee a backhanded compliment, "You're not the pretty one, but you're the best waitress."

Iowa's largest city, Des Moines, is lapping into northern **Warren County**. The open space between Des Moines and the Warren County towns of Norwalk and Carlisle is closing with the accelerated growth in these two suburbs. Commuters to Des Moines are also fueling growth in Indianola. The city has grown about 10% since 2000 and is closing in on a population of 15,000. **Warren County** is the fourth fastest growing county in Iowa. However, there are still about ten miles of open countryside between Des Moines and Indianola. **Indianola** stands alone with its own identity.

It is an identity of which the residents can be proud. Cultural attractions are a

two-way street with Des Moines. The Des Moines Metro Opera is staged in the Blank Theatre for the Performing Arts; there is the national Balloon Classic; the Iowa Wine Festival is held each year on the square; and weekly events like Bluegrass Tuesdays and Friday Night Bike Night are big draws.

The Des Moines Metro Opera has a reputation as one of the finest—if not the finest—regional operas in the United States. Its founder and artistic director, Robert Larsen, is an Iowa treasure. The Simpson College professor of music lives opera and has presided over DMMO's growth from $22,000 budget 36 years ago to $2 million today. Connie and I have regularly attended these operas and lectures on opera by Professor Larsen. We are in awe of the talent, intelligence and graciousness of this humble man who chooses Iowa as his stage. He also has a cool sense of humor.

The first, manned free flight of a hot air balloon took place in Paris in 1783. In 1960, Paul Yost and three others formed Raven Industries in Sioux Falls, South Dakota, and developed the modern hot air balloon and propane gas burner. That

was the beginning of the present-day sport of hot air ballooning. In 1970, the preliminaries of the National Hot Air Balloon Championships were held in **Indianola** with the finals at the Iowa State Fair. The following year, the complete event was held in **Indianola**. For the next 18 years, Indianola was the capital of hot air ballooning as the home of the Nationals. In recent years, the Nationals have moved around to various parts of the country. However, much of the history remains at the National Balloon Museum housed in a cleverly designed building on the north side of **Indianola**. And there is still a big-time, annual festival known as the Indianola National Balloon Classic.

Education was important to Warren County's Methodist settlers and they set the tone that it was inclusive by opening the Indianola Male and Female Seminary in 1860 that evolved into Simpson College. This inclusiveness again manifested itself in 1887 when Simpson College accepted the application of a former Missouri slave named George Washington Carver. Carver studied art at Simpson and was good at it, but he was

Simpson College

Great Western Trail, Martensdale

John Wayne birthplace

encouraged to pursue science for better job opportunities. In 1891, he transferred to Iowa State University. He was a devout Christian and gave God credit for leading him in his scientific discoveries. Simpson bestowed an honorary doctorate degree on him in 1928 and, in 1941, he returned to give the commencement address.

Simpson has grown into a first-rate, liberal arts college of 1,500 full-time and 400 part-time students. It provides well-rounded educational opportunities in academics, the arts and athletics. Robert Larsen heads up a music department that is widely acclaimed locally and nationally. Opera, combining music and theatre, is the bridge to a fine theatre department. And there is a full range of visual arts classes. Eighteen athletic teams compete in the NCAA sanctioned Iowa Intercollegiate Athletic Conference (IIAC). They have captured 65 conference championships and count ten, professional football players and Kip Janvrin ('88), an Olympic decathlon athlete, as alumni. And they have a great rivalry with Central College.

Area outdoor recreation destinations include one of Iowa's oldest state parks

Winterset Chamber of Commerce

Barbara Birlingmair Rasko

Banner Lakes at Summerset State Park, Warren County

and its newest. Lake Ahquabi State Park is located six miles south of **Indianola**. It was dedicated in 1936 and many of the structures built by the Civil Conservation Corps (CCC) are still in use. It is popular for boating, fishing, swimming, camping and picnicking. A stone lodge, constructed by the CCC, overlooks the lake and is the venue of choice for many family reunions. Banner Lakes at Summerset State Park, Iowa's newest, was dedicated in 2004. Located halfway between **Indianola** and Des Moines, it offers a two-mile bike loop that connects with the 11-mile Summerset Trail, as well as good fishing and picnicking. The lakes were formed by Iowa's largest strip mining operation. In 1932, forty feet of earth and shale were removed by the Banner Coal Company to get at a four-foot vein of good grade coal. The resulting lakes are deep enough for trout and pleasing to look at as vegetation covers the scars.

In 1918, Iowa was the sixth largest wine producing state in the union. Prohibition, pesticides, soybeans and corn took their toll and the industry virtually disappeared. It's back! And its heart is in central Iowa. *Make Mine Wine*, a glossy, 48-page, full-color magazine, is trumpeting the return to glory. We had the opportunity to talk to Barbara Birlingmair Rasko, the founder and publisher of the magazine. She told us that Iowa's wine industry with 70 wineries and 300 vineyards is at about the same stage of development as California's was 30 years ago. She conceived the Indianola-based publication to provide a forum for blending wine with food and fun and reporting on and promoting winemaking in the Midwest. Progress is being made to improve quality and quantity with experts from Iowa State University and courses at Des Moines Area Community College.

Presently, there are five wine trails in Iowa and that includes an excellent 18-winery trail in central Iowa. We recommend you take to the trail on your own or with a group and sample the variety of wines produced in your backyard. Whether your tastes run sweet or dry, we assure you'll be sipping some delicious wines as you drive through the lush Iowa countryside. And you don't have to travel 2,000 miles for the experience.

On to **Winterset** and **Madison County** where John Wayne was born and Robert Kincaid and Francesca had their illicit affair. Hollywood connections aside, **Madison County** is a beautiful place. The drive from Indianola to **Winterset** provided many lovely vistas. And if you leave the main highway, you can drive along densely-wooded river valleys and observe limestone bluffs and historic covered bridges. We don't know how many covered bridges were built but there is evidence that the first one was built in 1868. In 1870, the board of supervisors laid down rules for bridge building and it required that they be covered. In 1872, a wrought iron bridge was built over the Middle River and that signaled that the end of covered bridges was imminent. As we drove over the latest in bridge construction (concrete), we observed the picturesque covered bridges of old in their natural setting. Six remain and they are easy to find with well-marked signs showing their locations.

Marion Robert Morrison was born May 26, 1907, to Clyde and Mary Brown Morrison. Clyde Morrison, an alumnus of Simpson College, was a kind gentleman who served as a pharmacist at Smith

Madison County

Winterset

Old County Jail Antique Shop, Winterset

Drugstore on the Winterset square. Mary was a tiny, vivacious, redheaded bundle of energy. Marion changed his name to John Wayne and went on to become the greatest box office star in Hollywood history. There is an impressive collection of John Wayne memorabilia in the restored house of his birth. It includes his *True Grit* eye patch and letters from the greatest stars of the day.

Robert Kincaid's favorite restaurant, the Northside Cafe, on the north side of the square was our choice for lunch. Stools line a counter on one side and booths line the wall on the other side. The ceiling is acoustical tile and the walls are sheet paneling. Connie's friend from Spanish class, Sarah Frahm, joined us. She lives with her husband Mike on an acreage near **Winterset**. She enjoys walking around Winterset with her dog—admiring the big, old houses and enjoying the city park. She also likes antique shops and she insisted we join her on a tour of the Old County Jail Antique Shop.

Cheryl Weltha has always enjoyed dealing with antiques. She started with garage sales, and then moved on to dealers which led to opening a booth at the

90

Madison County Courthouse, Winterset

Sarah Frahm

Cheryl Weltha, Old County Jail Antique Shop

Old County Jail Antique Shop

Brass Armadillo. When the Madison County Jail in **Winterset** came up for sale, she saw some real possibilities for a unique antique store. She set up shop in the sheriff's booking area, the holding tanks, maximum-security cells, minimum-security cells and the yard. The exercise yard is now a side garden. Treasures are displayed on the metal bunk beds, hung from the cell bars, set in the cell toilet and sink and there is a nice display case for jewelry in the booking area. The walls that are not exposed rock or brick are sanded down—revealing several layers of different colored paint. They wisely did not paint over this beautiful texture. She and husband Roger reside in the sheriff's living quarters. Roger says that in the antique business Cheryl is the manager and he is the laborer. It's her dream and he is happily along for the ride. Connie and I truly enjoyed browsing in this special store. Connie found a neat ring and the price was right.

Winterset is another one of those wonderful Iowa towns with a square and stately courthouse centered there-in. It was built in 1876 with locally quarried limestone. The construction was executed by English, Welsh, Irish and German immigrants with a Frenchman as the stonecutter foreman. The big, black, walnut newels at the foot of each stairway were carved with hammer and chisel wielded by a judge. I believe public buildings like this inspire people to lead quality lives and this seems to be the case in the classy town of **Winterset**.

We took a side trip to see St. Patrick's Irish Settlement Church. It was very quiet with a misty rain as we stood by the church and looked at the cemetery and the valley beyond. It was another one of those spiritual experiences looking at the Irish names on the headstones and sensing these were people who had worked hard and enjoyed a good life in the rural Irish Settlement of **Madison County**. Pope John Paul II made it one of his stops when he visited Iowa in 1979.

Howell's Tree Farm was also on this loop so we stopped for a visit. Trees are actually a small part of this operation. There are fields of flowers, different types of animals, a greenhouse and a large barn with gift and floral shops on the lower level and a huge drying area in the haymow. Pumpkins, gourds and squash are harvested in the fall and a corn maze is created to add to the fun. There is no winter hibernation at Howell's as it is a year-round business. There is an abundance of Christmas trees to choose from, as well as other holiday needs such as swags, wreaths, candles and potpourri. This is one, unusual, impressive enterprise.

We approached **Adair County** along its northern border. Our first stop was **Stuart** where we observed the remaining structure of All Saints Catholic Church. Years ago we attended Mass at this incredibly beautiful church, a rare example of Byzantine and Romanesque architecture in the Midwest. Not long after that experience, an anti-Catholic arsonist set it on fire which completely destroyed the interior and much of the exterior. It hurt terribly to read that news. In 1996, Project Restoration was formed to renovate the structure to serve as a cultural center and as an institute of peace with emphasis on teaching tolerance and understanding. The project is still in the fundraising stage.

Clinging to the county's northern border we entered **Casey**, a small town

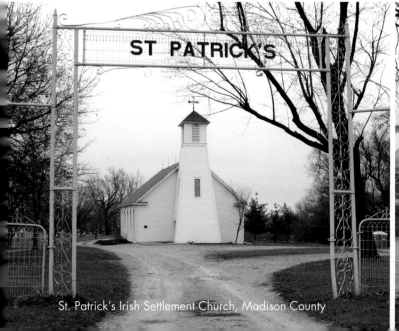
St. Patrick's Irish Settlement Church, Madison County

Howell's Tree Farm, Madison County

Artist Ray "Bubba" Sorenson's tribute to veterans, Casey

Denna Mitchell,
Adair County Free Press

Adair County Courthouse, Greenfield

Iowa Aviation Museum, Greenfield

92

with a few active businesses at its core, dominated by antique shops. There is a thoughtful memorial to our veterans painted on the side of a downtown building by Ray "Bubba" Sorenson. "Bubba" is also known for painting Patriotic Rock, located on Highway 25 between **Casey** and **Greenfield**. Prior to every Memorial Day, he paints a different tribute to American veterans.

There is another rock of note located on the next north/south road to the west. It is named Slayton's Rock and at 500,000 pounds, it's one of Iowa's largest, fully-exposed glacial deposits.

Further down the road, about a mile and a half east of **Adair**, is a large steam engine wheel mounted on a concrete slab. It marks the spot where the James-Younger Gang staged the first robbery of a moving train. They derailed the Rock Island Express and mounted the train expecting to find a $75,000 gold shipment. There was no gold and they rode off with a take of only $3,000. The derailment killed the engineer.

We left the northern border and drove to centrally located **Greenfield**, the county seat. We stopped at the library for

Slayton's Rock, Adair County

Greenfield

our customary research.

Adair County is part of the rolling prairie transition from the southern hills of Iowa to the flat lands of north-central Iowa. There are no natural lakes or major streams. Elk, red deer and buffalo found abundant grazing land before the white man came. Along creeks and minor rivers were found beaver, mink and other furry creatures. There is no evidence of significant Indian activity. Individual Indians chose to camp there to avoid inter-tribal conflict. It was those four or five tepee camps that the pioneers first encountered. Settlers were also attracted to the area and soon forced the Indians to move out.

Greenfield (named for the lush green countryside) was born in 1856. The first business established was a stage station. The first coaches to make the **Greenfield** stop ranged from farmers' wagons to the Concord coach made famous in western movies. Weather, breakdowns and lack of communication made overnight stays frequent at a stage stop. In 1858, the same man who built the stage station built the Kirkwood Hotel. In 1859, the first store was established, selling general merchandise that had to be

hauled in from St. Joseph, Missouri—a two-week trip. There was a county seat war with Fontanelle that went on for years before the Iowa Supreme Court ruled in **Greenfield's** favor in 1875. Greenfield was on its way to becoming the progressive community it is today.

Movie producer Norman Lear thought **Greenfield** was perfect for filming his movie, *Cold Turkey*. It was about a typical, small, Midwestern town where every resident was asked to give up smoking so the town could win a multi-million dollar prize. An all-star cast included Dick Van Dyke, Pippa Scott, Tom Poston, Bob Newhart, Jean Stapleton, Graham Jarvis and Greenfield extras. *Cold Turkey* premiered in Des Moines on January 30, 1971, and was first shown in Greenfield on February 3 of the same year.

Time magazine columnist Hugh Sidey was a hero of mine. I always felt he and fellow-Midwesterner Eric Severeid were the most common sense, fair-minded commentators on the national scene. They were wordsmiths who expressed their views eloquently. Hugh's roots are in **Greenfield** and his family has operated the *Adair County Free Press* since

1889. His grandfather, Edwin J. Sidey, founded the paper and originally named it the *Adair County Democrat*. He didn't want to take sides politically so he changed Democrat to Free Press. With the first press, they had to hand set type, one letter at a time. Today, it is made press-ready on computers and sent to Creston for printing.

The common sense, fair-minded approach to journalism is also the hallmark of the *Free Press*. Hugh's brother, Ed Sidey, carried on the Sidey tradition as editor/publisher until his death this year. Ed and Hugh were very close and very supportive of the Greenfield community. Ed was no less a great man because he chose the smaller stage. **Greenfield** benefited greatly as he carried on the Sidey ethic of caring, thoughtful news reporting. This philosophy continued when Linda Sidey, Ed's wife, took the helm as editor/publisher. We had the privilege of conversing with her about the **Greenfield** experience. She said, "Greenfield is an active, progressive community; good forefathers kept it alive and mapped it well." She also volunteered an entertaining story about

Cardinal IG, Greenfield

Fontanelle Bar and Grill

Sandy McPeak

Dave Nichols

Supplying Genetics Worldwide

Lillian Nichols

Iowa cowboys, Nichols Farms

Nichols Farms

the *Free Press* winning the INA (Iowa Newspapers Association) Blooper of the Year award. A headline was intended to read, "Half of the town is feeding the other half." A typo replaced the 'd' in feeding with an 'l.' The townspeople called or stopped in to ask where the line formed and what half they were in!

Cardinal IG, the world's largest producer of insulated glass units, has a plant in **Greenfield** that employees 600 people. There are a couple of lakes for water sports, camping and fishing and the Middle River forest area is good for canoeing and primitive camping. Good schools, a golf course and other recreational facilities add to the amenities. Nearby tourist attractions include the birthplace of Henry A. Wallace and the Iowa Aviation Museum. The Henry A. Wallace Country Life Center honors the high achieving Iowan who founded Pioneer Hi-Bred Seed Corn and also served as U.S. Secretary of Agriculture and U.S. Vice President. The Iowa Aviation Museum opened in 1990 with a gift of eight vintage aircraft from the John and Yvonne Schildberg airplane collection. The collection has since grown

Henry A. Wallace Country Life Center and birthplace

and an Iowa Aviation Hall of Fame has been added that features some very high profile aviators from Iowa.

As we moved down the road, we stopped in **Fontanelle** for lunch. This little town that lost a bid for county seat has a restaurant loaded with character. Sandy and Robert McPeak own and operate the Fontanelle Bar and Grill. The walls are covered with memorabilia, beer signs (some very old) and patriotic banners and flags. Sandy was a delightful waitress and her husband was a good cook. She agreed with Connie that it was a nice arrangement to have a man working in the kitchen.

Adair County's Nichols Farms is not nearly as vast as the famous King Ranch in Texas, but Iowa's largest farm/ranch operation comprises 5,000 acres of Iowa soil, the richest in the world. The King Ranch is the size of Rhode Island but it is arid and mostly scrubland. There is no scrubland on Nichols Farms; it is all very productive as are the people who run it. They raise all the hay and corn necessary to feed a large herd of purebred Angus cattle. They are a national, full-service genetic provider with locations in four states. They utilize high technology and employ good people. In addition to the 2,000-plus calves harvested each year, they export embryos and semen to countries around the world.

We stopped for a visit at the office located in the end of one of their barns. We entered a room with a desk by the door and an old couch and two chairs along one of the walls. The couch and chairs were occupied by three Iowa cowboys attired in billed caps, jeans, sweatshirts and knee-high rubber boots. A smattering of springtime mud on the boots was no problem in this very casual office. Lillian Nichols, a sister-in-law of Dave Nichols and a full partner in the business, occupied the desk. Soon Dave emerged from his office and invited us back. Again, the furnishings were old and it appeared he had no problem with hired hands entering his office with their boots on. One of the walls was covered with Marilyn Monroe photos that were mostly gifts because people know his favorite movie is *The Seven Year Itch*. The other walls had photos of cattle and people in the business. Small statues of bulls and a cowboy on a horse crowned his roll-top desk. Nichols Farms is an impressive, high-tech operation run by some very unpretentious people.

Dave and his brother Lee started building this enterprise when they took over their father's 240-acre farm. They had built the farm to about 1,000 acres when, in 1981, Lee died. Dave was in charge of genetics, sales, promotion and planning and Lee had managed the day-to-day operations. Dave had made the decision to sell because he didn't feel he knew Lee's side of the operation well enough to continue. Lee had trained his men well and they came forward one by one and assured Dave they could handle various aspects of daily operations. Lee's wife, Lillian, quit her job as high school librarian and Dave's wife, Phyllis, who had been volunteering for everything, quit that life to join in on saving the business. The crisis was met and they never looked back. Lillian, Phyllis and Dave are equal partners and they treat everyone who works for them as equals.

Our overnight stay was at the Harrisdale Homestead B&B on a Cass County Heritage Farm (150 years in the same family) owned by the Harris family.

Mick & Kitty Sheref

Adair County

Cass County

Cass County

The family has kept it even though none of them live on the property nor do they farm. The land is rented out and LaVon Eblen manages the B&B. LaVon told us about a farmer-owned railroad that connected **Atlantic** and **Kimballton** that used to run past the farm. When they built the tracks, they arrived at Elkhorn by Christmas, but needed to reach **Kimballton** by first of the year to receive grant money. The only solution to meet the deadline was to move the city limits south, which they did. The development of **Kimballton** fell far short of this expanded city boundary. The train operated from 1907 to 1932. People could flag it down anywhere along the line if they needed a ride.

We unpacked, returned to our car and drove to **Atlantic** for dinner at the Main Street Grill. This spacious restaurant takes up the first floor of an old hotel. The reservation desk was formerly the hotel reservation desk. The décor was a little confused—basically Victorian. Paintings on the walls were done by the owner's mother. I thought an eight-ounce, top sirloin with a Jack Daniels glaze sounded good. It wasn't quite what I

Harrisdale Homestead B&B

LaVon Eblen

Atlantic Park and pioneer cabin

expected. Piled high atop the steak were deep-fried onions and, I think, mushrooms. The glaze had a gelatin-like quality. The steak wasn't easy to find, but when I did, I ate it with a small amount of "pilings." The taste was fine. Connie enjoyed a healthy stir-fry of grilled chicken and a variety of vegetables.

We spent the night in the classic, foursquare farmhouse from the 1920s. We were the only people in the house that was located at the end of a dead-end county gravel road. A thunderstorm raged through the night with some thunderclaps so loud that I'm sure lightning struck some farmstead object. We survived and LaVon fixed us a hearty breakfast the next morning and we were on our way.

Another stage of spring was happening in the countryside—random bursts of subtle green were appearing in the wooded areas as buds began leafing out. After the heavy rains, the grass was greener, the fields muddier and the streams swollen. Ah, but it was spring and the daffodils were blooming—adding color from the warm side of the color wheel.

These days, crime is generally more prevalent in heavily populated areas than in rural areas. In pioneer days, the opposite was true with Indian/white clashes and bullies and ruffians terrorizing small settlements. **Cass County** had the Crooked Creek Gang to make things miserable. Whiskey was their first love and, under its influence, they became dangerous, lawless characters who delighted in fighting, destroying property and shooting up villages. Carl Strahl and his son Roll were prominent members of this gang of knuckle-draggers. Roll and another gang member got intoxicated on a February day in 1883 and, as they headed home riding in the back of a sled, Roll shot into a group of bystanders on the street with a double-barreled shotgun. As the Crooked Creek boys were having their fun, an unknown rifleman shot Roll in the head. He died the next day. Looking to avenge his son's death, Carl confronted a young, expert marksman named George Halleck whom he was convinced shot his son. Carl leveled his gun at Halleck and started cussing him out. Halleck replied with a shot to Carl's neck that proved fatal. The demise of the Strahls was greeted with applause and ringing of church bells.

In 1834, another bit of sad violence in **Cass County** was the death of Chief Mahaskah of the Iowa tribe. This great leader, who has an Iowa county named after him, was shot in the back by a skulking, cowardly Indian enemy.

The first permanent settler in the **Cass County** area was Vincent M. Conrad who arrived in 1850 with his wife and one child. He built a 15- by 32-foot log cabin and added on to provide overnight shelter for travelers. Other settlers were more transient, staying long enough to harvest a crop and then moving to what they perceived to be a better place.

A forerunner to **Atlantic** was the town of Grove City. In 1856, it began as a quiet city with a post office, saloon, hotel, doctor, school and a fire-and-brimstone preacher. When the railroad bypassed it in favor of Atlantic, its residents and some of its buildings moved a few miles northwest to **Atlantic**. Grove City was born, flourished and died within a few years, but it provided **Atlantic** with its earliest citizens and businesses.

Franklin H. Whitney deserves most of the credit for founding Atlantic although he had help from B. F. Allen, a banker

Southwest Iowa Egg, Cass County

Cass County Courthouse, Atlantic

Atlantic

CYCLES
GOODRICH CYCLES
Norton
AJS

Baxter Cycle, Marne

Bob Anderson

from Des Moines, and from John P. Cook, who owned most of the land on which the town was built. They formed the Atlantic Town Company in 1868. **Atlantic** was well located but the railroad probably chose it because the promoters owned the land. The moving of the county seat from Lewis to **Atlantic** aided its growth. Whitney helped survey the railroad right-of-way, built a hotel, opened a bank and generally served the community as a caring citizen. His two sons followed in his footsteps. Incidentally, this founding trio was responsible for the town's name. They noted that there was no town between the Pacific and Atlantic Oceans named Atlantic. Why not Atlantic, Iowa?

Atlantic has a railroad town layout with the business district streets running up a hill from the tracks. There is no town square. An attractive, 1934, art deco style courthouse sits on top of the hill. Leaded glass windows and art deco motifs adorn the exterior and the theme is carried out with flair inside. A beautiful city park with a historic log cabin and veterans' monument occupies space between the business district and courthouse. Recent

Randy Baxter and Italian buyer

98

Atlantic

street-scaping with trees, plantings and brick-trimmed sidewalks enhance the restored, turn-of-the-century buildings.

Lively, fun festivals start in August with Atlantic Fest and continue into fall with Harvest Fest and Coca-Cola Days. Coca-Cola has regional offices and a bottling plant in **Atlantic**.

We took a little time to talk to **Atlantic** resident, Bob Anderson. Bob is a retired nutritionist who worked for Walnut Grove Products, a once booming company that no longer exists. He spends his time gardening, volunteering, serving as an honor guard for veterans, tutoring and auditing high school classes. Right after we talked to him, he was off to sit in on a calculus class. Calculus? Man, that's keeping the aging brain active. Bob gives the Hunt family, successful farmers and bankers, much credit for Atlantic's good quality of life. They donated land for the hospital and new high school and have made many more contributions to the community. He says that Atlantic is a great town with its new modern high school, community center and YMCA.

Marne, a Cass County town of 150, is home to a unique international business. Thirty-plus years ago, Randy Baxter threw open his garage door exposing a collection of junk motorcycles and exclaimed, "This is how I'm going to make a living." A welder by trade, he used his mechanical talents and love of British-made motorcycles to create a niche business that draws customers from around the world. Baxter Cycle is a franchise dealer for Triumph, Royal Enfield and MotoGuzzi motorcycles. They have a complete stock of parts for British motorcycles—1950 and newer. They also have a ton of used parts and salvaged parts-bikes. And there is a complete service and machine shop. Three buildings house the aforementioned departments, a showroom and warehousing for vintage bikes-restored and in various stages of repair. There are probably only one or two similar businesses in the United States and Canada. On the day we stopped in, they were loading 30 classic bikes into a shipping container mounted on a semitrailer. Randy and an Italian buyer were supervising the process. As we were looking around the facilities, we struck up a conversation with James Friddle, a British bike collector from Arkansas. He has 65 antique bikes, has been to England's Motorcycle Museum and he visits Randy every three or four months. I love people like Randy who pursue a dream while staying true to their roots.

More traditional antiques were in store for us as we moved on to **Walnut** in **Pottawattamie County**. Walnut, a town of about 900, was established in 1871. In the late 1800s, the complete downtown of wooden structures burned down. The new buildings that replaced them were built with brick and used sturdier construction techniques. They remain today and the majority of them are antique stores. There are a total of 17 antique dealers in Walnut—making it Iowa's antique capital and a destination for collectors. Every Fathers' Day, **Walnut** hosts Am Vets Antique Show. It begins Friday morning and ends Sunday evening. It draws hundreds of dealers and thousands of shoppers from all over the United States and Canada. It started in 1982 as a fundraiser for Walnut's American Veterans.

We took Highway 83 out of **Walnut** to **Avoca**, the home of Pottawattamie County Fairgrounds. At **Avoca** we con-

Walnut

Walnut

99

Oakland

Gold Mine Bar and Grill, Council Bluffs

Pottawattamie County Courthouse, Council Bluffs

nected with Highway 59 and turned south to **Oakland** where we encountered the smell of Oakland Foods, a 300,000-square-foot beef, pork and poultry processing plant. Downtown Oakland has a lot of character with a curved street and ornate buildings. Leaving **Oakland**, we took a right on Highway 6, which is the road to Council Bluffs.

Approaching **Council Bluffs**, Highway 6 became a roller coaster. We would crest a hill and drop into a valley and up a hill and into a valley. This went on for several miles. The fields in this area were mostly terraced. The next scene on the horizon was the Loess Hills which we traversed into **Council Bluffs**, the **Pottawattamie County** seat and, at a population of 58,000, the largest city we had experienced so far.

Our stomachs were suggesting that we have lunch the first thing when we entered town. We found a place called the Goldmine Bar and Grill in a blue-collar area of town. It was a bustling place with vinyl covered chairs and booths, wood paneling and typical tavern wall décor. However, beer promotion was taken a step further with large, wind deflectors

Council Bluffs

Council Bluffs

Kanesville Tabernacle, Council Bluffs

from semi cabs hanging on the walls. One had the Budweiser logo and the other Miller Lite. We split a tasty, filling, super-club sandwich.

History abounds in **Council Bluffs** and **Pottawattamie County**. French explorers worked their way up and down the Missouri River in the 1700s, long before the United States purchased this territory from the French and almost a century before the Lewis and Clark Expedition. Lewis and Clark spent five days in this area and held council in the bluffs with Missouri and Otoe Indians, thus the name **Council Bluffs**. However, this wasn't the original name. Colonel Thomas Kane was sent by the United States government to check on the Mormons who were using the area that is now **Council Bluffs** as a staging area for wagon trains embarking on the Mormon Trail to Utah. They were feared as a military, anti-government group. Kane ended up being sympathetic to their plight and the community was named Kane, and then Kanesville, in his honor.

More than 30,000 Mormons passed through Kanesville in the mid-1800s. They organized churches, schools, gov-

ernments, courts and newspapers for their members as they made Kanesville and the surrounding area a temporary home before continuing on to Utah. Kanesville became the midwestern headquarters of the Mormon Church. In 1847, a group of 200 men constructed a large log structure in less than three weeks. It was at this temporary tabernacle that Brigham Young was sustained as the second president of the Mormon Church on December 27, 1847. The original tabernacle deteriorated and was torn down. In 1996, an authentic replica was built.

By 1852, the majority of the Mormons had left for Utah and Kaneville's population dropped from 7,000 to 2,500. In 1853, the name Kanesville was changed to **Council Bluffs**. The town continued serving as a staging site for homesteaders and gold rushers preparing for the final push west. In 1859, a young lawyer for the Rock Island Railroad, named Abraham Lincoln, came to **Council Bluffs** to examine a tract of land he held as security for a loan. He also met with Grenville Dodge, a railroad engineer and later a Civil War general. They spent three days discussing the possibility of

building a coast-to-coast railroad. Dodge went on to become **Council Bluffs'** leading citizen and an adviser to Presidents Lincoln, Grant, Johnson, Hayes, McKinley, Roosevelt and Taft. Five of them were guests at his elegant Victorian home that was designed by the same architect who designed Terrace Hill, the Iowa governor's mansion.

The railroad came to **Council Bluffs** in 1862. At one time, seven rail lines served it and it became the mail-handling center for the American West. Rapid growth followed and **Council Bluffs** developed into a bustling center of commerce. By the 1880s, the city was ranked second in the nation as a wholesale farm implement center. In 1954, railroading supported one quarter of the city's population and it was ranked as the fifth largest railroad center in the nation. After some economic stagnation in the late twentieth century, **Council Bluffs** is on the move again.

Enthusiastic chamber of commerce employees, Diane Hestness and Chrissy Caniglia, gave us a verbal tour of present day **Council Bluffs**. Diane is the office manager and Chrissy is the director of

Rails West Museum, Council Bluffs

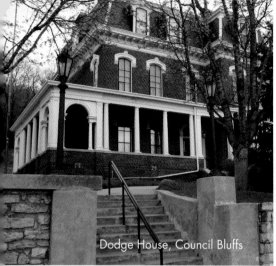
Dodge House, Council Bluffs

Bayliss Park, Council Bluffs

Diane Hestness and Chrissy Caniglia

Squirrel Cage Jail

group tours, sports marketing and the convention and visitors' bureau. The first thing we learned was that they sincerely love this city and find their job of promoting it a pleasure. Chrissy, who grew up in a small Iowa town and lived in New York City for two years, said, "I went from really small to really big to just right." **Council Bluffs** lives like a small town, yet has the amenities of a metropolitan area of 800,000. Omaha is an easy commute to the other side of the Missouri River, but **Council Bluffs** is no suburban, bedroom community. It has its own culture and economic base. What commuting is done, goes both ways.

Railroading has declined in **Council Bluffs** as it has across the country, but the city is still served by five freight lines and Amtrak. Interstates 29 and 80 provide excellent north/south and east/west connections. Dynamic growth is evidenced by the construction of more than 4,000 new housing units within the city limits over the last decade. Beautiful sculptures and a spectacular fountain adorn Bayliss Park in the center of the business district. A large, attractive, new library is located in the heart of downtown. The old

Carnegie library building has been converted into the Union Pacific Railroad Museum. The complete story of railroad history is told in the displays—following the technology revolution from steam power to diesel hybrids and signal lanterns to remote control. There are historical sites all over town, telling of the city's fascinating past. One of note is the Squirrel Cage Jail. Prisoners were locked up in a three-story revolving cage with pie-shaped cells. This was supposed to make it less labor intensive for the jailer. I'm not sure how. The 8,000-seat Mid-American Center is a premier entertainment and convention center. There is an abundance of recreational activities and they have good Iowa schools. A cost of living well below average for a metropolitan area makes it all a bargain.

Then there are the casinos. **Council Bluffs** has three and Connie had the arduous task of checking the looseness of their slots. At Harrah's, she lost $10 in 20 minutes. At Ameristar, she came out 75 cents ahead after 30 minutes of play. At the Horseshoe Casino, she lost $10 in 26 minutes. The running score after six casinos is $7.25 ahead.

Squirrel Cage Jail

Council Bluffs Public Library

DeSoto Bend Visitor Center observation area

Shooting carp, DeSoto Bend National Wildlife Refuge

The *Bertrand*, Visitor Center

Bertrand cargo, Visitor Center

eaving Council Bluffs, we took I-29 on a short drive north to **Harrison County**. At the U.S. Highway 30 interchange, we exited and motored west to the DeSoto Bend National Wildlife Refuge. We passed through the park gate and proceeded to the Visitor Center. It was a sunny, warm day in early May and the foliage was reacting in a very positive way. Yellow-greens dominated the wooded areas as leaves were unfolding from their buds. More flowers were joining the daffodils with their colors filling out the remaining blanks on the color wheel.

DeSoto Bend National Wildlife Refuge is one of 500 refuges in the United States devoted to preserving and restoring habitat for migratory waterfowl. It is located on what was a looping bend of the Missouri River. The Army Corps of Engineers rerouted the river in 1959 to eliminate this loop, thus creating DeSoto Lake. Each spring and fall since the end of the Ice Age, migrating waterfowl have made this wetlands and river a stopping point on their north/south journey. They put on spectacular shows that can be observed from an enclosed observation area at the Visitor Center. Bald eagles fol-

Visitor Center

DeSoto Lake

Boating Regulations
- Limited To No-Wake, 5 MPH Speeds
- Must Comply With State Regulations
- Flotation Devices Required For All Passengers
- Open Alcoholic Beverages Prohibited During Boat Operation
- Boats May Not Be Left Unattended

No Waterskiing   No Swimming

low the geese in the fall and many winter there until March. Peak numbers occur in December and again in March. As many as 145 have been counted at one time. Other types of wildlife enjoying this protected environment are deer, cottontails, raccoons, coyotes, opossums, fox squirrels, beaver, muskrat and mink. Fish are not given the protection of their above-water colleagues. Angling is allowed from shore and from boats traveling at no-wake speed. Game fish include largemouth bass, walleye, crappie, bluegill, channel and flathead catfish. Spear fishing and archery are allowed for non-game fish, such as carp. A beach and trails provide other recreational opportunities.

The Missouri River is, and always has been, a treacherous river for commercial traffic. Its flow is faster and there are more hidden snags and sandbars than on the more benign Mississippi. Between 1819 and 1936, 400 steamboats either sank or were wrecked on a stretch of the Missouri from St. Louis, Missouri, to Fort Benton, Montana. Even though the average steamer survived only about three or four years during the 1800s, the "Big Muddy" was a vital artery for ship-

ping supplies to frontier settlements, fur trading posts and mining towns. A new steamer, the *Bertrand*, didn't even survive its first trip as it sank trying to navigate around the loop at DeSoto Bend.

The *Bertrand*, built in 1864, was a mountain packet sternwheeler designed for shallow, narrow rivers. It measured 178 feet long and, with a wide, flat hull, it was estimated it could carry from 250 to 400 tons of cargo. For its maiden voyage up the Missouri, it docked at St. Louis to load supplies for the gold mining fields of Montana and other settlements along the way. The departure on March 18, 1865, was timed to take advantage of rising water levels caused by the spring melt and rains. After a stop in Omaha to pick up a few passengers and a new pilot, it continued powering upriver about 25 miles until it hit a snag and sank in 12 feet of water. Before it sank, the pilot was able to maneuver it close enough to shore so that a gangplank was dropped for the passengers. There were no deaths. Salvage operations began two weeks later but were temporarily halted when divers were called to another sinking vessel upstream. When they

returned to the *Bertrand*, the river had already claimed the boat and further efforts were hopeless.

Over the years, the Missouri changed course leaving the *Bertrand* buried under 25 to 30 feet of silt and clay. Salvors Sam Corbino and Jesse Pursell, using a sophisticated metal detector, discovered a large concentration of buried metal. They began excavating after further evidence convinced them they had located the *Bertrand*. They started with heavy equipment in the spring of 1968 and continued through the summer with a variety of excavating techniques, including 210 well points, as they dug 18 feet below the water table. After a winter break, they resumed the next spring and by mid-summer, they had cleared the deck. They salvaged 10,000 cubic feet of hand tools, clothes, foodstuffs, furnishings, munitions, mercury, household goods and more—200,000 artifacts total. All this cargo is on display at the Visitor Center and I swear it looks like 200,000 artifacts is a lowball number. It is impressive.

After a pleasant drive circling the park, we returned to U.S. Highway 30 and drove east to the town of Missouri

Visitor Center

View of Missouri River valley from Loess Hills

Small's Fruit Farm

Old Home Cafe, Pisgah

Valley. **Harrison County's** largest town (3,000) butts up against the Loess Hills. The town's heritage is a classic railroad town and market for the area's agricultural products. The town was platted by the railroad and from the beginning was intended to be an important feeding stop for cattle being shipped to eastern markets. By 1888, there were 12 trains a day and that expanded to 25 per day in 1896. In 1900, there were 500 railroad workers living in **Missouri Valley**. The Depression, more powerful locomotives that needed less servicing and a national system of good highways contributed to a decline in railroad activity in smaller towns. **Missouri Valley**, however, continues to reap many benefits from its relationship with the railroad. Tracks have been upgraded throughout **Harrison County** and many trains use these tracks every day. The Union Pacific has made investments in the town and has made material and monetary donations.

   Missouri Valley lost the competition for the county seat but they out-hustled the competition for hosting the county fair with a building spree in 1872. The first fair's attractions were exhibits of the

Small's Fruit Farm

Loess Hills

Harrison County Fairgrounds, Missouri Valley

best in agricultural products that were judged with 50-cent to five-dollar awards for the winners. There were footraces and horse races in the beginning; sporting events like baseball and football were added later. The agricultural aspects of the fair are basically the same today with more youth involvement through programs such as 4-H. The emphasis is still placed on local talent, but carnivals, tractor pulls and professional entertainment add to the festive atmosphere.

Iowa Western Community College owns a parcel of land five miles southeast of **Missouri Valley** that played a role in the Cold War. It was the site for an Atlas missile launch complex. The missiles rested on their sides in a bunker and had to be raised to a vertical position before firing. The process was too time-consuming so they quickly became obsolete and were replaced in the mid-'60s with underground silo types. It was a sobering sight to see the 82-foot-long missile armed with a nuclear warhead raised in the vertical position.

Our lunch stop in **Missouri Valley** was the Willow Creek Bar and Grill. It was a vinyl-covered stack chair, beer sign type atmosphere. A sign on one wall asking for RAGBRAI XXXVI volunteers is probably part of the décor of many businesses in town as they plan to host the departure of the 2008 Register's Annual Great Bike Ride Across Iowa. On the menu, I noted they had two sizes of hamburgers so I figured if I ordered the smaller size, I could avoid the super-size sandwich that many restaurants like to serve. I received a burger containing a one-inch-thick patty. I give up.

We left **Missouri Valley** driving on scenic byways weaving through the Loess Hills. We stopped at Small's Fruit Farm in **Mondamin** where we observed apple trees in bloom. The store on the premises was open but unattended. The honor system was in play with a box for depositing money for any item you wanted to purchase. We continued driving through the hills to **Pisgah** where the Old Home Keep On Truckin' Café is located. It was made famous in the Midwest by my favorite TV commercial of all time. C. W. McCall was the truck driver and Mavis was the gum-chewing waitress in an ad selling Old Home Bread. The casting was perfect for those delightful characters and the gentle humor of the ad made you feel good. It was created by Chip Davis when he was an ad man in Omaha. **Pisgah** is also home to the Loess Hills State Forest Headquarters and Visitor Center.

We exited the hills and drove into rolling prairie farmland. The farmers were in the beginning stages of working the fields. I hadn't noticed any plowed ground but had seen planters in stubble fields. It appeared no-till farming was catching on. *The Des Moines Register* reported on May 6 that about 18 percent of Iowa's intended acres have been planted, compared with the past year's pace of 42 percent. It has been a rainy spring.

Logan, the **Harrison County** seat, owes its location to a narrowing of the Boyer River—making it an ideal dam site for a mill. We found a very informal atmosphere at the Logan Public Library where we learned that bit of history. A lady who was using a library computer had a large dog lying at her feet. When we walked in, the dog took notice and got up to check us out. The lady gently called him back and told him to sit, which he did. Then the process was repeated a couple of times until she told him she was

Irrigation rig, Missouri River valley

107

Agribusiness, Portsmouth

SHELBY COUNTY HISTORICAL SETTLEMENT

LOG CABIN DAYS

SUNDAY JUNE 1
ENTERTAINMENT
FOOD DRINK

almost finished and that seemed to settle him down. The librarian making copies for me was holding a baby in one arm as she deftly turned pages and flipped the book on the copier. The baby reacted to my little gestures with big smiles. It was an enjoyable visit.

Harrison County was host to the Lewis and Clark Expedition when they camped at the mouth of the Soldier River on August 2, 1804. For many years after that occasion, hunters and trappers followed streams into the county and brought back news of the fertile valleys covered with tall grass. In 1846, Daniel Brown, who had been with the Mormon encampment at Florence, Nebraska, made a hunting trip up one of those streams and found a spot that appealed to him. He built a cabin, brought his family over and established a home. The settlement of **Harrison County** had begun.

The first **Logan** mill was built in 1856 by Henry Reel, founder of Logan. It served the early settlers by grinding corn, wheat, rye, buckwheat or any other grain. Money was scarce so Reel was generally paid with a set percentage of the milled grain. A trip to the mill was usually a

Antique rock crusher, Logan

Debbie and Joe Pennington

108

Harlan Haus B&B

Mary Secress

Harrison County Courthouse, Logan

family outing with picnic dinners and activities with other mill patrons. They visited, had wrestling matches, pitched horseshoe and dropped a line in the millpond where fish were plentiful.

Leaving **Logan**, we drove past a huge limestone quarry where rock was being crushed. There was a large, antique crusher sitting next to the road that must have provided a lot of rock for country roads in days gone by.

Shortly after crossing the **Shelby County** line we entered the town of **Portsmouth**. It is a clean little community built on a hill rising out of the rolling prairie. A well-kept cemetery with religious statuary and German names on the tombstones crowned the hill. The adjacent St. Mary's Catholic Church was a few feet lower in elevation. At the bottom of the hill were a couple of agribusinesses that appeared to be prospering.

Continuing down the highway, we entered **Harlan**, the **Shelby County** seat. We drove around the square and found our lodging just a half block off the square. The Harlan Haus B&B is a one-story building that was originally a combination residence and print shop.

Innkeeper Mary Secress spruced up the residence part and moved in. The print shop was remodeled into a B&B suite that includes a kitchenette, dining area, queen-size bed and sitting area. A beautiful quilt, made by Mary, hangs as a divider between the bed and sitting area. Quilting is Mary's passion and this suite is often occupied by quilters on a retreat organized by Mary.

Next door to the B&B is a small, white, steel building with a bright red sign proclaiming Rusty's Shoe Repair. **Harlan** is lucky to have a business that has become less common in our throw-away society. Roger Rust will repair anything made from leather and he draws business from far beyond **Harlan**.

After checking in, we retreated to the Rosman Glendale Shelby County Golf Course located five miles north of **Harlan**. Walking on the lush green grass and stroking the little white ball was a therapeutic way to end the day and work up an appetite. The appetite was satisfied at Joe's on the Square.

Joe Pennington, a Texan, and his wife Debbie, a Nebraskan, followed Debbie's family members who had been drifting

into western Iowa. Joe and Debbie ended up in **Harlan** where they opened this charming gourmet restaurant. For five years they have been serving a wide range of specials to tempt the taste buds. The decor is cozy and elegant with plants and smart art posters on the walls. We ordered the special of the evening—pork chops with a sauce that included chocolate in the ingredients. The meal was delicious from the salad and bourbon-molasses sweet potatoes to the buttered, brown sugar carrots.

Joe also serves as a pastor of a non-denominational church that meets every Sunday morning at the Hansen Brothers Coffee House—another neat establishment on the square. It is a cleverly done recycling of an old downtown building where they presently serve breakfast and lunch along with their coffee.

Anyone who follows high school sports associates **Harlan** with championship football. They expect to go to the UNI-Dome every year and they have come close to meeting that goal. Since 1972 the Harlan Cyclones have won the 3A state championship 11 times and have finished runner-up eight times. We met a

Roger (Rusty) Rust

109

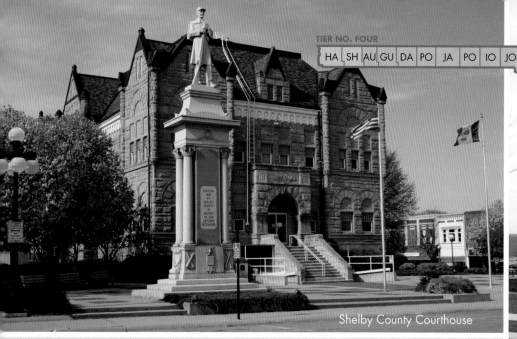
Shelby County Courthouse

76-foot-tall steel sculpture, Shelby

WELCOME TO MERRILL FIELD
HOME OF THE Cyclones

1972,1982,1983,1984,1993,1995,1997,1998,2003
2004,2005

1981,1985,1986,1988,1989,1992,2000,2001

Gary Christiansen (right) and coffee group

group of their boosters who were enjoying their daily coffee meeting at Burger King. All topics are fair game with this group, except politics. They are fairly evenly divided on that topic and no one has been able to convince the other of the error in their ways, so they don't try anymore. Unity comes in supporting the Harlan Cyclones.

Gary Christiansen, the mayor of **Harlan**, agreed to break from the group and talk to us. Gary, a former mail carrier who walked his routes, says, "I used to be 6 feet 5 inches tall but shrank from carrying that heavy mailbag for 30 years." He played guard on the **Harlan** football team back in 1954. Their line averaged about 145 pounds, as opposed to a recent team's line whose average was close to 300 pounds. Harlan's success begins with the mental attitude of believing they are the best. If they lose, they work that much harder to be successful. At the beginning of the season, a mother of one of the athletes asked the coach how things looked. He replied, "It looks pretty good down to the third grade." Football is the marquee sport but **Harlan** students excel at everything. They grow up in a nurturing

Shelby County

Willow Creek Glass Chapel

UltiMilk Dairy Company rotary

community that is well equipped to develop their talents and character. Gary said, "It's a great Midwestern town. If people can find work, they stay here."

North of **Harlan**, near the town of **Kirkman**, is an impressive dairy operation owned by UltiMilk Dairy Company. The structures on the complex barely break into the horizon but sprawl out over a large piece of real estate. In the office we were greeted by Donna Olson, administrative assistant and our tour guide. She is a **Shelby County** native and her in-laws farmed the very land of this dairy's location. She first took us to a glass-enclosed room that overlooked the milking parlor. It was a dramatic introduction. We looked down on two, carousel-like mechanisms called rotaries. Each rotary has 72 stalls and they were each filled with a cow in the process of being milked. The rotaries rotate slowly and never stop. The cows step on from one holding pen and step off to another. The five workers on each rotary spray iodine, wipe, attach milking equipment and spray after milking. RFID tags scan production and health records on each cow. The dairy milks approximately 5,000 cows

four times a day and 600 cows twice a day. Seven 5,000-gallon tankers make daily trips to the Anderson Erickson Dairy in Des Moines.

The cows lead an indoor life and it has its advantages. The barns are cross ventilated with cool cells dripping water on the north side and fans on the south side pulling the cooler air through. The air movement lowers a hot day's temperature about 15 degrees and keeps out the flies. The cows' diet is consistent and healthy. They sleep on sand bedding and the manure is scraped twice daily. We visited on a hot day and the odors were typical of a barnyard on a farm of any size. They were present but not overwhelming.

UltiMilk Dairy Company is an investor-owned corporation managed by a board of seven directors. Steve Weiss is president and Dr. Matthew Van Baale is vice president and general manager.

The town of **Shelby**, located in the southwest corner of the county, is worth a visit. There is a biking/hiking trail that crosses a historic, stone-arched railroad trestle. A 76-foot-tall, steel sculpture and garden symbolize the commodities produced by area farmers—corn, beef and

pork. There is an antique Coke sign on the side of a downtown building. An 80-acre, working farm exhibit and a railroad depot in the process of being restored are other points of interest.

Out in the country near **Shelby**, is a beautiful, non-denominational chapel located in a ravine with a creek and willow trees. It has an elegant, contemporary design with a 360-degree view of the serene countryside. Its name, Willow Creek Glass Chapel, says it all. It is privately owned and rented for weddings, baptisms, renewals and funerals. One client said, "It is like having an outdoor wedding, only it's climate controlled."

Peg McCool's niece in Missouri asked her to help find a place for her wedding. They visited many venues and Peg took mental notes on what they saw. Her niece selected a chapel in the woods, which proved to be a delightful setting for the ceremony. Peg thought to herself, "Why not do something similar on our farm?" She and her husband Eugene came up with a design, took it to an architect for finishing touches and built it. It is a unique and attractive chapel.

Our stomachs were calling for food as

UltiMilk Dairy Company cattlebarn

Danish Immigrant Museum, Elk Horn

Elk Horn

we approached **Elk Horn** and the Danish Inn with its well-known buffet answered the call. The choice and quantity were our decisions as we pushed our trays past the delectables. We decided on a wide variety while holding the volume in check. That meant taking a tablespoon portion of each offering. The dining atmosphere was pure Danish with 1x4-trimmed walls and simple Danish modern furnishings. Hanging on the far wall of one of the dining areas was a large photo of the *Little Mermaid* that graces the harbor of Copenhagen. And each sample from the buffet was delicious.

Elk Horn and nearby **Kimballton** make up the largest, rural Danish settlement in the United States. **Kimballton** is only three miles to the north but the **Audubon County** line runs between them. Both towns show their Danish pride with their architecture and Danish flags. In **Elk Horn** you can experience an authentic 60-foot windmill that was originally built in Denmark in 1848. It was dismantled and shipped to Iowa where it was rebuilt in 1976. There is also a recently constructed (1994) museum in **Elk Horn** that displays Victor Borge's

112

Kimballton

Little Mermaid, Kimballton

Elk Horn

Victor Borge exhibit, Danish Immigrant Museum

first piano, among other impressive immigrant exhibits. Its exposed post-and-beam architecture is in itself worth seeing. In **Kimballton** there is an actual-size replica of the *Little Mermaid*.

After **Kimballton**, we pushed further into **Audubon County** without stopping until we were faced with a Hereford bull that stood 30 feet tall with a horn span of 15 feet. Albert the Bull sits in a park on the edge of the county seat town of **Audubon**. He was built out of steel and concrete in 1963 as a tribute to the nation's beef industry in which the Audubon area is a major player.

The story of Albert the Bull has its roots in a promotion called Operation T-Bone. Back in the early 1950s, local cattlemen shipped their prime-grade beef to markets in Chicago. This was a little more comfortable than early western cattle drives in that cattle rode on a train and the drovers (shippers and businessmen) rode in a Pullman. **Audubon** banker Albert Kruse named the trip Operation T-Bone. The excursion was picked up by news services and it received worldwide press. Albert the Bull was named after the banker and Operation T-Bone is still cele-

brated each year in August.

There is no evidence that Indians made permanent homes in **Audubon County**. They typically preferred living near larger rivers, but the settlers did experience Indians making hunting forays in this part of Iowa. The Indian/white relationship was generally friendly with some wariness on each side. On one occasion some young, white, male settlers thought it would be fun to take their girlfriends to visit an Indian camp. One of the camp's Indians stood 6 feet 6 inches tall with a well-proportioned body. He had put in a tiring day of hunting and was stretched out along the side of a tent and was covered with a blanket when the adventuresome couples arrived. The Indians weren't big on chairs so when one of the ladies tired, she noted there was a blanket-covered bench beside a tent. She sat down and the big Indian stayed motionless for a while but eventually rolled over. She sprang up with a scream that caused uproarious laughter from all, including the big Indian.

Bayard Taylor, a nineteenth-century writer, claimed the Nishnabotna Valley was as beautiful as the Rhine in Germany

and the Thames in England and he complimented Audubon on its stone and brick buildings of fine architectural designs. It is still a lovely place and the townspeople are continuing to work on it. In the center of a downtown park there is a statue of the town's namesake, John James Audubon, with pen and sketchpad in hand. Sidewalks, brickwork and landscaping are new or still in the construction process. Commemorative tiles are being placed along the walks. And it appears they are doing it right. A recent addition to the town's Carnegie library is another example of good design and workmanship. One wall inside the addition is the brick façade of the old library. Gail Richardson, the head librarian for 24 years, filled us in on things of interest and the good life in **Audubon**. Gail says, "I like Audubon because of the opportunity to raise children in a community where they have the freedom to go swimming and to walk downtown with their friends." The original library and the addition were designed by the same architectural firm—Brooks, Borg and Skiles of Des Moines. The Carnegie structure was renovated and is now called

ALBERT THE BULL
AUDUBON IOWA • 50025

Gail Richardson

11

Audubon County Courthouse, Audubon

John James Audubon statue, Audubon

the John James Audubon Culture Center. In it are displays of the work of the famed artist-naturalist. A collection of Royal Copenhagen Danish Christmas plates rests along a shelf above the bookcases.

The first settlers were of mixed heritage but they were followed by a heavy influx of Germans. Danes have spilled into **Audubon** from the Elk Horn/Kimballton area. Many of those ethnic settlers came as hired hands who eventually bought their own farms. Some residents of the county still carry on pioneer-like pursuits such as trapping and fishing along the rivers.

Audubon County has two museums that illustrate and report on the early days. Nathan Hamlin Park, located immediately south of **Audubon**, is named after the county's first settler. This complex includes an 1890, Victorian brick house; a corn museum; 18 antique windmills; a little red schoolhouse and a machinery building of antique farm equipment. The latter includes a 200-foot mural depicting a ranch/farm-to-market process. The second museum in **Exira** is housed in the first courthouse of **Audubon County**. It contains histori-

Our Saviour's Lutheran Church, Audubon

Sheila Kearney—Washington Street Hardwood Floors, Exira

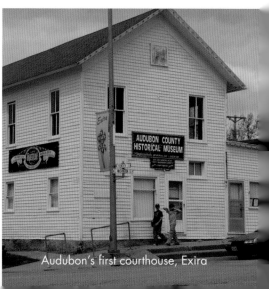

Audubon's first courthouse, Exira

Audubon

cal artifacts, a genealogy library and a video and newspaper clipping of a devastating, Nishnabotna River flood in 1958.

Exira is also home to a unique business—Washington Street Hardwood Floors and Décor. This business has its roots in a do-it-yourself project performed by Sheila and Alan Kearney. Alan crafted a beautiful floor of patterns using different hardwoods. He received so many requests to do something similar in other homes that he decided to make it a business. He and Sheila set up shop in a vacant downtown store. They gutted the store and divided it up into three display areas in front with a shop in the rear. In the basement space, there is a display room for Alan's hardwoods and another room where Sheila can work on her projects. Alan's flooring design and workmanship shine in the store where Sheila has antiques and specialty items arranged in appealing displays. The finished woodwork and painted walls are examples of the finest craftsmanship.

An important addition to the recreational amenities of **Audubon** and neighboring counties is the Littlefield Recreation Area. A 70-acre lake, com-

plete with beach and bathhouse, was finished in 1982. Camping sites, hiking trails and picnic areas complement the lake and there is a 100-acre hunting section that is clearly marked.

After viewing the man-made lake and recreation area, we took a little side loop on gravel roads to view the Sheeder Prairie Preserve—a small piece of original prairie that man has not altered. In itself, it is not very spectacular. You have to visualize that this was typical of the open areas of the state before settlement.

We entered **Guthrie County** and returned to the paved roads and continued our trip through farm country. As we drove, we observed that more fields had exposed black dirt indicating the use of disks for minimum tilling. Do they use the plow anymore? We'll clear that up the next time we talk to a farmer.

It was a perfect spring day in the middle of May when we entered **Guthrie Center**, the county seat. Elementary school kids were swarming the high school track and football field in celebration of their annual track and field day. The town's aquatic center was being filled with water in anticipation of the

Memorial Day opening. People were out walking and everyone we encountered was in a good mood. When you go through a winter like we had this year, you deserve the nice weather and you appreciate it more.

We made our customary stop at the chamber of commerce to look for printed material on **Guthrie County** and **Guthrie Center**. Most of the information we were looking for was contained in a booklet of which they had no more copies. They suggested we check the Guthrie County State Bank for a copy. Two women who were employees at the bank informed us that they didn't have any copies either, but they immediately began calling all over town and nearby Panora trying to track down a copy. At that moment, Lorrie Stringham, the designer of the elusive piece, entered the bank and joined in the quest. She assured us she would find one and catch up with us at our next stop, which was the library. We had just begun our research when she bounced in with a copy in hand. I love it!

Location, location, location were the three most important reasons for staking a claim on unsettled land. Settlers needed

Track and field day, Guthrie Center

Guthrie Center

115

Guthrie County

Guthrie County Courthouse, Guthrie Center

Guthrie County

water, timber and tillable land. They could claim a maximum of 320 acres, which figured to be a square of 1,500 average paces on each side. A stake or some other marker was placed at each corner to define the boundaries. To retain his rights to a tract of land, the settler was required to cultivate at least five acres and construct a cabin measuring at least eight feet high. To receive a patent endowing him the owner, he had to pay Uncle Sam $1.25 an acre. Few settlers had the funds to pay the full amount, which led to claim jumpers who would come in and pay Uncle Sam the full amount and virtually steal a settler's claim after he had made many improvements. Later, laws were passed to discourage that practice.

Benjamin F. Kunkle, a blacksmith from Pennsylvania, was **Guthrie County's** second settler, but the first to stick it out. He prospered by planting corn and potatoes in the rich soil. He harvested prairie grasses for hay and his cattle had free range. He brought with him 24 hogs, four cows, a team of oxen, a team of horses and several adult sons to help with the work. And his blacksmith

116

Yale

Karen and Jim Sievers

Guthrie County Historical Village, Panora

skills were invaluable.

Other settlers came and prospered; thus, towns like **Guthrie Center** and **Panora** sprang up and the customary fight for the county seat began. Panora, the oldest county town, first had the honor of being the home of **Guthrie County** government. However, **Guthrie Center** was intentionally located dead center in the county with the idea of taking the county seat away from **Panora**. Votes were held and votes were held and more votes were held. In 1859, the first vote to move the seat was defeated; in 1860 the second vote went in **Guthrie Center's** favor; in 1869, Panora got it back; in 1870 another vote was held and Panora won again; in 1873 the voters again waffled and the seat went back to **Guthrie Center**. Voter fatigue must have set in because there have been no more moves.

You can imagine yourself as an early resident of the county by visiting Guthrie County Historical Village located on the south side of **Panora**. The village features an antique and artifacts building, log cabin, general store, Milwaukee Railroad depot and caboose, church,

school, blacksmith shop, implement exhibit and coalmine display. There are other destinations and events in the county where you can use skills that would have been handy in those days. There are two archery ranges, a skeet shooting range and areas for hunting and fishing.

The Primetime Restaurant in downtown **Guthrie Center** has a sports theme bar and a country theme dining room. When we checked in for lunch, it was very busy. I commented to the cashier, "The food must be very good here." She responded, "Yes, it is and it's also the elementary school's track and field day." After a couple of minutes, a booth opened up and we took it. Our waitress was efficient, but the sheer numbers slowed the service. A French dip sandwich with cheese was delicious.

After lunch we drove to Springbrook Conservation Educational Center located adjacent to Springbrook State Recreation Area. The CEC is a hands-on center, operated by the DNR, which offers outdoor and indoor classrooms for teaching conservation and resource use. Recipients of the instruction include teachers, students, conservation personnel, communi-

ty leaders and other groups. The recreation area includes 763 acres of parkland and a 114-acre lake, where you can fish, swim and camp. There are also two public hunting tracts on the north and south sides of the park. Another outdoor venue is Leon Mills Park and Wild Life Area on the banks of the Raccoon River. There are 1,236 acres available for camping and fishing and there is a canoe access.

Located approximately halfway between **Guthrie Center** and **Panora** is the Prairie View B&B, our choice for an overnight stay. And a good choice it was. Two guest rooms and a suite are immaculate and expertly decorated with art and art objects, as is the rest of the house. Looking out the rear windows, you see a pool in the foreground and, in the countryside beyond, you see the edge of the part of Iowa that was flattened by an ancient glacier. On the other side of the house, the landscape is rolling prairie.

Mounted on the back of our car were two bicycles. We brought them along in anticipation of riding the Raccoon River Valley Trail, which goes through **Panora**. This 56-mile trail stretches

Prairie View B&B

Springbrook Conservation Educational Center

Lake Panorama

Historic Washington Township Consolidated School, Guthrie County

from Waukee, a suburb of Des Moines, to Jefferson. In Waukee you can link up with Des Moines' metro area trails that in turn link up with other country trails. There is another trail in the planning stages that will go north from Waukee to Perry and then west to Herndon on the RRVT, thus creating a riding loop. Iowa has done a commendable job of developing this biking and hiking trail system and they continue to work on it.

After we parked our bags at the B&B, we headed for the **Panora** trailhead. As noted earlier, the day was perfect at about 70 degrees and no wind. We started down the trail with big "life is good" grins until a swarm of gnats wiped the smiles off our faces. We continued the ride with more sober expressions. On our 15-mile trip, we rode through tree canopies, open prairie and the small town of Linden. We saw about 12 different varieties of birds—the most beautiful being the bluebirds. We smelled the flowers and the aromatic lilac bushes. It was exhilarating.

Dinner that evening was at The Port located at the Lake Panorama Marina. The dining room had a panoramic view of Lake Panorama. It is laid out so that all

118   Blacksmith shop—Guthrie County Historical Village, Panora

Don and Pam Parsons

Lake Panorama

tables have a good view of the lake. There is outdoor seating on two deck levels. We ordered a "United Nations" meal with a quesadilla hors d'oeuvre and a Maui chicken sandwich.

Back at the B&B as we were preparing to go to bed, Connie started picking up the bed's decorative pillows and was looking for a corner to pile them when she commented, "There are too many pillows in the world." We dealt with the pillows, watched a little TV and dozed off.

We awoke to another sunny day and were treated to a breakfast of ingredient-enhanced scrambled eggs on English muffins with an assorted fruit dish. Innkeepers Karen and Jim Sievers joined us. They are former teachers from the Des Moines' metro area who opened this B&B about five years ago. They are eco-minded people who recycle, compost and are contemplating the installation of a wind turbine to supply electricity. They are loyal Midwesterners who could have taught anywhere. They said, "Everywhere else is just for visiting."

They had a good Iowa story for us about some young men on a river kayaking trip. The adventurers packed some beer and embarked from Coon Rapids, but the beer supply was depleted shortly after breakfast. As they paddled along, they saw a guy on shore who waved and asked how they were doing. They replied, "Fine, but we're out of beer." He asked, "Do you have any money?" They said, "No." He then instructed them to look for a rock before the next bridge a ways downstream. As they approached the bridge, they saw sitting on a rock a 12-pack with one can missing.

About thirty-plus years ago, Connie and I received some promotional material inviting us to visit a new development called Lake Panorama. We accepted their free lunch offer and, out of curiosity, we took a look. There was the lake, a modest lodge and a few houses. Some financial setbacks followed, but somewhere along the line, the project got wings so that today, the lake is rimmed with upscale homes. We talked to Pam and Don Parsons who moved to the lake from Des Moines eleven years ago. They first bought a spec house on a man-made channel. Then they built an upgraded home on a lakeshore lot. As their enthusiasm for boating waned, they built what they claim is their final house on a lot bordering the Lake Panorama National Golf Course. Pam said this moving scenario is not unusual for residents of this community. Don commutes daily to Des Moines, where his company Wood Roofing has its offices. For several years Pam also worked in Des Moines. She said it was an easy commute to which Don replied, "Ya, that's because you'd sleep all the way!" But, Don says he doesn't mind the drive because he enjoys the Panorama community so much.

Dexter was the first town we encountered as we entered **Dallas County**. It received national attention in 1933 when the Barrow Gang and the Des Moines police had a shootout in nearby Dexfield Park. That resulted in the capture of part of the Barrow Gang. It was the bloodiest scene in the movie *Bonnie and Clyde*. Another attack took place 60 years ago at the National Plowing Match held near **Dexter**. "Give 'em hell" Harry Truman was running for re-election for president when he gave a speech at the plowing match blaming Congress for farmers' problems. It was considered an important speech and may have turned

Dexter Community House

Guthrie County

119

Adel City Hall, Raccoon River Valley Trail and renovated railroad station

NO MOTORIZED VEHICLES

Dallas County Courthouse, Adel

the tide in his favor. And on a sweeter note, you can buy a box of chocolates at Drew's Chocolates made in **Dexter**.

At the county seat, **Adel**, we found brick streets, a town square and a classic, old courthouse being renovated. The old courthouse didn't have enough office space for **Dallas County's** growth so they have annexes in downtown buildings. The eastern part of the county is no longer rural as the Des Moines' metro area keeps expanding westward. However, **Adel** retains its quaint character. Downtown historical buildings house antique and specialty shops alongside traditional businesses. City Hall is located in a smartly renovated, brick railroad building. Nearby is a new library. The railroad station has been restored and is home to law offices. The beautification and restoration process is ongoing.

Seven tons of free sweet corn is the draw in Adel's Annual Sweet Corn Festival held the second Saturday in August. Adding to the fun are a parade, craft and food vendors, a beer garden, street dance, art show and kids' activities. The Dallas County Fair in July, the Brick Street Classic Car Show in June and the

RACCOON
RIVER VALLEY TRAIL

DALLAS • GUTHRIE • GREENE
COUNTY CONSERVATION BOARD

Brick factory, Adel

Tiling, Dallas County

Grain storage, Redfield

Farmers Market held on Saturdays (June through September) are other enjoyable events that draw people to **Adel**.

July 19, 1918, was the birth date of a boy who grew up in Adel to become one of the most talented, decent people to walk this earth. He was a scholar and all-around athlete who was constantly thinking about self-improvement and turning weaknesses into strengths. He was successful in that it was difficult to pinpoint any weaknesses as he grew into a man. In 1936, he enrolled at the University of Iowa and initially competed in baseball, basketball and football. He dropped baseball after his freshman year but was Iowa's second leading scorer in basketball as a sophomore. However, football was where he made his mark with a senior season of unmatched success. Iowa's famous Iron Men of 1939 was a group of football players with outstanding stamina; an outstanding young man named Nile Kinnick led them. He was a multiple threat halfback who played 402 of a possible 420 minutes and set 14 school records, six of which still stand. The team ended up ranked ninth in the AP Poll with a 6-1-1 record. Kinnick won virtually every major athletic award in the country—the most notable being the Heisman trophy and the AP Male Athlete of the Year, where he beat out Joe DiMaggio, Byron Nelson and Joe Louis. Through all this, he maintained a 3.4 grade point average and most importantly, he continued being a modest, caring person. He answered America's call to serve by joining the Army Air Force. An oil leak in a military aircraft Kinnick was flying on a training mission caused the engine to freeze and the plane crashed in the ocean off the coast of Venezuela. He was 24 years old. That oil leak robbed us of what possibly could have been an effective world leader of high moral principle.

One of Kinnick's teammates on a Junior Legion baseball team was future Hall of Famer Bob Feller, a **Van Meter** native. Bob ("Rapid Robert") Feller was probably only a couple of years away from the majors at that point as he was a starter for the Cleveland Indians while still in his teens. They didn't have radar guns to clock his fastball when he played, but it is estimated it was between 100 and 110 miles per hour. No one in the history of the game has thrown it harder. He was just wild enough that no one dug in on him. He has a museum in **Van Meter** that contains two rooms of memorabilia, as well as items from his personal collection. He periodically returns for personal appearances and autograph signing.

Perry, a **Dallas County** town of about 8,000, is quite a story. Harvey Willis, a California '49er, bought land where **Perry** now stands and convinced the railroad to lay track on said land. When construction on the railroad was well under way, Harvey and his brother John platted the new town. Train service began in **Perry** in 1869, and by the next year, 70 people had taken up residence.

For approximately 110 years hence, railroading defined **Perry**. This era came to an end when the Milwaukee Railroad discontinued operations. The town didn't waste any time making the adjustment. Within six weeks they raised $1 million to build a meat packing plant. Tyson Foods, Inc., presently occupies that facility and it is the town's major employer and the majority of those employees are Latinos—about one-third of the town's population. In the *Perry Resident Guide 2007*, Mayor Viivi Shirley writes,

Van Meter

Perry

121

Hotel Pattee, Perry

Thymes Remembered Tea Room, Perry

"The Perry community has been immeasurable enriched by the culture and economic impact of these new citizens."

In 1913, the magnificent Hotel Pattee was opened in downtown **Perry**. It had the latest in amenities, including its own bowling alley and a telephone in each room. As grand as the original was, it could not compare to renovations it underwent in the late 1990s. Roberta Green Ahmanson, a 1967 graduate of Perry High School, came back to her hometown and spent millions restoring the Pattee and adding to its original grandeur. Throughout the hotel, two guestrooms from the original hotel were combined into one guestroom. Each had a different theme that was elaborate and exquisitely done. The Arts and Crafts style was recreated in the public areas and enhanced with classy, professional artwork. Connie and I spent a night there a few years ago. It is the most beautiful hotel I've ever seen—much less stayed in.

About a year ago when I heard the Pattee Hotel was closing its doors, a tear came to my eye and I started praying that someone would buy it and reopen the doors. I'm sure there were many similar

Salvador Lepé (right) and employees—Casa de Oro Restaurant, Perry

Perry

122

Perry

prayers and it looks like they may be answered. The word is that it sold and will be reopened in July 2008. Yes!

Adding to the variety in this interesting town is Thymes Remembered Tea Room. Jim Birdsell, a railroad worker with carpenter skills, and his wife Ramona, who had artistic talents, decided to develop a gift shop. They chose a building that had been a paint shop and went to work. They began with a one-room shop, then added another and another. A tea room was added and expanded. At present, the tea room and shops cover over 6,000 square feet and there are new owners—Vicky and Dwight Taylor. It is all very elegant and the food is delectable. It has become a **Perry** landmark.

We decided to save the tea room for another time as we chose Hispanic fare for lunch. Casa de Oro, in the heart of downtown, is a clean and brightly decorated restaurant with excellent food and service. Connie ordered a chimichanga and I requested a taco and enchilada combination. Connie tried some of her Spanish and the waiter graciously listened and told her he understood. His

name is Salvador Lepe and his family owns the restaurant. They also own restaurants in Creston and Harlan. They moved from Seattle about ten years ago and are very happy in Iowa.

Back on the highway, we headed toward the Des Moines' metro area. As we drove, it seemed like the suburbs were coming out to meet us. They have encroached into **Dallas County** far enough to make it the fastest growing county in the state. The newest and largest shopping mall in the state is in the **Dallas County** part of the metro area. Jordan Creek Town Center has many upscale shops and major anchor stores at the corners. A theater complex and row of restaurants are part of the development. The restaurants have outdoor patios that overlook a pond with geyser-like water sprays. On adjacent properties, big box stores and other retail business have sprung up to complement the mall. Rimming these developments are new office buildings and beyond that are apartments and houses. It is all brand new and well designed.

We drove into the metro's more established areas as we took I-235 toward the

central city. We passed Valley West Mall that was **Des Moines'** largest mall prior to Jordan Creek. Merle Hay Mall and Southridge Mall are additional, large, enclosed malls located within the city limits of **Des Moines** proper. In addition to the four major malls, there are many, smaller, neighborhood shopping districts; specialty shops; and strip malls for shopping opportunities.

As the skyscrapers of downtown came into view, we exited on Martin Luther King Jr. Parkway and drove into the heart of this beautiful city. We motored south observing the huge Woodland Cemetery on our right where the deceased rest in the shade of stately oak trees. On our left was the Sherman Hill district of old, inner city homes that urban pioneers are restoring to their original splendor. New town houses and apartments are springing up in the area where Martin Luther King Jr. intersects with Ingersoll Avenue. If we had taken a right on Ingersoll, we would have driven through an older distinctive commercial strip that serves **Des Moines'** west side residential neighborhoods. If we had continued south, Martin Luther King Jr. becomes Fleur Drive, a

Jordan Creek Mall, West Des Moines

123

Meredith Corporation, Des Moines

Water Works Park, Des Moines

street that is as pretty as its name. The first impression air travelers receive of **Des Moines** is a drive down Fleur with its flower medians, tree-lined views of a golf course, well-kept homes, Gray's Lake Park and Water Works Park.

We turned left at Ingersoll and worked our way down to Locust Street where we headed east toward the state capitol, which is centered on Locust. The first office buildings we passed were the headquarters of Meredith Corporation, one of the largest and probably the most successful publishing company in the United States. *Better Homes and Gardens®* is their flagship publication. Other magazines include *Successful Farming*, *Wood*, *Midwest Living*, *Traditional Home*, *Ladies' Home Journal* and about 40 or 50 more. They also have book and broadcasting divisions. There is lot of talent working in those two buildings.

The most dominant building in the skyline is the home office of the Principal Financial Group. Three architecturally-significant buildings make up the campus of this insurance/financial giant. Many more insurance companies call **Des Moines** home—making it the second

124

Gray's Lake, Des Moines

Bill Davis

Des Moines

largest insurance center in the country.

As we drove past Meredith, we passed a large, open park area between Locust Street and Grand Avenue. This is the future home of a sculpture park that will be as impressive as any in the country. John and Mary Pappajohn have generously donated seventeen, world-class sculptures, valued at $30 million. The Pappajohns are philanthropists who have a history of giving back. **Des Moines** is blessed with a business community that works in cooperation with city government on projects that enhance the quality of life in Iowa's largest city.

On the east end of the park is the city library with its contemporary, bright, copper-colored exterior wall panels. This one-of-a-kind structure was designed by British architect, David Chipperfield. Adjacent to it is a restored Masonic Lodge that now houses a music conservatory, theatre, elegant restaurant (Centro) and a Starbucks coffee shop.

We continued driving through this cosmopolitan city passing the 2,700-seat Civic Center for the performing arts and the 17,000-seat Wells Fargo Arena. If we had drifted further south, we would have seen the new Science Center with an I-Max theatre and the beautiful, 11,000-seat, Principal Park baseball stadium. However, we continued east and drove across the Des Moines River where a riverwalk park is under construction. It is another project, led by Principal Financial Group, where businesses and the city are combining resources.

On the east side of the river, in the shadow of the Iowa State Capitol, turn of the century buildings are being restored and recycled into shops, galleries, restaurants, bars, clubs and residences. There are also a number of new, trendy buildings under construction. The area has been given the name East Village.

Further east beyond the Capitol is the Iowa State Fairgrounds, home to America's signature state fair. Continuing east we came to the eastern suburbs, which are home to two of the metro's biggest tourist draws—Adventureland Amusement Park and Prairie Meadows Race Track and Casino.

The art lover is well served by many galleries in East Village, on Ingersoll Avenue and in Valley Junction, which is the historic downtown of **West Des Moines**. The Des Moines Art Festival held each summer is nationally ranked in the top five. The Des Moines Art Center, designed by Eliel Saarinen with additions by I. M. Pei and Richard Meier, has an art collection worthy of these architects.

We stopped at Olson-Larsen Galleries in Valley Junction and visited briefly with Marlene Olson. Marlene has owned the gallery for 29 years. She represents 65 artists—mostly Midwesterners or artists with connections to the region. This includes artists who live in Colorado, Washington, New Hampshire and Arizona. It is a beautiful gallery and her stable of artists are first-rate professionals. My favorite works are the Iowa landscapes. Marlene says, "There has been a lot of growth in the visual art scene since I began 29 years ago. There are more galleries and venues for exhibiting art such as coffee houses and restaurants."

We also visited a couple of other people who make up the fabric of the **Des Moines'** community. Bill Davis is a private banker at Bankers Trust in downtown **Des Moines**. He has lived in Iowa since he was a four-year-old when he moved with his family to Cedar

Valley Junction Art Fair, West Des Moines

Marlene Olson—Olson-Larsen Galleries, Valley Junction

125

Des Moines

Civic Center of Greater Des Moines

Des Moines Art Center

Rapids. He developed his academic, athletic and music skills in Cedar Rapids' schools. Upon graduation, he attended the University of Dubuque for one year where he majored in music and then transferred to Coe College where he switched his major to business. He was a hurdler in track and his music talent found an outlet in playing bass. He played string bass in both the Dubuque Symphony and the Cedar Rapids Symphony for ten years and played for jazz groups over a 16-year period. In 1972, he brought those talents to **Des Moines** where he has been a successful banker. The bass is gathering dust, but he stays athletically active playing a mean game of tennis. Bill loves **Des Moines** and Iowa; four of his five children have chosen to stay in Iowa.

As an African American, Bill recalled that America's race relations weren't very good in the '40s and '50s. There were probably less than 1,000 African Americans in Iowa when he moved here as a four-year-old and he doubts that any of them were in banking. He said race wasn't a great hindrance growing up but that dynamic was always in play—you

126

Kathy and Gene Needles

Iowa State Capitol, Des Moines

were conscious of potential problems. Generally, he says progress has been made; African Americans are more empowered and there are more open discussions of issues. Banking is a tremendous business to learn and it's very rewarding to see more young, male and female African Americans involved.

Gene Needles, a Chicago boy, met Kathy Coleman, a **Des Moines'** eastsider while they were both attending Drake University. "Chicago cool" won over the lovely Des Moines' lass; they married and began a life together starting with law school for Gene and modeling for Kathy. After graduation Gene secured a job with Travelers Insurance and Kathy became a model mother. Over the years, Gene served as assistant Polk County attorney, director of liquor enforcement for the state of Iowa and commissioner of public safety. For the public safety job, Governor Harold Hughes, a Democrat, appointed him. After three years in private practice, Gene was appointed to the bench by Republican Governor Robert Ray in 1980 as an Iowa district court judge. Is that kind of non-partisanship possible today?

You don't serve that long on the bench without hearing or being the object of some good stories. Gene told us about his colleague, the late Judge Wade Clark, who had just sentenced a guy to ten years for breaking and entering. As the guy was leaving the courtroom he turned toward the judge and said, "You're a dirty S.O.B." The assistant county attorney looked at the judge and asked, "What are you going to do about that?" Judge Clark promptly replied, "I'm going to deny it!"

The Needles credit the suburban community of **Urbandale** and its schools as a wonderful environment for their three children. One daughter became a prime time news anchor for the leading television station in the Twin Cities. Another daughter earned a law degree, and after five years of private practice and ten years as a U.S. attorney, decided to go back to her artistic roots. She makes high-end decoupage plates and trays, which she sells in her New York West Village shop. Their son served as a CEO of a large corporation in Houston, Texas.

Brain drain? No! Call them Iowa exports if you like, but remember their father was a Chicago export to Iowa. The point is that the Iowa environment and educational system prepare our young people well. If they are of value in other parts of the country or world, we have done our job. The people who choose to stay or return to Iowa must also have a few brains and talent because we keep turning out these special young people.

Drake University, located in the heart of the city is Iowa's largest private college. It is home to the Drake Relays, a track meet that annually draws worldclass athletes to **Des Moines**. It got its start in 1910 and today it is the second largest collegiate track and field event in the United States. This year, the storied oval will host the National Division I NCAA track and field championships. The 2007/2008 Drake men's basketball team was in the national spotlight after winning the Missouri Valley conference championship when the forecast had them finishing ninth. Coach Keno Davis was National Coach of the Year. The women's team was also MVC champion, as was the men's tennis team. The 1969 Drake basketball team reached the final four before losing by three points to eventual champion UCLA.

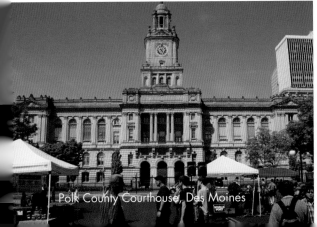
Polk County Courthouse, Des Moines

DRAKE UNIVERSITY

127

Grand View College, Des Moines

River Ridge Ranch, Polk County

Pioneer Pavilion, Iowa State Fairgrounds

Athletics aren't the only qualities defining Drake—it also has a strong academic reputation and the arts flourish. It ranked seventh out of 142 Midwestern universities in the *U. S. News and World Report's*, "Great School, Great Prices." The law school is the oldest in the country west of the Mississippi and boasts of many stellar graduates.

Grandview College, a four-year, liberal arts college affiliated with the Evangelical Lutheran Church in America, is located on **Des Moines'** east side. With 1,800 students and an average class size of 14, students get to know their professors well. Also special is Grandview's partnership with leading businesses and organizations in the **Des Moines** area. This has resulted in challenging internships and 100 percent job placement or continuing education. Leadership qualities are developed through campus organizations, which include intercollegiate and intramural sports, speech and theatre groups, major department clubs, student government and college choir. Sports teams compete in the Midwest Collegiate Conference of the National Association of Intecollegiate Athletics. Athletic

State Pony Show at Pioneer Pavilion

River Ridge Ranch

Doug Vail

scholarships are available.

Leaving the eastern suburbs of **Des Moines**, we drove about eight miles to River Ridge Ranch, a thoroughbred horse farm. The late Jim Rasmussen and Doug Vail were a pair of horse lovers who made their living in the construction business. With the arrival of Prairie Meadows Race Track, Jim began looking into developing a thoroughbred horse-breeding operation. He bought an old, 40-acre apple orchard on a ridge above the Des Moines River and the process began. He asked Doug to work for him for 90 days, which led to another 90-day stint, which led to Doug's permanent employment as farm manager. Together they used their construction skills to renovate old buildings and build new ones; they developed roads around the farm, which eventually expanded to 180 acres. Eleven miles of rail fences, made from Kentucky oak, cordon off the pastures. They have a state-of-the-art foaling facility on a nearby farm where Doug and his wife Sharon live. Sharon is computer-savvy and is also good at sensing whether a veterinarian is needed to treat a horse. She is also presently president of the Iowa Thoroughbred Breeders

and Owners Association. Jim's wife Sandra continues to be an active owner. River Ridge Ranch has been the leading breeder in Iowa for nine consecutive years. Being located in Iowa has the advantage of readily-accessible, top quality grain and hay. An indoor exerciser and other facilities deal with winter elements. Connie and I thoroughly enjoyed the fascinating tour Doug gave us of this sophisticated, pleasing-to-the-eye, horse farm. Doug is a happy Iowan. He says, "I like the people of Iowa and being around family. (One of his sons and a daughter-in-law work on the farm.) I would miss the pronounced seasons anywhere else."

That evening, after having visited River Ridge Ranch, we took in the races at Prairie Meadows. We generally bet unsuccessfully, but occasionally our bet on a favorite to show paid a couple of dollars. We still enjoyed the action and watching the sleek, athletic steeds run. And since there is a casino connected to this facility, Connie was obligated to test the slots. She lost the $10 allotment in about ten minutes. I think she was anxious to get back to the track. The running score after seven casinos is minus $2.50.

It was late May when we entered **Jasper County** and spring had sprung. The trees were fully leafed out. Darker greens were meshing with the early spring yellow-greens. In the farm fields, tiny plants were sprouting in neat rows giving the fields a pin-striped look, which contrasted nicely with the lush, green carpet of pasture.

Straddling the Polk/Jasper County line is the town of **Mitchellville**—home to the Iowa Correctional Institute for Women. It is located on what was originally a college campus and later a girls' training school. In 1984, it was converted to its present use as a women's correctional facility. I had the opportunity to visit the grounds and talk to prison chaplain Kay Kopatich.

After we passed through security, Kay led me to a courtyard buzzing with activity. Much of that buzz was the power mowers operated by several inmates mowing grass. After a short walk we entered the chapel, which had a barren look because it had just been cleaned. The altar and chairs had been stacked to the side of the room. Kay told me that when she first came to the facility in

Grandstand, Iowa State Fairgrounds

129

TIER NO. FOUR

HA SH AU GU DA PO JA PO IO JO CE MU CL SC

Cemetery near Prairie City

Prairie Learning Center

1991, they had a very small chapel that seated only 60 people. Because of the space restrictions they had to use the gym for services. Consequently, Kay was asked to spearhead a drive to raise money for a new chapel. She traveled the state making presentations at churches where she was warmly received. The funds were raised and the chapel was built.

Kay says being chaplain of this correctional facility is the most rewarding job she has held. Ninety percent of the inmates come from the lowest economic level and a large percentage of them are victims of abuse. Sixty percent have some form of mental illness. Yet, she finds the inmates to be very open, generous and receptive to God in their lives. The facility has a staff of good professionals and the best drug program in the state. The patients are put in an environment for a period of nine straight months 24/7 in order to modify their behavior and to develop a new mindset. This is not a cure for everyone and not all inmates fit the aforementioned profiles, but this institution does its best to turn lives around and it does a commendable job.

We entered the western edge of a sec-

Jasper County

Kay Kopatich

NEAL SMITH NATIONAL WILDLIFE REFUGE

PRAIRIE LEARNING CENTER

Jasper County

tion of Iowa designated as the Silos and Smokestacks National Heritage Area. Thirty-seven counties in the northeast quarter of the state represent an agricultural legacy of crop, dairy, beef, pork and poultry farms, as well as vineyards and museums. Heavy industry in the area's cities produce farm tractors and machinery. The smaller towns have towering elevators, livestock auctions and packing plants. The terrain varies from some of Iowa's flattest land to the spectacular limestone bluffs along the Mississippi. No other region in the United States shares this rich agricultural heritage. It is affiliated with the National Park Service.

One of the pioneers getting things started in **Jasper County** was Adam Tool. He and four other rugged individuals worked their way up the Skunk River and staked claims on prime land in the spring of 1843. In the fall of 1843, his family joined him but there wasn't enough room in his small cabin so the sons temporarily slept in their covered wagon. Soon a shed was added so they could all sleep under a roof. Then they got ambitious and built a much larger log house. The nearest sawmill was 70 miles

away so, with axes in hand, Adam and his strong sons felled trees, hewed the logs and erected a house that soon became a pioneer tavern—an oasis for Oskaloosa to Des Moines travelers.

In the early days there was a substantial wolf population in Iowa. Some pioneers had greyhounds that were capable of chasing down a wolf and disposing of him. In the winter of 1846–1847, the snow was very deep and the greyhounds tired of running in the snow and would give up the chase. One pioneer decided to take matters into his own hands. He grabbed a club and mounted his horse whose longer legs could catch the wolves that were slowed by the snow. Seven wolves did not survive that day.

While Adam Tool was off to fetch his family, some low-lifes from Missouri migrated north and seeing the empty cabin, moved in. When Tool returned he decided that rather than stirring things up, he would pay them $15 to move out. They went on to claim land nearby and build a cabin. Then they continued in their profession of thievery. It wasn't long before one of them was making frequent trips home to Missouri to see his father.

The Indians hated to see him go because it meant he would steal their ponies along the way. The thieving continued until frontier justice was administered.

Following the early pioneers into **Jasper County** was William J. Gannon, the ancestral father of the numerous Gannons who populate the northwest corner of the county. He came from a farm family in Ireland where the tradition is that the oldest son inherits the farm. He was not the oldest so his farming future was elsewhere. He chose America and ultimately, **Jasper County**, Iowa. As soon as he could, he sent travel money to Kate Rooney, his 16-year-old, Irish girlfriend, so she could join him. Her parents did not approve so she ran away. She came through New Orleans and went on to Chicago where she joined her love on the front steps of a Catholic church. They lived into their 90s and died within 30 days of each other.

We visited William J. Gannon's great-grandson and namesake at his home in **Mingo**. I think the old Irishman would be proud of the accomplishments of this descendant. He has been a public servant, serving three terms in the Iowa House of

Neal Smith National Wildlife Refuge

Bill Gannon

131

Former Hotel Colfax is now home of Teen Challenge of the Midlands

Ol' Lonely at Maytag Park, Newton

Representatives where he was elected Democratic floor leader. In 1970, he ran statewide for the Democratic nomination for governor but lost to Bob Fulton. In 1972, he was the Democratic nominee for lieutenant governor and lost. Then he lost one more attempt for the Democratic nomination for governor. Bill summed it up by saying he was a three-time loser. A loser, he is not. First, it takes a winner to get to that stage. Second, he went on to be a successful John Deere dealer for 25 years and is presently farming 800 acres of cropland with his nephew. Third, and most important, he and his wife Kathleen have raised three, bright, talented children who are all involved in politics. Matt, Tim and Clare are the kind of good citizens you want in the political process.

As we have driven through the Iowa countryside and observed the action in the fields, some questions have come to mind. Connie and I both have farm backgrounds, but it is a whole new scene today from when we were doing the chores and working in the fields. The farming operations are much larger and more specialized; the tractors are huge, as is the machinery they tow. What hap-

Colfax

A vineyard in Jasper County

Maytag Park

pened to the plow? Bill Gannon enlightened us on some crop farming methods. The plow has become an antique and is rarely used today. Soybean residue from the previous harvest is generally left undisturbed in the next year's planting. This is called no-till planting. Corn residue is rougher and can make no-till planting difficult so generally, these fields receive a minimum till treatment. That means they get disked or chiselplowed. When the plants emerge, there is no cultivating. The weeds are controlled with herbicides. There is virtually no soil erosion from no-till and it's minimal with minimum till. Adding grass filter strips along streams and gullies further retards any soil runoff. The tonnage of Iowa's topsoil flowing to the Mississippi Delta has dropped dramatically.

One hundred fifty years ago, tall grass prairie covered 85 percent of Iowa. Today, only one-tenth of one percent of that prairie remains. At the Neal Smith National Wildlife Refuge in southeastern **Jasper County**, 8,600 acres are being restored to their original prairie character. The new, elaborate learning center with exhibits for all ages is a good place to

start a visit at this one-of-a-kind park. There are walking and auto trails and a drive-through buffalo and elk range.

On the many trips I've made between Des Moines and Newton, I have noticed a Spanish-style structure protruding above the tree tops on a hill just east of **Colfax**. I've been curious about it for some time. On this trip, we didn't drive by—we stopped to check it out.

In 1875, miners digging for coal discovered a mineral spring. That immediately attracted people looking for a magic mineral water cure for their ailments. A modest hotel was built and a bottle works was constructed to corral the wonderful liquid. The first hotel burned down on Thanksgiving Day in 1881. A more exquisite, 100-room hotel named Saratoga of the West took its place. The hotel's peak year was 1900 when a record 13,000 guests came to stay. A crash came a few years later and the property was sold at a sheriff's sale. Colonel James P. Donahue bought it and enhanced the property adding the latest equipment in the hotel and developing a six-hole golf course and generally beautifying the grounds. Dances were held in the dining

room and famous entertainers frequently appeared. The success of this era came to an end when it was closed during World War I. Then, the U.S. government leased it to be used as a hospital for veterans. In 1946, the Fox Chemical Company purchased it and penned hogs in the basement and auctioned them off in the dining room. Next, it was a hospital for the rehabilitation of alcoholics. A monastery and Catholic retreat house followed.

Since 1986, it has been home to Teen Challenge of the Midlands. Teen Challenge is a Christ-based ministry designed to help those struggling with life-controlling problems such as drug and alcohol abuse. It was founded in 1961 by Dave Wilkerson, author of *The Cross and the Switchblade*.

Newton, the **Jasper County** seat, is in the process of reinventing itself. This town of 15,500 people was the home of Maytag Corporation, the maker of the iconic, quality washer that never needed a repairman. The Ol' Lonely ad campaign was classic and was an accurate portrayal of the product at its inception. Somewhere along the line, the corporate culture shifted and the acquisition

Maytag Farm, Jasper County

Newton

Annette West

Jasper County Courthouse, Newton

Newton Public Library

game became more important than concentrating on making a better product. A company that at its peak employed up to 4,000 Iowans was sold to Whirlpool in 2006. Whirlpool shut down the manufacturing plant and corporate offices, putting 1,800 people out of work. Whirlpool now has a virtual monopoly on washing machine manufacturing in the U.S.

It hurt, but **Newton** quickly put it behind them and moved on. For 99 years Maytag was not only Newton's largest employer but was responsible for many amenities that make the town a desirable place to live. Annette West, executive director of the Greater Newton Area Chamber of Commerce, said, "We have things no other community has because of Maytag and this is a great asset in attracting new business." This adversity brought out the best in the community and the kindness and concern from other communities was overwhelming. Annette added, "It was pretty darned impressive."

Almost immediately after the closing, Iowa Telecom announced it would buy the former Maytag headquarters building. Manufacturing firms began looking into using some of the vast, vacated industrial

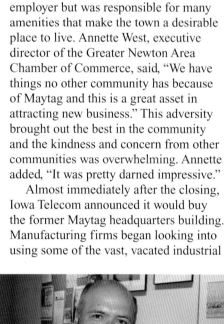
Mark Montgomery

Iowa Speedway, Newton

buildings and others looked at the potential workforce. Many former employees tried their entrepreneurial skills and started their own businesses. Jordan Bruntz, former head of Maytag research and development, founded Springboard Engineering and staffed it with all 65 members of his former R&D team. Their first contract was with Whirlpool.

Another quality Maytag product is staying true to its roots. In 1919, E. H. Maytag, the son of the appliance maker's founder, established a herd of award-winning Holstein dairy cattle. His son, Fred Maytag II, heard about a new process for making bleu cheese that was developed by Iowa State University. This time-consuming process was adopted by Magtag and is still in use. Each batch of cheese is monitored during months of aging in caves. When the peak flavor is reached, it is packaged and sold. It may be the best bleu cheese in the world.

Quality continues to define **Newton** with the addition of the Iowa Speedway designed by Rusty Wallace. It is the nation's most state-of-the-art racing facility and the first ever designed by a driver. I don't think there is anyone in the racing

community who is more respected and well liked than Rusty and this track is his baby. It is beautiful. On the day we visited, there was a Richard Petty driving experience event where race fans could either drive or ride in a racecar around the 7/8-mile oval. Consequently, we were allowed to enter the infield. After seeing how the drivers were stuffed into the car through the side window and then handed the steering wheel, Connie and I both decided we didn't need the ride or driving experience but were thrilled to be observing the action and facility close up. There are 2,500 Newton Club seats, 25,000 grandstand seats and 104 RV spaces on the backstretch. The Iowa Corn 250 is an Indy Racing League event held at the end of June and there are many other quality events during the year.

Leaving the Iowa Speedway, I revved the engine of my Avalon stock car and tore down I-80 at the 70-mph speed limit. I was loosing the race, however, as I kept getting passed by young girls with ponytails. I gave up at the **Grinnell** exit and left the freeway for a quiet drive into town. We located Saints Rest Coffee Shop where we met Mark Montgomery,

an economics professor at Grinnell College. The name Saints Rest is derived from early days when **Grinnell** was a very religious, straight-laced town. It was a tag outsiders gave it. Mark and his wife Irene were East Coast outsiders when they accepted a shared teaching position at the college. It was an adjustment coming from the crowded East Coast to the open spaces of Iowa. Some early experiences included Irene getting stopped for speeding a couple of times and getting used to allotting five minutes rather than 30–45 minutes to run an errand. They happily made the adjustment and have enjoyed the good life in **Grinnell** for 19 years. Mark also likes the natural beauty of Iowa. He said, "It's a beautiful place, even though there is nothing topographically spectacular. It is hard to explain." I understand totally. As Mark gave examples of things he enjoyed, he mentioned taking his dog to the Jacob Krumm Preserve. A lady at the next table couldn't let that pass without telling us that her husband's uncle was the Jacob Krumm who donated the land. The degrees of separation in Iowa don't go very far.

Irene has Iowa roots; she grew up in

Grinnell

Iowa Speedway

135

Grinnell Farmers Market

Grinnell College

Jewel Box Bank, Grinnell

Cedar Rapids where her father taught at Coe College. As a young woman, she lived in Africa, then Delaware and on to graduate school at the University of Wisconsin. Mark also chose the U of W for grad school. They met, got married and took teaching jobs at Mount Holyoke College in Massachusetts. Their daughter was born in Massachusetts, educated in the town of **Grinnell** and attended Grinnell College where she majored in history. Mark and Irene also have two adopted sons. One is African American and the other is a native African from Sierra Leone. The boys are doing well in school and are active in sports.

Grinnell and Grinnell College were but a gleam in the eye of Josiah Bushnel (J.B.) Grinnell when he was a congregational minister in New York in the mid-1800s. He was a rock solid man with strong beliefs. He denounced slavery in his sermons, which was a controversial stand at the time. A hoarse voice cut short his preaching ministry so he began exploring another dream. He envisioned starting a colony out west of like-minded people who opposed slavery and drinking and, for the most part, led moral lives. He

Fremont Farms of Iowa, Poweshiek County

Grinnell College

also emphasized the importance of education. J.B. and three other men found an Iowa location that fit their dream so they staked their claim. Soon their wives and other settlers joined them and the town began to grow. The strong leadership of J.B. prevailed in decisions on the town name, as well as the locations of the business district, the cemetery and the future college. He was a generous man who welcomed hungry newcomers by giving them hams. He served two terms in the United States Congress where he continued his anti-slavery fight. Returning to **Grinnell**, he played a major role in its development until his death in 1891.

The town of **Grinnell** has taken on the moniker, "Jewel of the Prairie." It is gaining national attention. Norman Crampton's publication, "The 100 Best Small Towns in America," lists **Grinnell** among its top communities. The town has pride in the upkeep of the town's properties and has been recognized as one of 60 of the "Prettiest Painted Places" in the country by Rohm and Haas and the Paint Quality Institute of Philadelphia. It thrives with agriculture-related businesses and more than 20 factories and pro-

cessing plants. The Merchants National Bank in downtown **Grinnell** was designed by legendary architect Louis Sullivan—Frank Lloyd Wright's mentor and the inventor of the steel-framed skyscraper. The front facade features a very detailed, jewel box motif that is an appropriate symbol for **Grinnell**, the "Jewel of the Prairie."

Then there is J.B. Grinnell's other offspring, Grinnell College. He emphasized quality education from the beginning and that spirit has prevailed. In 2003, *Newsweek* rated it as the top, all-around college in the country. Academically, this college is in a class with the best, including Ivy League schools. No college in the United States has a larger per capita endowment. It is selective, but has grants and scholarships available so that no qualified student is turned away for financial reasons. The students come from a mix of cultures throughout the country and the world, yet there is a strong Midwest influence with 45 percent of the student body from this region.

The arts are central to life at Grinnell College. Celebrated artists, musicians, dancers and theatrical groups are regular

visitors. Seventy-five percent of the students are engaged in one or more arts program. The Buebsbaum Center for the Arts is the hub of **Grinnell's** arts expression. Designed by Cesar Pelli, it provides more than 129,000 square feet of space for classrooms, studios, a recital hall, two theatres, a scene shop and studio theatre. The Faulconer Art Gallery hosts international traveling exhibitions.

Grinnell played in the first intercollegiate football game west of the Mississippi and was one of the leaders in establishing gender equality in sports. Most students are involved in some sports activity, which includes pursuits like rock climbing or ultimate Frisbee. Varsity teams compete in the Division III Midwest Conference.

After the **Grinnell** experience, we drove west on Highway 6 until we came to Highway 63 where we turned south. We passed a huge, corporate farming operation owned by Fremont Farms of Iowa LLP. Our curiosity piqued—we'd have to ask the locals about it. We continued on 63 to just north of **Montezuma** where we turned onto a gravel road that led to our overnight stay at the English

Brooklyn flags from each of the fifty states and the four branches of the military

137

Fishing for catfish with stink bait, Diamond Lake

Montezuma

Valley B&B. Innkeeper Stacy Helm greeted us as we pulled in and proceeded to show us the facility, which consists of a farmhouse and old-style, red barn. The barn has been converted into the Heritage and Bunkhouse Rooms on the lower level and a banquet and party room in the upper level haymow. Stacy's bright and precocious daughter Shelby joined us on the tour and pointed out many features.

They went to a lot of work for our room. They jacked up the house, dug a deeper basement, put in a new foundation and finished it exquisitely with leather, upholstered, western-style furnishings. Our room had a king-size bed and a bathroom with a shower and whirlpool tub.

After we unpacked, we drove to **Montezuma** for dinner. The folks at the Apple Basket Restaurant on the square gave us a warm welcome and showed us to our table. The theme was country with upside-down apple baskets serving as shades for the dining room lighting. Water and beer were served in fruit jars and the water pitcher was an old-fashioned, metal coffee pot with a blue and white speckled enamel finish. Owner and Chef Dale Miller had exten-

Poweshiek County Courthouse, Montezuma

138

Malcolm

Pin-striped field of corn, Poweshiek County

The Helms—Doug, Stacy, Shane and Shelby

English Valley B&B

sive experience working in upscale restaurants in other parts of the country but chose to come home and open his own restaurant. My crab cakes were seasoned well and had a nice texture with chunks of crab. Connie had beef tenderloin tips in a brown sauce with tomatoes, peppers, onions and mushrooms over pasta. Nicely done, Dale.

After dinner, we backtracked north to **Malcolm** where we enjoyed an after dinner drink and conversation at the Pour House. One of the subjects we brought up was that corporate farm just a couple miles north of **Malcolm**. We learned that it is a hen laying operation; one patron estimated it houses 6 to 7 million chickens. He said it is the third largest in the country and easily the largest in Iowa. The consensus was that the people who manage it are nice people who contribute money to town projects and provide scholarships to local high school graduates and, generally, try to be good citizens. When we drove by the operation we did not notice any odors, but the locals said the smell can be pretty strong on hot days. Our impression, looking at the facility, was that it was well planned to be

efficient and a professional operation. It is not my intention to take sides in a controversy with this type of business, but to report what I see and hear.

After a good night's rest in our plush room, we went upstairs to a breakfast of blueberry pancakes, fruit, scrambled eggs, cinnamon cake and apple-cinnamon bacon. The latter was processed at Dayton's Locker in **Malcolm**. After breakfast we lingered long enough to learn a few things about the Helm family. Stacy and her husband Doug were high school sweethearts, who graduated from the University of Northern Iowa where they prepared to become math teachers. Stacy taught seven years and Doug taught and coached basketball for ten years. Eventually, they found farming was in their blood so they returned to their roots. Doug works with his family to farm 3,500 acres that includes some rented land. They use technology and advanced equipment such as a yield monitor on the combine and GPS auto steer on the tractors. When planting with auto steer, you program a straight line in the field and after that, all the operator has to do is turn the corner at the end of a row and

start back the other direction. He then pushes a button to start the auto steer; the tractor positions itself perfectly and travels in a straight line with accurate spacing. They keep a few cattle so their children, Shelby and her brother Shane, can raise a bottle calf. Doug once had a New Yorker brag to him that he had to pay about as much for a square foot of Manhattan apartment space as what an acre of Iowa farmland is worth. Doug thought to himself, "That makes him smarter than I am?" Then he just smiled without commenting.

Montezuma was located and laid out to be the **Poweshiek County** seat in 1848, but wasn't incorporated until 1868. A beautiful, brick courthouse was built in 1859 and still serves the county today. No county seat wars here—no other towns could compete with that courthouse. Some local veterans of the Mexican-American War gave the town its name. Montezuma was the last emperor of the Aztec civilization.

Montezuma is a down home community of 1,500 people with many amenities, especially for the outdoors lover. The southern-most ski slope in

Malcolm

139

HA SH AU GU DA PO JA PO IO JO CE CL MU SC

Poweshiek County

Beau and Paula Long

Iowa County Courthouse, Marengo

Iowa is located two and a half miles southwest of town. It features a snow-making machine, lifts, lighted slopes, a snack shop and a pro shop. A half mile north of town is Diamond Lake where campsites and fish are plentiful. It is a premier area for pheasant hunting. Many area farmers will open up their farms to hunters. And, they have a pretty golf course with a large swimming pool.

Industries include Sig Manufacturing Company—a manufacturer of balsa wood, screen printed decals and model airplane kits for an international market. Streetrod Productions manufactures customized golf carts that are sold worldwide. Brownells is a mail order distributor of tools, supplies and accessories for gun repair and maintenance.

We left **Montezuma** and drove east. It was after an overnight storm and the cloud formations interplayed beautifully with the freshly washed landscape. The countryside along the English River has a lot of pastureland and groves of trees where grazing cattle are living the good life. This scene continued with variations as we drove into **Iowa County** and headed for **Williamsburg**.

140

Williamsburg

Iowa County

To Connie, and many other shoppers, the name **Williamsburg** conjures up a vision of Tanger Outlet Center located near Interstate 80. While a good selection of brand name merchandise has its appeal, one should be informed that a mile south of the interstate is a town worth visiting. **Williamsburg's** city center is very pleasing to the eye. The town square contains a well-maintained, shady park that invites you to people-watch while sitting on one of the numerous benches. Surrounding the square are brick streets with brand new pavers and the commercial buildings lining the streets share this new/old look. Also, pleasing to the eye and healthy for the body, is the recreation complex. It consists of an aquatic center, soccer fields, softball fields and an indoor recreation center of 30,000 square feet where you find three sports courts, fitness equipment, workout rooms and running track.

On to **Marengo**, the **Iowa County** seat. **Marengo** owes its name to its resemblance to a plain in Italy where Napoleon won the Battle of Marengo in 1803. **Marengo**, Iowa's beautiful plain, is the rich bottomland of the Iowa River valley. The Iowa River is central to the amenities of this hamlet of 2,500 people. At Gateway Park and Preserve located on the river, you can watch for bald eagles and other wildlife from a tower or launch a canoe. You can explore the river further on new hiking trails. And, the locals boast of some of the best hunting and fishing in the state.

The river and woods of the Iowa River valley were perfect for Indian habitat. Whole tribes of Sauk and Fox congregated in this region until the Indian Agency moved them further west in 1843. One of the first white men to move in after the area was opened up for settlement was Horace H. Hull. He was also the first merchant in the county. Money was scarce and skins were plentiful so there was a lot of trading skins for merchandise. For a pound of sugar, a man would give the merchant a coonskin and probably get a rabbit skin in change.

While researching at the Marengo Public Library, we observed a young mother and child in the children's section. She was guiding her three-year-old son's exploration of the library's learning tools—computers, puppets, puzzles. This nurturing session was such a delightful scene, that we decided to engage them in conversation. Paula Long is a native of **Marengo** and she has no desire to leave. That attitude runs in the family. Her parents and three sisters also call **Marengo** home. She said, "It's a friendly town. We all know each other and enjoy impromptu gatherings." In his hushed, library voice, her son Beau excitedly informed us, "I have a real fishing pole with a real hook." Before, the only line he was allowed to put in the water had a bobber, but no hook. A worm on that real hook might mean catching a fish. When we asked him about that, he said he'd throw it back.

The broad, rich plains of the Iowa River valley also beckoned a tribe of a different character—the Community of True Inspiration. This was an organization of German Lutherans who were pacifists; they advocated freedom of speech and worship and refused to send their children to German public schools. This did not sit well with the authorities and the persecution began. Like many persecuted religious groups before them, they looked to the New World to escape

Williamsburg

Amana

Jam session at Amana Visitor Center

Europe's tyranny. They first established a colony near Buffalo, New York, where they adopted a communal living system. There was a common ownership of shops, mills and farmland; individual needs were provided for by the community. As needs for more farmland increased, the group looked west where attractively priced land was available. The Iowa River valley was their choice for the new communal community.

In 1855, Werkzeng Christian Metz and his followers came to Iowa and built a village. They chose the name **Amana** from the Song of Solomon 4:8. **Amana** means "to remain true." Five more villages were built: Middle Amana, High Amana, West Amana, South Amana and East Amana. In 1861, after the purchase of Homestead, the community owned 26,000 acres of land.

Day to day life revolved around worship, home and work. Children attended school six days a week, year around. They had the requisite professionals to take care of their health and spiritual needs and the community provided the material needs. They prepared their meals at communal kitchens. That was their

142

Amana

Ox Yoke Inn, Amana

Amana

way of life for 89 years.

In 1932, the communal system was replaced by a new, profit sharing, joint stock corporation and the Amana Society was formed. For the first time, members worked for wages and owned their own homes and businesses. Today, the Amana Society farms the land and operates a variety of businesses. The Amana Church remains a vital part of the community.

Present day **Amana** is a tourist destination and their dollars add another dimension to the society's income. It is truly a German experience. The terrain and weather are almost a carbon copy of the farming regions of the homeland. The original buildings that are still in use are authentic German in style. Newer structures have been designed to fit in. You can order classic German cuisine in the restaurants. Shops feature merchandise crafted by these German-Americans and, in some cases, by native Germans. Nature trails and a beautiful golf course add to the attractions. Full-service hotels, condos and B&Bs are available for those seeking a unique getaway.

We crossed the **Johnson County** line the first week in June. It was a sunny,

70-degree day and the countryside looked great because of all the recent rains. The shades of green were incredibly beautiful. Unfortunately, there had been a bit too much rain. Swollen streams and rivers had overflowed their banks and more rain was in the forecast. There were fears there might be another summer like 1993 when Iowa had its worst flooding in recorded history. That was not something we wanted to dwell on so we continued our journey into **Iowa City**, enjoying the present weather.

When it was decided the capitol of the Iowa Territory should be located further inland rather than at one of the Mississippi River ports, a commission was set up to find a location. They had already decided on the name of **Iowa City** and were searching for a location of beauty, good water and convenience to timber and stone suitable for building. They chose a site with a natural amphitheater of hills, bluffs and a river valley located about two miles north of Napoleon, a settlement of two houses that had capitol ambitions of its own. With the establishment of **Iowa City**, the Napoleon settlement disappeared. Its for-

mer location is marked by Napoleon Park on the southern edge of **Iowa City**.

A survey was completed, lots were sold and in July of 1839, the first log cabin was built. One year later, **Iowa City** had a population of 500. Even though it was the county seat of **Johnson County** and the capitol of Iowa, it had no government of its own until 1853 when local citizens finally agreed to incorporate. The capitol moved to Des Moines in 1857.

Probably the first white people to set foot on the location of **Coralville** were Nathaniel Fellows and his family in 1838. To get to the other side of the Iowa River, Nathaniel dismantled his family's wagon at Napoleon and took it across the river in an Indian canoe, one piece at a time. After bringing his family across, one at a time, Nathaniel reassembled the wagon and pitched a tent. They found a friendly tribe of Indians down river with whom they shared food and lived with peaceably for three years.

In 1843, the damming of the Iowa River to provide power for mills being constructed on its western banks marked the beginning of **Coralville**. By the

143

Coralville Lake, Johnson County

Iowa City

Hotel Vetro, Iowa City

Old Capitol,
University of Iowa

144

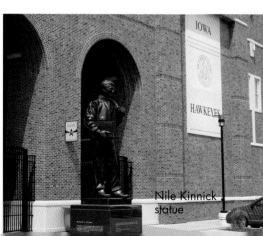

Nile Kinnick
statue

time of its incorporation in 1873, its population had grown to 300 with typical frontier establishments from a blacksmith shop to saloons. In 1866, a Harvard professor gave a speech at the University of Iowa talking about the samples of fossilized coral he found in the limestone bluffs surrounding the mills—thus, the name **Coralville**.

On the evening of June 20, 1840, **Iowa City** inhabitants were startled by the sound of a steamboat puffing upriver. Everyone in town ran down to meet the boat with visions of a great river port occupying their minds. Those dreams were never realized because the railroads came and replaced water travel as a superior way to move cargo.

A hotel is typically one of the first commercial establishments built in a new settlement and Iowa City's Lean Back Hall was a doozie. It was built in a matter of days and contained a bar, dining room, kitchen and one bedroom. In the bedroom, there was one bed that ran the length of its shed-like structure. The mattress consisted of slough grass a foot deep covered with heavy blankets. There were two, very long pillows made of

Art Building West, University of Iowa

muslin and stuffed with prairie chicken feathers. The floor in front of the bed was carpeted with wild hay. The bed could accommodate 36 to 56 men depending on their size. Those who couldn't fit on the bed, sat on the carpet of hay and leaned back against the wall for their slumber. My guess is that most of those fellows had patronized the bar before they turned in. Can you imagine the volume of snoring noise? I can't either, nor do I want to.

Iowa Citians have done a much classier job of development in the years following the notorious Lean Back Hall. In contrast, Hotel Vetro is elegant in design and luxurious in its accommodations and there are many other fine places to rest your body after experiencing present-day **Iowa City**. The appeal of the city is no secret as it is continually receiving national recognition as a good place to live. *Morgan Quitno Press* ranked **Iowa City** No. 3 on its "most livable" list. *Expansion Management* magazine ranked the **Iowa City** metro region No. 7 in the nation for "quality of life." It is the third most educated metro area in the country with 47 percent of **Johnson County** adults having a

bachelor's or graduate degree. And, of course, a major factor in this good life is the presence of the University of Iowa.

No one wanted the job of president when the University of Iowa was founded in 1847. The lack of money might have had something to do with the lack of interest in the job. It was September 1855 before the doors opened to students. It was coed from the beginning, and by the next school year, there were 83 men and 41 women students. It was the nation's first public university to admit men and women on an equal basis. The first building was the old state capitol building, donated to the university after the capitol moved to Des Moines. It still sits like a matron on a hill overlooking her offspring—the rest of the campus.

Openness to all people prevails today. Of the University of Iowa's 30,000-plus students, 9.3 percent are African American, Hispanic, Asian or Native American. International students from 113 countries represent 6.5 percent of the student body and 62 percent are from Iowa. The faculty is distinguished with three Pulitzer Prize winners, three former clerks for U.S. Supreme Court justices,

two National Medal of Science winners and four Howard Hughes Medical Institute investigators. It is home to the world-renowned Iowa Writers' Workshop, the National Advanced Driving Simulator and one of America's best hospitals. The arts thrive on this campus. In addition to the Writers' Workshop, the visual, music and performing arts departments boast of graduating outstanding artists, musicians and actors. The Museum of Art's collection includes Jackson Pollock's *Mural 1943* and one of America's most important collections of African art. Hancher Auditorium, a 2,500-seat performance theatre, hosts some of the most respected names in music, dance and theatre.

Then there are the Iowa athletic teams. Iowans love their Hawkeyes! They fill the 70,500-seat football stadium and the 15,500-seat basketball arena to watch their favorites take on Big Ten conference foes and non-conference foes. Those who can't make it to the games, tune in on radio or television. Varsity competition includes 12 women's teams and 10 men's teams. Their wrestling teams dominate the country with more Division I national championships than any other college.

Kinnick Stadium, University of Iowa

Reflection of Iowa Advanced Technology Laboratories in Museum of Art window, University of Iowa

145

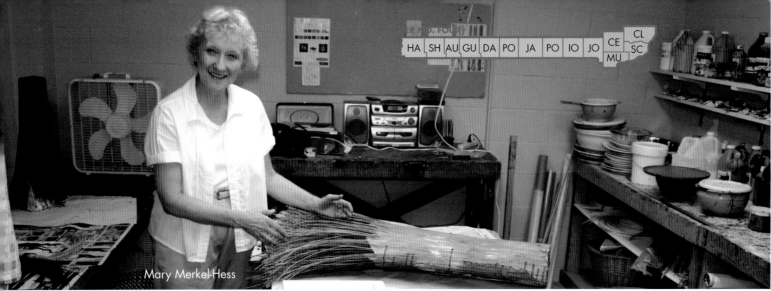
Mary Merkel-Hess

Johnson County Courthouse, Iowa City

After tooling around **Iowa City** and the university campus, we stopped for lunch at the Hamburg Inn No. 2. This restaurant specializes in good ol' American food and is a favorite campaign stop of politicians. It was featured in a 2005 episode of *The West Wing*. It evidently has been written up a few times as the walls were covered with newspaper and magazine clippings. Ronald Reagan and Bill Clinton have stopped in and so have we. I probably ordered the same thing Bill did—a hamburger. It is one of their specialties and it was perfect.

Mary Merkel-Hess, a fiber artist, is an active member of the **Iowa City** arts community. Even though she exhibited art talent at an early age, she did not see herself pursuing it as a career. She chose Marquette University for her undergraduate study in sociology and philosophy. However, art was still in her psyche so upon graduation from Marquette, she enrolled at the University of Wisconsin where she gradated with a BFA in metal smithing. A MFA in metal smithing from the University of Iowa completed her formal education. We visited her studio in the basement of her **Iowa City** home. I

Bo Ramsey and Pieta Brown

Greg Brown

Hamburg Inn No. 2, Iowa City

146

University of Iowa

didn't see any evidence of metal smithing art but she was working on some very creative fiber projects. She is known for her fiber vessels where she adds layers of reed-like fibers over a form to make sculpture pieces in her unique style. She also had other art in process where a special paper is stretched over a framework. She draws her inspiration from her life's experiences and visual environment.

My favorite radio program of all time is *Prairie Home Companion*. I love Garrison Keillor's sense of humor, his cleverly written sketches, his choice of talent to guest on his show and the way he needles upper-midwest Scandinavians. When I first started listening to *Prairie Home Companion*, Iowa City folk singer Greg Brown was a regular on the show and I have been a fan of his ever since.

I caught Greg's act at a recent concert in Des Moines at Hoyt Sherman Place Auditorium. His daughter Pieta opened with Bo Ramsey accompanying her. This was the second time I'd heard Pieta in concert and she is growing on me. She is a tall, attractive girl with a nice, folk singer voice who can play some pretty good licks on the acoustical guitar. Bo is

a tall, slim, down-home, guitar picker sporting a straw cowboy hat. He had about five guitars lined up on stage and he used all of them. I have one of his CDs on which he sings and plays the blues as well as anyone. I love that CD.

Bo also accompanied Greg when he came out for the second half of the show. They go back a long time and they complement each other perfectly. Greg sat in a chair with an Australian outback-style hat on his head and cowboy boots on his feet. When they performed, Bo would weave and bob with the music and kind of hover over Greg who sat back and strummed away. Greg has a gritty, deep voice that clearly tells a story as he sings. When he sings, I make a real effort to listen to every word of the poetry in his lyrics. He has written songs for Willie Nelson, Carlos Santana and Mary Chapin Carpenter. Greg and Bo are true Iowans and great performers.

Greg graciously consented to visit with us when we were in **Iowa City**. We called on him at his home. The first thing we saw upon entering his 1920's, Craftsman-style house was a shiny, black, baby grand piano. We learned that his

wife Iris Dement is a country/folk artist who plays the piano. They take turns going out on weekend gigs so that one is home with Sasha—their nine-year-old, adopted, Russian daughter.

Growing up, Greg moved around a bit due to his father's call to the ministry. As his father served first in the Baptist church, next in the Open Bible and finally, in the Methodist, they lived in Missouri, Kansas and Iowa. Greg graduated from Dubuque High School and moved on to the University of Iowa where he won a talent contest and was invited to New York. He never did find the New York contact but he stayed and found work in small clubs around Greenwich Village. That led to performing around the country during the hippie era. Those experiences, coupled with the environment in his home with his guitar-playing mother and her musical family, provide rich lyrics for his songs. Character runs deep in his family. He told us about his grandpa, a fireman on steam locomotives, who didn't like the switch to diesel. He enjoyed the tinkering with the steam engine. He derisively said, "All you have to do with a diesel is turn it on and

Iowa City

Cedar River rising at Cedar Bluff

Cedar County Courthouse, Tipton

West Branch

it goes." He quit the railroad and managed to get one of those old locomotives hooked up to power a sawmill he ran in Douds, Iowa. Greg and his cousins worked for him and, on their own time, they made music together. After visiting with Greg Brown, I'm going to enjoy his music even more.

A few miles out of **Iowa City** we crossed the county line into **Cedar County**. The first town we came to was **Cedar Bluff**, located on the Cedar River. The rising river was coming close to some small vacation cabins. I was surprised to see boats still tied to floating docks. I expected, at any moment, someone would come down and pull the boats out of the water to higher ground.

We drove on to **Tipton**, the **Cedar County** seat. Tipton, a town of 3,200 residents, is a "town-square" town with turn-of-the-century stores on the perimeter of the square. The centerpiece of the square, however, is a contemporary courthouse. **Tipton** is, and has always been, the hub of commerce in **Cedar County**. At one time it was referred to as the "agriculture and livestock center of the world." There are several historical

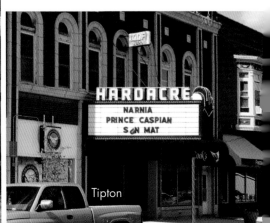

HARDACRE

NARNIA
PRINCE CASPIAN
S N MAT

Tipton

148

Law Enforcement Museum, Tipton

places of interest. One was a classic, county sheriff's house with an attached jailhouse. Built in the 1800s, it remained in continuous use until 2001 and is now a law enforcement museum.

Pride in the community was apparent as we observed newly painted buildings—some in the process with old paint scraped off and a new brick-lined streetscape. We learned that **Tipton** is into a ten-year project to improve infrastructure and amenities. It includes work on water and waste water systems, gas and electric systems and the storm sewer system. Street reconstruction and repair and adding a new, family aquatic center to the city park are other examples of the ten-year project. I congratulate them.

Tiptonians like to celebrate with festivals and events ranging from the 4th of July to Ridiculous Days where merchants take their merchandise to the streets and cut prices. There is also the Hardacre Film Festival, held in the historic Hardacre Theater on the square. The summer of 2008 marks the eleventh year of its existence. The festival was started by Hollywood set designer Troy Peters and he ran it for nine years. In 2006, Peters

announced there would be no festival because of his busy schedule and some difficulty in securing the theater. This meant that local lodging, restaurants and shops would have to forgo a two-day boost in business. After one year of not having the festival, the Tipton Chamber of Commerce took over and put Community Development Director Travis Alden in charge. The festival was brought back in 2007 and Iowans were once again treated to a program full of cutting-edge, thought-provoking and entertaining films from Iowa filmmakers, as well as independent films from other parts of the country and world. The Hardacre Film Festival is held the first week in August.

After a full day of research and exploration, we thought it might be good to stretch our legs and play a little golf. We chose Fox Run Golf and Country Club in West Branch because we were going to meet a high school friend of Connie's for a late dinner in **West Branch**. We teed off and started down a hill heading for the first hole. All the recent rain had made the ground squishy on the hillsides and there were tiny ponds throughout the course's low spots. Things weren't well

marked so after the first hole, we headed off in the wrong direction in search of the No. 2 tee box. With no tee box in sight, we realized we had made a mistake and retraced our steps back to where we discovered the tee box behind some trees a few yards from the first green. The next hole was 450 yards and mostly uphill. Gnats accompanied us up the hill and, at the top, they turned us over to the mosquitoes. This scenario continued for the next few holes as we walked with mud oozing up between Connie's sandal-shod toes. My tennis shoes were no longer white and we both had mud splatters on our legs all the way up to our shorts. On hole No. 6, there was a creek to cross with no bridge. There was a spillway that a cart could drive across but, for us walkers, it meant ankle deep water and the possibility of our pull carts being dragged downstream. We decided to forgo that hole even though we had hit our balls across the creek. We found a bridge on the next fairway where we crossed and were about start play again when we heard the town siren go off. It was 7 p.m. so we knew it wasn't the noon whistle. A couple in a cart drove by and informed us

West Branch

CHAMPAGNE'S

Von and Carol Baily

Herbert Hoover birthplace

Pines on the Prairie B&B

150

it was a tornado warning. We trudged back to the clubhouse (all uphill) as fast as we could pull our mud-encrusted carts. When we arrived at the clubhouse, we went inside and asked where we could take cover. The pro shop guy was engaged in a card game with a buddy. After some hesitation, he folded his cards and informed us the siren was being tested for the possibility of later tornadoes. We went back outside, loaded our clubs and drove downtown to a restaurant named Champagne's.

The name Champagne's was not chosen to be uppity; it is a family name of some Cajuns who moved from Louisiana to Iowa after losing everything during Hurricane Katrina. Carol and Von Baily accepted the invitation of Carol's brother Bob Champagne, who had previously settled in Iowa City, to open a restaurant in a building he had purchased. Bob handles the finances; Carol and Von run the restaurant. Iowans have taken to the Cajun-spiced food and business is good. We ordered some deep-fried alligator for an hors d'oeuvre. Connie and friend Carol Clemens chose shrimp creole and I had a big bowl of gumbo. Good food!

Carol Clemens and Connie

Herbert Hoover Presidential Library-Museum

Carol Clemens retired four years ago from the position of treatment director at the Oakdale Iowa Correctional Facility near Iowa City. She devotes much of her time these days to her Dobermans, Dustin and Abigail. She socializes with like-minded dog lovers and enjoys going to competitions with them. Dustin is a certified therapy dog, has good manners and is stable. Therapy dogs are used to lift the spirits of people in hospitals and care facilities. Carol said, "People who have dogs live longer and have happier lives."

West Branch is the birthplace of Herbert Clark Hoover, the thirty-first president of the United States. The Herbert Hoover Presidential Library-Museum and the gravesites of Hoover and his wife Lou Henry Hoover are on the grounds near his birthplace cottage. Connie and I have toured this library-museum, as well as those of Lyndon Johnson in Austin, Texas, and Harry Truman in Independence, Missouri. I hope we have the opportunity to visit more presidential library-museums in the future. They do an excellent job of projecting the personalities of the presidents and clearly present their accomplish-

ments and failures and report what the world was like during the respective president's term. I find them very interesting.

Mention President Hoover and the first thing that comes to mind is the Great Depression. He was undeserving of the scorn heaped upon him as he was made the scapegoat of the economic disaster. Programs he submitted to Congress to deal with the crises were sabotaged. His opponents in Congress, for their own political gain, unfairly labeled him callous and cruel. Had his ideas become law, there is no assurance they would have worked, but there is no way this man did not care. He had a history of great humanitarian accomplishments. He risked his life saving Chinese children during the Boxer Rebellion in China; at the outbreak of World War I, he formed a committee to help 12,000 Americans return safely to the United States; and during the war he headed the Food Administration and kept the Allies fed while avoided rationing at home. After the war he organized shipments of food to starving Europeans including famine-stricken Soviet Russians. When a critic suggested he was aiding Bolshevism by

feeding Russians, Hoover retorted, "Twenty million people are starving. Whatever their politics, they shall be fed." He was a great man!

Donovan Trana, the innkeeper at the Pines on the Prairie B&B, assured us the door would be open for our late arrival after dinner. True to his word, the porch light was on and the door open when we arrived at about 9:45 p.m. He also arrived at about the same time, riding his Harley. We heard a friendly, "Hi," as he cruised by. One last climb for the day was up the stairs to our room where we cleaned up and fell into bed and slept soundly. We awoke the next morning to bright light filtering through lace window treatments. A nice breakfast of fruit, muffins, ingredient-enhanced scrambled eggs and ham was delivered in a basket to our room. After breakfast I went outside to see what this rural acreage looked like in daylight. It was clean and well maintained. The 99-year-old farmhouse was in excellent condition and looked like it could easily survive another 99 years. I took a couple of pictures and went back inside for a little dialog with Connie and Donovan.

Donovan and his wife LeAnn have

Hoovers' burial site

151

Thelma and George Nopoulos

Candy Kitchen, Wilton

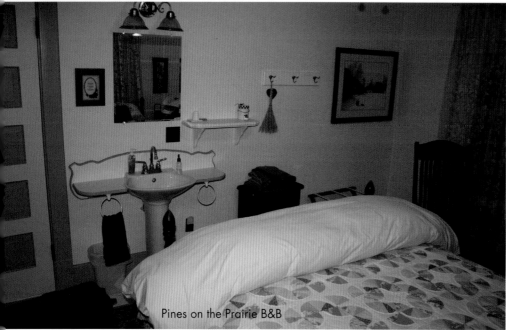

Pines on the Prairie B&B

lived on this acreage since 1993. They raised six children whom they home-schooled. After the children left the nest, LeAnn went to college at St. Ambrose in Davenport and earned a degree in occupational therapy. Donovan owned an auto glass business in **Muscatine** to support his family while the kids were growing up. He presently has a cottage industry operating out of his garage and another out-building. He and a couple of coworkers assemble and ship auto glass products he has developed. These include: an auto glass cut-out knife; a velocity bridge and injector; and a velocity repair system kit. Of Iowa, Donovan says, "I like the big sky, rolling land and the seasons. Iowans are polite and laid back. They ponder and think about things. Be prepared to slow down when dealing with Iowans. They are connected to the land and would rather work with nature than fight it."

Leaving the B&B, we drove south, crossed the **Muscatine County** line and almost immediately entered the town of **Wilton**. Donovan recommended we stop at Wilton Candy Kitchen. After all, if Brooke Shields and Gregory Peck sought it out, there must be something

152

Donovan Trana with his Equalizer Velocity Repair Kit

Donovan's St. Bernard

Gerdau Ameristeel, Wilton

special about the place and, indeed, there is. The first amazing thing is the building itself. In most towns we have covered, the wood frame buildings built in the 1850s have burned down or have been razed. The Candy Kitchen building, built in 1856, survived three, major, **Wilton** fires. The soda, confectionary and ice cream parlor business in this little old building traces its beginning to 1860, one year before the beginning of the Civil War. That makes it the "Oldest Ice Cream Parlor/Soda Fountain in the World."

In 1910, a young, Greek immigrant named Gus Nopoulos, who invented the banana split sundae while working for his uncle in Davenport, bought the store. From that day on, Wilton Candy Kitchen has been open seven days a week, 365 days a year to the present-day. Gus's son George (88) and George's wife Thelma (76) are the ones putting in the hours these days. I asked Thelma if anyone was in line to take over and she quickly replied, "We are not done yet!" I'll ask her again at the 150-year anniversary of the business on August 27, 2010. It was obvious that they have received a lot of attention from writers and reporters.

When I told Thelma what I was up to, she immediately phoned George and told him to come to the store. She then orchestrated the photo shoot suggesting they stand behind the fountain. She whipped together a strawberry soda topped with whipped cream and a cherry and sprinkles and placed it on the counter for a prop. After all that, she gave me permission to snap the picture. I felt like I had danced with a lady who led me all over the dance floor. I love strong women.

When the name **Muscatine** is mentioned, there might be some confusion as to whether you are referring to the city or the county, but it will not be confused with a city in any other part of the world. It began as "Casey's Woodpile" (that's kind of catchy) and was incorporated as Bloomington in 1839. That caused confusion in mail delivery because there were already many Bloomingtons in the Midwest. When they changed the name to Muscatine, there was no doubt where a letter with that address was going. It is believed the name was derived from the Muscaoutin American Indian tribe.

From 1840 to the beginning of the Civil War in 1861, **Muscatine** had

Iowa's largest African-American community. Alexander Clark, an African American, came from Pennsylvania to initially work as a barber. He rose to become a successful timber salesman and real estate speculator and one of the most prominent men in the community. He was a leader in getting state government to overturn racist laws and assisting fugitive slaves. In 1868, he successfully desegregated Iowa's public schools by suing the **Muscatine** school board when his daughter was turned away from her neighborhood school. His son Alexander Jr. became the first African American to graduate from the University of Iowa where he received a degree in law. At 58 years of age, the senior Clark became the second African American to graduate from the U of I. He said, "I want to serve as an example for young men of my race." This remarkable man also rose to prominence in the Republican Party. I am proud of my state's early gender and race equality efforts and successes.

Manufacturing is the mainstay of **Muscatine's** economy. It was once the "Pearl Button Capital of the World." Fresh water clams stacked up in the bend

The Button Factory, Muscatine

The Button Factory

153

Muscatine

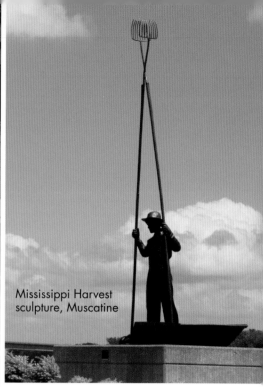

Mississippi Harvest sculpture, Muscatine

Muscatine County Courthouse, Muscatine

Allsteel reception area, Muscatine

Scott Livermore

of the Mississippi and were harvested for their pearl-like surface. German immigrant, John F. Boepple, a skilled button cutter, started punching buttons out of clamshells in 1887. At its peak in 1905, 1.5 billion buttons were manufactured by 37 companies. Fifty percent of the city's workforce was involved in the industry.

While the button industry waned (there are still a couple of companies making plastic buttons), other industries grew and prospered, keeping the unemployment rate low. Bandag is a leading manufacturer of tire-retreading material and equipment. Bandag's owner Roy J. Carver started the Carver Pump Company, a solid performer in manufacturing industrial pumps. The Grain Processing Corporation is a world leader in manufacturing corn-based products. HNI Corporation (Muscatine's largest employer) is the second-largest manufacturer of office furniture in the world and the leading manufacturer and marketer of gas- and wood-burning fireplaces. You'll recognize these brand names: HON, Allsteel and Heatilator. Another familiar name is Stanley Consultants. As one of the top engineering firms in the world,

154

Pine Creek Grist Mill, Wildcat Den State Park

you'll frequently hear their name mentioned in major projects. They are headquartered in Muscatine. H. J. Heinz, Kent Feeds, Monsanto and Musco Lighting also have operations in the community.

We talked to one of the employees who does his part to make the **Muscatine** area a desirable place to do business. Scott Livermore, who works in the Allsteel division of HNI, has two job titles: supply chain continuous improvement manager and supply chain manager for steel products. His responsibilities include working on plant layout efficiency, supply efficiency and buying steel. Allsteel manufactures office furnishings for contract sales as opposed to the HON brand, which is mainly retail. While at the University of Iowa, Scott was enrolled in ROTC. When he graduated he served eight years in the Air Force as a navigator. He continues his Air Force career as a member of a National Guard unit in Peoria, Illinois. They have been deployed in the Mideast for Iraq war duties four times. Scott is proud of the company he works for and the community he calls home. The Livermores chose to live in Iowa because of its quality education sys-

tem. The parks and recreation facilities are an added attraction and a nice venue for the activities of Scott, his wife Jen and their three children.

We ate lunch at the Button Factory, which as the name suggests, occupies an old button factory building. We sat outside in a screened-in porch with a great view of the Mississippi waterfront. The food and atmosphere were superb.

South of **Muscatine** is a rich, truck farming area where there is a bit of sand in the soil making it ideal for growing melons. **Muscatine** melons are known throughout Iowa as the best.

We drove northeast on the Great River Road to Wildcat Den State Park. We stopped to look at the Pine Creek Grist Mill located within the park. This old mill, built in 1848, is quite a sight and it is still operating. Weathered clapboard siding distinguishes the four-story mill and water running over an adjacent dam adds to the charm. Looking at the massive beam structure on the inside, you realize this building isn't going to collapse anytime soon. The heavy machinery is also impressive. Sitting next to the mill site is a fully-furnished, nineteenth-centu-

ry, country schoolhouse. The park itself has primitive camping and a beautiful trail through woods and rock formations.

As we continued our drive along the Mississippi, we contemplated some facts about this great river. The largest cargo carried by a steamboat in the 1800s was that of the "Henry Frank" which arrived in New Orleans in 1881 with cotton bales stacked so high that the vessel itself was barely visible. The cargo weighed 2,390 tons. Today, it is common to see a tow of 12 to 15 barges, laden with 20,000 tons of cargo, powered by one sturdy diesel towboat. Can you imagine the skill it takes to maneuver that water train up and down the river? Typically, the upstream cargo consists of petroleum products from Texas and Louisiana and coal from southern Illinois and western Kentucky. For downstream cargo, it is the most economical way to transport the bounty of the Midwest grain harvest to the World Port of New Orleans.

It was another perfect day in the middle of June as the weather patterns settled down. The dry days allowed the Iowa rivers to crest and begin receding from record floods in early June due to

Button punch, Muscatine History and Industry Center

Muscatine

155

Figge Art Museum, Davenport

Figge Art Museum

Davenport

Davenport

unprecedented rainfall. It has been a character-building year weather wise. The winter was the coldest and snowiest in my memory. Prior to the flooding, there were an unusual number of tornados and some were severe. Interestingly enough, at times like this, there is less complaining and more resolve to roll up your sleeves and deal with it. That is the positive of having to face adversity. People come together and forget their differences and petty problems; when the sun shines again, life is better than ever.

The sun was shining on the Quad Cities even though the Mississippi was still at flood stage. The Quad Cities is a metropolitan area of **Davenport** and **Bettendorf** on the Iowa side and Rock Island and Moline on the other side of the river in Illinois. The combined population is over 350,000. The cities interact with cooperation that allows them to provide the amenities of a larger city.

As we entered **Davenport**, we noticed that the waterfront area of downtown was under water. That included John O'Donnell Baseball Stadium and LeClaire Park. Due to some extraordinary sandbagging, the field of the historic sta-

Scott County Courthouse, Davenport

dium was dry. Sandbagging and flood-fighting measures—short of building a levee—are a well-developed science in **Davenport**. The citizens love the aesthetics of the river and they don't want a levee spoiling the view. If you have experienced the waterfront during normal water levels, you understand their sentiment. We observed people matter of factly going about business even though the river was cresting at one foot below the record flood of 1993. I commend their spirit and character. Their reward is living in a beautiful Mississippi River city.

An attractive new addition to the waterfront is the Figge Art Museum. The high water was lapping at its floodwalls but its extensive collection, including works by Grant Wood and Thomas Hart Benton, was high and dry and so was the entrance to this outstanding piece of architecture. The Figge Foundation's $12 million gift provided the impetus; David Chipperfield Architects, London, provided the plan. The results are stunning. At 100,000 square feet, it triples the size of its predecessor, the Davenport Museum of Art. Fifty percent of its space is dedicated to educational and social program-

ming. It has one of the Midwest's largest and best venues for art exhibitions.

The arts flow throughout the area. **Davenport's** historic Adler Theatre hosts the Quad Cities Symphony Orchestra and traveling professional acts, including Broadway musicals. Talented local artists, musicians and actors are inspired by the river and the colorful character of the metro area.

Festivals abound along the river and beyond. The weekend following our visit, the festivities were slated to be overhead when the Quad City Air Show performers would do their stunts. In August, there is the Great River Tug Fest where Port Byron, Illinois, challenges LeClaire, Iowa, to a tug of war contest with a rope strung across the Mississippi. River traffic is stopped for the event. The daddy of all the celebrations is the Bix Jazz Fest in July. It honors **Davenport's** own Bix Beiderbecke and it draws world-class, traditional jazz bands. One of the celebration's events, the Bix 7 Run, draws world-class distance runners.

The "Father of Waters" has always been a world-class draw. The name the Indians gave it conveys the respect they

had for it. The early white explorers felt its pull and the earliest settlers of trappers and fur traders began tapping its economical potential. The river's value as a major transportation waterway was understood by the waves of settlers who arrived in the mid-1800s. The entrepreneurial spirit kicked in and big time projects were undertaken. Huge steamboats were built to transport people and cargo. Large rafts of logs from the north were guided downstream by steamers headed for sawmills in Clinton, Davenport and Muscatine. The architect of this process was Rock Island native Frederick Weyerhaeuser. At the turn of the century, the source of Upper Midwest lumber dried up and the Iowa mills on the Mississippi shut down. The name Weyerhaeuser became synonymous with the lumbering industry as he moved on to new ventures in the American Northwest and South.

The first lock and dam built on the Upper Mississippi was between **Davenport** and Arsenal Island. It was built in the early 1930s at the height of the Depression. It was a major economic lift for the area. By the end of the 1930s, twenty-six locks and dams were in place

Mississippi crests at one foot below 1993 record flood stage

Halligan-McCabe-DeVries
Funeral Home, Davenport

Tom Frandsen

Mac's Tavern, Davenport

to create stair steps for river traffic.

The arduous task of plowing the Iowa prairie was difficult enough without having to stop frequently to clean the dirt buildup on the cast-iron plows. A blacksmith named John Deere surmised that a highly-polished, steel plow would clean itself. He built the plows and farmers eagerly bought them. That was the humble beginning of the world's largest manufacturer of farm machinery. The company is headquartered in Moline and has major manufacturing operations in **Davenport**. Alcoa is another large presence with a sprawling plant that is spread along the **Bettendorf** waterfront for what seems like miles.

Davenport native Tom Frandsen says, "I wake up every morning and give thanks that I live in Davenport, Iowa." He is a funeral director at the Halligan-McCabe-DeVries Funeral Home—the oldest funeral home in Scott County. Funerals bring former residents back to **Davenport** for the services and Tom feels privileged to serve them. He is a delightful person and a good storyteller. He told us about the Fairmount Crematory that used to have bodies

Palmer College of Chiropractic,
Davenport

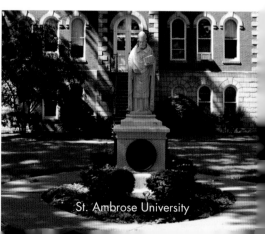

St. Ambrose University

St. Ambrose University, Davenport

shipped from Chicago. They had a setup where the aggrieved would see the deceased placed on a bed that would subsequently be lowered into the crematory room below. I hope they didn't take that as symbolic of the direction the soul might be headed.

Tom lives on a hill in an established neighborhood near downtown and the river. He has marveled at the increase of bald eagle sightings from rare—when he was a kid—to common today. During the comeback period, he noticed some fish innards on his lawn and wondered where they came from. His question was answered when he almost got hit by a sampling while standing under a tree. An eagle was sitting up there dining on the better cuts of the fish.

In his younger days, Tom served as a bartender at Mac's Tavern in downtown **Davenport**. He said Al Capone used to visit the establishment when in town. A secret elevator took him upstairs to a private room where he liked to play cards. I asked Tom, who is in his 30s, if he ever served him. "No," he laughed, "but I think a couple of the waitresses I worked with might have." My next question was

if Mac's was still in business and if they served food. His answer was, "Yes, and the food is great."

You guessed it! We were off to Mac's for lunch. A large, curving bar with stools graced one side of a long room. Along the other wall there were leather booths. Adorning the walls above the booths were Bix Jazz Festival posters. The background music was traditional jazz and the food and atmosphere were great.

St. Ambrose University began as a seminary and school of commerce for young men in 1882. Davenport's first bishop, John McMullen, D.D., founded it under the auspices of the Diocese of Davenport. The affiliation remains strong today. Temporarily housed in the old St. Marguerite's School, it moved to its present location in 1885. The site was chosen for its secluded grove of oak trees and that it was far removed from the "corrupting influences of town life." In 1908, the name was officially changed to St. Ambrose College. In 1968, it became coeducational; in 1977, graduate courses were offered with the master of business administration program. In 1987, St. Ambrose College became St. Ambrose

University—offering graduate programs in 15 academic disciplines.

Today, the campus is no longer secluded or far removed from town. It is still a beautiful setting with attractively designed buildings and it embraces the town of **Davenport** as one of the amenities. Academically, St. Ambrose offers 75 majors with a 15-to-1 student-teacher ratio. They emphasize hands-on and interactive learning. An excellent program of intramural and varsity sports leads the way in extra-curricular activities. Eleven intramural activities encompass a wide range of choices from tennis to bowling to euchre. There are nine varsity sports for men and nine for women. St. Ambrose varsity athletes not only compete—they excel. The football teams and women's basketball teams consistently win conference titles and go on to national competition. One year, the teams won four conference championships and were runners-up in eight others.

Daniel D. Palmer believed that correcting a spinal misalignment would release a normal nerve supply that enhances natural healing. He performed his first spinal adjustments in 1895,

World's largest truckstop, Walcott

LeClaire riverfront

Grasshoppers Gifts-Antiques-Wine, LeClaire

which led to relieving deafness in one man and heart trouble in another. Arrangements were made to train others in the application of the chiropractic principle. Bartlett J. Palmer (Daniel's son) took responsibility of the resulting school in 1904 and led it through some difficult years of development until it secured a place among the health sciences before his death in 1961. A guiding influence in B.J.'s life was his wife Mabel who became a doctor of chiropractic in 1905. She was an anatomy instructor at the school for 30 years. B.J. and Mabel's son, David Palmer, assumed the presidency in 1961. Under his watch the name was changed from Palmer School of Chiropractic to Palmer College of Chiropractic and it was established as a non-profit. Today, it has a modern, well-equipped campus in Davenport and a west campus in San Jose, California, and south campus in Port Orange, Florida.

The Quad Cities has three riverboat casinos. On the Illinois side, there is Jumer's Casino in Rock Island; on the Iowa side, there is Rhythm City Casino in **Davenport** and Isle of Capri in **Bettendorf**. We were obligated to test

160

LeClaire

Patrick's Steakhouse, Clinton

Nutan Bhakta

Timber Motel, Clinton

only Iowa casinos and that was cut in half because the entrance to Rhythm City was under water. After half an hour of playing the quarter slots in the Isle of Capri, Connie walked out seven dollars to the good. The running score after eight casinos is $4.50 above the line.

Leaving the Quad Cities, we took Highway 67 north to **LeClaire**. It was named after the founder of Davenport. When it came time to name the city he had helped lay out, Antoine LeClaire asked that it be named after his good friend, Colonel George Davenport. The generous LeClaire, who was married to Sacagawea's granddaughter, donated the land where the Scott County Courthouse stands. A tidbit of **LeClaire** history—it's the birthplace of Buffalo Bill Cody.

LeClaire is an attractive, clean town of 3,000 with a historic business district on high ground bordering the river. South of town on a road that fronts the river there are some nice houses with boat docks and a couple of marinas. The river's high water was close to the road but wasn't causing any damage.

If we had taken Interstate 80 west to **Scott County's** border we would have

stopped at the World's Largest Truck Stop near **Walcott**. We have done that previously and I assure you, it is worth a look. It is enormous, well designed, very clean and has every facility and service an over-the-road trucker could want. In the main building there are restaurants, a gift shop, a convenience store, automotive supplies, a theater, a barber, a dentist, a laundry, showers and more. It is a pleasant atmosphere with vintage truck displays and well-done murals and photos on the walls. There are truck wash bays, repair shops and motel rooms. I'm sure I'm leaving something out.

We headed north on Highway 67 crossing the Wapsipinicon River into **Clinton County**. We continued the drive to the edge of **Clinton** where we checked into the Timber Motel. The saws mounted on the lobby walls carried out the theme that pays homage to the 1800s' lumber industry in **Clinton**. Chad and Nutan Bhakta, who emigrated from India to Canada to the United States, own the motel. They have been in the motel business for about nineteen years.

Our choice for dining in **Clinton** was Patrick's Steakhouse and Brewery located

in the old Clinton Paper Company building. The pub atmosphere with exposed brick walls was pleasant; the steak and Cajun/chicken/Caesar salads were tasty.

The next morning after eating the motel's minimal, continental breakfast, we began our exploration and research of **Clinton**. As we drove to the central city, we noticed some heavy industry structures with bustling rail activity in the foreground. We learned later that the mile-long conglomeration of tanks, smokestacks, pipes and buildings are all part of Archer Daniels Midland's (ADM) corn-milling operation. There is a gold-dome structure for storing the coal that is used to create steam for generating electricity and running some of the processes. There are several end products. A PHA bio-plastic plant, in partnership with Metabolix, will join the complex in early 2009, which will add 114 new jobs to the 600-plus work force.

ADM isn't the only economic force in town. Over a dozen Fortune 500 companies have operations in **Clinton** and many smaller manufacturing, distribution and service industries contribute to the area's economic health. The **Clinton**

ADM complex, Clinton

Clinton

Clinton Showboat

162

Clinton County Courthouse, Clinton

community is the most industrialized per capita in the state.

A major factor in the industrial successes is the availability of transportation services. The Union Pacific takes an east/west route through the city and Burlington Northern Santa Fe runs a north/south route, as does the Iowa Chicago and Eastern Railroad. Railroad spurs hook up to one of the busiest river ports on the Upper Mississippi. It has three active barge terminals with cranes for loading cargo. U.S. Highways 30 and 67 intersect at **Clinton** and provide easy access to the interstate system. Clinton Municipal Airport can accommodate corporate jets and the Quad Cities Airport is only 35 miles away.

Much of the aforementioned information was conveyed to us by Steven Ames, President and CEO of the Clinton Regional Development Corporation. Steven is a southeast Iowa native with a well-rounded education. He attended a community college and Augustana College and then St. Ambrose for his B.A. in economics. He earned an M.A. in both economics and urban planning at the University of Iowa. His job at CRDC is

Steven Ames

Clinton levee

to: (1) work with existing businesses, (2) market the area, and (3) represent six communities, including three in Illinois. He is enthusiastically pursuing these duties to enhance Clinton-area life.

Downtown, generally in good shape, has some rough edges. My impression is that it is a work in progress. They have done a beautiful job restoring the Van Allen Building—a classic Louis Sullivan design. There is a massive, solid levee that keeps the business district dry when the Mississippi River waters rise. It is attractively finished with a street on top, grassy slopes on the land side and riprap on the water side.

There was no levee to get in the way of the huge log rafts that came downriver from Wisconsin and Minnesota in the mid- to late-1800s. Their destination was the **Clinton** area sawmills where they were cut into lumber and shipped throughout the country via the river and railroads. **Clinton** was the sawmill capital of the nation in those days. Production peaked in 1892 with mills turning out 195 million board feet. Mansions along Fifth, Sixth and Seventh Avenues attest to the wealth generated by this industry.

Depleted forests ended the sawmill era in 1900, but with the railroad and river transportation systems in place, manufacturing and heavy industry moved in.

Clinton was originally platted as the town of New York in 1836. Early on, it showed little promise while Lyons, the next town to the north, was prospering. Lyons was blessed with a great leader in Elijah Buell. He doctored early settlers, served on the school board, served eight terms as alderman, offered his home for worship services and co-owned the Lyons-Fulton Ferry that transported thousands across the Mississippi. Lyons went on to become a grain and milling center, and later a lumber manufacturing community. Ah, but as luck would have it, the Chicago, Iowa and Nebraska Railroad announced it would cross the "Big River" at sleepy New York. In 1855, the Iowa Land Company was organized to buy the tract of land that New York occupied. They renamed the town Clinton after New York Governor Dewitt Clinton, one of the driving forces behind the Erie Canal. The railroad came and **Clinton** grew and a fierce rivalry developed between **Clinton** and Lyons. A mon-

strous cottonwood tree was the dividing line. In 1895, **Clinton** annexed Lyons and, in the following years, the rivalry gradually abated.

Today, they all work together to make **Clinton** a pleasant place to live. The arts are healthy with a resident ballet company and a professional symphony orchestra. Summer repertory theatre of musicals and comedies are performed in the Lillian Russell (Clinton native) Theatre aboard a restored paddle wheeler on the riverfront. You can cheer for the Clinton LumberKings, a minor league professional baseball team, and you can buy food fresh from the fields at the Farmers Market. Of course, there are festivals and parks and recreation venues worthy of a city of close to 30,000. We stopped at the beautiful Eagle Point Park for a spectacular view of the widest part of the entire Mississippi River.

Before we left **Clinton**, Connie had to test the slots at the Wild Rose Casino, which is presently on a riverboat but is in the process of moving to a land-based operation. During her half hour of gambling, she lost $5.50. The running score after nine casinos is $1 below the line.

Clinton baseball park

163

Clinton

Eagle Point Park, Clinton

Clinton

Van Allen Building, Clinton

174

Clinton

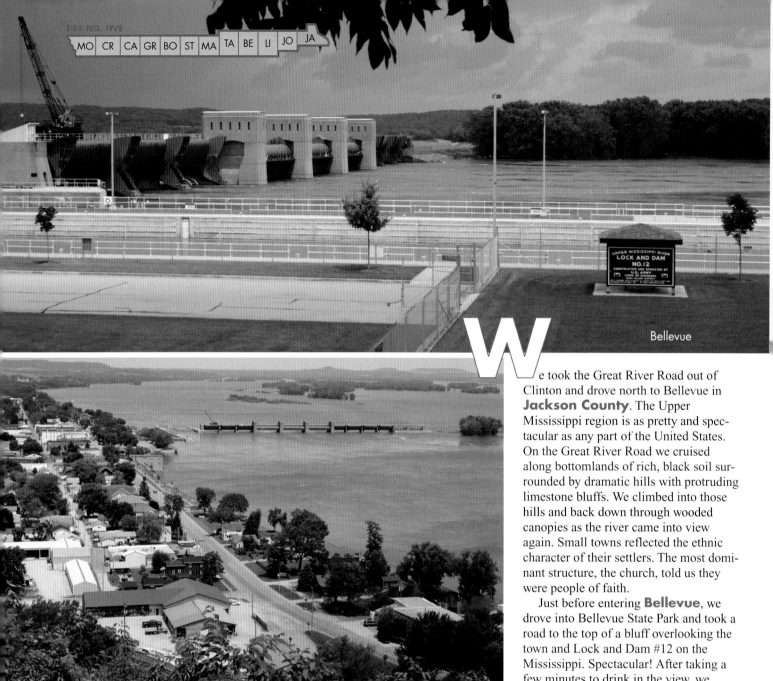

Bellevue

Bellevue

We took the Great River Road out of Clinton and drove north to Bellevue in **Jackson County**. The Upper Mississippi region is as pretty and spectacular as any part of the United States. On the Great River Road we cruised along bottomlands of rich, black soil surrounded by dramatic hills with protruding limestone bluffs. We climbed into those hills and back down through wooded canopies as the river came into view again. Small towns reflected the ethnic character of their settlers. The most dominant structure, the church, told us they were people of faith.

Just before entering **Bellevue**, we drove into Bellevue State Park and took a road to the top of a bluff overlooking the town and Lock and Dam #12 on the Mississippi. Spectacular! After taking a few minutes to drink in the view, we drove back down the hill and returned to the highway. We crossed Big Mill Creek into **Bellevue** and immediately turned left to Potter's Mill on Big Mill Creek.

Potter's Mill was built in 1843 by Elbridge Gerry Potter using massive, hand-hewn oak beams to frame the structure. It was originally powered by a 20-

166

Potter's Mill, Bellevue

Bellevue

Stations of the Cross

St. Donatus Catholic Church and
Pieta Chapel (on top of the hill to the left)

foot diameter overshot wheel. Later the dam was raised and the water rerouted through six turbines. By the time Potter retired, the mill was producing 200 barrels of flour a day and buying wheat from as far away as St. Cloud, Minnesota, and Portage, Wisconsin. Eventually, the flour milling shifted to feed milling for livestock. It finally shut down in 1969 after 126 years of service. Today, you can eat and sleep amongst the old beams and machinery as it is now a B&B and restaurant. It is very well done.

Three years prior to building the mill, the good people of **Bellevue** formed a posse of outraged citizens to rid the area of a loathsome band of outlaws led by a man named Brown. He was an attractive looking man who seemed to be cultured and he had the town fooled for a while. The band of no-goods—27 members strong—performed every kind of illegal act from stealing horses to murder. Brown had been informed of the impending arrest and quickly assembled his men and sympathizers at his house. They were armed and ready for a fight. Sheriff Warren, leader of the posse, initially tried to negotiate the arrest of Brown and his

men. While they were parleying, Brown's men were drinking freely and becoming boisterous. No agreement was reached so Sheriff Warren returned to the posse and they marched toward the house. Before reaching the house, one of Warren's men was taken out by a shot from a second story window. In the ensuing fight, many people were killed or wounded. Brown was among those killed. This is known as the "Bellevue War." Thirteen prisoners were taken and a jury of 80 men voted on the penalty by dropping colored or white beans into a ballot box. The choice was to hang or to whip and exile the criminals. The whipping and exile sentence won by three beans. The lashing was administered and the men were sent downstream with a warning to never return. At their new location downriver, many of them continued a life of crime. Colonel George Davenport was killed during a robbery at his home by seven of those miscreants.

Today, **Bellevue's** 2,400 residents enjoy a peaceful life along the Mississippi. The business district borders the river with a park that overlooks the lock and dam. A street one block west of the river has an active railroad track run-

ning down the middle.

We chose the River View Restaurant for lunch. Sheet paneling covered all the walls; vinyl-covered booths with an early American trim and vinyl stack chairs at the tables provided the seating. Photos of old **Bellevue** hung on the paneling. The breakfast menu was still available so I ordered hamburger steak and eggs. Health-wise, it was not a good move, but I had never tried the combination before. The hamburger steak was ten ounces and the hash browns were piled high. I assured the delightful, little old lady who waited on us, that the food was delicious, even though I could eat only half of it.

More spectacular scenery greeted us as we drove Highway 52 to the town of **St. Donatus.** Our first glimpse of this Luxembourg settlement was the stucco and stone St. Donatus Catholic Church sitting on the brow of a high hill. To the west of the church, on the peak of the hill, is the Pieta Chapel. Between the church and the chapel are 14 brick alcoves set into the wooded hillside. They represent the Stations of the Cross. Each one contains an original lithograph print illustrating Christ's journey to his cruci-

Jackson County

Bellevue

167

St. John's Lutheran Church, St. Donatus

Cheryl Clark

Maquoketa Caves State Park

168

Hurstville Interpretive and Visitors
Center, Maquoketa

fixion. It is beautifully done and a very moving pilgrimage through nature.

This little hamlet of 150 people lives big with the largest and best collection of Luxembourg nineteenth-century architecture outside of Europe. A bed and breakfast and a restaurant occupy a couple of the buildings. It's a very charming place.

As we turned and drove south, we saw another impressive church on a hill across the valley from **St. Donatus**. In 1919, Germans built St. John's Lutheran, an attractive brick church to replace a stone structure built in 1864. A recent addition to the front of the church has a contemporary look that complements the original, traditional style architecture.

As we traversed Jackson County on the way to **Maquoketa**, we passed through some very picturesque, dairy farming country. We saw freshly harvested hay in round bales scattered over a hay field. Holstein cows were munching grass on the hillside pastures. Some farmsteads had stone houses and red outbuildings and other were painted all white. We saw one large scale operation but the rest appeared to be family farms. Ninety-five percent of them had a neat,

Hurstville lime kilns, Maquoketa

Jackson County

clean look. It was a pleasant drive.

Maquoketa, the **Jackson County** seat, takes its name from the Maquoketa River. The Indian word translates to "Bear River," so named because of the numerous bears that once inhabited its banks. The bears are gone but plenty of wild life remains. **Jackson County** has a national reputation for producing trophy, white-tailed deer. Many landowners welcome hunters and there are generous seasons for bow, shotgun and muzzle-loading hunting. Wild turkey, pheasants and migratory fowl are also abundant and, of course, there is no shortage of rabbits and squirrels. Spring spawn and fall migration mean good walleye and sauger fishing on the Maquoketa River. Small-mouth bass will take your bait on the South Fork of the Maquoketa and channel catfish are plentiful everywhere. And trout fishing has become an option as some of Iowa's southernmost trout streams are in the area.

We stopped at the Maquoketa Chamber of Commerce office and had a nice chat with administrative assistant Cheryl Clark. She was quick to point out all the advantages of her hometown. As it

has happened so many times before, the first words out of this Iowan's mouth were, "It is very friendly and you know almost everyone." It might be a cliché, but it's true, and a real plus to small town life. She went on to say, "There is a lot of natural beauty and **Maquoketa** is convenient to larger cities." Her husband Andy manages the Super 8 Motel. He tells of folks from Indiana who make an annual trip for the sole purpose of hunting mushrooms. Cheryl is proud of Old City Hall Gallery and Banowetz Antique Mall. She also recommended that we check out the Hurstville Interpretive Center, Hurstville Lime Works and Maquoketa Caves State Park. We did.

The Hurstville Interpretive Center is located in a wetlands area that is the habitat of a couple of swans as well as other waterfowl. It is a multipurpose facility that allows visitors to explore natural resources, environmental education and resource protection.

The unique limestone structures known as the Hurstville Lime Kilns were used to burn lime into the whitest, purest and most adhesive qualities on the market in the late 1800s and early 1900s. At one

time the operation employed over 60 men and provided an excellent market for firewood. The railroads also benefited as the product was shipped throughout the Northwest. The last time a Hurstville kiln was fired was in 1930.

The Maquoketa Caves State Park is something special. There are 13 caves with varying degrees of accessibility. There are also limestone outcroppings and bluffs and there is a natural bridge. A beautiful trail system links the caves and takes you through a nature wonderland.

Western **Jackson County** and **Jones County** occupy a part of Iowa that takes the rugged hills and bluffs along the Mississippi and introduces them to rich, interior farmland. This is Grant Wood country. After experiencing other parts of the world, he chose to come back and paint **Jones County**. It is easy to understand why. There is roughly an equal mix between cultivated and uncultivated ground. Trees cluster around a network of meandering streams and rivers and on the steeper hillsides. Ribbons of strip farming wrap around the gentler hills and appear as though they are a natural part of the landscape. This is

Jackson County Courthouse, Maquoketa

A huge heat exchanger on its way to Clinton traverses Jones County

Ray and Mary Finn

rich soil and farms are generally prosperous and have an attractive appearance.

Our first stop in Grant Wood country was an organic farm near **Cascade** on the northern border of **Jones County**. It is a pioneer farm that Ray Finn's Irish family settled in 1842 and Ray is the fourth generation of continuous ownership. A half century ago, he married a Cascade High School classmate and she joined him in preserving the family farm.

Mary and Ray began conventional farming in 1966. During those first years, their cattle had chronic health problems. After the hospital births of their first two children, they decided on a more natural approach for their third child with a home birth aided by a midwife. This experience put them in contact with people who emphasized the natural approach to life. In 1978, they decided to take another step in natural living by converting to organic farming. With no chemicals washing off their fields, the health of their cattle improved considerably. The yields on the crops weren't quite as good, but this was offset by the higher prices organic foods command. They have kept their costs down by growing their own food. Mary is

Finn organic farm

Kelly's Country Oven, Monticello

TIER NO. FIVE

MO CR CA GR BO ST MA TA BE LI JO JA

Jones County Fairgrounds, Monticello

a vegetarian now and Ray is close to it. When they ate more meat, they did their own butchering and even made soap from the tallow. They are virtually self-sufficient as they currently raise 80–90 percent of what they eat. We thoroughly enjoyed walking through their gardens and touring their nicely-appointed, country home, which they spent five years building. It is gorgeous including the vistas from their perch on a hill. Mary gave me a list of the plants you will find on their farm. Hold on a few minutes, as it will take me a while to count them. The results are: 34 fruits, 54 vegetables, 25 herbs, 63 perennial flowers, 14 annual flowers, 2 flower bulbs, 2 mushrooms, 39 trees and shrubs and 5 vines.

We left **Cascade** and took Highway 151 to **Monticello**. If it had been the 1840s, we would have been driving or riding our horses on the Old Military Road from Dubuque to Iowa City. It connected the small mining town of Dubuque to the territorial capital in Iowa City. Iowa Highway 1 and U.S. Highway 151 are located almost precisely on the Old Military Road.

General George Wallace Jones, while serving as Wisconsin territorial representative in Washington, D. C., was responsible for gaining recognition of the Iowa Territory in 1838. Eight years later, in 1846, Iowa gained statehood. Jones went on to become one of Iowa's first two senators. **Jones County** was named to honor the state's founder.

Monticello lost out to Anamosa in the fight for the county seat but negotiated a compromise to be the site of the county fair. They immediately took advantage of the privilege by staging the first fair in 1852, thus making it the oldest fair in Iowa. During the middle of July, the 156th annual Great Jones County Fair will once again entertain attendees. In addition to being the oldest, it is the second largest county fair in the state. Name entertainers, such as Josh Turner, will grace the grandstand stage and the traditional events of harness racing and stock car racing will compete on the oval. Fairgoers will need earplugs for the truck and tractor pulls and their appetites for the tenderloins, kettle corn and funnel cakes. There will be lemonade to quench thirsts and fresh-faced, young exhibitors to renew faith in the next gen-

eration. A midway crowded with rides will round out this Americana experience.

We experienced an Americana setting when we ate lunch at Kelly's Country Oven in **Monticello**. We ordered the appropriate food—a tuna salad sandwich and a chilidog. Country music was playing at the appropriate volume. It was a perfect, down-home atmosphere.

Continuing on the Old Military Road, we arrived in **Anamosa**. Originally named Lexington, the town's name was changed to Anamosa to give it distinction. They did not want to confuse the postmasters with another Lexington. It was named after an attractive, young Indian girl. **Anamosa** is an Indian word for "White Fawn."

In contrast with the pretty Indian girl association, the name **Anamosa** is associated with Iowa's second-oldest penitentiary. The prison is an incredible structure and there is a great story behind its construction. It was built almost entirely with inmate labor. In 1872, its first prisoners were 20 convicts transferred from Fort Madison's penitentiary. They were temporarily housed in wooden cells and were employed at the stone

Monticello

Monticello

Prison Farm, Anamosa

Grant Wood Art Gallery, Anamosa

Jones County Courthouse, Anamosa

172

quarries nearby. Two weeks later, they had their first escape as three men slipped away while working in the quarries. Construction continued over the next 65 years. The prison foundry molded iron and the blacksmith shop fabricated window bars. There was a carpentry shop for woodwork and a stone cutting shed for carving stone. The end result was a striking, limestone structure in Romanesque Revival style with some Gothic Revival detailing. In 1992, it was placed on the National Registry of Historic Places.

Ruth Ann Bungum recalls working as a secretary for the assistant warden at the penitentiary in the early 1970s. It was called a reformatory then as the emphasis had changed from punishment to reforming inmates. Her job was a top security position and she had to be escorted by guards through part of the prison. There was a prison rule that women could not wear slacks and the fashion at the time was the mini-skirt. That made the daily trip very uncomfortable for Ruth Ann. After two and a half years at the prison, she took a job with **Jones County** as deputy treasurer in charge of the motor vehicle department. She enjoyed working

Stone City blacksmith shop

Anamosa Limestone quarry

for the county and stuck with it until retirement 25 years later.

Ruth Ann's husband Pete is a retired educator. His last 35 years were spent teaching seventh grade geography in the **Anamosa** school system. During that period he earned two distinctions. In 1972, he was the Jaycees' Outstanding Young Educator of the Year. In 1974, he earned the Anamosa Education Association Educator of the Year. He used innovative methods to hold the attention of his students and the feedback he receives from alumni is rewarding.

Pete and Ruth Ann consider **Anamosa's** size (5,000), good people, good schools and good recreational opportunities to be a good family environment. Their son and granddaughter live in Denmark. Pete and Ruth Ann generally make the trans-Atlantic trip once a year. However, they won't have to do it this year as their granddaughter is going to spend a year in **Anamosa** and experience attending an American high school. The Bungums are looking forward to that. Their daughter who lives nearby has blessed them with two more grandchildren. It will be fun for the

cousins to get together in the coming year. Pete and Ruth Ann have purchased burial plots in the cemetery where Grant Wood is buried. When the time comes, their remains will spend eternity within 175 steps of the great artist.

Probably the most famous painting executed by an American artist is *American Gothic*. Grant Wood's iconic painting is definitely the most parodied. Wood was born and raised in Anamosa. After gaining fame with *American Gothic*, Wood started an art colony in **Stone City** where he had found inspiration for much of his work. It was his aspiration that this setting would have the same effect on other artists. He converted a turn-of-the-century, limestone mansion into studios and dormitories. That was in 1932 and it only lasted about a year. The Grant Wood Art Festival has had much better lasting power. It started in Anamosa and was shifted to **Stone City** for 30 years before it returned to **Anamosa** in 2006.

Stone City grew out of the successful limestone quarries along the Wapsipinicon River. Limestone as building material was in demand and the city

grew with buildings made of stone. That included a magnificent hotel and opera house and the mansion Grant Wood used for his colony. Those structures were destroyed; however, a church, a blacksmith shop and a few other stone buildings remain. After the advent of Portland Cement in the early 1900s, the quarries began to shut down.

A revival of the quarries began in 1952 under the ownership of C. B. Dewees and William C. Weber. Mike Deutmeyer, Weber's grandson, is the present owner. A couple of years ago, Mike gave us a tour of the operation and it is big time. The quarry goes on and on. The equipment is massive and they use huge trucks that look like they belong in an open pit iron mine. Anamosa Limestone has a national reputation as a beautiful building material.

We cannot leave Anamosa without telling the remarkable story of John and Jill Parham. The motorcycle bug bit John early in life. When he was 16, he bought a 650 BSA that he quickly turned into a chopper. He developed a passion for Harleys and dreamed of owning his own motorcycle shop. The dream became a

Ruth Ann and Pete Bungum

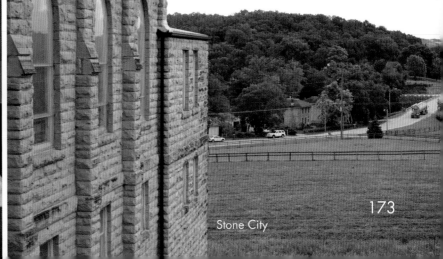
Stone City

173

National Motorcycle Museum, Anamosa

J&P Cycles, Anamosa

reality in 1975 when he partnered with his high school science teacher to open his first shop. Four years later, he and his partner split and John moved his business to a rented garage outside of town. When John was laid off from his factory job, Jill went to work full time because she believed John would do well if he could devote all his time to his business. That proved to be prophetic. After surviving an electrical fire where everything was destroyed, they started in again. With a little insurance money and lot of help from family and friends, they began the rebuilding process. That evolved into continued growth. Today, the headquarters in **Anamosa** occupies 150,000 square feet of space. The brand name is J&P Cycles and it is America's largest mail order and retail business of aftermarket parts and accessories for Harley-Davidson and Metric Cruiser motorcycles. John and Jill complement each other. John looks to the future and can identify new trends and Jill keeps it all together by overseeing day-to-day operations. They employ 300 people. In the fall of 2006, John was inducted into the Sturgis Motorcycle Hall of Fame.

Cornell College, Mount Vernon

John Parham

Quaker Oats plant, Cedar Rapids

In 2000, John was asked to take over as president of the National Motorcycle Museum in Sturgis, South Dakota. Running the museum from Iowa proved difficult so the museum was moved to **Anamosa**. Whether you love motorcycles or not, the exhibits at this museum are a must-see. The antique and customized machines, the posters, engines, clothing and other items are fascinating. The displays are clean and professionally done. In 2007, there were 17,000 paid admissions and some came from as far away as Australia and Japan.

We returned to the Old Military Road and followed it to **Mount Vernon**. At that point we were on the Iowa Highway 1 section. The **Linn County** town of **Mount Vernon** is perched on a hill (not a mountain) and on the highest ground there is a wonderful, small, liberal arts college whose entire campus is listed on the National Register of Historic Places. The college's name is Cornell and it gets confused with Cornell University in Ithaca, New York. I recall several years ago reading about the larger school in New York suggesting the Iowa school change its name. The folks at Cornell in

Iowa said, "Wait a minute; we were here first." Founded in 1853, it preceded the New York Cornell by 15 years. They don't back off when it comes to the quality of education, either. The Iowa Cornell has a higher percentage of alumni listed in Who's Who in America than their New York counterpart.

Cornell College was originally known as the Iowa Conference Seminary. It was renamed in 1857 after William Wesley Cornell, a devout Methodist and distant cousin of Ezra Cornell, founder of Cornell University in New York. The affiliation with the United Methodist Church continues today, but students from all religious traditions and from all non-religious perspectives are welcome. Women were treated as equals from the beginning and a resolution was adopted in 1870 that color or race would not be a qualifying factor for college admission.

Cornell has a unique "one-course-at-a-time" academic system where students immerse themselves in one academic discipline per three-week course term. Ninety-seven percent of the college's tenure track faculty hold the highest degree in their field. Eighty-eight percent

of Cornell's 1,200 students live on campus. There are more than 100 clubs, organizations and special interest groups ranging from the film club to the mountaineering club. Their varsity sports teams compete in the Iowa Intercollegiate Athletic Conference at the NCCA Division III level. Four of their student athletes have earned Academic All-American honors and 19 have earned Academic All-District honors. There are 40 intramural sports.

Our next destination was Iowa's second largest city, **Cedar Rapids**. This beautiful city was the victim of the worst natural disaster in Iowa history. In the middle of June, the Cedar River that flows through the middle of the city crested at twelve feet above the record prior to this year. Twelve feet! How is this possible? It has been labeled a 500-year flood. While the water was rising, a family was moving into a house they thought was out of reach. It wasn't, nor were 7,200 other commercial and residential properties. People lost not only their homes—but also their jobs—if their place of employment was flooded. The Quaker Oats plant, the world's largest

CORNELL COLLEGE

175

Flood damage, Cedar Rapids

TRESPASSING
FORBIDDEN
UNDER PENALTY OF THE LAW
CEDAR RAPIDS AND IOWA CITY RWY.

Dave and
Pat Miller

cereal factory, is located downtown on the river. PepsiCo, the parent of Quaker Oats, has proved to be a good corporate citizen in the treatment of its 1,100 workers during the crisis. First, it worked full speed ahead to clean up its plant and bring it back into production—one step at a time. Second, it continued to pay its workers while the plant was idle. Third, it provided food, water and temporary shelter through an employee assistance center. Using temporary power, Quaker Oats lit its landmark sign for a short time as a symbol of hope.

We drove through an area where the flooding was at its worst. There was virtually a continuous pile (six to ten feet high) of flood damaged furnishings and appliances along the streets on both sides. There was a truck with a powerful claw-like apparatus picking up the trash and dropping it into a dumpster that was also mounted on the truck. Many people were working to clean up the mess and a few were sitting on their porches with a resigned looks on their faces. We also heard the sound of hammering. To me, it was the sound of hope. It was painful to see what the disaster did to these people.

Cleaning up after the flood, Cedar Rapids

Victorian Lace B&B (former summer kitchen), Cedar Rapids

Jim and Renee Condit

Jessica Morley of Cedar Rapids hiking in Palisades-Kepler State Park

But I predict that you will hear more hammers pounding and I will again be proud of the resiliency of Iowans.

We Iowans acknowledge and express appreciation for the help that came from beyond Iowa's borders. The Federal Government, individuals and organizations made major contributions. Jay Leno gave the entire proceeds from two of this Las Vegas shows to the Greater Cedar Rapids Community Foundation. He said, "I don't see anyone in Iowa asking for money. These people are not looking for favors. I don't see anybody whining. I see people working hard, with shovels and brooms trying to clean the places."

We spent the night at the Victorian Lace B&B in suburban **Marion**. Our accommodations were in an outbuilding that was formerly a summer kitchen. The wall hangings and objects in the suite included everything, even the kitchen sink. Jim and Renee Condit got into the B&B business about ten years ago when they bought the 100-year-old farmhouse and outbuildings. They first got to know each other when they shared a rug during quiet time in kindergarten. Eventually, they went their separate ways, got mar-

ried, divorced and got together again at their 20-year class reunion. Renee works full time at Rockwell Collins and Jim runs the B&B and works a couple of other part-time jobs. He is also a licensed minister by way of Internet courses and non-denominational Christian ordination.

After breakfast, we met for coffee with Dave and Pat Miller. Dave and Pat met in the Quad Cities where Dave taught and coached at Rock Island High School and Pat worked in admissions at Marycrest College. After they were married Dave began selling insurance part time and was so successful that the income from sales superseded his teaching salary. The insurance company, Continental Western, encouraged him to open a general agency in **Cedar Rapids**. After three years, Life Investors approached him to take on a job in sales management. It meant a cut in income but getting in on the ground floor of a young company appealed to him. Life Investors prospered and was bought by Dutch insurance giant, Aegon. Dave retired as Chief Marketing Officer in the Life Investors division of Aegon. Pat worked until their first child was born

and then she became a full-time mother and volunteer. Their daughter is president of St. Luke's Foundation at St. Luke's Hospital in **Cedar Rapids** and their son has worked his way into his dad's old position at Aegon. When asked about Iowa, Dave and Pat agreed, "It's hard to get beyond the people—the spirit and attitude of the people. They have a great work ethic and they care. They believe other people are important."

Robert Fulton invented the steamboat in 1807. I am curious as to how many steamboats were built since that invention. In the mid-1800s, the Mississippi was clogged with large steamboats and smaller ones chugged up the big river's tributaries. I had no idea that the Des Moines, Iowa and Cedar Rivers once had steamers plying their waters. **Cedar Rapids** began as a milling town and when the merchants heard that paddle wheelers were coming up the Iowa River, they thought, "Why not the Cedar?" In 1843, the *Maid of Iowa* was the first steamer to make it to **Cedar Rapids**. For the next decade extensive trade developed between Cedar Rapids, Burlington, Keokuk and St. Louis. There was also

Rockwell Collins   Headquarters

TIER NO. FIVE
| MO | CR | CA | GR | BO | ST | MA | TA | BE | LI | JO | JA |

National Czech and Slovak Museum (after flood), Cedar Rapids

Brucemore Estate, Cedar Rapids

Linn County Courthouse, Cedar Rapids

Mount Mercy College, Cedar Rapids

steamboat traffic between **Cedar Rapids** and upriver towns of Waterloo and Cedar Falls. One of the boats, the *Black Hawk*, was built in Cedar Rapids.

Today, **Cedar Rapids** provides a cross section of jobs for its inhabitants. In addition to Quaker Oats, there are more agriculture-related businesses such as National Oats, Cargill, General Mills and Archer Daniels Midland. Aegon employs 3,600 people at its North American headquarters. Rockwell Collins, headquartered in **Cedar Rapids**, is high tech personified with its engineering and manufacturing expertise in sophisticated communication products for aircraft, including space projects Mercury, Gemini and Apollo. The company employs 20,000 worldwide. **Cedar Rapids** and Iowa City combine to make a technology corridor that spawns new high tech industries.

The arts are an important part of life in **Cedar Rapids**. The Cedar Rapids Museum of Art houses the largest collection of Grant Wood paintings in the world. The 1920s' Paramount Theatre is home to the Cedar Rapids Symphony Orchestra, one of the best west of the

Grant Wood's studio, Cedar Rapids

Cedar Rapids

Mississippi. The U.S. Cellular Center hosts sporting events, exhibitions, concerts and political rallies. Grant Wood's studio at 5 Turner Alley has been preserved. The National Czech and Slovak Museum is located in Czech Village.

Muslims have had a presence in **Cedar Rapids** since 1895 when immigrants arrived from the Beqaa Valley in today's Lebanon and Syria. It is the location of the National Muslim Cemetery—the first in the United States. The Mother Mosque of America, dedicated in 1934, was one of the first permanent structures built specifically to serve as a mosque in the United States.

Mount Mercy College is located on a hilltop in the heart of **Cedar Rapids**. It is minutes from a variety of malls, movie theaters, restaurants and museums. Its 40-acre campus is in a leafy neighborhood with a view of the city skyline.

Mount Mercy College is a Catholic institution founded by the Sisters of Mercy. It uniquely blends liberal arts learning and professional training with an emphasis on leadership and service. Its 1,500 students consist of traditional, residential, transfers, adult-accelerated and

graduate. Recent graduate offerings include a master of business administration and two master of arts in education programs: special education and reading. Internships that often result in full-time employment are numerous in the thriving city of **Cedar Rapids**.

A student newspaper, the *Green Club* and multiple community service clubs are included in about 30 organizations. Six men's teams and six women's teams compete in the Midwest Collegiate Conference, a member of the NAIA. These teams have combined for over 30 conference championships. Mount Mercy athletes regularly move on to regional and national competition and frequently earn NAIA Academic All-American honors. Intramural sports are also offered.

Cedar Rapids' other private college, Coe College, claims the shortest name of any American institution of higher learning. Its first name was a bit longer. When the Reverend Williston Jones founded the college in 1851, he named it The School for the Prophets. Classes were conducted in his parlor to prepare young men for the ministry in the Midwest. Two years later, while canvass-

ing churches in the East for money to send three of his students to Eastern seminaries, a Catskill farmer named Daniel Coe gave him $1,500 and urged him to start his own college. The gift had one stipulation—that the proposed school be made for education of females as well as males. Two lots on the edge of town and 80 acres of farmland were purchased to build the coeducational college. In 1868, it was named Parsons Seminary in an effort to secure money from the Lewis Parsons' estate. That failed and the institution was reestablished as the Coe Collegiate Institute in 1875. In 1881, it was incorporated under the name Coe College and it has operated continuously since then. It was a complicated process to get to that simple, three-letter name.

A high quality liberal arts education on an attractive urban campus is Coe's calling card today. It draws students with an average high school GPA of 3.5 and ACT score of 25. Virtually all of its 1,300 students live on campus in residence halls or apartments. Coe offers an abundance of out-of-class opportunities, including student-faculty collaborative research, honors projects and internships. There is

Islamic Center, Cedar Rapids

NASSIF HOUSE

Coe College

Vinton

good balance between art, music, science, education and business courses. All have strong programs. Opportunities abound for physical activity. On-campus facilities provide for complete, all-around sports competition and physical development. Varsity teams compete in the Iowa Intercollegiate Athletic Conference. Twenty-one Coe athletes have earned NCAA Division III All-American honors.

We drove back out into the country and crossed the **Benton County** line on the way to county seat Vinton. The terrain flattened out a bit and developed a gentle, rolling character. The crops looked good and the view was extremely beautiful. Billowing white cloud formations on a partly-sunny day and an azure sky met a landscape of well-tended fields with groves of trees seemingly placed just right aesthetically. The mostly white farmsteads added sparkle to the scene.

This was not the orderly scene that greeted **Benton County's** first settlers in 1843. In fact, they could see very little when, at midnight on May 1, 1843, they were allowed to stake their claim in what is now **Benton County**. Dawn revealed a confused mess that had to be

Benton County Courthouse, Vinton

More than knee high on the Fourth of July

Vinton

settled by compromise or, in a few cases, violence. After it was all straightened out, homesteaders began living the pioneer life. Cabins were built with large, open fireplaces dominating the rooms. The floors were dirt and the furniture was homemade. The whole family worked from dawn to dusk. They did take some time off to visit neighbors and enjoy celebrations such as dancing after a house raising or a husking bee. They were generally a friendly, hospitable people. Many came from Eastern states such as Massachusetts and Ohio and they adopted the education systems of those states. With that sturdy foundation, succeeding generations prospered.

Vinton began building on that foundation, opening its first store in 1848 and erecting a courthouse in 1849. A Vinton banker, George Horridge, helped build the *Black Hawk* riverboat and was a passenger on its maiden voyage up the Cedar River in 1858. When it arrived in Vinton, almost the entire population was there to greet it. **Vinton** was another Iowa city with a company that harvested fresh water clamshells for making buttons. There was an abundance of clams in the

Cedar River, as there was in the Mississippi. The Iowa Canning Company was a major industry from 1892 to 1959. It canned corn grown on a thousand acres near **Vinton**. A beautiful, bowl-shaped swimming pool was built in 1930 to entice youngsters away from swimming in the Cedar River. It served admirably until it was replaced in 1955.

Today, **Vinton** is a vibrant county seat town of 5,100 people. A community theatre provides an outlet for the performing arts and entertainment for the townspeople. They have a community band for the musically inclined. Parks, ball fields, a golf course, a pool and an indoor recreation center are there for the physically active.

Vinton is home to the Iowa Braille and Sight Saving School. The roots of the school go back to 1852 when Samuel Bacon in Keokuk founded it. At Bacon's urging, it was moved to Iowa City and became a state school. When larger facilities were needed, an offer was made to locate the new campus in a community that was willing to donate 40 acres and make a gift of $5,000. Vinton came through. The following are the names of

the school from day one until today: Asylum for the Blind; Institution for the Instruction of the Blind; Iowa Institution of the Education of the Blind; Iowa College for the Blind; Iowa School for the Blind and, finally, the Iowa Braille and Sight Saving School.

Little House on the Prairie author, Laura Ingalls Wilder, had an older sister who became totally blind at the age of fourteen due to brain fever. Laura and her sister Mary were living in De Smet, South Dakota, at the time. Laura spent hours reading aloud to Mary and helping her memorize pertinent material. There was no school for the blind in South Dakota. A traveling missionary told them about the school in **Vinton** and the family decided to enroll Mary even though it was a struggle to make ends meet without added expenses. Mary rewarded them with exceptionally high academic achievements and she received 100 percent in deportment. In 1889, at the age of twenty-four, Mary graduated and returned to the family home in DeSmet, South Dakota. The Ingalls' story is one chapter in the overall success of this remarkable institution. The school contin-

Benton County

Pierce Lumber Inc., Belle Plaine

ues to teach the visually impaired how to adapt to their handicap and lead full lives.

After strolling around the **Vinton** downtown area, we stopped in at the Peony Chinese Restaurant for lunch. The atmosphere was bright and clean with the color green dominating. Chinese lanterns hung from the ceiling and wall hangings with Chinese motifs graced the walls. Chinese music soothed us as we dined on delicious Chinese food.

Leaving China we hit the road again with **Norway** as our destination. That's Norway, Iowa, a little town in southern **Benton County**. A Norwegian immigrant named Osman Tuttle founded the town in 1863. Evidently not many of his countrymen followed because in 1875, when the population reached 500, there was no Lutheran church. There were, however, Baptist, Methodist and Catholic churches. St. Michael's Catholic Church overlooks Norway's well-manicured baseball field, immortalized in the movie, *The Final Season*. **Norway** has a rich history of successful high school baseball teams that have produced major league players. The movie was about its last team before the school was consolidated

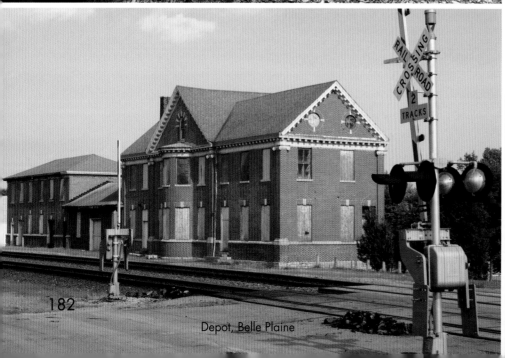

Depot, Belle Plaine

Belle Plaine

Norway

with another district. Mike Boddicker, a star pitcher for the Baltimore Orioles, and Hal Trosky, a slugging first baseman for the Cleveland Indians, are **Norway's** most notable baseball alumni.

As we have visited Iowa towns—large and small—we have noticed well-maintained parks and recreational facilities. When we talked to the locals and questioned why they like their town, good schools was typically the first quality mentioned. Sometimes I noted this when I wrote about a town, but it would be redundant to repeat it again at each stop. Suffice it to say that good schools and easy access to recreation venues are virtues of almost all Iowa towns.

Sports aren't the only statewide high school competitions. There are statewide contests in orchestra, jazz, choral singing, debate, and *The Des Moines Register* sponsors an Academic All-State recognition program for deserving scholars.

From **Norway** we drove west to **Belle Plaine**. On the east edge of town, we noticed a large sawmill operation with a sign stating, Pierce Lumber Inc., Buyer of Standing Timber. On further investigation, we learned that the company was a producer of fine Northern hardwoods and kiln-dried lumber.

The name **Belle Plaine** has a roaring west ring to it and the downtown buildings fronting the railroad had a character to them that reinforced that image. There was a tavern with a sign featuring a sexy girl and the name Oasis Tap. I visualized an interior atmosphere of ragtime music and dancing girls. As I was observing an imposing depot with boarded up windows, a mainline freight came roaring through town at full throttle. In the old days that train would have come to a halt. In the late 1800s, the Chicago and Northwestern selected **Belle Plaine** as the terminus of the Clinton division. A roundhouse with 30 stalls was built and 120 workmen were employed in the shops and yards. Needless to say, that stimulated growth.

In 1886, a well was drilled in **Belle Plaine** that turned out to be Iowa's most famous artesian well. A two-inch borehole was drilled 193 feet to trapped water that was under extreme pressure. The water came up with such force that it enlarged the hole from two inches to three feet and boiled up to eight feet in height. It threw out an estimated 400 carloads of sand, rocks and debris. Its estimated 3,472 gallons per minute flowed into two ditches to the Iowa River. It took over thirteen months of continuous effort to finally cap the well and stop the flow.

We followed the Iowa River out of **Belle Plaine** to the twin towns of **Tama** and **Toledo**. The picturesque drive is designated as a Scenic Byway. We soaked in the scenery of wild areas blending in with farms and small towns. Another option of appreciating this area would be sliding a canoe into the river and paddling downstream. The towns and farms would disappear leaving a landscape that has changed little from pre-white settlement days. Speaking of pre-white settlement days, the Iowa River valley has long held an attraction for Native Americans. And, it still does. The present day Meskwaki Indian Settlement is located on the banks of the river.

Note that the aforementioned Indian lands are referred to as a settlement rather than a reservation. The Meskwaki Tribe can trace its history back to their Algonquin origin in the Eastern woodland area of the St. Lawrence River

Peony Chinese Restaurant, Vinton

Sheridan Store, Tama County

183

Meskwaki Settlement

Johnathan Buffalo

valley. The French explorers gave them the name of Fox but they have always identified themselves as Meskwaki. Pressure from white settlers and encroachment from other tribes pushed them west. They didn't go easily. In the Fox Wars of 1701–1742, they fought the French so fiercely that the King of France declared war on them and called for their extermination. That is the only time in history that a European power has declared war on one Indian tribe. In 1735, the Meskwaki allied with the Sauk Tribe to fend off Europeans and other tribes. After the Blackhawk War of 1832, the U. S. government combined the two tribes for treaty-making purposes. They were named the Sac and Fox. The new name was for treaty-breaking purposes also, as you know the story of forcing Indians west as new waves of white settlers arrived. When the Sac and Fox (Meskwaki) were moved to a reservation in Kansas, they were removed from their bioregion and adapting was a problem. Some of the tribe hid in Iowa and others returned. In 1857, they bought 80 acres on the present settlement location. (They have since purchased another 7,000

184

Suzanne Wanatee and Connie

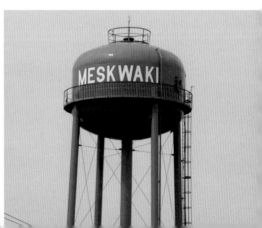

Meskwaki Casino/Hotel

acres.) That differed from Indians being relocated on federal lands called reservations and it caused a jurisdiction ambiguity between federal and state governments. The Meskwakis lived a relatively independent lifestyle for 30 years. In 1896, Iowa ceded all jurisdiction over the tribe to the federal government. Today, they are classified as Federal Indians. However, they live on a settlement they own as opposed to a reservation owned by the federal government.

We had the privilege of visiting with Johnathan Buffalo, the Meskwaki Settlement's historic preservation director. He formerly taught history at the settlement school and those teaching skills were evident as he told us about his people. The Meskwakis are proud of their heritage and have no desire to abandon their culture. Presently 80 to 90 percent speak the Meskwaki language and they have hosted an annual powwow for more than 93 years. They are making efforts at economic development without corrupting their traditional culture. Residents of the settlement do not individually own land—it is owned by the tribe, which is governed by a seven-member tribal coun-

cil. Some tillable land is leased to farmers and some is used by residents for gardens up to an acre in size. There are approximately 1,400 acres of timber—walnut, black oak, hard/soft maple and white pine. The Tribal Council has chartered the Meskwaki Enterprise Corporation with four directors appointed by the Tribal Council and three seats are filled with representatives of area businesses. The Meskwaki Casino/Hotel complex is the tribe's primary revenue source. Income from all enterprises goes into the tribal treasury with equal per capita payments made monthly from a general fund. It appears to be working. We observed well-maintained homes as we drove around the settlement. A new high school was under construction.

Johnathan's wife Suzanne Wanatee is clerk of court for the Tribal Council. She also spoke to us about the tribe's proud heritage. Even though history has not treated them kindly, present day Meskwakis have realized economic gains while holding onto their traditions. And, they live on a beautiful piece of land on the revered Iowa River.

At the Meskwaki Casino, Connie lost

her $10 allotment in 15 minutes. After ten casinos, the score is an $11 deficit.

Tama County takes its name from the wife of Poweshiek, a Sac and Fox (Meskwaki) chief. The word means "beautiful." It was the beauty of the open prairie and an abundance of timber in the Iowa River valley that attracted the first settlers—the Isaac Asher family. When they arrived in 1849, Indians in war paint met them. Initially the Indians strongly encouraged them to turn around, but after a long council of the two parties, they were allowed to settle peacefully. The first obstacle was dealt with; now all they had to do was face up to the other frontier challenges. An especially daunting task greeted them in the winter of 1857. The snow began on the first of December and continued falling for days until it reached a depth of two feet with drifts as high as twenty feet. Snow remained on the ground for three months. The barrier to travel or movement of any kind caused an inordinate amount of suffering.

The town of **Toledo** began as a mail drop-off site at the home of James H. Holden. Mr. Holden took the name from a book he was reading which was entitled

Meskwaki Settlement

185

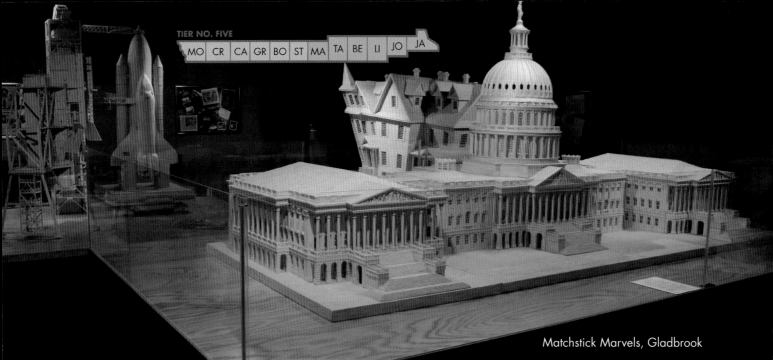

TIER NO. FIVE

| MO | CR | CA | GR | BO | ST | MA | TA | BE | LI | JO | JA |

Matchstick Marvels, Gladbrook

Tama County Courthouse, Toledo

Knights of Toledo in Spain. His house was located on the north side of the Iowa River and the stagecoach route was on the south side. That meant that twice weekly he had to cross the river to retrieve the mail—sometimes by swimming. A commission was formed in 1853 to locate a county seat site. The process became so frustrating that one commissioner randomly drove a stake into the ground and said, "This is it." The stake missed its mark as far as the railroad was concerned so another town named Iuka was platted on the Chicago & Northwestern Railroad line. The postal department changed the name to Tama City in 1866 and, in 1887, the word City was dropped from the name. Today, the two towns are located adjacent to each other and each has a population in the 2,500 to 3,000 range.

After observing the unique Lincoln Highway Bridge in **Tama**, we drove to **Toledo**. As we entered the town, we noticed a bronze cow and calf sculpture perched on a hill with a large oak tree backdrop. It was created by Neal Deaton to honor Norma "Duffy" Lyon of Iowa State Fair butter cow fame. The **Toledo**

186

Traer

Toledo

Tama

native used butter rather than metal as a medium for sculpting cows, people and objects at the Fair. After 46 years of creating topical scenes, she retired in 2006.

The Wieting Theatre was the latest in opera house construction when it was built in 1912. It was a gift to the people of **Toledo** by Mrs. P. G. Wieting in honor of her husband. It is still in use with movies shown on most Friday, Saturday and Sunday evenings. Actors, singers and dancers take the stage on numerous other occasions.

Additional **Tama/Toledo** attractions include: a 200-acre ATV park located along the Iowa River; the John Ernest Vineyard and Winery; the Tama County Historical Museum and Genealogical Library; and the 1866 historic courthouse with a completely restored, 1914 Seth Thomas clock.

"Wind Up in Traer" is the slogan in the north **Tama County** town of **Traer**. Inspiration for the slogan is an unusual spiral staircase located on the street side of a downtown sidewalk. It rises to a platform that leads to a second-story entrance. In 1894, it was public access to a newspaper office.

James "Tama Jim" Wilson, from **Traer**, was the longest-tenured Secretary of Agriculture in U.S. history. He was appointed to the post by President McKinley in 1897 and continued to serve under Presidents Theodore Roosevelt and William Howard Taft. At the beginning of his term, there were 2,444 employees; by 1909 the force had increased to nearly 11,000. Under his watch, the Food and Drug Act was passed, which set standards for parity in food and drugs. He was a politician for the people. In 1867, he ran for a state legislature seat with "fencing in cattle instead of crops" as one of his issues. Up to that point, rich cattlemen let their herds roam and the poor crop farmers had to do the fencing. You can learn more about fair-minded Wilson at the Traer Historical Museum.

We made one more stop in **Tama County** to see Matchstick Marvels in **Gladbrook**. This is an amazing, "How does he do that?" kind of exhibit. Patrick Acton, a native of Gladbrook, constructs large-scale models using matchsticks and Elmer's glue. The U.S. Capitol, churches, ships, the space shuttle and launching apparatus, as well as figures, are some of

his subjects. And, he does it in his spare time. He is employed as a career counselor at Iowa Valley Community College District in Marshalltown. He has sold 15 pieces to *Ripley's Believe It or Not*. There are approximately 15 large models at the Matchstick Marvels Tourist Center.

We took Highway 96 out of **Gladbrook** heading west to Highway 14 where we turned south with **Marshalltown** as our destination. As we approached Marshalltown, the Marshall County Courthouse came into view. Sitting erect and elegant on a rise in the landscape, it could have passed for a state capitol building. Entering downtown, it came into full view; it is an exceptionally attractive example of Italian Renaissance style architecture. Located half a block from the courthouse is the Tremont on Main Inn, our overnight accommodations in **Marshalltown**. It was late in the afternoon so we checked in, deposited our luggage and returned to the car for a twenty-minute trip southwest to The Harvester Golf Club.

There was no intent to play golf on this trip—we just wanted to take a look.

Toledo

Traer

187

Marshall County

Marshall County Courthouse, Marshalltown

The Harvester is Iowa's premier golf course. Shortly after it was built, it was rated by *Golf Digest* as one of the nation's ten best new golf courses. In 2006, *Golf* magazine rated it in the top twenty for your money. It sits back away from the surrounding farmland in a lush valley with mature oak trees dominating the wooded areas. Blue water ponds, bright green fairways and ochre-colored grasses in the roughs round out the palette. I played it years ago and it was the ultimate golfing experience for me. I came prepared with a bag of balls to replace the ones I expected to lose on this challenging course. As it turned out, I had a better than average round with a minimum loss of my ball inventory. A lodge and condominiums are available for overnight stays. There is a small commercial area; new home development in the communities surrounding the course is ongoing.

After leaving the classy golf course, we returned to our classy room at the Tremont Inn. The Tremont building has been a **Marshalltown** landmark since 1874. The original hotel was destroyed by fire and rebuilt in 1904. The rebuilt Tremont survived and it has recently been

188

Marshalltown

Jennifer and J. P. Howard

The Harvester Golf Club, Marshall County

lovingly restored and refurbished by Jennifer and J. P. Howard. It now houses two restaurants, four condominiums, six hotel rooms, meeting rooms and the Howard's residence. The Howards gave us a tour of their spacious apartment. It is uptown elegant!

Our room was also spacious and elegant with a high ceiling and a king-size bed. The decorative pillows on the bed were nicely understated. After freshening up a bit, we took the stairs down to the Tremont on Main Restaurant where we dined on a bleu cheese/chicken pasta dish and listened to Brian Joens, a folk/jazz singer who puts his style into popular songs. His voice and guitar playing had a distinctly pleasing character and the volume was just right. A perky, attractive young lady waited on us as we relaxed in the soft glow of candlelight. We were truly having a cosmopolitan experience in Marshalltown. We decided to linger with an after dinner drink.

We slept well and the next morning we met the Howards at the Italian Grille, their other restaurant in the Tremont building. This restaurant had a coffee shop atmosphere and again the Howards did a superb job. Jennifer is a Marshalltown native. After graduating from the University of Wyoming with a degree in journalism, she moved to Phoenix where she bought two coffee shops. Twenty-two years later, she returned to her roots and opened a coffee shop in Marshalltown. She met J.P. in front of the Tremont. J.P., a native of Cresco, Iowa, had also decided to try life in another part of the country. He went the other direction to West Palm Beach, Florida. Upon his return to Iowa, he started a golf distribution business serving Iowa and Nebraska. Ten years later, he retired from the golf business and bought the Tremont building. That was in 1998 and the first move was to relocate Jennifer's Muddy Waters Coffee Shop to what is now the Italian Grille. They stuck with the renovations one step at a time and now have the satisfaction of sharing the results with their customers.

Taking one last swallow of coffee, we moved on to our next appointment with another remarkable **Marshalltown** resident. Dean Elder, Jr. is a broker associate with Coldwell Banker and an unabashed **Marshalltown** booster. We definitely got a feel for the community during our session with him. Quality manufacturing, an Iowa staple, is manifested in **Marshalltown's** large and small companies. Fisher Controls was founded as Fisher Governor Company in the 1880s when William Fisher invented a pressure pump governor. It is now the world's leading supplier of control valve technology, products and services. The company continues to expand their **Marshalltown** operations and presently employs about 1,000 people. The Fishers are good business people and they have a strong interest in the arts. Iowa State University's C. Y. Stevens Auditorium and Fisher Theatre are beneficiaries as is the Fisher Community Center in **Marshalltown**. The latter is a beautiful complex with an impressive art gallery and outdoor sculpture collection and is home to the Martha-Ellen Tye Theatre for the Performing Arts.

Marshalltown was only 27 years old when Dave Lennox moved from Chicago looking for new opportunities. Fifteen years later, in 1895, he designed and built the heating industry's first riveted steel furnace. It revolutionized the

Tremont Hotel, Marshalltown

Italian Grille, Marshalltown

189

Fisher Controls, Marshalltown

Fisher Community Center, Marshalltown

industry and the Lennox brand has been a leader ever since. Today, about 1,200 employees produce quality heating and air conditioning products at the **Marshalltown** plant. There are 40 additional manufacturing and technology companies ranging from Marshalltown Trowel to Fake Space—a high tech, virtual reality company. Marshalltown is also the home of Wolfe Eye Clinic, a national leader in eye care.

Agriculture-related industries are led by a Swift and Company plant that processes over 17,000 hogs per day. Recently, some illegal immigration problems came to a head at this plant. It is difficult to come to any consensus on what measures should be taken. But, again, it was reported to me that the Hispanic immigrants have been assimilated into the community and there is generally a mutual respect.

Dean Elder, Jr., a life-long resident of **Marshalltown**, has been in the real estate business for over 40 years. He said, "We're so happy we live in Iowa. We have just as big of TV screens as they do in New York. **Marshalltown** is very vibrant and resilient. We rise to the occa-

Community Y, Marshalltown

Dean Elder, Jr.

Martha-Ellen Tye Theatre for the Performing Arts, Marshalltown

sion. Bond election issues pass. The community does include downtown. We've been making trips to Washington, D. C. to get things done. There are a lot of caring people."

A generous endowment of $28 million by Virginia Horne Henry spearheaded the building of the Community Y, a combination YMCA and YWCA. This magnificent complex tops a list of many recreational options in **Marshalltown**. It is good to have these facilities to work off the food featured in the town's festivals. BBQ, Buggies and Tunes Festival features a barbeque competition, a classic car show and live bands. Sounds like a perfect mix! The Central Iowa Music Festival, combining a diverse music offering with sweet corn and pork, also sounds like fun. Then there is the Octoberfest in September that is named Octemberfest.

Marshalltown has been blessed from the beginning with good, pragmatic leaders. Central Iowa Settlement began in 1846 and, by 1851, there were about 350 settlers in **Marshall County**. That was when a young, determined man named Henry Anson arrived. Anson's goal was

to find an ideal site to establish a town. He found it on a ridge between Linn Creek and the Iowa River valley. He immediately began lobbying for the county seat and went through the typical Iowa county seat fight.

In 1853, a town was platted and Anson persuaded a man by the name of Greenleaf M. Woodbury to use his milling experience to build a flour mill on the Iowa River. The courthouse fight was finally settled in 1858 when Anson's community of Marshall donated a 40- by 60-foot, two-story building to use as the courthouse. Woodbury used his influence to get the nation's first transcontinental railroad routed through Marshalltown. By coincidence, the first telegraph line across the continent was strung through the city at the same time. Thanks to these men, there is now a striking, imposing courthouse perched on a ridge overlooking a thriving, can-do community.

Henry Anson's son, Adrian "Cap" Anson, was a **Marshalltown** baseball star before he turned pro and signed with the Philadelphia Athletics. He later became captain of the Chicago White Stockings and was a leading hitter in the

National League. He played professionally for a record 27 years. "Cap" Anson is in the Cooperstown Baseball Hall of Fame and he was the first inductee into the Iowa Athletic Hall of Fame.

About twenty miles west of **Marshalltown** is **State Center**. This is the geographical center of Iowa. It is also bills itself as the "Rose Capital of Iowa." Continuing down the road we crossed into **Story County** and drove to the county seat of **Nevada**. It is pronounced (neh-VAY-da) and there is no gambling. In fact, it was named ten years before the western state of the same name. However, both the state and the Iowa town take their name from the Sierra Nevada mountain range.

Nevada might be named after a mountain range, but it is located in the flattest part of Iowa. This glacerized landscape extends down from Minnesota through the central third of northern Iowa. The flatness is interrupted by river valleys—most notably the Des Moines River valley. The countryside becomes rugged again for a few miles when you approach Iowa's largest interior river. Early **Story County** settlers found this

Blades arrive for the construction of wind turbines in Story County

Bergen Lutheran Church, Roland

Ben Britton's sculpture garden, Zearing

open country inhospitable, but over the years, conditions and markets changed so that, today, it is the most valuable agricultural land in the state.

The present, post-modern Story County Courthouse in **Nevada** is the fourth incarnation of the first courthouse. It was built in 1967. County government and Donnelly Marketing are the major employers in this town of about 7,000 people. Donnelly Marketing's primary business is direct mail advertising. In 1995, Norman Crampton selected **Nevada** as one of the "100 Best Small Towns in America."

Years ago we bought a metal sculpture for our garden from Ben Britton at a Des Moines' art festival. It is a turtle constructed from farm machinery parts. We love it and it prompts many positive comments. We have read articles and have seen pictures of Ben's sculpture garden at his home in **Zearing**. We decided to swing by and see the real thing. We located the garden and his home and knocked on the door seeking permission to look at and photograph the garden. Ben wasn't home, but wife Carolyn okayed the request. She is also a talented artist work-

192
Nevada

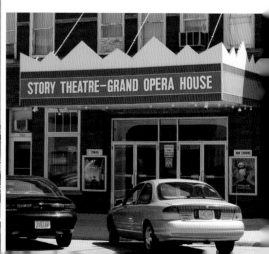

Story County Courthouse, Nevada

ing with ink and colored pencil.

The Brittons started the garden in 1994 and have hauled in several hundred tons of rock and planted a variety of bushes, trees and perennials. They dug three ponds in 1996. Rock and pebble art throughout provide a natural environment for Ben's numerous metal sculptures. It is beautiful. As impressive as it is now, it is still under development and probably always will be. It has been featured in numerous television programs and newspaper articles. They periodically have "Art in Our Yard" festivals.

Leaving **Zearing**, we again headed west toward **Story City**. As we passed through **Roland** we noticed an attractive, brick and stone church with the name Bergen Lutheran Church. Could this be a Norwegian community? Indeed it was and it is also the hometown of a remarkable athlete, Gary Thompson.

Iowa has its own *Hoosiers* story of a very small town taking on the city schools and beating them in the game of basketball. In 1951, Roland High School, led by its star sophomore guard Gary Thompson, made it all the way to the finals of the Iowa state basketball cham-

pionship. In those days, the schools were not divided into classes based on size. Roland had to beat schools like Waterloo West and Des Moines East for the privilege of meeting mighty Davenport in the finals. They led Davenport for three quarters before losing in the last three minutes. Little, 5-foot-6-inch Gary was all over the floor harassing the bigger players, stealing their dribbles and making baskets from every angle. He went on to star for Iowa State University in basketball and baseball, earning All-American honors in both sports. In one notable Iowa State game, a Gary Thompson-led team upset Kansas, the number one team in the country. Wilt Chamberlain, the 7-foot, All-American pivot man was on that team. Wilt showed some class by going to ISU's locker room after the game and congratulating them. Gary played five years of AAU ball for the Phillips 66ers, coached them another four years and then became a nationally known broadcaster. He is a wonderful man who has been a strong supporter of ISU and Iowa in general. And at 73, he is one of the state's top senior golfers.

There were some Danes, Swedes and

Germans joining the Norwegians in settling **Story City** but it appears the Norwegian culture became the dominant ethnic character. However, the Scandinavian Days festival name also celebrates the Danes and Swedes but leaves out the Germans unless they are Scandinavian wannabes. At any rate, we drove into town to see the Norwegian (Scandinavian) touches. There are Norse motifs here and there but the overall look doesn't tip off its character. The downtown Story Theatre/Grand Opera House is Iowa's oldest, continuously operating theater. In North Park there is a 1913 carousel with hand-carved horses, pigs, dogs and roosters you can ride or you can sit in a chariot or whirling tub. Restoration has made them look new; during our visit, they were merrily circling paintings of Indians, cowboys and landscapes while the 1936 Wurlitzer military band organ played on.

On the other side of town, just beyond the business district, is the Cottage on Broad Restaurant. We have read excellent reviews about their food and atmosphere. Award-winning chef Chris Hansen owns it. It was our intention to eat lunch there,

Story City

Story City

193

Jack Trice Stadium, Iowa State University

USDA
United States
Department of
Agriculture
Animal and Plant
Health Inspection
Service
Veterinary Services

Center for
Veterinary
Biologics -
Laboratory

National
Veterinary
Services
Laboratories

1800 Dayton Avenue

Ames

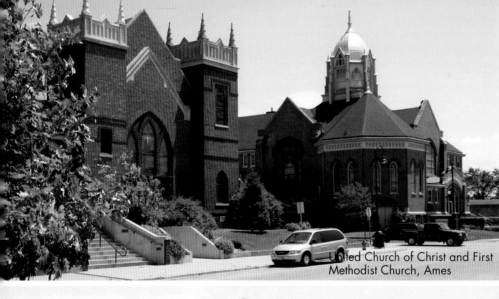

United Church of Christ and First Methodist Church, Ames

but we arrived after their 2:00 p.m. lunch-hour closing. Our next choice was the Royal Café where we missed the noon buffet. That was not a problem, as we preferred their barbecue sandwich. The décor was clean and unadorned and our servings were placed on little paper doilies—a Norwegian/American touch.

On to **Ames** where we met Tom Flack at the Café Diem Coffee House for an after-lunch iced tea. Tom is a semi-retired pharmacist who continues to work part-time as a relief pharmacist. He is a volunteer who has served on boards such as Youth Shelter Services and Heartland Senior Services. He has read for IRIS (Iowa Radio Reading Services for the Blind and Print-Handicapped) in both Des Moines and **Ames**. And, he is a past winner of the Ames Unsung Hero of the Year award. He enjoys Ames mainly because of Iowa State University's contributions to the culture with its many attractions. He also says, "We are fly-over country and we get mistaken for Ohio and Idaho, but it is good to live where you don't fear your neighbors." It was an enjoyable tea break.

Ames was established in 1884 to

Tom Flack

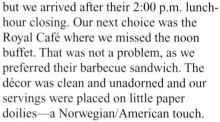

194

Barilla pasta plant , Ames

C. Y. Stephens Auditorium, Iowa State University

serve the Cedar Rapids and Missouri River railroads. Presently the Union Pacific runs 60 to 70 trains per day through town. They maintain a small yard between **Ames** and Nevada. There is also a small branch line that extends north to Eagle Grove. Iowa State University and the Iowa Department of Transportation are the major employers in Ames but there is diversification in jobs with the National Animal Disease Center, 3M, Hach Companies, Sigler Companies, Sunstrand, Ball and Barilla.

In addition to typical Iowa recreational amenities, the Iowa Games Annual Sports Festival is held in **Ames**. Everyone—young, old and weekend athletes—has an opportunity to compete in Olympic-style competition. Choose your event and if it isn't available, it probably will be next year. It is very popular and great fun.

In 1859, **Story County** was chosen as the location of the State Agriculture College and Model Farm. In 1862, it became the first institution designated as a land-grant college. It was coeducational from the beginning and, in addition to career training for the farmer, courses were offered in mechanical, civil, electri-

cal and mining engineering. Iowa State University has built on that solid footing into a highly rated school that is presently numbered among the top 50 public universities in the nation. It ranks number two in licenses and options executed on its intellectual property and number five in licenses and options that yield income. The world's first electronic digital computing device, the Atanasoff-Berry computer, was developed on ISU's campus. Today, strong curriculums in business, humanities and the arts have been added to its engineering and agriculture roots. The College of Veterinary Medicine is a national leader.

In 1895, an Iowa State football team was sent to Evanston to play a highly rated Northwestern team and they beat them 36-0. The next day the *Chicago Tribune* headline read, "Struck by a Cyclone: It Comes from Iowa and Devastates Evanston Town." The Cyclone moniker stuck. The present day Cyclones compete in the powerful Big 12. Their strongest sport over the years has been wrestling where they have been national champions eight times.

Two hundred works of art grace a

campus of 160 buildings. The American Society of Landscape Architects listed the 20-acre central campus lawn as a "medallion site" in 1999. Yale and the University of Virginia were the only other schools to receive that designation.

A major artistic feature in the library is a mural executed by artists under Grant Wood's direction. It was a federal public works project designed to give unemployed artists work in the 1930s. My favorite building, C. Y. Stephens Auditorium, was named Iowa Building of Century (1900–1999) by the Iowa Chapter of the American Institute of Architects. I agree!

Another element of extraordinary beauty was added to the campus when the horticulture gardens were moved to a new site where dramatic improvements were made. Bobbi and Roy Reiman of Greendale, Wisconsin, made the move possible with their financial gift. It is situated on 14 acres just south of Jack Trice Stadium, creating a striking entrance to Iowa State University. It consists of eleven distinct gardens, an indoor conservatory, an indoor butterfly area, a gift shop, a café and five supporting green-

Reiman Gardens, Ames

Reiman Gardens, Ames

195

Kate Shelley Bridge with its concrete replacement showing through the steel girders

Boone County Courthouse, Boone

houses. Reiman Gardens has become a major central Iowa attraction.

A little further west on Highway 30 is another town that owes its start to the railroad and still embraces it whole-heartedly. The Boone and Scenic Valley Railroad offers train rides over a trestle bridge and through the scenic Des Moines River valley. Pufferbilly Days, an annual celebration of railroad heritage, has grown to be one of Iowa's top five festivals. They have a historical museum that features early **Boone** railroading and coalmining, as well as many other things of historical interest. Five miles south of **Boone**, in the town of Moingona, there is a memorial park and museum dedicated to Kate Shelley who, as a young girl, performed a heroic act that prevented a train disaster.

Boone is also the county seat of **Boone County**. And it was named after the famous frontiersman's son Captain Nathan Boone. He and his entourage camped in what is now **Boone County** while on a mission to become acquainted with great Sioux Chief Wabasha. That was in 1835 and, in 1847, the county was established. The

196

Hindu Temple and Cultural Center, Madrid

Backpackers at Ledges State Park

Ledges State Park

railroad came in 1865 and along with it came the town of **Boone**.

Kate Shelley was an infant when her parents emigrated from Ireland to America in 1865. After a brief stay with relatives in Freeport, Illinois, the family moved to a 160-acre farm near Moingona. In 1878, her father died in a railroad accident and her mother was in poor health, so 13-year-old Kate helped support the family by doing farm work and hunting. On July 6, 1881, a flash flood on Honey Creek took out some timbers that supported a trestle bridge. A pusher locomotive sent to check track conditions plunged through the weakened bridge into Honey Creek. Kate heard the crash and rushed to the scene. She told surviving crew members she would get them help and then started crawling across the damaged span with only lightning as illumination. Once across, she ran a half mile to the Moingona Depot to sound the alarm and stop an eastbound passenger train. She then led a party back to the accident scene where they were able to rescue two crewmembers. Two other crewmembers were lost in the floodwaters. The train with 200 passengers aboard was stopped in **Ogden**. She was recognized nationally for her bravery and she received numerous awards and gifts. In succeeding years, she served as a teacher and stationmaster. She never married and she continued to take care of her mother until she died in 1909. Kate passed away in 1912.

The world's longest and highest, double-track railroad bridge goes from hilltop to hilltop across the Des Moines River valley a couple of miles west of **Boone**. This 100-year-old, steel trestle structure bears the name of heroine Kate Shelley. However, the days are numbered for this historic bridge. It is on a main line of the Union Pacific and trains are slowed to a crawl as they cross the bridge. With an average of 70 trains a day, bottlenecks are created. A new bridge of reinforced concrete and steel is under construction. It will still retain the honor of being the world's longest and highest, double-track bridge. And two trains will be able to meet on the bridge traveling at 70 miles per hour.

One of the oldest and most visited state parks in Iowa is located in the hills of the Des Moines River valley just south of **Boone**. The Ledges State Park offers picnicking, camping, hiking trails and beautiful scenery. It takes its name from unusual sandstone rock formations and fossilized trees. An unfortunate side effect of developing Saylorville Lake downstream near Des Moines is that, during high water when the lake pool rises, it floods the Lower Ledges. After this year's floods, most of the park was closed for cleanup. That prevented us from taking a scenic drive through the park. We have taken that trip in the past and it is truly a beautiful part of Iowa.

Central Iowa diversity continues to grow and manifest itself. The latest proof is a new Hindu Temple and Cultural Center south of **Madrid**. The location was chosen to serve an estimated 1,000 Indians within a 60-mile radius that includes the Des Moines' metro area and Ames. Many are drawn to central Iowa's growing need for skilled workers in the technology and science industries. The incredible detail on the temple's towers and figures is rendered in concrete by sculptors from India. They have had to adapt to the Iowa climate for much of the year, but on the hot and humid day we

YMCA Camp, Boone

Boone

Boone

Ogden

visited, they should have felt at home.

There are many other things of interest in **Boone** and the surrounding area. Mamie Eisenhower's birthplace has been restored and welcomes visitors. The Boone Speedway is another Iowa dirt track with a national reputation. The one-third mile oval hosts weekly races April through August and the IMCA (International Motor Contest Association) holds its Super Nationals at the track. The 378-acre Iowa Arboretum, containing hundreds of species of trees, shrubs and flowers in a scenic setting, is located in the heart of **Boone County**. The Snus Hill Winery produces wine from American and French-American grapes. Adult and youth camps dot the Des Moines River valley and its hills.

After a morning of checking out **Boone's** amenities, we took a healthy lunch break at Van Hemert's Dutch Oven Bakery. We split a club sandwich and each of us ordered a cup of soup and skim milk. We fought off the temptation to buy any of the delicious pastries.

We left **Boone** heading west and almost immediately descended into the Des Moines River valley. As we crossed

198

Des Moines River, Boone County

David Williamson

Boone County

the river, we noticed a couple of canoes with their passengers absorbing a lovely natural environment disturbed only by an occasional bridge. They might have rented those canoes from the Seven Oaks recreation complex on the west side of the bridge. This business offers other summer outfitting and activities such as kayaking, tube floating, paintball, tent camping, mountain biking/hiking trails, motocross and lodge facilities. During the winter, north-facing slopes, snow-making and a chair lift provide the best central Iowa has to offer in snow skiing, snow boarding and snow tubing. They liked this last winter's weather.

Prior to making our foray into **Boone County**, we received a lead on an interesting person we should visit. His name is David Williamson and he lives in a home made of recycled material on an acreage west of **Ogden**. When we pulled onto his property, there was no doubt we were at the right place because the buildings were unique to say the least. An exuberant man greeted us and we entered into non-stop dialogue as we explored his digs.

Almost every non-conventional mater-ial you can think of or would never have thought of was included in the construction of his house. He said he only spent $4,500 in materials but there was probably $1 million worth of his labor. There is no air conditioning; stoves he built provide the heat. Much of the recycled material was taken from abandoned farm-steads on land that was consolidated into larger farms. An outbuilding with corrugated steel siding and a sign proclaiming RANCHO WEIRDO provides space for his sculpture work. Behind that building there is an ample amount of found treasures ready to be recycled into sculptures or whatever. When I asked him in what setting he would like to be photographed, he replied, "I can fire up the forge so that the photo can capture the flames while I hammer some steel." This was on a humid day where the temperature was pushing 90 degrees.

David has a self-deprecating sense of humor and is an original but he is no weirdo. He is a very intelligent and talented man. In addition to his sculpture and recycled projects, he is a poet extra-ordinaire and a business consultant— teaching creativity as a survival skill in today's economy. He sells thoughts, not things. In the last year, he has given workshops in Seattle, Boston, Philadelphia, Portland, Savannah, Jackson, Tucson and South Padre Island. He volunteers for AWARE (A Watershed Awareness River Expedition) helping them clean junk out of Iowa's rivers and create sculptures from said junk. The sculpting is done live at the Iowa State Fair. At one point while we were sitting at a table and talking, he started telling us about his son playing with farm toys. As he continued talking, I realized he had morphed into reciting a poem he had written. It's a beautiful and heart warm-ing piece entitled "Farming at My Feet."

We continued our drive through the flattest part of Iowa. It is not table-flat. As we motored along, we came to high points where we could see for miles. From those elevations the countryside looks like one, huge, productive garden. The enjoyment of that pleasing sight was interrupted by our first whiff of livestock confinement odors. We had covered over half the state at that point, so it seemed the odor problem was not that prevalent. However, I'm sure this is no consolation

Williamson's home

Williamson's home

199

Spring Lake Park, Greene County

Shannon Black

to those who have to live with it. The problem needs to be dealt with, as well as any other pollution problem. We support the good people looking for solutions.

As we approached the outskirts of **Jefferson**, we were greeted with huge storage bins and elevators sporting the West Central logo. This is a full service, farmer-owned co-operative with a national and international presence. Incorporated in 1933, it is currently one of the nation's 20 largest grain companies. More than 3,000 farmers have paid a one-time $100 membership fee to own stock. Dividends are based on the amount of business a member has done with the company. Co-ops buy, sell and ship grain and in most cases provide other services and products for the farmer.

Greene County's soil, that yields gold in the form of corn and soybeans, was once thought to have gold of the mineral sort. In 1875, word spread that gold had been found in paying quantities in a small stream. A company was quickly formed and the stream was dammed and hopes ran high. Then the spring floods came and washed out the dam and, if there was any gold, it was flushed

Greene County Courthouse, Jefferson

200

Mahanay Memorial Carillon Tower, Jefferson

Jefferson

Bikers Vicki and Mike Lauzon of Boone (Jefferson trailhead)

downstream. Other efforts at finding treasure in the earth yielded attempts at coalmining but the veins weren't very thick in the area and the resulting mines didn't do very well. However, coalmining efforts revealed large deposits of fine potters' clay that was used to manufacture tile and brick.

One natural disaster that is non-existent in Iowa today is a prairie or forest fire. This was not always true. Before the open grasslands were fully cultivated, grass fires were major, fearful events. Firebreaks in the form of two parallel belts of plowed furrows were made to protect settlements. When an approaching fire was seen, the grass between the belts was lit on fire to widen the firebreak. The people would vigilantly watch for any embers that blew across the break and quickly extinguish them. In the aftermath, the prairie was black and desolate until new growth emerged and renewed the spirits. It was symbolic of the despair and renewal of pioneer life.

The first pork from **Greene County** to reach eastern markets was driven on foot 200 miles to Keokuk. Uncle Billy Anderson was the drover and

it is assumed that several of his 17 children accompanied him. There is no information on how much market weight was lost on the trip.

John C. Harker of Hardin Township was a farmer, inventor and successful businessman. He also fed his cattle well. In the early 1900s, John and his brother Simon, owned the two largest steers in the world. The larger one was 7 feet 1 inch tall, 12 feet long and weighed 3,970 pounds. The steers were shown around the country and when they died, they were mounted and displayed in a San Francisco museum for about 50 years.

A structure of imposing size in today's **Jefferson** was built in 1966. The Mahanay Memorial Carillon Tower can be seen for miles and, if you take the elevator to the top, you can see for miles. The late William Floyd and Dora L. Mahanay's will provided the finances and directive for the construction of the 162-foot tower. An electronic carillon belted out tunes as we strolled around **Jefferson's** attractive square.

A small screw had dislodged itself from Connie's glasses and we were hoping there would be an optical shop in

Jefferson to replace it. We parked our car just off the square and looked up and there it was—Eye Care Associates, P. C. Shannon Black, a delightful, young lady behind the reception desk assured Connie she could fix her glasses. Connie started thinking she might be able to help in another way—by answering our questions about life in **Jefferson**. She willingly agreed and the conversation began.

Upon graduating from Jefferson High School, Shannon enrolled at DMACC and then Lincoln (Nebraska) Southeast Community College, majoring in restaurant management. With this training she secured a job in Lincoln, managing a restaurant for five years. She didn't like the restaurant hours and she preferred small town life so it was back to **Jefferson** and she couldn't be happier. Her husband Chad was born in Des Moines, raised in Texas and is presently assistant manager at a Home Depot in Des Moines. He tolerates the hour commute because he also loves **Jefferson**. Getting together with friends on weekends for grilling and socializing while watching their two children play in the neighborhood with their friends' children

David Williamson sculpture, Jefferson Public Library

West Central Cooperative, Jefferson

201

Darwin Pierce, Whiterock
Conservancy farm manager

River House, Whiterock Conservancy

North branch of Raccoon River, Greene County

is a favorite activity. Shannon was active in high school with cheerleading and golf. She continues to be very active in the community by serving on the city council, Bell Tower steering committee, swim team board and Kiwanis. The Bell Tower Festival, held the second week in June, is her favorite celebration. It features an hour-long parade and draws alumni back for reunions. Athletes around the world use equipment manufactured in **Jefferson**. AAI produces gymnastic equipment—their logo will be seen at the Olympics. Power Lift specializes in weights for strength training.

As we left **Jefferson** we were not sure which street would take us to Highway 4. We stopped to ask some people in a church parking lot for directions. I looked one of them in the eye and as I began to ask my question, I realized I was talking to Chuck Offenburger of Iowa Boy and RAGBRAI fame. Much of my pre-trip knowledge about Iowa was gleaned from his Iowa Boy columns that used to appear in *The Des Moines Register*. During that time, he also served as a RAGBRAI (Register's Annual Great Bike Ride Across Iowa) leader and

John Deere implement dealer, Manning

Ben Teuch,
Carla and Chuck
Offenburger

Photo in Garst farmhouse

Campers at Whiterock Conservancy

Giant cottonwood dwarfs
Connie at Garst house

reporter. He, his wife Carla and Ben Teuch were discussing plans for the next week's RAGBRAI overnight in Jefferson. They agreed to have their photo taken and then Chuck helped us find our way.

Highway 4 took us across the north branch of the Raccoon River. After crossing the bridge we stopped to view a pretty pastoral scene. The river had a meandering quality with a large, sweeping bend in the foreground and a sandbar in the crook of the bend. Lush meadows with trees randomly placed in a pleasing pattern completed the picture.

In 1959, Soviet Premier Nikita Khrushchev wanted to see how modern agricultural practices in America could help feed his country and the world. That was one of the few positive exchanges between the two countries during the Cold War. The farm chosen to showcase America's agricultural know-how was owned by Roswell Garst. This colorful man was an innovator in hybrid seed corn, fertilizer and cattle feeding. I recall a picture I saw in the newspaper of him throwing a shovel full of corn at some reporters/photographers who were crowding him. He and Khrushchev seemed to

be at ease with each other.

The farm is now part of the Whiterock Conservancy, which includes the Whiterock Resort. It is a gift of the Garst family of about 5,000 acres that runs along the Middle Raccoon River valley south of **Coon Rapids**. Through Whiterock Resort, the Conservancy hopes to help people see the strong connection between people and the land by providing a place they can interact with the environment. Fishing, canoeing, hiking, camping, biking, horseback riding and additional activities provide opportunities for this interaction.

We spent the night in the farmhouse that the Roswell Garst family lived in at the time of Khrushchev's visit. He didn't stay overnight but my guess is he would have been put up in the room we occupied. There was a photo of him arm in arm with Roswell and Adlai Stevenson. There were many other photos of the big event throughout the dining and living rooms. It was a nice, comfortable home without pretension. The exteriors of the buildings on the farm needed some sprucing up. Other areas of the complex that we checked out were also a bit shy of

top condition. An exception was the River House located on some well-manicured grounds with beautiful flower gardens and a great view of the Middle Raccoon River valley. The total complex is a work in progress with great potential.

We drove to **Manning** for our evening sustenance. **Manning's** identifying character is its German heritage and love of music. The Manning Liederkranz, a singing society for men, began in 1891. They practiced every week and performed regularly until World War I when they decided it would be prudent to quit singing German songs. They resumed after the war and were a forerunner to a plethora of music groups and bands to follow. In 1996, groundbreaking was held for the rebuilding of a hausbarn (combination house and barn) that had been dismantled in Germany. German workers with the help of local volunteers labored diligently to put the components back together. The thatched roof required 6,500 bundles of six- to eight-foot reeds.

Cliff's Place on **Manning's** main street made minimal efforts at developing a German theme. There was a small pic-

Original Garst Seed Corn plant

Hausbarn, Manning

203

Carroll

Kevin Boersma

Restored Carroll Depot

ture of a man in traditional German lederhosen on the men's restroom door. I didn't check the women's. The menu was straight American. We had a couple of glasses of Miller High Life draws as we waited for our food. The beer's taste took us back to our younger days before they started corrupting this delicious beer with all their new varieties. The place wasn't particularly busy, but our order was taking a long time. I was about ready to inquire when several employees came parading out of the kitchen with armfuls of carryouts. We received our food very shortly after that.

In 1917, the Eighteenth Amendment to the U.S. Constitution was passed making the sale of alcoholic drinks illegal. The law made an activity which was practiced by close to a majority of the people illegal. That led to a whole new class of lawbreakers. Al Capone immediately saw the potential and built an organized crime empire that is the model for today's underworld. During that period illegal distillers around the **Carroll County** town of **Templeton** developed a rye whiskey that gained a reputation as the "good stuff." It reportedly was Al

Carroll County Courthouse, Carroll

Capone's favorite drink and through his distribution, Templeton Rye gained a reputation as the best whiskey in Chicago. The bootlegging was a matter of survival for many families around Templeton and the basis for expanded criminal activity in other areas. Bootlegging was the answer to a very bad law. I'm not going to be judgmental here.

Scott Bush's great-grandfather and other family members were involved in the illegal production of whiskey in **Carroll County**. This bright young man graduated from the University of Iowa with honors and earned a master's degree from the MIT Sloan School of Management. After achieving business success on the East Coast, he decided to return to Iowa and revive an old family enterprise—only this time around distilling the whiskey was going to be done legally. Now you can buy Templeton Rye at your grocery or liquor store.

The Templeton Rye Distillery is housed in a steel building in **Templeton**. Kevin Boersma, the distillery manager, gave us a tour of the growing enterprise. The recipes are the same as the illegal product and sales are good. At the end of the tour we were treated to a sip at a bar in a very attractive hospitality room. It was smooth and smoky-oak delicious.

An older established business on Highway 141, just south of **Templeton**, is the Corner Station Café. Donna and Joe Kemper have been serving up good ol' Midwestern staples for 25 years. There were a couple of semis parked alongside the highway and a few pickups in the parking lot. Donna was cooking and Joe was serving and kibitzing with customers. He made us feel right at home; the pork tenderloin and chicken sandwiches were good, too.

As we drove to **Carroll**, the county seat of **Carroll County**, we noticed some old fashioned advertising—five Burma Shave signs. They read: The guy who drives/so close behind/is he lonesome/or just blind?/Burma Shave. Do they still make Burma Shave?

Ninety percent of the total farmland in **Carroll County** is cropland with the remainder in pasture and woodlands. In a typical year there is a yield of 23 million bushels of corn and 7 million bushels of soybeans. **Carroll County** is ranked sixth in the state in hog production and second in cattle production. The headquarters for West Central Cooperative is in Ralston; POET Biorefining (ethanol) is in Coon Rapids; Iowa Corn Processors is in Glidden; and Devansoy is in Carroll. Agriculture is big in **Carroll County**.

The county seat town of **Carroll** is lively and progressive. The amenities for recreation, education and social activities are well-above average. A beautiful, 33-mile hiking/biking trail that connects two state parks runs through town. Pella (windows), American Home Shield (warranty protection) and Farner-Bocken (wholesalers) lead the way as employers.

Sheriff Doug Bass has the responsibility of maintaining law and order in **Carroll County** these days. He has been in office for four terms of four years each. He told us that in Prohibition days, the sheriff worked with illegal distillers. When he got word the "Feds" were coming, he would emerge from his office without his hat. That signal enabled the distillers to shut down and hide equipment. Doug acknowledges there might still be some illegal whiskey made but it is not a problem and he keeps his hat on

WPA paintings by Ed Paulson, Carroll County Courthouse

Joe and Donna Kemper

205

TIER NO. FIVE

| MO | CR | CA | GR | BO | ST | MA | TA | BE | LI | JO | JA |

Crawford County

Doug Bass

when he leaves his office.

Stories about Templeton Rye were part of the fun when we sat down for a visit with Doug. We heard that kegs were buried in the ground for aging. Transactions were made by the customer handing cash to the bootlegger and not getting anything in return. Three days later, there would be a nondescript bottle of rye whiskey in a sack on the customer's doorstep.

People in **Carroll County** are open about drinking. Social imbibing is part of the culture. Small towns throughout the county sponsor festivals and celebrations. At the 125-year anniversary parades of Halbur and Dedham, many of the floats handed out free beer rather than candy. Most of the festivals double as fund raisers to make community improvements. **Willey**, a town of 100, cleared $96,000 in one of their fundraisers. The money went to the remodeling of a church.

Doug and his wife Pat have one child who lives in **Carroll** and another in New Jersey. Photos in his office show his affection for his five grandchildren. Doug, who grew up in **Coon Rapids**, has lived in **Carroll County** all his

RAGBRAI cyclists relax after a day's ride

RAGBRAI TRAFFIC AHEAD

206

The original Iowa Beef Processors (IBP) plant in Denison (now owned by Tyson)

life. He says, "People take care of each other here. If you are down on your luck, someone will help you. Living here all my life, I can walk through a crowd and someone always asks if I need anything."

At the end of each July, the humidity rises and the winds shift from the west and come out of the east. That lasts about a week for the Register's Annual Great Bicycle Ride Across Iowa (RAGBRAI). This year it made its way from Missouri Valley to LeClaire. It was coast to coast (Missouri River to the Mississippi River) with overnights in six interior towns. Ten thousand registered riders and an estimated 5,000 unregistered bandits descended in hoards on small towns and large. They were welcomed by volunteers serving up drinks, food, entertainment and friendly "Where are you from?" greetings. The riders are from all over the United States and other countries. They include old, middle age, young, Joe Blows and celebrities. Lance Armstrong rode a couple of days last year and was scheduled to appear again this year. It is the first and best ride of its kind and is celebrating its thirty-sixth annual running.

On the first of August we entered **Crawford County**. The bike riders were back at their home bases telling RAGBRAI stories. The prevailing winds were again coming from the west and the past week's humidity had made the corn grow another foot or so it seemed.

The first permanent settler to enter **Crawford County** was Cornelius Dunham Sr. who arrived in 1849. He brought a son and daughter along to help prepare a homestead for the rest of the family. His wife and five more children arrived in 1850. Cornelius was a talented, hardworking, good man. He was an outspoken abolitionist who entered into hot debates with opponents. He caught and tamed a number of elk and turkeys. At times forty or more turkeys would roost on trees near the cabin. That proved to be a mistake on their part. Roast turkey was a delicious complement to fried cakes, plum pudding and gooseberry pie.

In 1863, Dunham took the first **Crawford County** shipment of Chicago-bound cattle and hogs to the nearest railhead in Marshalltown. The cattle were fattened on native pasture and the hogs on rye mash and cornfields. The trip to Marshalltown was an Iowa cattle

(and hog) drive with a covered wagon and camping gear. Some of the fat hogs decided they had enough after a short time on the trail and were allowed to return to the farm on their own. Generally everything was successful and the livestock sold on the high end of the market. Their next shipment in 1864 was easier because the railroad had made it to Boone by that time.

In 1855, J. W. Denison, a Baptist minister, entered a tract of land in the interest of the Providence Western Land Company. He wrote a letter back to the company saying, "I stood on a hill where two rivers meet and I really enjoyed being there." The resulting town was the first in Iowa to be platted without a single resident within its boundaries.

Development began with a log house, a store building and a steam gristmill. The town was named **Denison** in honor of J.W. He continued to work on the town's behalf by negotiating for the county seat. Judge Basset, a traveling district judge, was given the responsibility of choosing the county seat location. J.W. knew that Judge Basset owned a shingle factory in Deloit. He told the judge that

Getting ready to boogie on a RAGBRAI stop-over

207

Crawford County Courthouse, Denison

Nathan Mahrt and daughter Sophie in front of their home

there would be many new houses built and they would need shingles from his factory. It was a good start for the present day, progressive community of Denison.

The only farm that Abraham Lincoln ever owned was in **Crawford County**. It was his reward for serving as a captain of a company of Illinois militia in the Blackhawk War of 1832. Although he never visited the piece of property, it stayed in his ownership until he died. His family held onto it for another 30 years before it was sold for $1,300. Signs on Highways 39 and 59 direct you to a historical marker of the farm's location.

German and English settlers were the dominant ethnic groups that increased **Crawford County's** population in the late 1800s. In fact, the Kaiser of Germany sent a group of soldiers with orders to obtain land in the county to be brought under Germany's control. That didn't happen because the German contingent decided it would rather be ruled by the United States government. The Germans maintained and exhibited their culture until World War I. The anti-German fervor during the war encouraged them to downplay their heritage;

Bluespace Creative art studio

Scott Winey

Denison

they removed German language signs and renewed efforts to speak English.

Nathan Mahrt, **Denison's** mayor, is of German descent and an all-around asset to the community. He teaches industrial technology in middle school, volunteers on community projects and is well-versed in the area's history. He, his wife Amber and their two children live in the oldest house in **Denison**. It is being lovingly restored by this handy man. He is also personable with a dry sense of humor and was a delight to interview. He gave us good insight into the community.

Ever since Cornelius Dunham sent his shipment of hogs and cattle to Chicago, livestock raising and processing have played a major role in **Crawford County's** economy. W. A. McHenry, a prominent Denison banker, took great interest in cattle breeding. Aberdeen-Angus cattle, named after two counties in Scotland, were being imported to the United States and taking their place as a premier breed of beef. McHenry spared no expense in purchasing the best animals from the best herds throughout the country. In 1892, at the Illinois State Fair, McHenry's herd of Angus competed

against the best from other states and he brought home the highest honors as the "best of the best."

In the 1960s, innovations at **Denison** packing plants led the way in modernizing the industry. They developed the disassembly line (the assembly line in reverse). Carcasses were put on line and various stations along the way cut away pieces. Prior to that, packing houses had butchers work on the complete carcass. Farmland and Iowa Beef Processors (IBP) got their start in **Denison**. IBP has since been sold to Tyson and they continue large-scale operations. The packinghouse jobs have attracted many Latinos to the city. They presently comprise one-third of the population. They bring in a younger community and enrich the culture. Nathan Mahrt said, "When immigrants move in, you find out who you are and what's important. We are reconfiguring the way our community operates. We look at the needs of both the new arrivals and the establishment. Iowans are easy-going; by and large, it has been a pretty easy transition with a few bumps along the way."

We interviewed Nathan in the lobby of

the Donna Reed Theatre. In the office space directly above us, there is a smart looking art studio named Bluespace Creative. After gaining experience working in large cities, Scott Winey returned to his hometown and opened his own studio. That was three years ago and it has grown to employ ten people and it serves 260 clients worldwide. They specialize in brand development and have in-house capabilities to support nearly all a client's communication needs.

Adjacent to the lobby in the Donna Reed Theatre is a room filled with Donna Reed memorabilia. This elegant, movie/television star epitomized wholesomeness and decency and she never turned her back on her Iowa roots. She was known to say, "No matter what I do, I am still a farm girl from Denison." This former 4-H girl and Denison High School homecoming queen went on to do quite a bit. She starred in over 40 movies, six of which are considered classics. *It's a Wonderful Life* was her favorite and is my favorite. In the movie *From Here to Eternity*, for which she won an Oscar, she was totally out of character. She received the best supporting actress award for por-

Connor's Corner B&B, Denison

209

Yellow Smoke Park, Crawford County

Iowa corn in August

Welcome To The Donna Reed Museum — A Tribute to Grover

traying a prostitute. She played "herself" as the loving wife and mother in *The Donna Reed Show*. The television series ran for eight seasons from 1958 to 1965. Her final role was playing Miss Ellie at the end of the long-running series of *Dallas*. She gave back in many ways to the world community and to her hometown of Denison. She passed away January 14, 1986.

The annual Donna Reed Festival for the Performing Arts keeps her memory alive. It began as a small film tribute the year after Donna's death. It has grown into a full-fledged festival of student workshops led by industry professionals and has a scholarship program.

Another **Denison** native missed attaining Donna Reed-like fame by two weeks. He was one of three contestants waiting in New York City in the spring of 1927 to be the first to fly non-stop across the Atlantic Ocean. They were looking for a break in the weather. When the clouds parted briefly, Charles A. Lindbergh took off and landed in France 33 hours later and instantly became an international hero. One of the two remaining pilots was Clarence

210

View from Loess Hills State Forest overlook

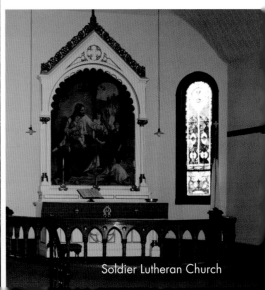

Soldier Lutheran Church

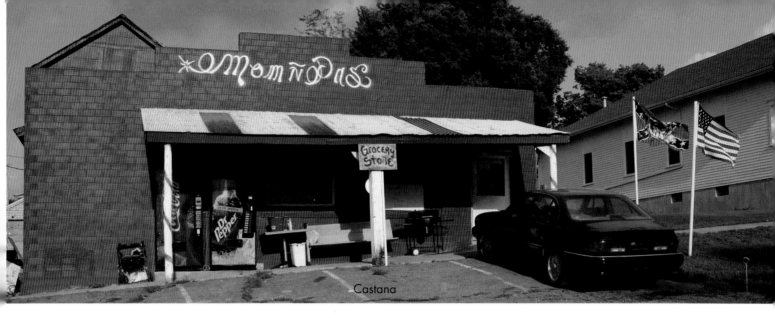

Castana

Chamberlain from **Denison**. He took off two weeks later with a passenger and flew faster and further than Lindbergh, landing near Berlin, Germany. Twenty-four days later the third pilot's effort ended in failure. Nathan Mahrt thinks the real reason Chamberlain wasn't first was because he wasn't political and glamorous looking and didn't have an aristocratic sounding name.

Denison has the typical amenities of an Iowa town of 7,400. One and a half miles east of the city limits is a 358-acre recreation area. Yellow Smoke Park is about 30 percent open grass; another 30 percent is woods and 40 percent consists of a lake and developed area. Park activities include picnicking, hiking, camping, swimming, boating, canoeing, sailing and fishing.

As we drove into eastern **Monona County** we entered an area settled by Norwegians. A couple of miles south of Soldier is the Soldier Lutheran Church. This Norwegian house of worship sits on a high spot in rolling hills farmland. A cemetery with tombstones bearing many names ending in "son" slopes away from the church on its west side. I'm sure it

has been an inspiration over the years for farmers to look up from their toil and see the gleaming white church on the hill.

The Loess Hills, that we have been driving in and out of as we traverse the state, reach a crescendo in **Monona County**. The deepest and widest loess deposits are found here. We took a Scenic Byway loop through the Preparation Canyon Unit—experiencing beautiful scenes every mile. The climax was reaching the Loess Hills State Forest overlook, a wooden platform on top of one of the hills. Looking out in all directions, I didn't know where to point the camera because the spectacular view was panoramic. I took some pictures but there is no way they will capture the vista. There was a path along the top of a ridge leading away from the platform. I hope to return someday and take that trail into one of God's unique creations.

A few miles from the overlook is the entrance to Preparation Canyon State Park. The name comes from a group of Mormons who rested there in 1853 as they prepared to continue their journey to Utah. The 344-acre park features hiking trails and seven backpack campsites. It

has one of Iowa's largest areas of native prairie and a burr oak forest. Unfortunately, it was closed to us because a recent tornado did extensive damage.

We drove out of the wilds into tamer Loess Hills terrain and on to **Castana**. It is a dusty little town with no paved streets and it doesn't look like the pioneers bothered to plat it either. There is a funky, little "Mom & Pa" grocery store and an abandoned miniature golf course with a Lewis and Clark theme. An abandoned brick schoolhouse has been sold twice on EBay, most recently to a Californian who plans to use it as a private residence. And there's the Dormitory Inn, our overnight accommodations.

The Dormitory Inn is a three-story house that was built in 1888 to provide living accommodations for teachers who taught in the school across the street. During the summers in the early 1900s, the school was used to teach Normal Training classes. The dormitory then housed teachers in training. When school space was limited in the 1920s to the 1950s, some grade school classes were held at the dormitory.

Eugene Hamman bought the building

Castana

Dormitory Inn, Castana

Eugene Hamman

Monona County Courthouse, Onawa

in 1995 and, after extensive renovation, opened it as a bed and breakfast in 1998. A café was added in 2000. The Dormitory Inn caters to family reunions and hunters. Eugene says the hunters that stay at his place are classy; they don't dress out the harvested game in the bathtub. The café and Eugene's living quarters are on the first floor. The guestrooms are on the second floor along with shared bathrooms. The third floor has been opened up for games and TV. The café is for reservations only and we didn't make any nor did anyone else that Thursday night; it was on to **Onawa** for dinner.

Before dinner we took care of the gambling obligation at Casino Omaha, located just west of **Onawa**. After 30 minutes at the quarter slots, Connie ended up $1 in the red. The running score after 11 casinos is $12 below the line.

We returned to downtown **Onawa** for a late dinner at the B&B Roundup. We entered a clean, small town tavern with a bar on the left and black vinyl booths on the right. A wide doorway on the end wall opened into a restaurant. We chose a booth in the tavern section where a waitress promptly appeared. She took

Keelboat at Lewis and Clark State Park, Monona County

212

Keelboat

Onawa Public Library

our drink order as we studied the menu. Connie decided on a steak sandwich and I thought the walleye fillet looked good. When we placed our order, the waitress informed me they were out of walleye and also out of carp. I settled for a shrimp basket. The waitress asked how Connie wanted her steak done. She said, "Medium, please." My compliments to the cook! The steak in that sandwich wasn't more than one-fourth to three-eighths of an inch thick, but there was a thin, pink line running through the middle. It was medium, as ordered.

After a good night's sleep in our dorm room, Eugene served us a delicious breakfast of French toast and a thick cut of prime ham. Eugene grew up in **Monona County**. He is a graduate of Moorhead High School and Morningside College. He cut his teeth in the restaurant business by working for Della McDonald of the Gold Slipper in Dunlap. In addition to the B&B/café business, he presently teaches title math at the Winnebago Indian Reservation in Nebraska.

Eugene had some printed material we were interested in but he did not have a copier. He suggested taking it to Iowa Computer just one dusty street down from the Inn. We did, and to our surprise, we found a thriving computer sales/repair business housed in a non-descript, white building. Sharing the space was Ink Spot, a silk-screen printing business for shirts, jackets, hats and signs. We have been running into several businesses like this that operate out of inexpensive properties in very small towns. I see a lot of potential here for Iowa's small towns.

As we were driving along the Maple River valley on our way to **Onawa**, I pulled over onto the shoulder to take a photo. The scene was some healthy looking corn in the foreground and the morning sun shining on the Loess Hills in the background. I took the photo, returned to the car and sat for a moment admiring my work on the camera LCD monitor. Through my peripheral vision, I noticed a car pull alongside ours. I wondered, "Oh, oh, what's up?" I rolled down my window and looked into the eyes of a kindly, gray-haired lady who asked, "Need any help?"

Onawa is an Indian word meaning "wide awake" and the town boasts of having the widest main street in the United States. Its four rows of parking spaces goes back to the horse and buggy days of the 1800s. Another claim to fame is the development of the Eskimo Pie. It was prompted by the indecision of a little boy who couldn't decide between ice cream and a chocolate bar. He said, "I want 'em both, but I only got a nickel." The clerk, Christian K. Nelson, started thinking, "Why not combine the two?" While experimenting with the idea, he came up with the necessary ingredient of cocoa butter to make the chocolate stick to the ice cream. In 1921, he secured a patent, hooked up with Russell Stover (yes, that Russell Stover), test marketed in Des Moines and began nationwide distribution. Nelson was flying high with success for about two years. Then the vultures came with imitations and patent infringement and they neglected to pay royalties. The brand name, however, has survived and today it is estimated there are 750 million bars sold annually world-wide.

Our first stop in **Onawa** was at their attractive library. The original building was a Carnegie library designed in the Prairie School of architecture style. An addition stays true to the classic architecture. After a little research we moved on

Wide main street of Onawa

Historic Mann School, Monona County

Cheri Hardison

Greyhound mother and puppies

to the Monona County Extension Office where we talked to Cheri Hardison, the county extension education director. County extension offices throughout the state were set up years ago by Iowa State University to educate rural communities on the latest in farming and farm living. They have done a tremendous job in helping Iowa become the world's leader in agricultural production and have contributed to the good quality of life enjoyed by farm families.

Cheri grew up in a Norwegian farming community in eastern **Monona County**. She was a member of the Soldier Lutheran Church to which I referred earlier. Her family still farms in the area. She attended Morningside College and Iowa State University, earning a degree from Iowa State. She filled us in on some facts pertaining to her home territory. One third of the county is flat river bottom with the Missouri River on its western edge. The Loess Hills fill in most of the remaining county. Tourism centers on the Lewis and Clark Center (there is an annual Lewis and Clark celebration every June) and the Loess Hills. ONABIKE (in its fifteenth year) is west-

ern Iowa's largest one-day bike ride with routes of 29 miles or 63 miles. Both routes go through the Loess Hills. **Monona County's** average size farm of 623 acres is the largest in the state. She concluded by saying, "I'm thankful this was my birthplace and I'm happy to be able to work and live here."

Our final question was an inquiry about her husband and children. She has a son in Portland, Oregon, and a daughter who is a senior in high school. When she told us that her husband raises and trains greyhound racing dogs, lights started flashing in my mind like a pinball machine. "Can we see his operation?"

We followed Cheri out to the Hardison spread a few miles west of **Onawa** on the Missouri River bottomland. Her husband Bob was on the road so Cheri showed us around. There were several sets of puppies—from the just-born to the equivalent of a teenager—whose bodies were taking on the sleek, greyhound shape. Bob owns over 100 dogs and he kennels more. He takes them to Oklahoma and Kansas for training. He races them at both Iowa tracks in Council Bluffs and Dubuque.

Teenage greyhounds

View of Sioux City from
Sergeant Floyd Monument

Sergeant Floyd Monument

WO ID SA CA WE HA HA GR BH BU DE DU

Anderson Dance Pavilion, Sioux City

Lewis and Clark Interpretive
Center, Sioux City

ver the years when I have visited
Sioux City in **Woodbury County**,
I have had the feeling that I was transi-
tioning from the Midwest to the West. On
my earlier visits there was still a large
stockyards adjacent to downtown. More
men choose cowboy hats over seed corn
caps even though they may have most of
their land in corn. Horses and cowboy
boots are more common here than even in
the adjacent county to the east.

The Loess Hills wear down just north
of the city where the Missouri River
leaves Iowa and wanders off into the
Dakotas. Its tributary, the Big Sioux
River, now becomes Iowa's western border. **Sioux City** is the navigational head
of the Missouri River. I find it a very
interesting and attractive city and area.

Anthropologists believe that Asian
hunters from the Stone Age crossed the
Bering Strait land bridges from Asia to
America in search of big game. That was
at least 12,000 to 15,000 years ago.
Evidence found along the streambeds and
lowlands of **Woodbury County** point
to the presence of elk and bison hunters
(Stone Age descendants) as far back as
10,000 years ago. The Indians/Asians had

Missouri River, Sioux City

evolved into agrarians as well as hunters by the time the first white explorers arrived in the county. The women tended the crops of corn, squash and beans on the river bottoms while the men hunted among the wooded bluffs and plains. The explorers also found a fierce nation of nomads who had been forced westward by white settlers in the East. French Canadians took a derivative from the Indian word Nadowessioux that meant "snake" and named the nomads Sioux.

Early French explorers, also known as voyageurs, made their living by trading furs. They developed personal relationships with the Indians and often learned their language. One such explorer, Theophile Bruguier, endeared himself to Yankton Sioux Chief War Eagle and the chief rewarded him by giving him two of his daughters. One of the maidens was stolen so the chief presented Bruguier with another daughter. The sisters Blazing Cloud and Dawn continued as his wives and bore him eight sons and five daughters.

Bruguier was born near Montreal and was well educated. After an unhappy love affair, the young man left the civilized

world for Indian country. In St. Louis he hooked up with the American Fur Trading Company and paddled up the Missouri River. After two years with the company he went into business for himself. In 1849, three years after Iowa became a state, Bruguier was ready to settle into a permanent home. He chose a site at the confluence of the Big Sioux and Missouri Rivers. He built a large, double-log house for his family. It was surrounded by a cluster of tents for Chief War Eagle and a large party of Yankton braves. And there were cabins for employees, trappers and stock herders. This little melting pot became a favorite stop for travelers.

In 1852, Chief War Eagle died and settlers were arriving who were more interested in farming the land and platting out cities than roaming free as trappers and hunters. This did not appeal to Bruguier so he sold out and moved on. He eventually became a widower. In 1862, he married a French woman. He returned to his Catholic faith and civilization and lived until 1896. He witnessed the transformation of the beautiful site he chose for his home to a colorful and important city.

Bruguier would have been totally disgusted with us as we drove our air-conditioned car up Interstate 29. The Indians we visited on the way were running a casino. We stopped at WinneVegas, our twelfth casino, to test their slots. They were pretty tight. Connie lost the $10 allotment in 25 minutes. The running score so far is $21 in the red.

Our next stop, the Floyd Monument in **Sergeant Bluff**, took us back in history again. Sergeant Floyd was the first soldier to die west of the Mississippi and the only member of the Lewis and Clark expedition to meet his demise. It is believed he died from an appendicitis attack in 1804. He was buried by his comrades on the highest bluff near the river. His remains were moved several times for various reasons until they were permanently placed in the concrete core of the lower courses of the obelisk monument that honors him today. The monument is impressive and so is the view of the Missouri River and **Sioux City**.

The dominant building in the **Sioux City** skyline is the Terra Centre, the home office of Terra Industries. Terra manufactures and distributes nitrogen-

Tyson Events Center with Terra building in background, Sioux City

217

Statue of Mary, Trinity Heights

Father Harold V. Cooper, Trinity Heights

based products for agricultural and industrial markets. It has the capacity to annually produce about seven million tons of nitrogen-based products per year.

Natives were wearing popcorn necklaces when they greeted Columbus in 1492. In 1620, the Native Americans brought bowlfuls of popcorn to the first Thanksgiving. In 1914 Cloid Smith and his son Howard shelled, cleaned and packaged the first branded popcorn in the United States. The brand was Jolly Time. Jolly Time has become an American icon and is still produced in many forms by the American Pop Corn Company headquartered in **Sioux City**.

The Missouri River's upstream-bound barges make their final stop in **Sioux City**. Beyond the shipping terminals the river takes on its original wild character and becomes a joy to recreational boaters. Chris Larsen Park is a beautiful strip of land that fills in an area between the river and Interstate 29. This pleasing setting is home to the Lewis and Clark Interpretive Center, a marina, Spirit of Siouxland statue, Anderson Dance Pavilion and the Argosy Riverboat Casino. Connie lost $5 in 30 minutes at the Argosy. The running

Woodbury County Courthouse, Sioux City

Sioux City

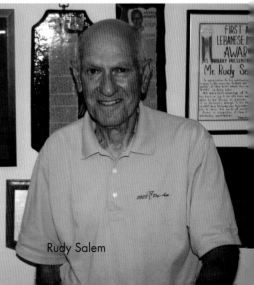

Rudy Salem

Last Supper wood sculpture, Trinity Heights

Sioux City reservoir

score after 13 casinos is minus $26.

I'm a fan of Prairie School architecture, so our first stop in downtown **Sioux City** was the Woodbury County Courthouse. It was designed by Purcell and Elmslie at the height of their careers and is the only major civic building designed by Prairie School architects. It was a totally original building when built in 1917 and is still a one-of-a-kind structure. Intricate sculpted details, painted murals and a stained glass dome compare with European Renaissance architecture but the shapes and layout of the building take on a completely different character than anything in the past. It's an incredible building. It's on the National Register of Historic Places and, in 1996, it was designated a National Historic Landmark.

A couple of years ago, Connie and I attended a concert by B. B. King in Sioux City's Orpheum Theatre. This is a turn-of-the-century, 2,500-seat theatre that was restored to its original glory in 2001. It has a rich, velvety, ornate 1890s look that is unrivaled by any theatre. B. B. King was pretty good, too.

The Sioux City Art Center recently moved its permanent collection of over 900 works into a new, contemporary building with a three-story, glass atrium. The collection includes a Grant Wood mural. There is gallery space for touring exhibits and children get their first experience in appreciating art in a specially designed, interactive gallery. The Sioux City Convention Center and the 10,000-seat Tyson Events Center/Gateway Area are venues for a wide variety of entertainment and sporting events.

Trinity Heights will give your spiritual side nourishment. We visited it on a day with a blue sky and white, fluffy clouds. I looked up into the faces of the 30-foot tall sculptures of Jesus and Mary and, as the clouds floated by, I felt like I had a glimpse into heaven. The stylized sculptures and the gardens are very well done. Another spiritual treat is the life-size, hand carved, wood sculpture depicting the Last Supper. This whole scene was inspired by Father Harold V. Cooper—who is honored with a sculpture of human proportions. The Jesus and Mary sculptures are constructed of stainless steel; they were designed and made by Dale Lamphere. Jerry Traufler carved the Last Supper sculpture.

Sioux City native Rudy Salem agrees that my positive impression of Siouxland is right on. He says, "People are friendly, salt of the earth, caring, love your neighbor people. There is no lack of things to do." Rudy, who is retired, made his living in the personnel business as a company personnel director and later in his Rudy Salem Employment Agency. He made his name as a play-by-play sports announcer and a critic of city government. Words flow easily when you talk (listen) to him. He grew up in a Lebanese family with five brothers. At Trinity High School he competed in basketball, golf and baseball. After high school, he started working in sales. While selling ads for a radio station, he was asked to do some play-by-play and, "Mama Mia," he proved to be good at it. ("Mama Mia" was his well-known reaction to a good play.) We were having an enjoyable conversation talking about **Sioux City** but we had to move on and Rudy had to join his all-Lebanese foursome for golf.

We took a lunch break at the Green Gables—an established **Sioux City** restaurant. It has a charming, garden-like character with its colors and art but does

Grandview Park, Sioux City

219

Battle Creek

Green Gables Restaurant, Sioux City

Woodbury County Fair, Moville

Woodbury County Fair

Holstein

not pretend to be a garden with phony motifs. The food was delicious and the service was professional.

Adding to the cultural strength of the **Sioux City** area are two, excellent, private, liberal arts colleges—Briar Cliff University and Morningside College. And after lunch we visited both of them.

In 1930, the Dubuque Franciscan nuns started a small, women's college sited on a hill overlooking **Sioux City**. The name Briar Cliff was inspired by the site and the first year's enrollment was 25 women. The Franciscans were dedicated teachers and, from the beginning, the school was academically strong. As the school grew, extracurricular activities were added and in 1965 men were allowed to attend. In 2001, it attained university status. Today, the enrollment of 1,100 students hails from around the country and there is a balance of male and female students.

Briar Cliff is a comfortable college community with most of the full-time students living on campus. It is technology rich with ports in every room and many computer labs. There are 35 student organizations for many activities and stu-

Woodbury County Fair

Briar Cliff University, Sioux City

dents have the opportunity to perform in theatre productions and the Cliff Singers.

Intramural sports from bowling to basketball thrive on campus. There are eight varsity sports for women and eight for men. Football was recently added for men and they are already competitive. Strong teams are the norm at Briar Cliff. Within the last decade, the women's basketball team has had ten All-Americans and they've gone to seven national tournaments. In volleyball they have had a winning record in 32 of 35 seasons and have produced 29 Academic All-Americans. The men have also enjoyed success with basketball as the marquee sport. They have had 14 seasons with 20-plus wins and have appeared in 16 national tournaments. Thirteen players have earned NAIA All-American honors and four players have been drafted by the NBA.

Morningside, the college on the other side of the metro area, began educating young folks in 1895. Fifteen ministers and twelve laypersons of the Northwest Iowa Conference of the Methodist Episcopal Church filed the Articles of Incorporation in December of 1894. Classes started the next fall. It was co-ed

from the beginning and maintains affiliation with the United Methodist Church.

Morningside College offers its 1,500 students a liberal arts curriculum combined with a diverse array of practical experiences. The learning takes place on a neat, well-trimmed campus with buildings in the classic styles of Romanesque, Italian Renaissance Revival and Art Moderne. New, contemporary buildings add to the mix.

Students can show their talents in over a dozen instrumental and choral groups. In theatre they perform four, annual, mainstage productions. Their mock trial team qualified to participate in the 2007 national championship in St. Petersburg, Florida. They beat Stanford in the process. There are over 50 student clubs and organizations. Twenty-one men's and women's varsity sports teams compete in the NAIA Division II Great Plains Athletic Conference. More than a third of the students participate in at least one intramural sport.

From the hallowed halls of learning to the exhibition barns of the Woodbury County Fair in **Moville**, we continued our Iowa experience. I love to observe

people grooming their livestock, eating their fair treats, climbing up on new farm equipment, getting a thrill on a ride, pointing out things of interest to children and greeting their friends and neighbors. This being western Iowa, there were many cowboy hats as well as caps. At the grandstand some of the men in cowboy hats appeared to be readying the arena for some type of horse competition. It was a great scene of good people coming together to celebrate rural life.

One of the booths we stopped at was looking for monetary pledges to build a new Tri-State Equestrian Center on the Woodbury County Fairgrounds. This would be a large building where horse and livestock shows, rodeos, motocross, tractor and trade shows could be held year around. It would be a first class facility that could host regional and national competitive equestrian events. We picked up a pledge card.

When we entered **Ida County**, we drove south to Highway 175 and entered the little town of **Battle Creek**. The downtown didn't look too prosperous but it is the home of a unique, offbeat attraction—the Battle Hill Museum of Natural

Morningside College, Sioux City

221

Crawford Creek Recreation Area

Ida County Courthouse, Ida Grove

Ida Grove Country Club

GOMACO paving machine

History. It was created by Dennis Laughlin to show off an array of stuffed, freeze-dried and skeletal animal displays. He built all of the exhibits, mounted the skeletons and wrote the descriptions. Two-headed animals and other freaks of nature are the norm. There are hundreds of skulls including those of Iowa's wandering moose. Two moose with parasites on their brain didn't realize they weren't supposed to live in Iowa. They crossed the Minnesota/Iowa border and found hostile country. A poacher killed the first one in 1989 and a truck hit the second in 1994. As the reputation of Laughlin's collection grew, it attracted even stranger happenings such as someone dumping a 12,000-pound, dead elephant on his lawn. He moved it with the aid of a tractor with an end loader, chopped it up with an axe, boiled the bones and mounted the skeleton in his museum.

We took Highway 175 out of **Battle Creek** and drove along the Maple River to **Ida Grove**. The view was a gentle landscape with rounded hills on both sides of the valley. Maturing crops blended with open, grassy areas and small groves of trees completed the picture.

Midwest Industries, Ida Grove

This is as close as we will come to experiencing the scene that greeted Judge John H. Moorehead in 1856 as he and his family came over a hill and saw the Maple River valley. Great maples lined the river of crystal clear water. The view of lush, green grassland was broken only by the cabin of an earlier settler named Smith. With its dirt roof planted in flowers, the cabin blended into the landscape. Wildlife cavorting freely and emitting pleasing sounds added to the Garden of Eden mode. The Mooreheads decided to halt their westward trek and put down roots in **Ida County** and the town of **Ida Grove** grew from those roots.

Judge Moorehead was a Renaissance man extraordinaire. A listing of the roles he played on the **Ida County** stage makes it appear that he was a one-man history maker. He was a farmer selling hogs, hay, corn and meat to travelers; a make-do pharmacist; a skilled negotiator with the Indians; a miller; and timber man. He opened his house to church services and school classes and ran an inn for transients and stagecoach passengers. With his sons, he ran a ferry service. In civic affairs he was a county judge, post-master, deputy provost marshal, city planner and political kingmaker. In his home he was a patron of the arts, and with his cultured wife Martha, he raised a family who would play a leading role in the county into the next century.

The Mooreheads and their fellow settlers faced a horrendous, snowy winter in 1856–1857 that kept them confined to their cabins. The Sioux Indians living on the open prairie were dying from starvation and exposure. They blamed their suffering on the settlers and, driven by hunger and revenge, they began raiding the white settlements. A band of lawless braves with their leader named Inkpuduta were so ruthless, they were even despised by the Indians. They kept on the move, headed north and became progressively more vicious. In addition to thievery, they began destroying cabins and their furnishings and terrorizing the pioneers. These raids culminated in the Spirit Lake Massacre where Inkpuduta and his band murdered 38 white settlers.

Despite that nasty turn of events, life continued to improve in **Ida County** with the arrival of the stagecoach. Born in the 1840s, stagecoaches flourished in the 1850s and 1860s. The rough-riding, slow stagecoaches were no match for the comfort of railroad travel so they were phased out of existence in the '70s. At any rate, they were welcome in **Ida Grove** as another step in developing a vital community.

A couple of farmer brothers, Harold and Byron Godbersen, have been the major contributors to the vitality of **Ida Grove** during the last half century. In 1954, Byron invented the hydraulic Bolster Hoist to empty grain wagons; this laborsaving device was an immediate hit. Midwest Industries was founded to manufacture Bolster Hoists and other farm equipment. Over the years, the end product has evolved from farm equipment to marine products. Production now focuses exclusively on ShoreLand'r Trailers and ShoreStation lakefront systems. The company employs over 300 people and their products are shipped worldwide. Sister company, Byron Originals, designs and manufactures molded parts. All the castle-like structures you see around **Ida Grove** are Byron's work. He lived with his wife LaJune in a castle/house complete with moat, watchtower and draw-

Ida Grove

Stage Coach Inn, Moorehead Park

Ida Grove

Marvin Whitham
Prairie Pedlar, Sac County

Rita Rohde

bridge. Byron passed away in 2003.

Harold Godbersen chose to go in a different direction than his brother in his personal style, but there are many similarities such as the success of GOMACO, his manufacturing company. GOMACO manufactures concrete paving equipment and is a world leader in slip-form paving technology. His company employs over 300 people and he also has other interests. GOMACO Trolley specializes in reconditioning antique trolley cars from all over the world. GOMACO University is a unique training facility that also houses Harold's collection of vintage, luxury autos and CrisCraft wooden boats.

Rita Rohde, the chamber of commerce secretary, is married to a first cousin to the Godbersen brothers. Her husband Bob Rohde owns a successful concrete construction company. Rita was complimentary of the Godbersens' contributions to the community. She said, "They give us everything. It's a nice town." The most recent contribution was $600,000 for an indoor swimming pool to add to the new recreation center.

The office in which Rita works shares space with an H&R Block accounting

Ida Grove

service run by Joan Bengford. Joan is also treasurer for the chamber of commerce and she is the mother of 17 children. She was not in the office the day we stopped because she was canning corn. This must be one organized lady balancing tax services with raising 17 dependents. And she can't write all of them off on her tax returns. I regret that we didn't get a chance to meet her.

Continuing the castle motif, the Skate Palace is Iowa's most unique, roller skating rink, ballroom dance floor and convention center. In contrast to the castle theme is an 1883 Victorian house that serves as the Moorehead House Museum. Moorehead Park, located one mile west of **Ida Grove**, has hiking trails, a fishing pond, a shelter house, primitive camping, a playground and a sledding hill complete with towrope. Also located in the park is a restored Stage Coach Inn that was an important stop between Fort Dodge and Sioux City.

Before we left **Ida Grove**, we stopped for lunch at The Family Table. It was an attractive restaurant with a menu that included Mexican as well as American fare and all-day breakfast

selections. Connie stayed on her healthy diet by ordering a salad. I couldn't resist the Western breakfast skillet. After placing the order, I took a closer look at the décor and menu graphics and became concerned we were eating at a franchise restaurant which is a "no, no" on this trip. I asked the cashier if this was the case and she replied, "I don't think it is a franchise but there are other restaurants of the same name." On further questioning, I learned there were about six to eight more and they were all in Iowa. If it is a franchise, it is a budding one and it got its start in Iowa.

We digested our lunch looking at flowers and other plants at the Prairie Pedlar just north of **Odebolt** in **Sac County**. It is a perfect, Iowa garden surrounding a classic, bow roof barn sheathed in gray, weathered boards. Jane and Jack Hogue, with the help of Jane's father Marvin Whitham and others, transformed a rundown farmstead into a garden showpiece. There are 75 theme gardens neatly arranged for viewing pleasure. It is available for tours and wedding celebrations; a refurbished country schoolhouse is available for other special

occasions such as reunions, club meetings and bridal showers.

A barn quilt is mounted near the peak of the barn's end façade. Barn quilts are eight-foot-square, plywood pieces painted in colorful motifs based on classic quilt patterns. They are mounted on barns or corncribs that are at least 50 years old. This project was started by Kevin Peyton of **Sac County** as a 4-H Leadership and Herbert Hoover Uncommon Student Award Project. **Sac County** has more barn quilts than any other county in Iowa. They can also be seen in Grundy, Greene, Pocahontas and Humboldt counties. They add a nice flair to old outbuildings.

We continued our drive into **Ida Grove** and stopped at the birthplace of another great entertainer who got his start in Iowa. Andy Williams spent the first eight years of his life in **Wall Lake** where his first public singing experience was with his brothers and parents in the local Presbyterian church choir. When Andy was eight he moved with his family to Des Moines where he and his three older brothers sang on the WHO radio station. They went on to perform in the National Barn Dance on WLS in

Andy Williams' birthplace, Wall Lake

225

WO	ID	SA	CA	WE	HA	HA	GR	BH	BU	DE	DU

Carnarvon

Loraine Quinn

Sauk Trail entrance

Chicago; on WLW in Cincinnati, they sang on a morning show called *Time to Shine*. After Andy's brothers returned from service in World War II, they formed a quartet called the Williams Brothers and started a nightclub act with Kay Thompson. In 1953, Andy struck out on his own and you know the rest of the story. In 1998, Andy and his family returned to **Wall Lake** for the dedication of his birthplace. He was given the key to the city and he responded by singing his signature song "Moon River." The family has contributed many pictures to the photo gallery in the restored house.

Next on the horizon was the town of **Lake View** that overlooks Black Hawk Lake, the southern-most glacial lake in the United States. Although the lake appears to be surrounded by homes and cabins, there is actually public access to fifty percent of the shoreline. Black Hawk State Park borders the southern edge. The usual lake amenities from camping to fishing to swimming apply to Black Hawk Lake. However, there is a special amenity for bicyclists—the Sauk Rail Trail. It runs from **Lake View** and Black Hawk Lake State Park to Carroll

Marsh along Sauk Trail

Marie Werkmeister

Stone piers on Black Hawk Lake built by CCC during Depression

and Swan Lake State Park. It is 33 miles of changing scenery from lakes to wetlands to old trestles to farmland to wooded canopies. In the winter the trail is available for cross-country skiing and snowmobiling.

On arriving in **Lake View**, we located Marie's B&B where we were to spend the night. It wasn't easy. I felt like I was going through a maze with optical illusions. The curving streets were charming but they left me confused, but I get confused frequently. Marie's is not the typical, antique-filled, Victorian B&B. A 1950s style ranch house (which she designed) housed only three antiques—a cupboard that was an heirloom from her husband's family, a nail that had the date 1936 stamped on it and Marie. We checked in and I unloaded our bikes for an anticipated ride on the Sauk Rail Trail.

After changing into our strategically-padded riding tights we rode out from the B&B looking for the trailhead. Even though the trailhead was only a few blocks away, the streets again got my head spinning and we rode up and down and around for about a half mile before we found the entry arch of old bikes. The

trail began by going through a canopy of trees that opened up to a wetlands where nature's sounds massaged the senses as we observed birds and waterfowl, including a small flock of cranes. Humans were frolicking in the water as we passed a sandpit. We rode under a trestle and through farmland to **Carnarvon**. That was all we had time for so we retraced our route back until we passed under the bicycle arch, and then wandered around until we recognized our B&B.

We freshened up and drove back out into the maze looking for the East End Supper Club on the other side of the lake. After stopping a couple of times to ask about its location, we found it and settled in for a beer and a sandwich. It had a roadhouse atmosphere with wood-patterned-Formica tables and durable, vinyl-covered, stack chairs. We each ordered the special—a Reuben on rye. It was as good a Reuben as I had ever eaten.

Back at the B&B we enjoyed a good night's sleep. The next morning our hostess Marie Werkmeister honored Connie's request for cereal and my request for fried eggs over-easy just like she used to do for her husband. It was love at first

sight when she met Roy and their marriage lasted 59 years until he recently passed away. A California native, Marie moved to Iowa to live with Roy on the farm where he was born. She still owns the farm, which explains the "Century Farm" sign sitting near her front door.

Before we left **Lake View**, we stopped to visit Loraine Quinn. She lives in a one-story house with a traditional cottage style and a wonderful, all seasons porch overlooking the lake. She invited us out to the porch, which was in its screened porch mode. We chatted about her life and **Lake View** as we snacked on watermelon, doughnut holes, juice and coffee. There was a light breeze and the morning sun was glinting off the lake and the lush foliage surrounding it.

Loraine grew up in Carroll, met her husband Ken in **Lake View** and they took in an Iowa State football game on their first date. They married, raised three children and lived in the country where Ken developed a complete popcorn operation. They grew popcorn and bought popcorn from farms in five different states. The processing plant was on their country property. The Quinn brand of

Marie's B&B

East End Supper Club

227

Sac City

Chautauqua Park, Sac City

popping corn was sold all over the world. They were also in the popcorn seed business. When Ken passed away, the business was sold and the Quinn brand has been phased out. After living in the country for 46 years, Loraine bought her present home five years ago and is very happy here. She says, "I love the seasons and beautiful trees. We have a very good library and I enjoy the bridge clubs."

Some fun times on the lake are Christmas in July, the Carp Fishing Contest and the Pelican Festival. The latter happens when the lake is white with migrating pelicans. There are some wild, white swans that live on the lake all year.

Eugene Criss knew what he wanted and had a plan when he searched the unsettled territory in western Iowa in 1855. He wanted to originate a settlement with access to waterpower. He chose a site that is now **Sac City**. He first built a log house, then established himself in the hotel business and kept a stage station and general store. That got things started and Eugene's dreams were realized as others picked up on this lead. In the late 1800s, industries such as a creamery, iron foundry, lightning rod factory, monument

Sac County Courthouse, Sac City

Angie Jergens

World's largest popcorn ball, Sac City

Chautauqua Park, Sac City

works and feed mill became part of Sac City's makeup. After incorporation in 1875, Eugene Criss was elected mayor.

Throughout history there has been a class of people who have trouble taking care of themselves. Cultures in the distant past typically ignored or abused these people. In Iowa, during the post-pioneer days of the late 1800s and early 1900s, efforts were made to care for the poor by providing a county farm where they could live and work. **Sac County** established such a farm near **Early** and in 1893 began accepting residents who were referred to as inmates. The facility was known as the "poor farm" and it was considered a disgrace to be sent there. Generally every effort was made to help those who were struggling with the last resort of sending them to the poor farm. When United States government relief programs were enacted, the poor farms were no longer needed.

At the turn of the century a movement began with the goal of educating adults. It started on Lake Chautauqua in New York State and in 1904 became an official organization with assemblies springing up all over the country. Generally they consisted of eight to ten days filled with music, lectures, plays, readers and elocutionists. Twelve thousand towns held chautauquas in the peak year of 1924. They were common in Iowa; I have referred to them in some of the counties we have visited. The Sac City Chautauqua Association got on board early when it was formed in 1904. In 1908, they built a permanent, 98- by 120-foot building with an octagonal front. It still stands in Chautauqua Park located across the North Raccoon River from **Sac City's** business district. There are no more traveling shows but the building is still used for church services, graduations, family reunions, wedding receptions and special breakfast events.

The aforementioned Quinn Popcorn wasn't the only popcorn operation in **Sac County**. **Shaller**, in the northwest part of the county was known as "The Popcorn Capital of the World" during the mid-twentieth century. Popcorn production facilities have gone but the crop is still grown in the area. That heritage prompted Harlan Schade to make the largest popcorn ball in the world. It is a Guinness record—3,100 pounds. The ball is shrink-wrapped and displayed in a building in the Sac City Museum Village.

On Highway 175 near the county line of Sac/Calhoun counties, a yard display of barn quilts, carved figures, metal and barn board birdhouses and feeders caught our attention. A sign on the end of a small building identified it as "The Yard 'n Garden." Angie Jergens owns and operates this artistic enterprise and makes many of the items that are for sale. She lives with her husband and four children in an adjacent, brick farmhouse. Her husband is a crop farmer. She is a delightful person and there is a lot of neat stuff in the yard and gift shop. We bought a metal bird feeder and a barn board birdhouse.

We continued down Highway 175 and as we approached **Lake City**, we read a sign welcoming us to the town that has everything but a lake. The oldest town in **Calhoun County** once had a lake but its namesake was drained. The claim that it has everything else is an exaggeration but it does have a lot going for it. It is a clean town with a prosperous-looking business district surrounding a square park with an attractive fountain and bandstand. The Carnegie Library, the

Sac City

Dobson Pipe Organ Builders, Lake City

Dobson Pipe Organ Builders

Community Building, Central School and some personal residences are on the National Register of Historic Places. Every summer near the Fourth of July, they celebrate Western Days with a parade, activities in the park and a USPRC-sanctioned rodeo.

Much of the quality of **Lake City** emanates from Dobson Pipe Organ Builders located on a corner of the town square. It was founded in 1974 by Lynn Alan Dobson, a man with exceptional artistic and business acumen. When you step into the tastefully appointed reception area and tour the drafting room and shop areas, you know you are observing a high-class business. Dobson's interest in architecture, gardening, the visual arts and nature intertwine into a single discipline that influences the building of exquisite pipe organs. Dobson was born in Carroll, attended a summer session for gifted students at the Minneapolis School of Art and graduated from Wayne State College in Nebraska with majors in art and industrial education. He rebuilt his first pipe organ while studying at Wayne State College. He is also a sculptor of note completing many commissions for

Lake City

Gary Class

Colin King

Carnegie Cafe, Lake City

homes, churches and other venues.

Dobson Pipe Organ Builders employs 20 people—half of whom have had experience in other shops. They each bring their special talents to create the whole. It takes about three to four months to build a medium-size organ. They build one at a time. No business operates in a vacuum—the well-being of the community is vital to the well-being of the shop. Dobson and his employees are very active in civic affairs.

An example of the community spirit in **Lake City** is their movie theater. It shows first-run movies, charges two dollars for a ticket and is completely run by the town's volunteers.

We stepped across the street into another quality establishment for lunch—the Carnegie Café. The décor was elegant with white tablecloths and a swag window treatment complementing the woodwork and fixtures from the old library. Shelves held pottery that was produced by local artists. Colin S. King is the owner and is also a potter. Connie had a salad and I ordered great-tasting French onion soup and half a club sandwich.

The early settlement of **Lake City** and Manson were at the opposite corners of **Calhoun County**. The first county seat was **Lake City**, but because of its location, it was destined to lose the designation. Pioneers didn't want to fight their way through snake-infested sloughs or waist-high prairie grasses any more than they had to, so it was determined the seat should be moved to a central location. John M. Rockwell came forward with an offer to donate every other lot in a 20-acre tract he owned that was located almost dead center in the county. In 1876, his offer was accepted and the town of **Rockwell City** was platted and given the county seat. Mr. Rockwell continued to be active in the growing town's affairs.

In the 1880s, farmers in northwestern **Calhoun County** went to great lengths to drain 20,000 acres of wetlands. They contracted a company in Ohio to dig a ditch through a 400-foot-wide strip so the sloughs could be drained into Camp Creek. The contractors used two steam dredges, each 18 feet wide and 70 feet long. I saw a picture of one of those contraptions and it is hard to imagine the effort it took to ship and assemble it. There were, of course, cost over-runs that caused some farmers to sell out before any profits could be made from the newly available land. Today, great efforts are being made to restore these wetlands.

At the library in **Rockwell City** we noticed a man in a Hawaiian shirt sitting at a computer. He looked interesting so we asked him a few questions. Gary Class was born in **Knierim**, confirmed in a German Lutheran Church and received his diploma from Rockwell City High School. After serving 12 years in the Navy and Air Force, he settled in Portsmouth, New Hampshire, where he worked in construction and in a naval shipyard. Twenty-five years ago, with a total of $400 to his name he decided to spend some of it on a bus ticket and return to **Rockwell City**. He described his first job back as being a ditch digger. Actually, he was laying tile. After a few more odd jobs, he took a position as a dispatcher for the sheriff's office on the 11 p.m. to 7 a.m. shift. He liked that job and stuck with it for seven years until he retired. As we talked, it slipped out that there was more to the story of his life on the East Coast. He was known as Bangor, Maine's "Beat Poet." No, he said he was

Wind turbine base passes through Lake City

231

Twin Lakes State Park, Calhoun County

Calhoun County Courthouse, Rockwell City

not a Beatnik but he did write and recite poetry and got paid for it. He was also living the life of a heavy-drinking creative. He said he didn't think the drinking was necessary for his creative effort but it did influence some his poems. When we asked if he could recite a poem for us, hc reeled off a couple without hesitation. They were good! One was entitled Valentine for Bankers and the other, The Yin and Yang of Growing Old. The latter is as follows:

And now as I grow long of tooth
My howl at best less full of moon.
I think of songs as yet unsung
I think of things as yet undone; and now
I think I end too soon
 but,
I'm gonna always squirm and wiggle in my seat
 'til recess comes.
I'm gonna always act different
When a pretty woman watches
I will live poor, and rich, and a little goofy
From now until time belly-flops into
The flames of my birthday cake.

When asked about living in Rockwell City he said, "It's a community like other

232

Pomeroy Museum

Pomeroy

towns in Iowa. In **Rockwell City**, everybody knows your business, but they mind their own business unless you need help. If you get dizzy, there'll be an ambulance to take care of you before you fall down." Gary's three favorite places are his front porch, his church and the library. He was free with quotes from Mark Twain to E. E. Cummings.

Rockwell City is known as "The Golden Buckle on the Corn Belt." It is the hub of Calhoun County, the nation's largest exporter of grain. **Rockwell City's** location on Highway 20 and a major railroad line contribute to its grain shipping capabilities.

The Calhoun County Historical Museum in **Rockwell City** is known for its large collection of horse-drawn machinery. Rockwell City also hosts the Calhoun County Farmers Market. Held every Thursday afternoon from mid-June to mid-October, it features a barbecue as well as fresh produce and baked goods.

Take a five-minute drive north of **Rockwell City** and you will arrive at Twin Lakes. The North Lake shoreline includes three state parks, two county parks and three boat ramps. This natural

lake is popular for waterskiing, sailing, swimming and camping. The more shallow South Lake borders a wildlife refuge, hunting and fishing areas and a nine-hole golf course.

A little further north from the lakes is the town of **Pomeroy**. I felt like I was in a Coen brothers' movie as I walked around the downtown of this hamlet of 700 people. Former prosperity was evident in two, brick, bank buildings across the street from each other. One of them had a glass front door that revealed an abandoned interior with no roof. Two, steel, vault doors mounted in a brick wall were half open. On the other side of the street, there was a similar style building with the front door open. Music that sounded like the soundtrack of an art noir movie of the '30s or '40s was wafting through the doorway. I cautiously entered and discovered a room with historic items displayed on the walls and in glass cases. Patriotism was the central theme with uniforms and war memorabilia from both World Wars. The steel, bank vault door dominated one wall. A vintage record player was spinning the vinyls. No one was there except possibly some ghosts. It

was a special, eerie feeling as I stood absorbing the atmosphere. I enjoyed it.

The doors to Pomeroy Artisans Gallery and Abbejas Glass Art were locked. However, the door to the Kaleidoscope Factory was ajar. I pushed it open and walked in and, again, there was no one there. Wood, junk and machines were randomly placed throughout the room. I didn't see anything that looked like a kaleidoscope being built. The eerie feeling continued as I walked back outside, looked around and realized that, on a late Friday afternoon, there was no one downtown. As we drove away, we noticed there was a grain train being loaded at the co-op and some folks standing in front of a nearby building waved at us. We're still in Iowa.

We drove west to **Manson** and passed through typical Iowa farmland. If we had been on this spot 74 million years ago, we would have been buried thousands of feet into the earth by a stony meteorite weighing 10 billion tons and traveling at 45,000 miles per hour. At least that's what scientists believe based on what they have discovered below the surface of this land. We saw nothing

Pomeroy Bank building

Pomeroy

233

Manson

because glacial deposits have filled the crater and erosion has leveled it.

Two thousand and eight was the year of the Olympics in Beijing, China. Two competitors who were favored to win the gold were Shawn Johnson of West Des Moines and Lolo Jones of Des Moines.

Johnson came to the Olympics wearing the crown of the world's best all-around gymnast based on recent world competitions. She and her teammates won the silver in team competition. In the individual all-around, her friend and teammate Nastia Liukin turned in the performance of her life to edge out Johnson for the gold and Johnson, in turn, edged out Yan Yilin of China for the silver. Johnson saw the gold slip away to a Romanian on the floor exercise that many felt she won. That set the stage for her last chance for the gold—the balance beam, her strongest event. She nailed it! The 4-foot-8-inch, 90-pound dynamo from Iowa handled the pressure and won the gold. At the age of sixteen she showed exceptional poise with a positive attitude and ready smile that made her America's sweetheart. When she failed to win the gold as a favorite in the individ-

Sherman School, Calhoun County

234

Fort Dodge

ual all-around event, she was quoted as saying, "I gave my heart and soul out there today. Today was Nastia's day."

Lolo Jones, a world champion in the 100-meter hurdles, thought this was her year and so did many experts. She failed to make the 2004 Olympic team and she used that setback to motivate herself to work tirelessly to make sure she was ready for 2008. Overcoming obstacles has been Jones' life since she was a little girl. She attended eight schools in eight years and lived with three families in high school while her single mother worked two jobs to support the family and while her father served time. In 2008, she was ready and came to Beijing as a favorite in the 100-meter hurdles. Ten hurdles and the best hurdlers in the world stood between her and the gold medal. She had the world's best hurdlers beat when she was taken out by the ninth hurdle. She knelt on the track holding her head in her hands. How could this happen? "I only hit a hurdle in one or two races a year—why the Olympics?" She regained her composure and was later quoted as saying, "It's hurdles—you have to get over all ten. And if you can't,

you're not meant to be champion. So today, I was not meant to be champion." Lolo is a beautiful woman. She is an intelligent, enthusiastic, caring person with a smile that competes with Shawn's.

I can remember that when I participated in high school and college sports in the '50s and '60s, we were coached to give it our best and be good sports. "It's not whether you win or lose; it's how you play the game." Then along came Ohio State's Woody Hayes who as I recall said, "Winning is the only thing." Others attribute that saying to Vince Lombardi of Green Bay Packer fame. I do not admire the attitude of either coach. My heroes are Lolo Jones and Shawn Johnson. They did everything they possibly could to win in Beijing; they played the game to the utmost and dealt with their disappointments with grace. They have an attitude of gold that shines brighter than a medal, a national championship trophy or a Super Bowl ring.

The weather in the first half of August has earned a medal—at least a silver, possibly a gold. It has been gorgeous with enough rain to keep the terrain lush with thriving crops and green grass meadows.

Ag-related businesses are a vital part of Iowa towns. It seems as if you can't drive more than five to ten miles before you come to another co-op with high-rise elevators for grain storage.

This highly productive north-central Iowa land was wild in every sense when Nathan Boone (Daniel's son) led the United States Dragoons on an exploratory mission up the Des Moines River. The Sioux Indians aggressively roamed the countryside that was inhabited by buffalo, elk, deer, bears, panthers, lynx, wildcats and catamounts.

In 1849, General Mason of the Sixth Regiment of the U.S. Infantry was directed to select a site for a fort. He chose to build it on the east bank of the Des Moines River where **Fort Dodge** now stands. It was originally named Fort Clark and was changed to **Fort Dodge** in 1851. The intended purpose of the fort was to deal with Indian problems. The problems proved to be exaggerated so the Sixth Infantry spent much of its time pursuing local bootleggers and deserters.

The officers at the fort were well educated and the families they brought with them were cultured as well as adventure-

Fort Dodge

Open pit gypsum mine, Fort Dodge

Robert (Barney) Patterson

some. The wives frequently joined their husbands on hunting excursions. Back at the fort there were painters, musicians and actors who were all active in pursuing their talents as long as it didn't interfere with their duties. The fun didn't last long. In 1853, orders were given to abandon Fort Dodge and move the troops north to help with rising Sioux problems.

William Williams, who was serving as a sutler (seller of provisions to the troops) at the fort, decided to quit the service and settle in **Fort Dodge**. At first he and his 14-year-old son occupied the abandoned fort. He was, however, determined to start a town so he bought up surrounding land from the state of Iowa. The simple grid of streets surveyed in 1864 still exists. Businesses that occupy these streets today evolved from the blacksmiths, wagon makers and stonemasons of early **Fort Dodge**.

A soft rock known as gypsum was first used by the settlers as building stone. George Ringland saw another, more valuable use for the rock. In 1872, he and his partners opened the first plaster mill west of Grand Rapids, Michigan. They named their company Fort Dodge

Webster County Courthouse, Fort Dodge

Blanden Memorial Art Museum, Fort Dodge

Fort Dodge

Rogers Park softball complex, Fort Dodge
(home of Iowa High School State Softball Tournament)

Plaster Mills but changed it to Cardiff Plaster Mills to cash in on the famous hoax of the nineteenth century. The Cardiff Giant was carved from gypsum and proclaimed to be a petrified man. Hucksters made a small fortune selling tickets to see this bogus, nude figure.

The gypsum in and around Fort Dodge is 145 million years old and is among the world's most pure. Today, there are three gypsum mining companies operating open pit mines. Four processing companies make drywall, a universal material in today's building industry. Each company employs about 150 people.

Another major employer in **Fort Dodge** is Fort Dodge Animal Health Laboratories. Seven hundred employees produce pharmaceuticals and vaccines for veterinarians in this sprawling complex. Ag-related businesses and plants round out the industrial side of Fort Dodge. Shipping needs spawned two, over-the-road trucking companies with home offices in the city.

Small businesses also thrive and we had the opportunity to talk to Robert (Barney) Patterson, one of the owners of Midstate Plumbing and Heating Com-

pany. His dad and a partner started the business in 1963. It has grown steadily every year. Today, the business employs 30 people and does commercial and residential work within a 60-mile radius of **Fort Dodge**. After graduating from Fort Dodge High School, Barney attended Iowa State for one year before deciding he would rather work in the plumbing business. He was the boss's kid but he got no special favors from his dad. He took his turn at working all jobs and completed a four-year apprenticeship course in Des Moines. He has no regrets. He and his wife Tracey have three sons. The youngest is in his third year of plumbing apprenticeship so it appears the business will be in the family for a while longer. Barney notes that there is a wide range of things to do in **Fort Dodge** highlighted by community theatre, city and state parks, canoeing rivers and an all-terrain vehicle park. When asked what he liked about living in Fort Dodge, he said, "I love the weather, the four seasons. It's a very friendly town. Everybody seems to get along pretty good."

Marvin Gardens was the name and the Monopoly game was the theme at a

downtown **Fort Dodge** restaurant. We sat in a polished wood bar with a window to the street and a Monopoly board motif on the wall opposite our table. The special of a club croissant and a cup of soup completed a pleasant dining experience.

If you want to see the Cardiff Giant, you won't have to shell out to a huckster. It is presently on display at the Fort Museum and Frontier Village. The museum's centerpiece is a replica of Fort Williams, the second fort in Fort Dodge's military history. It was built during the Civil War to protect against Sioux Indian raids. Much of Fort Dodge and **Webster County's** past is on display, including items from the Karl L. King era. You'll find a collection of memorabilia, photos and instruments from the remarkable bandleader and composer.

Fort Dodge's 77-year-old Blanden Memorial Art Museum is Iowa's oldest art museum. Charles Blanden, a former mayor of the city, donated funds to build the museum to honor his wife Elizabeth, a former Fort Dodge teacher. Its paintings collection includes works by Max Beckman, Joan Miro, Marc Chagall, Wassily Kandinsky and Maurice

Karl L. King statue

Oleson Park, Fort Dodge

Des Moines River at Dolliver Memorial State Park, Webster County

Equestrian campground at Brushy Creek Recreation Area, Webster County

Velkommen House B&B

View from Velkommen House B&B

Carol Larson serves Coffee with Swedish flair

Prendergast. Sculpture is represented by Alexander Calder, Isamu Noguchi and Henry Moore. American potters Dean Schwarz and James Logan are included in the ceramics collection. Three hundred sixty graphic arts works cover a wide spectrum of great artists.

We left Fort Dodge and drove out of the Des Moines River valley to some open farmland and back into the river's valley at Dolliver Memorial State Park. The Des Moines River is especially beautiful as it flows through this park. I'm sure fishermen, campers, hikers, canoeists and picnickers appreciate this as they pursue their activities. Two lodges and family cabins are also available for overnight stays.

Immediately south of Dolliver Memorial State Park is the town of **Lehigh**. The Des Moines River divides the town in half. The quaint little village has tourist potential with the recently developed Brushy Creek Recreation Area just a few miles to the east.

Brushy Creek is over 6,000 acres of land and water designated for outdoor recreation. There are two equestrian campgrounds with all the camping

238

Brushy Creek Recreation Area

amenities plus hitching rails for the horses. There is a beach campground for camping without horses. Forty-five miles of multi-use trails are available for horseback riding, biking, hiking, snowmobiling and cross-country skiing. Fishing and swimming are great at the 690-acre lake. There are also hunting areas and a shotgun range for clay target practice. And if all you want to do is picnic, there are three large areas for your pleasure.

The town of **Dayton**, in the southeast corner of **Webster County**, hosts a PRCA-sanctioned rodeo each Labor Day weekend. It draws ropers and bronco riders as contestants from throughout the United States and attracts thousands of spectators to its hillside amphitheater.

The Velkommen House B&B welcomed us as we neared the **Hamilton County** line. The grounds were immaculate, the buildings were freshly painted and the American and Swedish flags were waving prominently. We pulled into the driveway and parked the car. As we began unloading our luggage, a lively, petite, Swedish lady came out of the house and greeted us. She was wearing shorts and a sweatshirt (not the Mrs. Olson of Folgers

Coffee fame whom I envisioned). She directed us to our accommodations in a 1903 farmhouse that her grandparents built. This little house was constructed with home-sawn lumber—the next step up from a log cabin. It was abandoned when her parents built a new house. Shortly thereafter, chickens were allowed to move in, and when they left, it was used to store grain. It spent some time as a clubhouse for the kids and then it was totally neglected with random foliage growing up around it. That was the condition it was in when Carol Larson moved back to the farm of her youth. She told her mother she was going to tear it down. This was the house of her mother's youth and she opposed the plan. You don't cross your mother. So with her mother as a consultant, Carol restored the house. We had the privilege of spending a night there. We were thankful that Carol didn't overdo the authenticity—there was an indoor bath with a shower.

It was getting late and time to head out in search of a dining venue. We drove to **Stratford** and found Philly's—a clean, sparsely decorated restaurant. A sign indicated it was 15 minutes until closing

time. When they assured us they could still serve us, we asked if they sold beer. "No." Then we asked if the tavern across the street served food. "No." However, they immediately added that they would deliver. Perfect! The beer was cold and sandwiches accompanied by tasty French fries were delivered piping hot.

Carol, dressed in full Swedish attire, served us breakfast in the main house. After we had consumed the last piece of peach French toast, she sat down for some conversation. Her husband Wayne was the superintendent of Ida Grove High School when her childhood home became available. The desire to live in her favorite part of the world was so strong that they pulled up stakes and moved with only a part-time teaching job (kindergarten) lined up for Carol. Wayne tried selling insurance for a while. Then the superintendent position in **Stratford** opened up and the school district was more than happy to hire a man with experience in a larger school. Carol said, "God takes care of fools."

Carol told us how the homeless were taken care of when her mother was a child. There was a woman in their com-

239

Lehigh Riverside Tavern

Wilson Brewer cabin in Brewer Park, Webster City

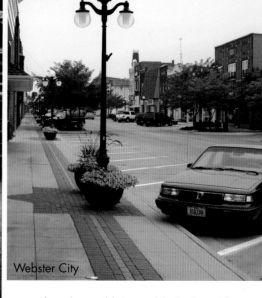

Webster City

Webster City Pulitzer Prize winners,
Clark Mollenhoff and MacKinlay Kantor

munity who couldn't provide for herself. She was given the name Tokalena. The community's families would take turns giving Tokalena board and room in their homes. Carol has a gospel clown routine where she gets an audience's attention with her Swedish clown attire and jokes. She follows that up with a serious message. Her clown name is Tokalena.

In 1847, a man by the name of Henry Lot brought his wife and three children up from Des Moines to settle on a site near the confluence of the Des Moines and Boone Rivers. He brought along a couple barrels of whiskey, some cattle, a horse and a few articles intended for trading with the Indians. Because he was the first settler in the area, the local Sioux tribe made it clear that he was not welcome. Lot decided to stick it out, believing the Indians would not follow through with hostilities. He, however, kept on the lookout and one day when returning to his cabin with his two older sons, he saw some Indians enter the cabin and heard his wife scream. His youngest son fled through the back door and ran toward the Des Moines River. Lot assumed the worst and brought the news to settlements to

Kendall Young Public Library, Webster City

Glenda and Donnie Wills

Hamilton County Courthouse, Webster City

the south that Indians had murdered his wife. The fact was she hadn't been murdered, but the force of hate and revenge had been unleashed. Lot evolved into an outlaw after his wife died the following spring. One of his criminal acts was the vengeful murder of Sioux Chief Sidominadotah. Inkpaduta, the leader of the Spirit Lake Massacre, was a nephew of the old chief.

Making a more positive impact on **Hamilton County** was a man from Virginia name Wilson Brewer. In 1854, he, along with William Frakes, platted a town on a horseshoe bend in the Boone River that reminded him of his hometown, Newcastle-on-the-James in Virginia. He named the town Newcastle. In 1855, Walter C. Willson and his brother Sumler bought the entire plat from Brewer and set about building a town.

Walter did the building and Sumler was the operator. First came a mill, then a log hotel, followed by a frame hotel that became a stagecoach stop. In 1857, Newcastle was renamed **Webster City** and the pursuit of a railroad began. John I. Blair, who had directed the building of the Dubuque and Sioux City Railroad as

far west as Alden, offered Willson enough money to build a new, larger and more elaborate hotel if he directed the building of the railroad from Alden to Storm Lake. Willson accepted the deal and set a record in laying track. Blair gave him the money to build a hotel and **Webster City's** growth continued. Altogether Willson constructed 133 buildings, four hotels and three railroads. In 1900, while he was supervising the unloading of some slag, a car that was being unloaded tipped over on him and killed him. His brother Sumler, who continued to manage many of the businesses, was also accidently killed when a horse bolted and threw him.

Glenda and Donnie Wills enjoy living in present day **Webster City**. Glenda works at Gilbert Flooring and Paint where she does everything but the installing. Donnie is employed by Hamilton Hospital in plant operations. He is also an EMT-trained volunteer on the Webster City Fire Department. Besides the fire chief, the department has one, full-time employee. The volunteers are divided into three crews that rotate every six months. Donnie is a lieutenant

who leads the interior attack on a fire; he answers all fire calls. Volunteers get paid a modest sum per call. Donnie says it is his way of giving back to the community. He also enjoys the camaraderie of the volunteers. The Wills have a long list of reasons why they love **Webster City**. Donnie commented, "We have a low crime rate, availability of things we need, good golf courses, stock car racing, enough restaurants, lakes and everyone knows you in town." Glenda added, "I can get to work in one minute. Neighbors are always watching out for you and people are generous."

Donnie's dad Don Wills was the postmaster in **Webster City** for many years. He and his wife Ina were known for their wit and love of partying with their family and friends in the CSP club. One story I love took place on a sunny Sunday at St. Thomas Aquinas Catholic Church. Don was sitting with his family and wasn't paying close attention. When he noticed the priest coming down the aisle carrying a holy water sprinkler, he asked Ina where the priest was going. She replied that he was going out to bless the cars. Don reacted in mock horror and in a

St. Thomas Aquinas Catholic Church, Webster City

241

Electrolux plant, Webster City

Stanhope

Williams

The Hemken Collection

loud whisper said, "Darn, I forgot to roll up the windows!" No one enjoyed his jokes more than Don himself; he'd be in tears before he got to the punch line.

Some amenities the Wills referred to include an abundance of city parks, one of Iowa's most challenging, public golf courses, walking/biking trails, the Boone River, nearby lakes and state parks. The Raspberry Festival is a favorite celebration. It is held at the 7B Ranch and features a pancake breakfast, amusements, stage entertainment, canoe rides, nature walks and one of the best fireworks displays in Iowa.

Products for the home dominate manufacturing in **Webster City**. Electrolux employs 2,000 people making washers and dryers and Beam central vacuum facility employs about 150. There are many successful smaller companies including a strong base of agriculture-related operations.

On the eastern side of Interstate 35 and in northeast **Hamilton County** is one of the nation's best vintage automobile collections. Take the Williams exit, drive a couple of miles to downtown **Williams** and you will find a building

242

Dr. Howard Hill and Mike Faga

Iowa Select gestation and farrowing barns, Hardin County

with a plastic sign proclaiming Goodwill Used Cars and gold letters on brick identifying the building's contents as The Hemken Collection. **Williams'** area farmer Daryl Hemken began collecting in 1958. Though the collection runs the gamut of vintage autos, there is an area of special interest—convertibles. For starters, there are 20 convertibles from the years 1947 and 1948. While on a trip to Hong Kong, Hemken ran into a trader of rare coins who happened to have a 1933 Roll Royce that the government of Brazil had given to President Franklin Roosevelt. Hemken had a coin the trader wanted and the trader had a car that Hemken wanted. The trade was made; the special car is part of the collection. The collection is open May through October in the afternoon or by appointment. It is another one of Iowa's hidden treasures.

We have been traveling through the heart of the heartland. It is Iowa's richest farmland and the evolution to larger operations is obvious. Abandoned farmsteads attest to the consolidation of acreages where large farm machinery is used to efficiently till the ground. Traditional barns are retained for their charm rather

than function. Specialization is replacing diversified farming. It is all very scientific and good management wins out. The world looks to Iowa for the latest in agriculture innovation and we were witnessing it as we entered **Hardin County**.

Iowa Falls was our destination and our first stop was at the headquarters of Iowa Select Farms. Iowa Select Farms was founded in 1992 by third-generation farmer and pork producer Jeff Hansen. He is presently the CEO of a hog production operation that has grown to be the largest in Iowa and the fourth largest in the United States. They employ over 950 people and have facilities in 43 Iowa counties. There are none outside of Iowa.

At the headquarters we sat down with chief operating officer Dr. Howard Hill and human resources director Mike Faga for a discussion on twenty-first century hog farming. Dr. Hill is a California native with B.S. and D.V.M. degrees from the University of California at Davis. A National Institute of Health Fellowship to study veterinary microbiology at Iowa State University brought him to Iowa. He earned his M.S. in 1972 and Ph.D. in 1974 from Iowa State. He has used his

considerable talent and education to Iowa Select's benefit since 2000. Mike Faga also makes a major contribution to Iowa Select's well-being in dealing with the company's most important asset—its employees. He grew up near Adair/Casey and is a graduate of Northwest Missouri State in Maryville.

We had an open and informed discussion with these two men. Iowa Select markets approximately three million hogs a year to the JBS Swift Packing Company. Sows are housed in gestation and farrowing barns. They are artificially inseminated and produce two and a half litters a year. When piglets are weaned, they are transferred to finishing barns. Every step of the process is monitored scientifically from how the pigs are fed to the treatment of waste. The men emphasized that they care about the environment as much as anyone. Dr. Hill said, "Present DNR regulations are about right. Water quality is improving, as is odor control. Knifing liquid manure into the fields prevents run-off and most odor."

When I helped my uncle Rudy with his hogs 50-plus years ago, I looked forward to a shower at the end of the day.

Bethesda Lutheran Church, Jewell

Gary Albrecht, an Iowa Select farm manager

Swinging footbridge, Iowa Falls

Metropolitan Theatre, Iowa Falls

When Mike took us on a tour of one of Iowa Select's gestation and farrowing barns, we were informed we had to shower <u>before</u> taking a look at the pigs. It is part of the bio-security process of keeping the sows and their babies healthy. Shower we did, and dressed in Iowa Select coveralls and boots, we marched down the barn's aisles observing sows and their litters. It was a clean place with healthy looking animals and the odor was mild. The only thing we questioned was the tight space. Mike said it prevents them from injuring each other and their offspring. He does not believe the pigs are uncomfortable with this arrangement.

We have now visited large crop, dairy beef and hog operations and have driven by and taken note of a large, hen laying operation. We have also driven by turkey farms but it seems like turkey farming has been a specialty for as far back as I can remember. The other livestock and commodities, in days past, were produced on diversified farms we now call family farms. Nostalgia for those days carries over into non-farm pursuits when most endeavors were done on a smaller scale. Times change and adapting to new ways

244

Iowa Falls Public Library

Camp David Restaurant, Iowa Falls

Ellsworth Community College, Iowa Falls

can be trying. You lose something and you gain something. Hopefully, you gain more than you lose.

The site of **Iowa Falls** was referred to by early settlers as the Upper Big Woods and the area below as the Lower Big Woods. It was a beautiful place with great rock columns of palisades rising 50, 60 and 70 feet above the Iowa River. Cool springs gurgled out of crevices in the valleys. A magnificent array of trees from cedar and juniper to oak and walnut to hickory and maple to huge cottonwoods grew in abundance.

In 1854, a Quaker by the name of B. I. Talbott bought a quarter section of land from early settler Samuel White and platted a town he named Rocksylvania. It seemed appropriate, given the character of the terrain. There was immediate objection to the name claiming that it was too long and cumbersome. In the days before a dam was built there was a rapids in the river by the town site. One of the objectors thought **Iowa Falls** would be a better name. Good decision.

The town grew and along the way the people dealt with the interesting and the mundane. In 1869, they had to pass an ordinance that it was unlawful for hogs, goats and sheep to run loose in the city streets. In 1871, a drought made water sources outside of town unfit so the town's herd of 150 cattle was driven to a slough north of town for water. They bolted for a nearby cornfield and gorged on roasting ears. Ten of them overdid it and died. In 1873, one hundred covered wagons passed through bound for the Northwest. In 1877, a Texas herder brought 700 horses to town to sell with prices ranging from $7 to $40. For every purchase he had to lasso and halter each critter to the delight of an assembled crowd of spectators.

Iowa Falls isn't as pristine as it was in the 1850s but it is still a beautiful city. The limestone bluff-lined Iowa River runs through the middle of the city. A dam creates a deep pool that is great for boating and water skiing. The woods now are interspersed with elegant houses. The business district is graced with the classic architecture of the Metropolitan Theatre where movies are now shown. It is also used for live productions. The old Carnegie library building sits proudly on a hill. Down the hill closer to the river is a smartly designed, new library.

We were very close to the river when we ate lunch at a restaurant named Camp David. We sat on a balcony overlooking the pool above the dam with the opposite shore of limestone cliffs. It was a nice place and the food was good.

Typically when we come to a town with a four-year college or university, we visit the campus and secure some information about the school. That leads to a two or three paragraph description of what we found. Iowa also has a wonderful, state-supported junior college system that has schools located strategically so that every Iowan is near a relatively inexpensive higher education opportunity. Students can pursue a four-year degree in a wide range of disciplines by taking the first two years of classes at an Iowa community junior college. Two-year associate degrees can be earned in an even wider range of subjects. The value of our junior college graduates to business, industry and agriculture cannot be overstated. Ellsworth Community College in **Iowa Falls** is an excellent representative of the Iowa community college network.

Sports have put the Ellsworth Panthers

245

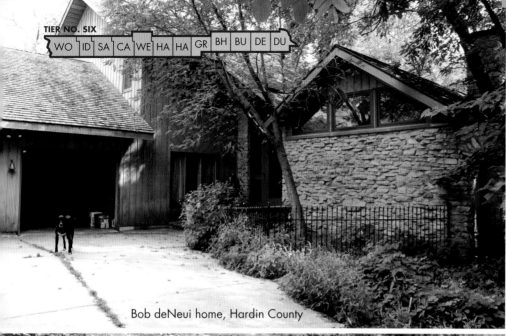

Bob deNeui home, Hardin County

Bob deNeui

Bob deNeui's driveway

on the pages of the sports section of Iowa newspapers. Golfers, wrestlers and cross-country runners typically advance to national competition. The football team has earned two national championships, 21 bowl appearances (17 wins) and 22 conference championships. Current professional football teams with ECC grads on their rosters are the Baltimore Ravens, Cincinnati Bengals and Green Bay Packers. Intercollegiate sports for men include baseball, basketball, football, cross-country, golf and wrestling. For the women, softball, cross-country, golf, basketball and volleyball are offered.

More importantly, the all-around quality from academics to student activities earned ECC the rank of "17th Best Community College in America" by *Washington Monthly* magazine. Agriculture, science, art, social sciences, computers, health care and skill trades are a sampling of the areas of study and there are numerous activities from musical groups to political organizations. It is a good school and representative of its sister schools throughout the state.

Complementing the rich farmland in **Hardin County** is the Iowa River

246

Pine Lake, Hardin County

Steamboat Rock house

Greenbelt. The Greenbelt is protected wilds of hills, bluffs, woods, rivers and streams along the Iowa River corridor. Combinations of public and individual efforts have been made to preserve and restore this land to its primitive state. One of the individuals involved in this effort is a man who built a house deep in the woods, a short distance from the river. We found our way through this sylvan wonderland of trees, meadows and wildflowers where a fawn crossed our path about 100 yards before we came to the house. Bob deNeui gave us a warm greeting and invited us into his unique, cleverly designed and decorated home.

Bob grew up on a farm in western Grundy County (borders **Hardin County**). He graduated from Steamboat Rock High School and continued his education at Dubuque University for three years. He transferred to Iowa State University where he earned degrees in chemistry and physics. Armed with those science skills, he landed a job with the U.S. government in Washington, D.C. as a nuclear engineer. He spent about eight years designing and building nuclear reactors for submarines and another

seven to eight years as an acoustic engineer looking for ways to make subs run quieter. It was exhilarating work but he eventually tired of the rat race and persuaded his wife Joell, a city girl, to return with him to Iowa.

They made the move in 1974 to a trailer situated next to the building site for their new home. They designed the house and, after it was framed, they spent the next four years doing the rest of the work themselves. He started out farming and later became a demolition contactor. He found many old treasures as he tore down old farmsteads, schools and other buildings. His main focus, however, was buying up additional wooded land to preserve it in its natural state. If a parcel he bought had a field, it was turned into a meadow with wild flowers. In some cases, trees were planted randomly to create more woods. He ended up with 800 acres of high quality woodland bordering the Iowa River.

Bob's legacy will be the effort he has made to protect this land. He says that there are four main "pillars." First was the donation of a conservation easement on 206 acres to INHF (Iowa Natural

Heritage Foundation). This allows the family to own the land while assuring future owners will never log, farm, mine or develop it. The second pillar was the addition of a second INHF easement of 100 acres. Pillars three and four were the sale (at a bargain price) of two, 40-acre parcels of dense, undisturbed woodland to the Hardin County Conservation Board. For his dedication to conservation, INHF presented him with the Lawrence and Eula Hagie Heritage Award given to "a person who demonstrates outstanding personal commitment to protecting Iowa's natural resources and encourages others to do the same." That's Bob!

On the road again, we drove south along the Iowa River Greenbelt, arriving at a point where man again has altered the river with a dam, creating Pine Lake. It is a beautiful alteration that provides wonderful recreation opportunities.

A little further south we came to the town of **Steamboat Rock**. It was named for the rock formation along the river that is shaped like the hull of a steamboat. It is one of the oldest settlements in **Hardin County**.

We continued our drive south to

CONRAD PUBLIC LIBRARY

Iowa River Tube Rides, Eldora

Eldora, the county seat of **Hardin County**. Its location, a few miles from the **Grundy County** line, would not qualify as a central location. They must have had faster horses in the western part of the county. More likely, the location is due to more established settlements in the east when the county seat was designated. At any rate, in 1892 they built a magnificent courthouse that stands today and is on the National Register of Historic Places. Architecturally, it combines Romanesque, Gothic and Victorian styles and makes it work.

Eldora is a pleasant town of about 3,000 people with the amenities of a new aquatic center, hiking/biking trails and recreation opportunities of Pine Lake and the Iowa River. The climactic scene of the 1996 movie *Twister* was shot in an **Eldora** house that is open to visitors. Also open to visitors is the Hardin County Farm Museum with displays detailing the history of agriculture.

There was a touch of fall in the air as we entered **Grundy County**. If your preference for weather is days in the 80s with low humidity and just enough rain to keep the countryside lush, you would

Hardin County Courthouse, Eldora

Eldora Methodist Church
and Civil War cannons

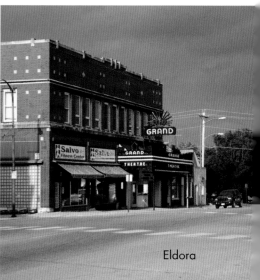

Eldora

Hardin County

have enjoyed this last August. With the approach of Labor Day, we mark the end of summer and beginning of fall. I love fall with its crisp, cool days and Indian summers and the dread of winter does not spoil it for me. I don't dread winter. In the few years I have lived in southern climates, I missed it. For you winter-haters, I'll spare you description on what I like about the season such as sitting by a fire and watching the snow fall or an invigorating walk in a winter wonderland or appreciating indoor activities more.

Grundy County is agriculture. I recall ten to fifteen years ago reading about the millionaire farmers of Grundy County. The west side of **Grundy Center** is anchored by a prosperous looking John Deere dealership and the east side is anchored by an equally prosperous looking Chase IH dealership. In between is a pleasant, county seat town of about 2,500 people that in the old days was simply called The Center. The town and county were named after Felix Grundy, a war hero senator from Tennessee, who never set foot in Iowa.

It took a pioneer with foresight to see beyond the tall grass and sloughs infested with rattle snakes and howling wolves. Maybe the intelligence of those pioneers could be questioned, but you can't question their courage and toughness. Again in this history, we find amazing generosity of the earliest settlers helping those who followed by sharing food and lodging in their small cabins. Two or three families might have been occupying a dwelling and they would still offer shelter to a traveler. In **Grundy County** many of the settlers were from Germany.

They first came in the early 1850s, and by the 1860s, much progress had been made. On a clear day in 1868, Jake Slifer took a telescope up on the roof of the frame courthouse in the village of The Center. The courthouse was on high ground and there were no trees large enough to obstruct his view. He scanned the horizon in every direction and counted over a hundred breaking teams turning over original sod. The courthouse itself was an all-purpose building. Its octagonal shape earned the nickname "the cheese box." In addition to the court and county offices, it provided space for grammar school classes, church services of all denominations and social gatherings.

In 1891, at the cornerstone laying of the new limestone courthouse, Judge D. E. Munn did some reminiscing. He recalled that he would reluctantly listen to hours of quibbling among lawyers and be impatient to adjourn so he could indulge in the prevalent sport of hunting prairie chickens. He also noted that the court treasurer took the county's funds home with him every night for safekeeping. He kept them in a little tin box that was no burden to carry (not many funds).

In 1909, Carrie Nation came to the eastern **Grundy County** town of **Reinbeck** carrying a Bible in one hand and a hatchet in the other. She was crusading against liquor, tobacco and sex; when she entered a saloon, the men cowered and no one interrupted her work. She broke windows, smashed bottles of liquor and hacked furniture to bits. She did what she could to destroy the alcohol industry. She didn't succeed but she made quite a few folks wish they hadn't gone into the saloon business.

Things have settled down in **Grundy County** these days. Jake and Wava Hemmen enjoy a relaxed life style—free from rattlesnakes, howling wolves and

Grundy Center

Grundy Center

249

Grundy Center

Jake and Wava Hemmen

fanatic reformers. They are natives of the county. Wava graduated from Grundy Center High School and Jake is an Ackley High School graduate. They met at a church youth rally. After high school Jake served in the U.S. Army. When he was discharged, he found a job at Simpson Furniture in Cedar Falls. His new bride Wava had earned a nursing degree and took a job at Allen Hospital in Waterloo. They missed their family and friends in **Grundy Center** so as soon as the opportunity presented itself, they secured jobs in their hometown. Jake found work at Frederick Furniture and Wava began working at the community hospital. After 18 years of working in the furniture business, Jake began a new career selling insurance for Grundy Mutual where he advanced to agency manager with 17 agents working for him. Wava is historian of her garden club and her gardening skills were evident everywhere around their home and garden. Daughter Staci, her husband Joe and family live in the Des Moines area. When she was in high school and went on a trip to Mexico with her Spanish class, Jake sold the family's cute, little, blue Fiat

250

Grundy County Courthouse, Grundy Center

Grundy County

convertible. He didn't think the convertible was very safe so he replaced it with a bright orange Pinto. Upon her return, Staci's reaction was not, "Magnifico!" She called the pinto a big pumpkin. The reasons the Hemmens live in **Grundy Center**? "It's the camaraderie of friends, family and neighbors. We go to football games and know almost everybody. We know our neighbors well."

Grundy Center has its priorities in order. They have recently built a new library and aquatic center. A very good hospital, spacious parks and excellent schools add to the quality of life. The YMCA is connected to the school so the workout facilities are easily accessible to students. Physical education gets a boost from the Polar Scholars program in which seven graduate students from the University of Northern Iowa spend a year teaching physical education classes to all grade levels. It's a program that uses high tech methods to improve the physical well-being of students. The prestige of the program is such that it was one of seven 90-minute presentations at the Pre-Olympic International Convention on Science, Education and Medicine in

Sports held in Beijing. **Grundy Center's** own Beth Kirkpatrick was one of the presenters.

Before we left Grundy's county seat, we stopped for lunch at Johnny Ray's on the west edge of town. It was a nice, clean, memorabilia-adorned atmosphere with an efficient waitress scurrying around. She noticed that we had bikes mounted on the car and commented on how much she enjoyed the area's trails. I suggested that the exercise she gets waiting tables must compare to the benefits of biking. She said she wore a pedometer once and it showed five miles at the end of an eight-hour shift.

Several of **Grundy County's** small towns are either growing or holding their own as bedroom communities for the Waterloo/Cedar Falls metro area. **Conrad's** growth has enabled it to build a new state-of-the-art library. **Dike**, located on Highway 20, has benefited the most because of its easy access to the cities. A new, 255-acre, conservation-recreation area with a lake and the usual amenities is located a half mile from town. **Morrison** is home to the Grundy County Heritage Museum where there

are excellent displays of farm history. A **Reinbeck** saloon didn't survive Carrie Nation, but many other enterprises did. Downtown you will find gift shops and a refurbished drug store with a soda fountain. The neat little town of **Wellsburg** flaunts its German heritage.

The first white settlers in **Black Hawk County** along the Cedar River where **Waterloo** and **Cedar Falls** are located came in 1845. The area was a favorite hunting ground for Indians and the location of two Meskwaki villages. William Sturgis, a farmer from Michigan, chose a spot on the river (where the Ice House Museum now stands) to build a dam and mill. George and Mary Hanna and their children were the first to settle on **Waterloo** turf. The mill became operational for sawing logs and grinding grain, thereby drawing people to the town. Waterloo was the winner in the battle for county seat. In the 1860s, the railroads came and so did the Danes. They settled for the most part in **Cedar Falls**. *Dannevirke*, a Danish language newspaper, began publication in 1882 and kept rolling off the presses until 1950. A Dane named Jens Nielsen invent-

Historic Wells Hotel, Wellsburg

Pioneer Reinbeck Production Plant

251

Waterloo

Bob Justis

Black Hawk County Courthouse, Waterloo

Waterloo

ed a rotary pump that led to the formation of the Viking Pump Company in 1911.

Industrious folks also settled in the town of Prairie Rapids Crossing— later renamed **Waterloo**. As the town grew, it spread across the river; today the river divides it into east and west sides. Diversification came early to Waterloo in 1911–1912 when a national railroad strike shut down the Illinois Central Railroad repair shop. The railroad reached into the state of Mississippi to recruit and transport African-American workers to Waterloo. From 1895 to 1915 there was rapid growth from 8,500 to 33,000 residents, fueled by manufacturing, rail transportation and wholesale operations. Another spurt was from 1925 to 1960 when the population of 36,000 doubled to 72,000. John Deere's operation in **Waterloo** and Rath Packing Company can take major credit for this growth. The agricultural recession of the 1980s hit Waterloo hard. John Deere cut 10,000 jobs and Rath closed down, eliminating 2,500 jobs. It is estimated that Waterloo lost 14 percent of its population during that time. Today, the city enjoys a broader industrial and commercial base.

Riding the Waterloo/Cedar Falls trails

252

Waterloo Center for the Arts

John Deere is still the lead employer with 5,100 workers. While we were visiting the city, news broke that Deere and Company was going to double a planned $90 million expansion to its tractor plant (the world's largest). Tyson Fresh Meats with 2,300 employees is another contributor to Waterloo's economic health.

Waterloo's culture is enriched by its diversity. Germans, Greeks and Croatians were early immigrants. As noted before, African Americans migrated from the South in the early 1900s and continue to have a strong presence. In the 1990s, an estimated 5,000 Bosnian war refugees were resettled in the city. And over 2,000 Latino residents add to the city's rich ethnic character.

The founder of Peregrine Financial, one of the nation's largest, commodities and forex brokerage houses, is a native of **Cedar Falls**. CEO Russ Wasendorf concluded that communication technology has reached a point where he felt comfortable moving the company away from the Chicago Mercantile Exchange to his hometown. They are building a 49,500-square-foot headquarters for an estimated $13 million. "Green" technology will be maximized in its construction. It will bring 72, new, high-paying jobs.

Bob Justis, the president and CEO of the Greater Cedar Valley Chamber of Commerce, is very enthused about the good happenings in the Waterloo/Cedar Falls metro area. He began life in Baltimore and moved here as a second grader in 1954 when his dad took a job with Rath Packing Company. He is a graduate of Cedar Falls High School and the University of Northern Iowa. Prior to taking the chamber position in 2002, he spent 20 years in public relations and fundraising for Allen Hospital in **Waterloo**. His wife Nancy, a former sports information director at UNI, presently edits and publishes the *Cedar Valley Athlete*. Bob maintains a close association with UNI sports as the public address announcer for football and basketball games. He is either "home or in the dome." He gave us some good insights as to why he chose to remain in the area when he was offered a good paying job in San Diego. He likes being involved in bringing back the downtowns of **Cedar Falls** and **Waterloo**. Cedar Falls has made a successful comeback and Waterloo is on its way. He considers the ethnic diversity with their businesses and festivals a strength. There are plenty of jobs that are also of a diverse nature. There are cultural advantages centered on the University of Northern Iowa. There is easy access to parks, lakes and the Cedar River. The 80 miles of bike trails weaving in and around the two cities are awesome. There is also a beautiful trail that follows the Cedar River to Cedar Rapids. Unfortunately, this year, the rampaging river damaged much of that trail. The record flood caused many problems in the cities as well, but dealing with it brought out the best in its residents. Thousands of people responded to the call by filling and stacking 200,000 sandbags that helped limit damage. Bob says, "This response is one of the reasons I live here. When I talk to people as a chamber person, I tell them I have had opportunities to leave. But there is no better place to work, play and raise a family."

Olympic gold medalist wrestler Dan Gable grew up in Waterloo. He won state championships in high school and national championships at Iowa State University. He went on to compile a

Grout Museum, Waterloo

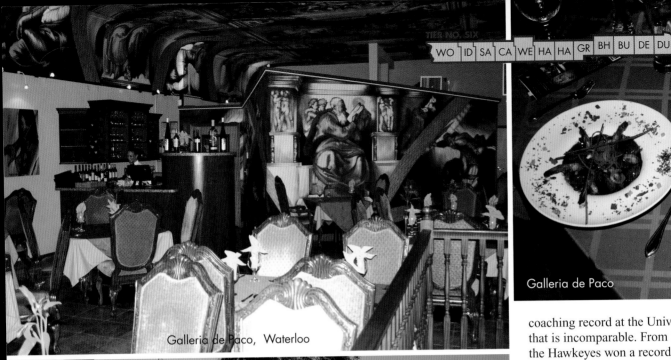

Galleria de Paco, Waterloo

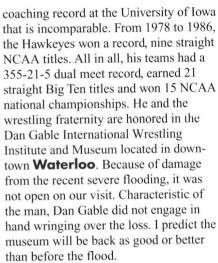

Galleria de Paco

coaching record at the University of Iowa that is incomparable. From 1978 to 1986, the Hawkeyes won a record, nine straight NCAA titles. All in all, his teams had a 355-21-5 dual meet record, earned 21 straight Big Ten titles and won 15 NCAA national championships. He and the wrestling fraternity are honored in the Dan Gable International Wrestling Institute and Museum located in downtown **Waterloo**. Because of damage from the recent severe flooding, it was not open on our visit. Characteristic of the man, Dan Gable did not engage in hand wringing over the loss. I predict the museum will be back as good or better than before the flood.

Brotherly love was behind the greatest World War II loss of members from one family in one military action. The five Sullivan brothers enlisted in the Navy with the provision that they would be allowed to serve together on the same ship. In the battle for Guadalcanal, their ship, the *Juneau* was hit twice with torpedoes from Japanese subs. The second torpedo caused the ship to blow up and it sank rapidly. Four Sullivans went down with the ship and the fifth was lost at sea.

Dam on the Cedar River next to Ice House Museum

254

Black Hawk Hotel, Cedar Falls

Black Hawk motel room, Cedar Falls

Paco and Jacky Rosic

Catacomb Lounge, Galleria de Paco

There is a myth that the Navy changed regulations so that members from the same family could not serve on the same ship. Even though it is highly discouraged, there is still no regulation against it. The Five Sullivan Brothers Convention Center and the new Sullivan Brothers Iowa Veterans addition to the Grout Museum keep their memory alive.

The Waterloo/Cedar Falls metro area has several museums displaying the past. The distinctive, round-shaped Ice House sits by a dam on the Cedar River adjacent to downtown **Cedar Falls**. Before refrigeration, six to eight tons of river-cut ice could be stored in this structure. Today, the story of ice harvesting is told through interpretive exhibits in its present function as a museum. An Italianate-style mansion named the Victorian Home and Carriage House Museum represents life in the 1880s. The Carriage House addition houses the Lenoir model train collection and the historical society's archives and research library.

We made reservations at the Black Hawk Hotel in downtown **Cedar Falls**. It is a classic luxury hotel of the late 1800s that has been restored and modern-ized. Unfortunately for us, the hotel was booked; but fortunately, they own a motel across the alley with beautiful, contempo-rary-style guestrooms that we enjoyed. The complimentary breakfast was at the hotel restaurant.

A dining experience unlike any in the world awaited us in downtown Waterloo. Tourists from Italy, France, England, Germany, Iceland, China, Japan and the country of Georgia have enjoyed the din-ing experience. Michelle Monaghan of *Mission Impossible III* celebrated her birthday there and Nicolas Cage visited with his family. The attraction? A paint-ing on the ceiling is a striking likeness to the Michelangelo painting on the ceiling of the Sistine Chapel in Rome. Artist Paco Rosic is a Bosnian refugee who moved to Waterloo with his family in 1997. Both he and Michelangelo had to lie on their backs when they painted but Paco used aerosol spray cans of different color paints to render his masterpiece. On the walls are more Paco Rosic paintings of a different subject but in the same, spray can style. It is an incredibly rich atmosphere. We were greeted at Galleria de Paco by Paco's father Jacky, an elegant man, who showed us to our table. A jazzy/classical blend of music played in the background at just the right volume. The food was beautifully presented and delicious. A level below the restaurant is the Catacomb Lounge with an atmos-phere far different than the early Christians in Rome experienced. Brightly colored booths and chairs contrast with black trim. Colorful floor tiles and Paco's aerosol art complete a look that is unworldly beautiful.

The next morning we visited the attractive campus of the University of Northern Iowa in **Cedar Falls**. It was established in 1876 as a Normal School for the special training of teachers for the common schools of Iowa. The one build-ing on the 40-acre campus formerly housed orphaned children of Civil War soldiers. It was renamed Iowa State Teachers College in 1909, and in the fol-lowing years, it attained a national repu-tation as a leading institution in teacher education. In 1961, the name changed again to the State College of Iowa as other degrees were added. Finally, in 1967, it was given its present name of the University of Northern Iowa to reflect the

Victorian Home and Carriage House Museum

UNI-Dome, University of Northern Iowa

Gary Kelley

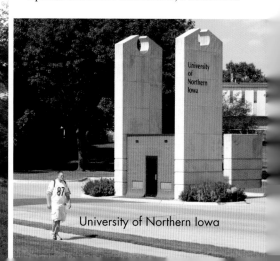

Robert Hellman

HELLMAN ASSOCIATES, INC.

University of Northern Iowa

addition of graduate programs. Today, about 12,600 undergraduates and 1,600 post-graduates attend a university that is on equal footing with Iowa's other two regent universities. Its schools in education and business rank among the best in the United States. Other disciplines in the arts and sciences are very strong, also.

About 220 student clubs provide opportunities for a variety of extracurricular activities. Varsity sports competition is provided with 18 Division I teams. Facilities include the new McLeod Center, a 7,000-seat field house for basketball and other sports, and the UNI-Dome—a 20,000-seat, indoor football arena. The football team has been ranked in the 1-AA top 25 almost every year in the last two decades and, in 2005, they lost a cliffhanger to Appalachian State in the 1-AA national championship game. The men's basketball team has made several NCAA tournament appearances, as has the women's volleyball team. Competition is also strong in other sports.

After working two and a half years as a graphic designer for Meredith Corporation's *Better Homes and Gardens*® Special Interest Publications, I struck out

256

Cedar Falls

on my own as a freelance graphic designer and illustrator. That was back in the early 1970s. I retained Meredith as a major account and in the process of doing their work, I came in contact with some exquisite illustration done for SIP (Special Interest Publications) magazines by Gary Kelley. He was just getting started at the time and I have followed his career ever since. His work soon started winning awards in leading art magazine competitions and shows. That was followed by glowing reviews and international recognition. To date he has been awarded 27 gold and silver medals from the Society of Illustrators in New York and has won Best-In-Show in New York and Los Angeles Illustrator Exhibitions. *Time*, *Rolling Stone*, *Atlantic Monthly*, *The New Yorker* and *Playboy* are among his clients. He has done work for the NFL and the NBA and was official artist for the 2002 Kentucky Derby. His work has been in prestigious fine art shows across the country and Europe. He has taught, given seminars and, in 2007, he was inducted into the Society of Illustrators Hall of Fame. I think he may be the best illustrator in the country and apparently

many experts agree with me.

Gary Kelley lives and works in **Cedar Falls**. Before we left town, we stopped at his studio in hopes of meeting him. To our delight, he was in and, to our further delight, we had an enjoyable visit with him. That morning he was working on four, large canvas panels for the World Food Prize headquarters in Des Moines. The art depicted Iowans Jessie Shambaugh, Herbert Hoover, Norman Borlaug, George Washington Carver and Henry Wallace—people who have made a significant impact on food production. Gary was raised in a musical family in Algona. He is a graduate of the University of Northern Iowa where he studied painting and design. He has an easy-going personality. He said he never set any goals—takes it as it comes and sees where it leads him.

Going back to when I still worked for Meredith's SIP as a graphic designer, there was a salesman from Hellman Design Associates in **Waterloo** who called on us. He had some illustration samples to present. Those first samples weren't to our liking so he didn't take back any business. After I went on my

own, I noticed SIP was buying illustrations from Hellman Design Associates and they were very good. Hellman was building a stable of artists of first-rate quality that included Gary Kelley before he went on his own. Hellman Design Associates grew to be a large, full-service art studio. In recent years, I had lost track of them. I had never met Robert Hellman, so while we were in the area, I decided to drop into his studio. Fortunately, he was in and happy to talk to me. The stable of illustrators is gone; the demand wasn't there anymore and the studio has evolved into an ad agency. Their motto is "Creative Solutions and Superior Results." We had an enjoyable discussion about the old days and present trends.

One more obligation before we left Waterloo—playing the slots at The Isle Casino. With her allotted time and $10, Connie chipped away at the $26 debt. She came out $1.50 to the good. After 14 casinos, she is $24.50 below the line.

I have never really appreciated how much farm-to-market activity goes on throughout the state until we started traveling county to county for our research. It is the end of August and nothing is being

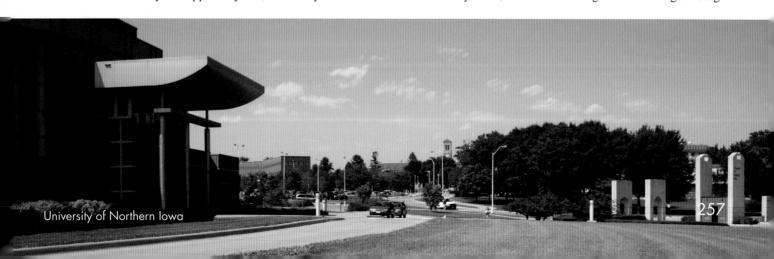

University of Northern Iowa

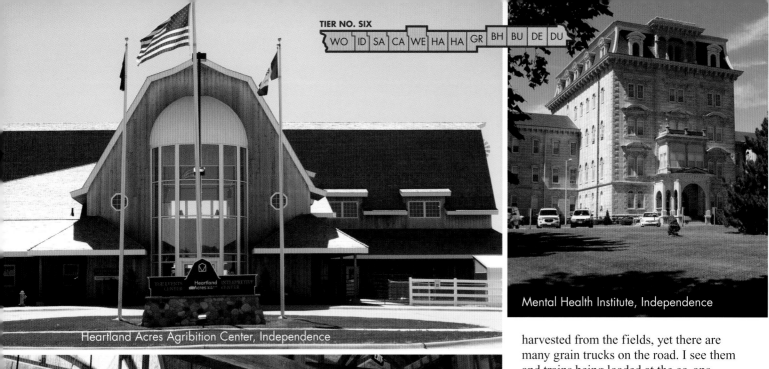

Mental Health Institute, Independence

Heartland Acres Agribition Center, Independence

Gift Shoppe

Big Tails Small Tails

Heartland Acres Agribition Center

258
Wapsipinicon Mill, Independence

harvested from the fields, yet there are many grain trucks on the road. I see them and trains being loaded at the co-ops. They must be clearing the elevators for the 2008 harvest.

Nearing **Independence** (the county seat of **Buchanan County**), we saw a new, large, barn-like structure dominating the landscape. Heartland Acres Agribition Center is Iowa's newest tourist attraction. Its interpretive centers lead you through the past, present and future of agriculture by means of interactive exhibits, equipment, simulators, historical displays, live farm animals and 66 acres of test/show plots. You have fun while you are being educated about Iowa agriculture. I recommend it for all ages.

Continuing toward **Independence**, we came to the Mental Health Institute (formerly called the Iowa State Hospital for the Insane). The French Second Empire style main building was built as a private mansion in the 1870s, and then later converted to a state health facility. It, along with the rest of the campus, is strikingly beautiful. It is presently a 181-bed state psychiatric hospital. It provides psychiatric hospitalization services to

New library, Independence

Independence

adults from northeast Iowa and children and adolescents from eastern Iowa. It also has a training school for nurses.

As we approached downtown **Independence**, its signature landmark—the six-story, brick Wapsipinicon Mill—loomed in the foreground. It is 112-feet long by 62-feet wide by 102-feet tall and it is a magnificent example of 1800s' architecture. Samuel Sherwood, the mill's builder, was no small thinker. When completed in 1870, it was the best flourmill west of the Mississippi. The old millstones were last used in 1942 to fill an order for the Burris and Soener Café. The mill delivered a ton of buckwheat flour for pancake "fixin's." Wapsi brand poultry and stock feed were produced when wheat production slowed. The mill was an electrical energy source from 1915 to 1940. It is now owned by the Buchanan County Historical Society and is open mid-May through mid-September.

America was sports crazy at the turn of the century; boxing, baseball and horseracing were the leading spectator sports. The latter mattered the most. Horseracing was divided into two rival pastimes—thoroughbred and standard bred (harness racing). Generally, thoroughbred racing (the sport of kings), was the most popular; but during the turn of the century, harness racing rose to the top. Dan Patch and Lexington, Kentucky, are names associated with the era but there was also big time harness racing in Independence and, at the time, it was competitive with Lexington. The frenzy in Iowa began when a horse racing association known as the Driving Park Association (DPA) organized one of the premier horse racing exhibitions in U.S. history. The race was between the two fastest trotting stallions in the world, Allerton and Axtel, and it was held at the 1889 Buchanan County Fair in **Independence**. Axtel won by two and a half seconds and Iowa horseracing fever rose several degrees.

Charles W. Williams sold Axtel and used the money to purchase 120 acres east of the old fairgrounds where he developed a kite-shaped track with seating for 10,000 fans. The stands were filled for the inaugural races in 1890 that drew 225 horses valued well over $1 million. Big time harness racing continued at the Independence track until interest waned in the early 1900s. The track site was returned to its agricultural roots and is presently a cornfield.

Racing machines with hundreds of horses under the hood draw fans to the Independence Motor Speedway at the present day fairgrounds. During the summer, over 120 IMCA cars and drivers enter the pit gates at the speedway each weekend. An average of about 3,000 fans cheer them on as they tear around a three-eighths-mile, dirt oval in pursuit of the checkered flag.

While we were in Independence we stopped to visit Betty Payne and her poodle Ginger. She identified with our project because she was working on her memoirs. She said it was slow going—she is still writing about her childhood. One of her three daughters teasingly suggested it might help if she used two hands when she typed. Flowers are another pastime. She is a master gardener, master flower show judge and belongs to a book club. She was a farmer's wife until her husband George passed away in 1995. They raised chickens, ducks, geese, rabbits, cattle and hogs on their 80-acre farm All they needed were some sheep, ponies

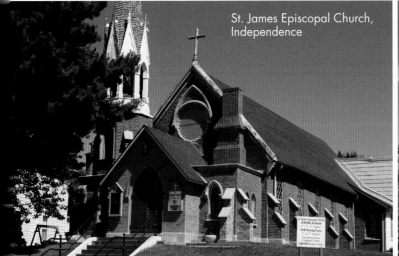
St. James Episcopal Church, Independence

Buchanan County Courthouse, Independence

259

Cedar Rock, Quasqueton

Betty Payne

and goats and they would have competed with Old McDonald. For additional income, George worked at Wilson Packing Company in Waterloo. When Wilson went on strike, George and his nephew Roy (also out of work) bought an old truck so they could cut pulpwood and haul it to Dubuque. It was always an exciting trip with frequent breakdowns. Anyone who recalls farm life in the '40s, '50s and '60s remembers the big debate of which tractor was the best. John Deere and Farmall had the most advocates. George was a Farmall man who later in life ended up with a John Deere lawn mower. He spent a lot of time cussing it and one day when it broke down, he took it to a John Deere shop for repair. When told the cost, he reacted, "If it was painted red, it would only be half as much." Betty says, " I have lived in Iowa all my life. I have no desire to move South. My neighbor plows my driveway and I have a chance to read more in the winter."

The river that powered its namesake mill got its name from an Indian romance tragedy. An Indian brave named Wapsi fell in love with an Indian maiden named Pinicon. Pinicon's father did not approve

Quasqueton Area Historical Society

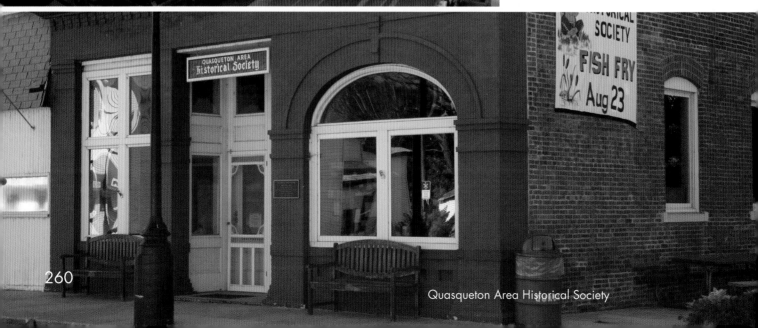

Quasqueton Area Historical Society

Wapsipinicon River, Quasqueton

and his efforts to break them up resulted in their plunging into the river and being consumed by the river. The beauty of this romance has sprung up from the waters into the countryside as the Wapsipinicon winds its way to the Mississippi. Boating, canoeing and fishing are great ways to enjoy this beauty. Veterans Park and Riverwalk Park grace the river's shores as it passes through Independence.

What is the town's premier festival? Independence Day, of course. The day features a tremendous Kidz Zone, live music, a coed sand volleyball tournament and the world pork burger eating contest. Capping the celebration is a breathtaking, fireworks show launched downtown over the Wapsipinicon River.

Downriver from **Independence**, we came to **Quasqueton**. The early history of this hamlet tells of being a county seat and having a substantial business district. The county seat was lost to more centrally located Independence and most of the business district was lost in a fire. A model of the business district is on display at the Quasqueton Area Historical Society Museum located in an old bank building. Volunteers were working on

expanding the exhibits when we stopped for a look. A sign on the building promoted the annual fundraising fish fry.

About two miles from **Quasqueton** is a house designed by Frank Lloyd Wright. It was the dream home of Iowa businessman Lowell Walter who was born and raised in **Quasqueton**. He owned and operated the Iowa Road Builders Company out of Des Moines. He sold the company in 1944 and made major investments in **Buchanan County** farmland. Cedar Rock is the name of the house and it sits on the brow of a hill overlooking the Wapsipinicon River. From its location just below the hill's crest (Wright didn't like to site at the top of a hill) to custom-designed furniture, this is a classic Frank Lloyd Wright house. Horizontal lines, lots of glass, large overhangs and the follow-through on choosing carpet, drapes and accessories are more Wright touches. When Walter died, the house was willed to the Iowa Department of Natural Resources. It is open to the public for tours from May 1 to October 31.

It was still early fall when we crossed the **Delaware County** line with

Manchester as our destination. The town was originally named Burrington and it was a latecomer in the early settlement of **Delaware County**. In 1840, when the county was first organized, the population was only 168. Despite the small population, the controversial task of selecting a county seat began. A site in the center of the county was selected and platted; the resulting town was named **Delhi**. Delhi grew quickly and by 1850 the population had reached about 1,800. It was during that year that Steiner Eiverson purchased a few hundred acres of land about six miles northwest of **Delhi**. Mr. Burrington bought this parcel of land in 1855, platted it, named it after himself and convinced the Dubuque and Pacific Railroad to run its tracks through town. The name Burrington got confused with the name Burlington so it was renamed **Manchester** (after Manchester, England) in 1858. With the arrival of the tracks and the agricultural boom during the Civil War era, **Manchester** took off with rapid growth. It became the most prosperous town in the county and its residents thought that entitled them to the county

Cedar Rock, Quasqueton

Manchester Livestock Auction

Manchester

Delaware County Courthouse, Manchester

seat. After an 11-year legal and political battle with **Delhi**, **Manchester** prevailed and the seat was relocated in 1880.

Before entering town we stopped at the Manchester Livestock Auction on the southern fringe of the community. Livestock auctions provide a competitive market for the sale of cattle. Special auctions are held from time to time for other animals, but cattle are the staple. At the Manchester Livestock Auction, slaughter cattle are sold every Tuesday. On the first and third Fridays of the month, sheep, goats and feeder cattle are auctioned off; on the second and fourth Fridays, dairy cattle are sold to the highest bidder. Packing house representatives and independent buyers bid for slaughter cattle; farmers provide most of the bidding action at the other sales. The auction house receives a commission on each animal sold. Hogs are generally sold directly to packing houses.

Marvin Waterhouse, manager and one of the owners of the Manchester Livestock Auction, is right out of central casting. A tall, slim man—he was attired in jeans, black shirt and black cowboy hat. A large, shiny, western belt buckle

Betty's Bread Basket, Manchester

Tirrill Park, Manchester

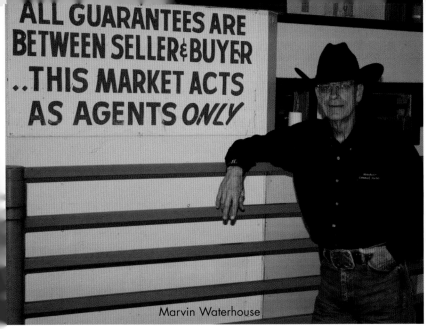

Marvin Waterhouse

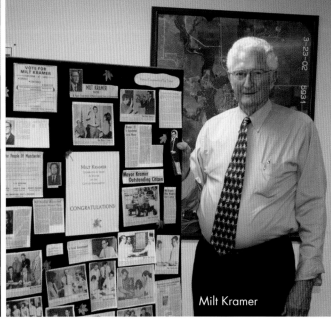

Milt Kramer

accented the look. Marvin grew up in the business. His father built a sale barn in Central City in 1949 for $48,000. In 1983, when Marvin and three other stockholders (his dad and two farmers) built the **Manchester** barn, the land alone cost $100,000. That was during a farming recession and 18 percent interest rates—the toughest time in farming since the Depression. They believed in what they were doing and they survived to be the successful operation they are today. Marvin, his son David and one other person presently own the business.

We continued our drive, crossing the Maquoketa River, into the business district of **Manchester**. It was bustling and appeared to be prospering as much now as it was in the late 1800s. We stopped at the chamber of commerce to pick up reference material, and as I exited the building, I noticed that City Hall was next door. I recalled reading a newspaper article about Mayor Milt Kramer, Iowa's longest-serving mayor of towns over 5,000. We decided to see if Mr. Kramer was still in office. He was and he agreed to take some time to visit with us.

The article marking 30 years of ser-

vice was written about four years ago and, to date, Milt has not given any thought to retirement. His political career began about 40 years ago when he was elected to the city council. After finishing out the terms of two mayors who passed away while in office, he decided to run for the office. He won and has been opposed only twice in the following elections. On the ceremonial side of serving, he has ridden an elephant and an ostrich, been in a dunk tank and judged a cutest baby contest at the fair. He said never again for the latter duty!

Milt is a graduate of Luther College where he used his 6-foot-5-inch frame to an advantage playing varsity basketball. Upon graduation, he taught social studies and coached basketball at Fayette High School. Four years later he took a similar position at Manchester High School. He initially thought of **Manchester** as a stepping-stone, but the community got a hold on him and his family and they decided to stay. He says, "The work ethic in **Delaware County** is phenomenal. We have a good chamber of commerce and a good industrial park. The amenities are also an attraction."

Our impression of **Manchester** as a bustling, prosperous community was no illusion and its success didn't just happen. Formed in 1986, Delaware County Economic Development (DCED) is the oldest, countywide industrial group in the state. Since inception, DCED has attracted and retained 17 companies including Exide Batteries Technologies (370 employees), Henderson Manufacturing (250 employees) and Rockwell Collins Air Transport (240 employees). DCED has also helped with nearly a dozen expansion projects of existing companies. In the last decade, over 600 manufacturing jobs have been created.

The downtown has a fresh look and a high occupancy rate that didn't just happen either. The town's business organizations have partnered to create an incentive program for retail businesses and property owners. The $850,000 program provides grants and loans for improvements to facades and interior rehabilitation of buildings. There are also property tax rebates as well as discounts for awnings and paint. A Chamber Downtown Design committee assists applicants. I love this spirit.

X-L Specialized Trailers, Manchester

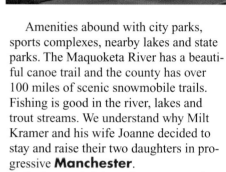

St. Francis Xavier Catholic Church, Dyersville

Amenities abound with city parks, sports complexes, nearby lakes and state parks. The Maquoketa River has a beautiful canoe trail and the county has over 100 miles of scenic snowmobile trails. Fishing is good in the river, lakes and trout streams. We understand why Milt Kramer and his wife Joanne decided to stay and raise their two daughters in progressive **Manchester**.

Before we left Manchester, we took a late lunch break at Betty's Bread Basket. It was almost 2:00 p.m. and we were happy they were still serving. Actually the restaurant was still nearly full with mostly elderly people enjoying the food and conversation. When I see a group of people like that, I always think they are older than I; in truth, they are my peers. At any rate, it was a delightful place and the food was superb.

Some attractions in other **Delaware County** towns include: **Edgewood** Rodeo Days; Civil War Days and the historical former Lenox College campus in **Hopkinton**; the Irish town of **Ryan**, home to Iowa's largest umpire statue; and a life-size replica of an Anheuser-Busch Clydesdale in **Greeley**.

264

National Farm Toy Museum, Dyersville

Biofuel plant, Dyersville

Just across the border in Dubuque County, we entered the town of **Dyersville**, made famous by the movie *Field of Dreams*. "Is this Heaven?" " No, it's Iowa." We Iowans really love those lines from the movie. The script was based on a book entitled *Shoeless Joe* and written by W. P. Kinsella, a University of Iowa Writers' Workshop graduate. Released in 1986, *Field of Dreams* became a classic that inspired millions. It earned an academy award nomination for "Best Picture of the Year."

The film site has become a Mecca for visitors from around the world. About 50,000 people a year gawk at the house and diamond, run out of the corn to the playing field and play baseball with friends or other visitors. It is open daily from April to November.

The Field of Dreams film site isn't the only reason to visit the quaint town of **Dyersville**. It is the home of one of only 53 basilicas in the United States. On May 11, 1956, His Holiness Pope Pius XII proclaimed in part, "Sacred for its works of religion and renowned for the nobility of its structure is the Church of St. Francis Xavier in the Archdiocese of

Dubuque . . . by viture of these letters we elevate in perpetuity the Church . . . situated in Dyersville, Iowa . . . to the dignity and honor of a Minor Basilica . . ."

German Catholic settlers in the **Dyersville** area first built a church in 1862 and the number of parishioners doubled by 1869. Because the population grew rapidly, the pastor and his people decided to build for the future and they did it with aplomb. There were no cranes jutting in the air during its construction from 1887 to 1889. Materials had to be hoisted to heights as high as 212 feet using the block and tackle of rope pulleys. Their methods seemed crude by today's measure but the craftsmanship was so superb that, to this day, there is not a single crack in the masonry. I was in awe as I gazed upon this imposing and beautiful, Gothic-style church. Can you imagine how those early settlers felt when they gazed upon the construction and completion of this sacred building?

I remember back in the '50s the implement dealers had toy, scale model tractors of their brand for sale. These toys were treasures to children and adults alike and they were manufactured in

Dyersville by a company named Ertl. Today, Dyersville is known as the "Toy Capital of the World." The National Farm Toy Museum features collections of toy tractors and model farm displays. There are five, farm toy stores and three, farm toy companies. The Summer Farm Toy Show, held annually on the first weekend in June, attracts dealers and collectors from all over the country. The Toy Farmers' National Farm Toy Show, held on the first weekend in November, attracts about 1,500 people each year.

For our trip from **Dyersville** to **Dubuque** we had another transportation option—biking. The Heritage Trail follows an old, rail right-of-way through rugged hill country, past old mining and milling towns. The 26-mile ride sounded very appealing but we had other stops in mind that were not on the trail.

The Trappist Monastery, New Melleray Abbey, is well off the trail but still in the county and there was a paved road leading to it. The Trappist monks embrace a hidden life wholly ordered to the contemplation of God. They support themselves "by the labor of their own hands." A 1,800-acre farm, of which

Stone water tower, New Vienna

St. Boniface Cemetery, New Vienna

265

New Melleray Abbey, Dubuque County

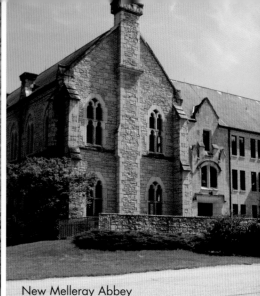

New Melleray Abbey

1,200 acres is timber, provides the resources for productive labor. Austere, elegant, limestone buildings house living, dining, study and worship facilities. I was moved by the simple natural beauty of the church's interior. Unadorned limestone walls, with windows letting in natural light, support exposed oak beams and rafters. The oak benches and organ have a simple, Shaker-like style. There was a feeling of serenity as I looked down the church's elongated shape—there was no question of God's presence.

Besides laboring on the farm, the monks work in a shop making pine and oak caskets. Trees from their own forest provide the lumber for the caskets. The trees are selectively harvested for long-term conservation. These old world caskets are still popular in Europe, but New Melleray Abbey is nearly alone in making them in the United States. Those on display at the Abbey exhibited simple elegance and fine craftsmanship.

Leaving the quiet of the monastery, we found our way to Highway 151 and eased into the flow of traffic heading for the city of **Dubuque**.

The Dubuque area was first explored

Ice Harbor, Dubuque

Dubuque

266

Dubuque Star Brewery building, (Shot Tower in background)

Grand River Center, Dubuque

in 1668 by French Jesuit missionaries who were sent to preach the Gospel to the Indians. The entire region was first claimed by France in 1682. They in turn lost it to Spain, but again gained ownership in 1800 and sold it to the United States in 1803 (the Louisiana Purchase). The first permanent settler was Julien Dubuque, a French Canadian pioneer, who arrived in 1785. For about 25 years, he lived with the Fox Indians at Catfish Creek where he mined lead—utilizing the labor of Indian women and older men. Between Julien's death in 1810 and the founding of the city of **Dubuque** in 1833, conflict ensued between white miners and Indians. From about 1830 to 1871, the Dubuque district was the most important lead-producing area in the United States. By the 1890s, almost all surface lodes of lead ore had been exhausted and deep mining was blocked by water tables.

When mining waned, **Dubuque's** lumber industry took off, providing jobs and creating great wealth. As early as 1837, there was a steam sawmill turning trees into lumber. From 1860 to 1900, lumber production peaked. Sawmills,

lumberyards, sash and door factories and planing mills employed hundreds. When the local timber supplies were exhausted, the companies invaded Minnesota and Wisconsin and floated huge rafts of logs downriver to **Dubuque**. During the late 1800s, the city became known for its sash and door mills. During peak production periods, two mills employed 3,200 people between them. Wagon and carriage manufacturing also became a major industry.

Before the Civil War, local butchers processed hogs for the local market. In the late 1860s, William Ryan opened the first genuine packing house with the capacity of processing 1,200 hogs a day. When Ryan died in 1891, the plant was closed and efforts at reorganization ended when fire destroyed the plant.

Boat building was also a major industry in the Port of Dubuque in the late 1800s. Rouse and Dean Shipyards pioneered the change of hulls from wooden to iron and later to steel.

The early industrial development drew poor immigrants from Germany and Ireland to work in the mills and other industries. They were all of the Catholic faith but they settled in opposite ends of

town. Germans chose the north side and the area still retains its working class roots and is home to some of the largest factories operating in **Dubuque**. The south side became the Irish neighborhood and was known as "Little Dublin." Today, Irish pubs and Irish import stores identify the ethnicity of the area. Both ethnic groups built beautiful churches that add to the classic character of **Dubuque**.

The farm crisis of the 1980s hit **Dubuque** with a knockdown punch. Deere and Company and Dubuque Packing Company were forced by the depressed agricultural economy to cut jobs. That contributed to a nation-leading 23 percent unemployment rate for one month in 1982. The city picked itself up off the canvas and started punching back. It diversified into more service-related businesses and the growth in tourism to 1,500,000 visitors annually has also helped the economy.

After our visit, I'm convinced that the tourism figure will double in the near future. The **Dubuque** folks have been enhancing their greatest asset—the Mississippi waterfront. They have been restoring and reworking old buildings

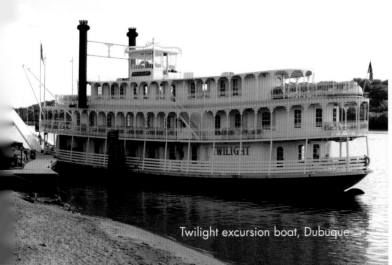

Twilight excursion boat, Dubuque

National Mississippi River Museum and Aquarium

267

View of the Mississippi from Eagle Point Park, Dubuque

Terry Greenwood

Eagle Point Park, Dubuque

while adding striking new buildings that contrast with the old in a complementary way. A stroll down the new riverwalk starts by the old Shot Tower and Star Brewery building. The Star Brewery is being converted to a bar, restaurant, shops and winery. Next in view is the spectacular Grand River Center with a glass-clad exhibition wing cantilevered toward the river. Handy to the conference center is the Grand Harbor Resort—a large, full-service hotel with an elaborate, indoor, aquatic play area. At the end of the riverwalk there is an excursion boat docked and ready to take sightseers on a river cruise. Ice Harbor looms up to the right as you leave the riverwalk. The Diamond Jo gambling riverboat and complex dominate the scene as you start your walk alongside the harbor. Several tugboats are tied up across the harbor. Walking past Diamond Jo's, you come upon Ice Harbor Park and boat docks; beyond is the National Mississippi River Museum and Aquarium.

At the museum you can buy your ticket and sit down to a film at the River of Dreams Theater where Garrison Keillor takes you on a river trip. Then you can

Four Mounds Inn and Conference Center, Dubuque

Marie Fitzgerald

1833 log cabin—the oldest Iowa structure in existence, Ham House grounds

Mathias Ham House, Dubuque

tour the National Mississippi River Museum and Aquarium where you'll enjoy your own trip of interactive experiences with river life from its live creatures to manmade artifacts and vessels. The museum is open year around.

Beyond the riverfront there are many more attractions. The Dubuque Museum of Art provides national, regional and local exhibitions. Eagle Point Park sprawls out on a bluff overlooking the river and its lock and dam. Beautiful Prairie School style buildings and new park structures grace the landscape that also supports picnic areas, tennis courts, a wading pool and playground equipment. The Fenelon Place Elevator is the world's shortest and steepest scenic railway. The Mathias Ham House and the Old Jail are museums worth seeing. During the winter you can enjoy the best skiing in Iowa at Sundown Mountain where you will find a 475-foot vertical drop, 7 chair lifts, 20 trails and a run of 4,000 feet. They have 100 percent snow-making capacity.

You don't have to convince Terry Greenwood of **Farley** that **Dubuque County** is a great place to live. We met

Terry, who works in **Dubuque**, at Café Mana Java for coffee and conversation. He is an employee benefits consultant for Cottingham and Butler and an active father of the Greenwood family. On the afternoon we met him, he was going home to two soccer games and one of his four children was having a birthday.

He and his wife Trisha (McDermott) represent the German/Irish Catholic settlements that dominate the county. Terry joked that he had to go to Creighton University (a Catholic school) to meet any non-Catholics. He graduated from West Dubuque High School in a rural public school district that is half the size of Rhode Island. There are many Catholic schools in the county. Terry's dad owned a grocery store in Farley to support his family of seven boys and one girl. Terry's mother died while most of the children were still at home so they had to help raise each other. Of course, they all took their turn working at Greenwood's Grocery, as did many other town kids. When his dad passed away in 1998, the wake began right after ten o'clock Mass. People were backed up for two blocks waiting to pay their respects. They were

many in numbers and they wanted to talk. Terry was stunned at the number of people who said, "Your dad was my first boss." One family had ten girls and five boys; nine of the ten girls worked for his dad and he found a job for the tenth next door at the drugstore. The boys all worked on the farm. I love this family/community commitment.

Following our session with Terry Greenwood, we checked into the Four Mounds Inn and Conference Center. Our room was in the main house—a 1908 mission/craftsman style mansion overlooking the Mississippi. There are also a rope course, hiking trails and a rental cabin on this beautiful estate. The property is owned by the city of Dubuque and managed by Marie Fitzgerald.

After stowing our bags in the guest-room, we got back in the car and drove out into the hills overlooking the Mississippi River valley. We enjoyed breathtaking scenery as we motored to Breitbach's Country Dining in **Balltown**. The restaurant is on a prime hilltop overlooking the big river in the heart of the Upper Mississippi River region. For my taste, this is the most

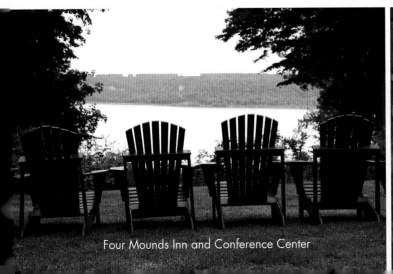

Four Mounds Inn and Conference Center

Old Jail Museum, Dubuque

269

Mississippi valley, Dubuque County

Black Horse Inn, Sherrill

beautiful terrain in the United States. The highway follows a ridge with spectacular views of woods and strip farming to the west and the main attraction—the father of waters—to the east. It cannot be captured with a camera.

Present owner Mike Breitbach's great-great-grandfather purchased an eating and drinking establishment in 1891 that had begun business in 1852. Since then the restaurant has been under the continuous ownership of the Breitbach family. Mike and his wife Cindy are doing their best to maintain the establishment's rich heritage. We doubt that there is another restaurant that can claim they have served both Jesse James and Brooke Shields.

We enjoyed our dinners. Connie ordered frog legs from the menu. They were large, meaty, lightly breaded and delicious. I chose the buffet and some good German food—brats, sauerkraut, pickled beets and the best hot potato salad I've eaten since my U.S. Army days when I was stationed in Germany.

Back in the car we retraced our drive back to **Dubuque**, enjoying the vistas as much as we did on the way out of town. We finished the evening by taking

Dubuque County Courthouse, Dubuque

Loras College, Dubuque

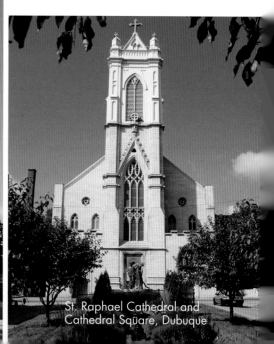

St. Raphael Cathedral and Cathedral Square, Dubuque

Mike Breitbach

Breitbach's Country Dining, Balltown

care of our gambling obligation. We began at Dubuque Greyhound Park and Casino where Connie parlayed $10 into $23.75 during her half-hour allotted time. At Diamond Jo's Riverboat Casino, she lost $1. After 16 casinos, the running score is $12.75 in the red.

The next morning we visited **Dubuque's** three, private, four-year colleges. We began with the oldest and largest of the three—Loras College. It was founded in 1839 by the Most Reverend Mathias Loras, the first bishop of Dubuque. It was given the name of St. Raphael Seminary and its mission was to educate young men for the priesthood and also provide higher education for the citizens of the area. After going through four name changes, the school finally adopted its present name during its centennial year in 1939. In 1963, when the Catholic University of America discontinued its branch graduate study program, Loras initiated its own graduate division. The college became coed in 1971.

Today, Loras offers 40 major and minor programs where active learning is emphasized with hands-on projects accompanying traditional, lecture-style teaching. The liberal arts curriculum provides a well-rounded education. Also adding to the complete college experience are campus ministry opportunities, 55 plus academic and social clubs, 90-plus intramural sports and 21 varsity sports. Competitive Loras College athletic teams go back to the beginning of intercollegiate competition. They compete at the NCAA Division III level in the highly respected Iowa Intercollegiate Athletic Conference.

In 1843, Mother Mary Frances Clarke founded a boarding school for local women known as St. Mary's Academy. In the early years, it operated out of several locations until 1881, when it settled into its present address on Clarke Drive. It was renamed Mount St. Joseph Academy and College. It became a liberal arts school in 1901 and was a four-year college by 1913. The academy portion of the school was closed in 1928 and, at the same time, it honored founder Mother Mary Frances Clarke by renaming the school Clarke College. In 1964, it began a graduate program and now offers three master's degrees and one doctorate degree. Men were first admitted in 1979.

On May 17, 1984, a disastrous fire destroyed four of its main buildings. The next day students displayed a large banner proclaiming, "Clarke Lives" and the mood was set for rebuilding. By 1986, a new library, music performance hall, chapel, bookstore, administrative offices and a massive, glass atrium were built.

Clarke has long been noted for its exceptional arts program with highly developed art, drama and music departments. Dedicated faculty members instruct courses that lead to 48 majors. Clubs and sports (intramural and varsity) round out the Clarke experience.

Dubuque's third institution of higher learning, Dubuque University, has been around almost as long as Clarke and Loras. The Reverend Adrian VanVliet founded the school in 1852 with the goal of training ministers to serve the great influx of immigrants to the Upper Midwest. He began by training two men and holding classes in his home. Although VanVliet was Dutch, classes were conducted in German until 1896. In 1864, the Presbytery of Dubuque assumed control of the school and renamed it the German Theological School of the

Bishop Loras, Loras College

Loras College

271

Clarke College, Dubuque

Clarke College

Northwest. In 1901, a liberal arts college and academy were added and the first college degrees were granted in 1906. One year later the college moved to its present site and in 1911 women were admitted. In 1916, the school, known as the Dubuque German College and Seminary, dropped the German part of the name due in part to anti-German sentiment during World War I.

Now known as Dubuque University, the school is going through another renaissance with the addition of new buildings and the upgrading of existing facilities. The first thing that caught our eye was an impressive, new football stadium—part of a sports complex that includes an 87,000-square-foot Recreation and Wellness Center. Like Loras, its varsity teams compete in NCAA Division III and the Iowa Intercollegiate Athletic Conference. It makes a nice, cross-town rivalry. It is strong academically and provides the typical extra-curricular clubs and intramural sports. Throughout its history Dubuque University has been known as a place of educational opportunity for all. Its diversity is still one of its strengths.

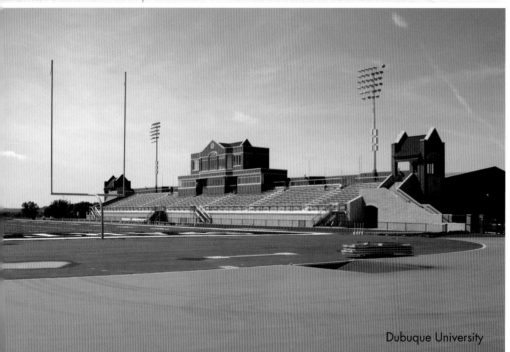

Dubuque University

Dubuque University

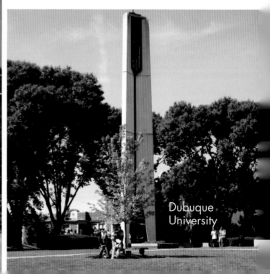

Dubuque University

View of Mississippi near Guttenberg

Guttenberg

e followed the gorgeous, spectacular terrain along the Mississippi from Dubuque County into Clayton County. **Clayton County** has numerous villages nestled in the hills along Mississippi tributaries and on the banks of the big river itself. The villages ooze charm and draw tourists but not in large enough numbers to make them touristy-appearing. This might change as the word gets out—I hope they retain their charm.

Word was out in the state of New York about the beautiful land beyond the Mississippi. In 1834, this promise prompted A. S. Cooley and his wife to make the move and, as early arrivals, they found a land in the very beginning of settlement. Dubuque consisted of two log cabins. In 1839, they eventually chose Garnavillo Township to build their home. The nearest trading points were on the Wisconsin side of the river at Prairie du Chien and Cassville, requiring a two or three day trip for supplies. While making this journey, Cooley had to leave his wife and children alone to deal with frontier life, including potentially hostile Indians.

The first wave of settlers to join the Cooleys were American-born residents of

274

New marina under construction, Guttenberg

The Landing Inn, Guttenberg

Lock and Dam #10, Guttenberg

the Eastern states. They were followed closely by European immigrants from Germany, Norway and Sweden. They found a county flush with game such as wild turkeys and prairie hens; fish were abundant in the rivers. Wolves and wildcats were an occasional problem but the timber rattlesnakes were a major problem. A bounty was soon enacted to deal with this slithering menace.

The American Indians did not understand land ownership on an individual basis. The early French explorers saw their point of view and established peaceful relationships by adapting a similar life style. In 1673, the explorers gave a Sac and Fox camping site on the Mississippi the name of Prairie La Port (the door to the prairie). In 1833, when the area was opened for legal settlement, a town grew on this site and served as a focal point for westward development. Germans began settling the town in 1845 and, by 1850, there was a considerable increase in population, nearly all German. They renamed Prairie La Port after Johannes Guttenberg, the inventor of movable type.

Today, **Guttenberg** retains the German flavor with many historic,

German-style, limestone buildings. The easily obtained limestone was used to construct over one hundred stone buildings in the mid- to late-1800s. With a population of about 2,000, it is the largest town in village-laden **Clayton County**. A business district of about four blocks runs parallel with the river. Between the street and the river, there is a lovely strip of parkland with benches on which you can rest your bones as you gaze at the scenery and river activity.

For our overnight stay we chose The Landing, an inn built into the shell of a former button factory. The rooms are new construction with each room bordering (and exposed to) the outside limestone wall of the original building. The upper floors are bi-level suites—nicely done.

After we checked in at The Landing and ate dinner at Doug's Steak House, we took a seat on a park bench overlooking the river and Lock and Dam #10. It's a slow pace on the river. River boys and old men fish offshore; barges (out of necessity) creep along; and trains lumber by. Traffic through the locks is laborious and fishing boats are in no hurry. The occasional speedboat looks out of place.

The Landing did not serve breakfast so we were on our own in the morning. We chose the Stadium Bar & Grill for our morning sustenance. The atmosphere was sports bar, but the patrons were pure, small town Iowa. A lively, elderly German waitress zipped between tables kibitzing with the customers. We couldn't hear all of her comments but she left tables laughing throughout the restaurant. At one point she spoke to the whole group saying, "You're gonna miss me when I'm gone." One of the regulars immediately piped up, "When are you goin'?" The sausage, egg 'n' muffin special was a perfect start to the day.

Another reason to visit the **Guttenberg** area is the 62-acre Turkey River Mounds State Preserve located south of town. It is the site of a large complex of ancient Indian mounds. At the summit of a narrow ridge near the confluence of the Turkey and Mississippi Rivers, there are 43 conical, linear, compound and effigy mounds. These ceremonial and burial sites were built between 500 B.C. and 900 A.D. There is no trail and the terrain can be rugged, but for the adventurous hiker, it is a rewarding trip.

Guttenberg

Guttenberg

275

Pikes Peak State Park

Standing: Ed and Cyndy Haley from New York
Sitting: Susan and Tom Church from Tennessee
Pikes Peak State Park

We left **Guttenberg** heading north via the Great River Road through the "Iowa Mountains." Our first stop on this trek was Pikes Peak State Park, just south of **McGregor**. It was named for the same man as the Pikes Peak in the Colorado Rockies. To say that Iowa's Pikes Peak can't compete in size is an understatement, but for my taste, the view from Colorado's Pikes Peak cannot compete for shear beauty. It is probably the most spectacular view of all the Mississippi overlooks. There is a map-like look at the confluence of the Wisconsin and Mississippi Rivers. And there are attractive campsites and picnic areas on the park grounds.

We left the park and descended into the west end of **McGregor's** main street. A Catholic church is built into the hillside and, if you stand on its front steps, you will be looking down the middle of the business district. The other end of the street, for all practical purposes, goes into the Mississippi.

In 1837, Alexander McGregor began operating a ferry across the big river between Prairie du Chien and the present site of **McGregor**. In 1847, McGregor

Clayton County Courthouse, Elkader

McGregor

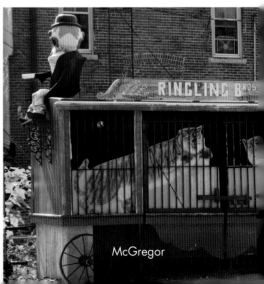

McGregor

View from Pikes Peak State Park

Marquette

laid out a six-block area for a town. It was quickly populated and, in 1857, it was incorporated. That same year the railroad reached Prairie du Chien. **McGregor** rapidly became a major commercial center where grain from Iowa and Minnesota was transported across the river and shipped east by rail. In the 1870s, the population exploded to over 5,500 as the city became the busiest shipping port west of Chicago.

Marquette, located two miles north of McGregor, began as North McGregor. It was a terminus for rail shipments from the western side of the Mississippi. It progressed as a railroad center when the east and west rail lines were connected by a pontoon bridge between Prairie du Chien and North McGregor. The fortune of **McGregor** declined as North McGregor's rail yards grew to employ up to 400 people as late as 1920, when the town's name was changed to Marquette.

Today, **Marquette** and McGregor's fortunes are still linked as they pursue tourist dollars. **Marquette** has a casino and winery and McGregor has a very picturesque downtown with antique and gift shops. The outdoor attractions are excep-

tional. The Mississippi and its tributaries are fun for boating and fishing. The bluffs and state parks are great for hiking and camping. As you traverse the area, whether on foot or wheels, you can feel the history and character of this colorful part of the world. The Ringling Brothers planted the seeds for their career by playing circus in the backyards of McGregor.

Connie risked $10 on the slots at Marquette's Isle of Capri and quickly lost it all. She renamed it the "Isle of Caput." After 17 casinos, the running score is $22.75 in the red.

We left the Mississippi for our journey west on the seventh tier of Iowa counties. We continued to drive through rugged country as we took Highway 13 to **Elkader**, the **Clayton County** seat. The charm of the town was immediately apparent as we approached the business district. The first building to catch our eye was the handsome Clayton County Courthouse. Red brick, arched windows, gleaming white trim with ornate touches and a cupola complete with clock, windows and vents all work harmoniously in this well-preserved building. As we continued our approach, we crossed the

Turkey River on a 119-year-old, limestone bridge. This beautiful, twin-arch structure is the longest of its type west of the Mississippi. To the right, as we crossed the bridge, we saw a vintage dam with water flowing evenly over its entire width. The remaining view from the bridge is of the backside of the downtown buildings lined up along the riverbank. The backside has its charm, but the fronts of these buildings and those across the street make an elegant turn-of-the-century townscape.

The town site on the west side of the river was occupied by Winnebago and Sac and Fox Indians when the first white settlers arrived in 1838. On the east side, a log cabin was built to house two families—the Boardmans and the Brownsons. Try to visualize the scene of these two cultures observing each other as they looked across the Turkey River. The two families could watch the Indian children playing on the west bank during the day and at night would clearly see their campfires while wolves howled in the distance. The wonderment must have been just as great for the Indians as they looked upon the strange ways of the white people.

Elkader

Motor Mill near Elkader

Former Mayor Ed Olson brought back this Abd-Elkader banner after trip to Algiers

1803 OPERA HOUSE

CITY HALL

OPERA HOUSE   OPERA HOUSE

Elkader

The town of **Elkader** was founded in 1846 by Timothy Davis, John Thompson and Chester Sage. Davis named the town after Emir Abd-Elkader who began the fight against French colonialism in Algiers. A true hero, this good man was a poet, philosopher, religious leader, humanitarian, statesman and military genius. While he was in exile in Damascus, Syria, he saved the lives of 12,000 Christians who were being threatened with death by the Druze during rioting in that city.

Elkader is the only town in the United States named after an Arab. This fact impressed Algerians who regard Abd-Elkader as their most revered hero. In January of 1984, the Algerian government invited the mayor and city council of Elkader to come to Algeria to sign Sister City resolutions with Mascara, Algeria, the hometown of Abd-Elkader. The folks from **Elkader** made the trip, were treated royally and, on their return, took steps to complete the Sister City agreement. The result is a wonderful, respectful and enjoyable exchange between North Africans and Upper Midwest Americans. **Elkader** has

MUSEUM   RURAL HERITAGE CENTER

Rural Heritage Museum, Elkader

STRAWBERRY POINT

Frederique Boudouani and Brian Bruening

Franklin Hotel, Strawberry Point

warmly entertained a steady stream of Algerian visitors including descendants of Abd-Elkader and seven ambassadors. It is my prayer that this inspiring story of very diverse cultures making the effort to appreciate each other (and succeeding) becomes more prevalent world-wide.

An Algerian presence in **Elkader** has taken shape at Schera's Restaurant and Bar. The restaurant is owned and run by New Hampton native Brian Bruening and Algerian native Frederique Boudouani. They met in Boston where they started a sideline business of catering while pursuing their individual careers. They both were tiring of city life and Boudouani began researching Islam in America. He discovered that the first mosque in the United States was in Cedar Rapids and that another Iowa town was named after Emir Abd-Elkader. Bruening, the Iowa native, knew what to expect when they decided to make the move to **Elkader**. Boudouani had never lived in a metro area fewer than two million people. They both wisely decided not to impose big city ways on the community even though there is a live-and-let-live attitude with most residents. They bought one of the

town's oldest buildings that had already been developed into a restaurant. They began the operation serving the basic menu of the previous owners and then slowly integrating Algerian cuisine as another menu choice. It was our pleasure to sample the latter as we experienced a very enjoyable lunch while seated on a back deck overlooking the Turkey River. We split an Algerian combo platter that included za'atar (pita bread topped with feta cheese and seasoned olive oil spread), bourek (seasoned ground beef rolled in phyllo dough and fried) and samosas (triangles of fried dough filled with spicy chicken). Superb!

More spectacular scenery awaited us as we returned to Highway 13 and drove to **Strawberry Point**. For a portion of the drive we were on high ground looking down into deep valleys variegated with field strips, woods, pastures and farmsteads. When we arrived at Strawberry Point, a welcoming sign with strawberry art greeted us. Many businesses have picked up on this motif in their name and graphics. A huge strawberry sculpture outside City Hall accentuates the theme.

Donna and Bob Johanns have enjoyed

the amenities of living in **Strawberry Point** nearly all their married life. It was a great environment for their four children who remain a close family. Two live nearby in Fayette and Manchester and the other two live in the neighboring states of Nebraska and Wisconsin. Donna and Bob do their best to give their 12 grandchildren equal attention, which means frequent trips to Nebraska and Wisconsin to watch kids' ballgames.

Donna grew up in Lanesboro, Minnesota, and started nurses' training at Mankato State but she got married before completing the course. She met Bob at the Playmore Ballroom in Rochester, a favorite '50s–'60s gathering spot for southeast Minnesotans and northeast Iowans. Bob, originally from Osage, had moved to **Strawberry Point** to work for SMI, a small masonry contracting company. Today, it has grown to employ about 500, making it the second largest in the country. It is still headquartered in **Strawberry Point** and Bob stuck with them for 40 years. He has a sideline of auctioneering house sales and charity auctions. One of his ideas was to sell high school football players for eight

Donna and Bob Johanns

SMI headquarters, Strawberry Point

Backbone State Park

Upper Iowa University

hours of labor. To date they have raised close to a total of $100,000 for the school. Donna does volunteer work for the SAFE coalition and the American Red Cross blood drive. Bob hangs with a coffee group of older guys who can't remember names. He also happens to be the first cousin of Mike Johanns, the former U.S. Secretary of Agriculture who is presently running for U.S. senator from Nebraska. Bob and Donna love the natural beauty of the area; the friendly, helpful people; and the convenience of being able to make a u-turn in the middle of town.

One of **Strawberry Point's** amenities is nearby Backbone State Park—Iowa's oldest and probably the best. Cabins equipped with heating and air-conditioning can be rented year around; there is also a lodge available for large groups. There are 125 camping sites (non-electric and electric) with showers and dumping stations. Activities include 21 miles of multi-use trails, lake activities, trout fishing and rock climbing.

After an enjoyable drive on a ridge that gives the park its name, we took Highway 3 to **Oelwein** in **Fayette County**. Oelwein is known as the "Hub

Upper Iowa University Alexander-Dickman Hall

280

Oelwein

Abandoned railraod yards, Oelwein

Hub City Heritage Railway Museum, Oelwein

Oelwein

City" because, at the end of the nineteenth century, three main branches of the Chicago and Northwestern (CNW) met there and the Rock Island line also ran through town. Extensive locomotive and car repair shops were built and Oelwein kicked off the twentieth century as a major railroad center. Chicago Italians and Italian immigrants invaded a predominantly Northern European ethnic area to work in the shops. In 1900, the town had grown to 5,142 of which 789 were immigrants. **Oelwein** remained a railroad town until the 1980s when most of the railroad business left. Transco Railway Products remains and employs about 70 people repairing railroad cars. The track from Oelwein to Waterloo is still in use.

The lookout tower on the western edge of downtown draws you to the Hub City Heritage Railway Museum. The CNW's first diesel, restored to its original paint scheme, sits on a track below the tower and next to the Railway Express Agency building where railroad memorabilia is displayed. The yard office building is also part of the museum and the depot is now City Hall.

Across the tracks from the museum

are the massive, abandoned shop buildings from the glory days of railroading in **Oelwein**. As I walked around taking photos of the ghostly buildings, I heard bluesy/jazzy music coming from a nearby dance studio. It was an eerie feeling.

The Italian character is preserved with the annual celebration of Italian Heritage Day held during the third week in August. Red Gate Park includes bocce ball courts along with the more typical Iowa recreational facilities of tennis and horseshoe. The railroad shops are abandoned but the rest of **Oelwein** is very much alive. There are 11 community parks. A new, 800-seat, performing arts center brings in professional entertainers. There is also a new library and wellness center that add to the quality of life.

In **Fayette County**, the eastern Iowa hills begin diminishing in size and become a rolling prairie terrain. In the town of **Fayette**, this less spectacular scenery retains its beauty with a university gracing a central hill and the Volga River flowing by. The rugged hills and river valleys to the east are easily accessible for recreation and the rich farmland to the west is an economic strength. The

town has less than 2,000 people, but it lives large with cultural advantages provided by Upper Iowa University. Due to consolidation, the town lost its high school, which gives it the distinction of being the smallest town in the U.S. with a university but without a high school.

Upper Iowa University's rich history began in 1854 when Elizabeth Alexander proposed the idea of a college. One year later, construction began on what is now named Alexander-Dickman Hall. This distinctive, limestone building first housed every function of the college—classrooms, administrative offices, the president's quarters and student rooms. Originally called Fayette Seminary of the Upper Iowa Conference, it changed its name in 1858 to Upper Iowa University. In 1861, a company of male students went off to fight in the Civil War carrying a flag sewn by UIU women. These brave volunteers fought in 17 major battles. In 1879, Susan Angeline Collins was UIU's first African-American graduate. She later became a missionary in Africa. In the late 1800s, more buildings were constructed, including an auditorium and gymnasium. The students chose blue and

Abandoned railraod yards, Oelwein

Pennington House B&B, Sumner

Connie visists with Lynn Manson and Faye Heath

Fayette County Courthouse, West Union

Sumner War Memorial

white as school colors and the peacock as a mascot. UIU icon John "Doc" Dorman graduated in 1900. He later established a dental business in **Fayette** and in 1907 became UIU's head football coach. Fifty years later he went down in history as having coached football at one college longer than any other person in the United States. He was elected to the National Coaches' Hall of Fame.

A major change in recent history was the 1972 launch of an external degree program that is the first (and most successful) in the United States. It provides opportunities for non-traditional students to earn degrees while working full time. Presently there are off-campus centers in Iowa, Illinois, Louisiana, Kansas, Wisconsin and Southeast Asia.

As a traditional student on the resident campus, you can earn bachelor of arts and bachelor of science degrees in business and liberal arts. Students can also participate in clubs, intramurals, varsity sports and music organizations of a typical Iowa private college. And a graduate program in education is available.

We left the UIU campus and motored west into farm country. Our destination

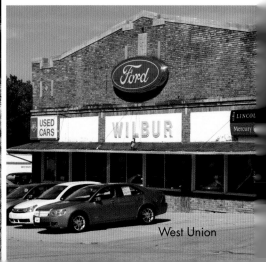

West Union

West Union

was the Pennington House B&B in **Sumner**. This beautiful, Queen Anne Victorian house was built by Charles Pennington in 1908. He was a prominent farmer and businessman who was a generous and influential Sumner citizen. He and his wife Martha had no children—he left most of his estate to the Sumner community. Lynn and Tom Manson did an excellent job in restoring the house to its original glory. As per our usual routine, we checked in and headed out for dinner.

Dinner was at the White Elephant Bar and Grill in downtown **Sumner**. Being late diners, we missed their spaghetti special (it sold out) so we each ordered a cordon bleu chicken sandwich. Connie jokingly envisioned a rolled up meat and cheese on a hot dog bun. It came with the ingredients laid out flat on a hamburger bun. It was a good sandwich and the french fries were crisp and tasty.

The next morning at the B&B, we shared a breakfast table with Faye Heath of Sebastopol, California. She was in Iowa to meet with some Internet friends, and while she was here, she decided to spend a few extra days exploring and photographing the countryside. She told

us she was impressed with the beauty of Iowa on her drive from Minneapolis. We inquired about her home area and gave her some tips on enjoying the Upper Mississippi region. It was a pleasant, stimulating conversation.

After a delicious breakfast we explored the northern half of **Fayette County**. An Ohioan named William Wells was a risk-taker who decided to move west. Rather than join the 1849 California Gold Rush, Wells chose to find his fortune in the newly opened territory in northeast Iowa. He headed for the area that **West Union** now occupies and bought an existing cabin. Then he and two partners bought 60 acres of open prairie with plans to lay out a town. The center of the 60 acres was a high point that a friend gave the insulting name of Knob Prairie. Wells, however, chose Union because of the partnership and added the word West because of the location in the "new west." **West Union** grew to be a vibrant county seat with a courthouse perched on a high point—the knob of the prairie.

The courthouse square is a center of activity in today's **West Union**. People

sit on its sloping lawn to view parades and to listen to concerts held in the gazebo. The town has developed a complex adjacent to North Fayette Community High School that includes athletic facilities, an aquatic center, a performing arts center and a 40-acre recreation area with many park amenities.

Clermont, another north **Fayette County** town, is known as Brick City because of its brick architecture and history of brick making. A New Yorker named Ezra Dibble began making bricks by hand in 1855. The industry expanded, so that by the 1860s, **Clermont's** brickyards used mechanical brick molding and pressing machines. Brickyards continued to be the town's most important employers until the late 1940s. The original Dibble Brickworks was later owned by William Larrabee, who went on to become governor of Iowa.

Montauk, one of Iowa's more impressive homes, was built by Governor Larrabee on a hill about a mile out of town. When Larrabee ran for governor in 1885, his slogan was, "A schoolhouse on every hill and no saloons in the valley." No one ever smoked in Montauk and

Near West Union

283

Clayton County bean fields

Iowa corn in mid-September

Montauk, Clermont

liquor was not allowed. When Anna Larrabee, the last of the governor's children, died at the age of 96, the heirs decided to turn the Montauk mansion over to the state. The house and furnishings are just like they were 100 years ago and are available for public viewing.

Before we left **Clermont**, we met Dick and Beverly Hinsenbrock at the Quarry Lodge next to Quarry Lake and Skip-A-Way Campground. We contacted Beverly and Dick through Sue Evans of Des Moines—who had been a roommate of their daughter Vicky at Iowa State University. Dick started the conversation by telling a story about Sue. The first time she came to visit them on their farm, she drove her mother's light-colored car. She parked in the lane where there were cattle. One of the cows was a bit sloppy in hygiene and rubbed up against the car and the manure transfer gave the car a new look. On another occasion, Vicky brought home an ISU friend who was from Hong Kong. This friend had more hang-ups than a little manure—the open space of the countryside unnerved her just as a walk down Hong Kong's crowded streets would do for us.

Frog Hollow Lake, Volga River State Recreation Area

Beverly and Dick Hinsenbrock

Terex Cranes, Waverly

Beverly and Dick, who have German pedigrees, grew up in Guttenberg. Dick is a 1955 graduate of Loras College where he majored in history with minors in philosophy and English. Beverly went to business school. Although Dick likes to philosophize (he has strong opinions), he made his living by farming. They raised hogs and pigs and did some dairying in the early years. Raising quarter horses and showing them was an enjoyable pastime for the family. Beverly still rides a couple of times a week. Present pursuits for Dick are reading, collecting old tools and writing letters to the editors of area newspapers. They love where they live. "We are Iowa bred and born. We live here because we found a farm we like. There are sincere people here."

It was the middle of September as we moved on to **Bremer County**. The lush green countryside looked like it was starting to collect a little dust. The foliage was losing some of its brilliance and, in spots, the warm colors of fall were breaking through. The approaching fall was most noticeable in the crops. Beans had progressed from green to yellow-green to primary yellow and were now turning to a yellow-orange. Corn had reached its full height and streaks of yellow ochre were running through the stalks and leaves.

Bremer County was named after Swedish novelist Frederika Bremer; one of its towns—**Frederika**—also honors her. However, that is the only Swedish influence you will find in the county. The earliest settlers in the 1850s came from states east of the Mississippi. They were followed by German immigrants and then more German immigrants. During the 1870s, there was a large influx of Germans into Iowa and into **Bremer County**, in particular. German Lutheran churches sprang up all over the county and the German language was more common than English. St. Paul's Lutheran Church in **Waverly** grew to be one of the largest of the Iowa synod's congregations, thereby attracting the location of church agencies to Waverly. Wartburg College, Wartburg Publishing House (later moved to Chicago), an orphanage and Lutheran Mutual Insurance (CUNA) grew from those roots.

Mills and agricultural markets developed in small towns around the county, drawing in merchants and other services such as blacksmiths. **Waverly** was especially blessed with ample fall in the Cedar River—ideal for the construction of mills. This waterpower soon turned the mechanisms of flour and saw mills. Early growth in the 1850s was instrumental in **Waverly** being chosen as the county seat and, unlike many other counties, the seat stayed in Waverly.

Waverly continues to be a progressive town with healthy businesses and industries. Nestle USA Beverage Division bought out the Carnation dry milk operation and its 300 employees presently produce hot cocoa mix, non-dairy creamer, instant breakfast drink, NESTEA and Nestle Quick. Cuna Mutual Life Insurance, whose roots go back to Lutheran Mutual Insurance, employs 750 people. Terex Cranes is the latest crane manufacturer to occupy the production facilities initially built by Schield Bantam Cranes in 1942. Terex is a major producer of earth-moving equipment and cranes. About 180 employees build these machines.

Limestone quarry operator Vern Schield thought a shovel crane mounted on a truck would be a real asset to his

Equestrian campgrounds, Volga River State Recreation Area

285

Waverly

Bremer County Courthouse, Waverly

lime operation. Lime, made by pulverizing limestone, was spread on farm fields to make them less acidic. In 1942, with the help of his brother Wilbur, Vern created the first Schield Bantam Crane from spare parts. The process evolved into assembly line built cranes that were mounted on a truck or a self-propelled crawler. The hardworking brothers kept pace with technology and their company became a leader in the industry. Their early efforts are on display at the Schield International Museum in **Waverly**. Also on display are artifacts gathered by Vern and his wife Marjorie from world travel to 70 countries.

In 1948, sale barn operator and auctioneer Arnold Hexom held the first Waverly Midwest Horse Sale. At the time the draft horse business was virtually nonexistent and Hexom, a lover of horses, set about to change that. The sale became a hit and awakened horse lovers across the country, due in no small part, to Hexom's colorful personality. He loved to joke and tell stories and he loved being the presiding auctioneer at the horse sales. He would call a sale for 12 hours straight, pausing only to take a swig of

286

Wartburg College Chapel, Waverly

Simon Estes

Home of the renowned
Waverly Midwest Horse Sale

orange juice to keep his throat moist. A restroom break after six hours took care of those needs. The next day he would do it all over again, enjoying every minute. It grew to be one of the largest and most prestigious horse sales in the United States. Hexom passed away in 1990 at the age of 77. His legacy is secure as the sale continues to attract thousands of national and international horse enthusiasts the last week in March and the first week in October. I picked up a flier for October's sales and its subhead proclaimed, "2008 Fall Draft Horse, Mule, Equipment, Miniature and Saddle Horse, and Light Driver Consignment Sale."

If visitors to the horse sale would like to linger a day or two, there are many **Bremer County** attractions. Small towns with gift and antique shops and restaurants with home-cooked meals are nice stops on a drive in the country. You can enjoy hiking, canoeing, hunting and fishing along the county's rivers. And visiting historic museums is always fun.

The 900-year-old Wartburg Castle in Germany was a center for German culture. Goethe, Wagner and Liszt found inspiration there and, for Martin Luther, it

was a place of refuge and accomplishment. During his year at Wartburg, Luther translated most of the New Testament into vernacular German. The castle's namesake, Wartburg College in Waverly, is also a refuge of inspiration and accomplishment to its present day students. It was a struggle to get to this point, however.

The ground was prepared in several places to plant the seed of a German Evangelical Lutheran Synod college. First was Saginaw, Michigan, in 1852, then Dubuque in 1853, on to St. Sebald in 1857, then Andrew in 1878 and Waverly in 1879. Stints in Galena and Mendota, Illinois, were also in the mix during this period. It is all very confusing and the seed's roots did not take hold with all the moving.

However, progress was made in **Waverly**; in the 1890s, the college and the town were cooperating on a plan to add a third building when Clinton made a dazzling offer to relocate the college. Through a land development scheme, they offered a new campus and an impressive main building. The college was thereby moved to Clinton with

Waverly keeping the teachers' seminary. For the next 40 years there were two Wartburgs. The synod leaders decided this was not working and Waverly, through some clever promotion, ended up with the permanent campus. Otto Proehl, the president of the Clinton school, was so bitter that he refused an honorary degree that was offered fifteen years later at a centennial celebration. After World War II, the campus quadrupled in size and today about 1,800 students walk the grounds of this beautiful college.

Balance is the key word in Wartburg's approach to educating its students. Academics are faith-based liberal arts with more than 50 majors. There are over 100 campus organizations. They have nation-leading programs in Division III intercollegiate athletics and they have won ten consecutive, Iowa Conference men's all-sports championships. Their musical ensembles perform in every region in the United States. The department has the added prestige of having Dr. Simon Estes, a renowned opera star as artist-in-residence. Estes, who has lived around the world, has moved back to his native Iowa. His youngest daughter

Wartburg College Hall of Pride

Bremer County

287

Anywhere in Iowa

Milt Westendorf

Blue Stem Winery,
Parkersburg

Tiffany will attend Wartburg after graduating from high school in Switzerland.

Before we left **Waverly** we paid a visit to Milt Westendorf, an old-time service station operator. Milt's dad was a mechanic and, of the five boys in his family, Milt was the one who liked to tinker. He owned a DX station in downtown Waverly that offered full service including mechanical work. At the time there were 13 full service stations, so you had to do a little extra to compete. Working six or seven days a week, he did a lot extra and was very successful. DX representatives kept offering him larger stations in Waterloo where he could make a lot more money but he said, "No, thanks, I like my life in Waverly." It was a busman's holiday when he got away from work because his hobby was, and still is, restoring vintage cars. He presently owns a '63 Chevy convertible, a 1915 Model T touring car, a '28 Model A sport coupe, a '37 Chevy business coupe, a '40s Indian motorcycle and a '60s Harley that he bought new. He also owns a railroad depot that he used to rent to the Star Clipper dinner train. It is presently a Sub City restaurant. With the advent of self-

288

Parkersburg

Sue and Tom Teeple

Bremer County

service gasoline, his station was converted to a mechanical service garage. His son Ed still runs Westendorf Auto and, up until last March, Milt helped out a couple of hours a day. Milt's wife of 53 years passed away about four years ago. She was a farm girl and had been raised like Milt and that is how they raised their children. His son and five daughters all live within six miles of **Waverly**. They are a close family.

The German culture prevailed as we moved into **Butler County**. It was originally settled by pioneers with no strong ethnic identity in the 1850s. As in Bremer County, Germans began arriving in the 1870s and the migration escalated in the 1880s. Many of the original non-German settlers moved out as the German contingent became dominant. Again, World War I brought about suspicion of the loyalty of the Germans who had maintained their language and Old World ways. Some super patriots made sure the German natives bought their share of War Bonds, planted large gardens and didn't hoard supplies that were scarce. No disloyalty was found.

The industrious settlers of the towns of **Aplington** and **Parkersburg**—both Germans and non-Germans—built progressive towns. Services and retail businesses were developed to serve the growing agricultural community. Original downtowns were built with frame buildings and the scenario of a fire starting with no equipment capable of dousing it repeated itself in these towns. In 1901, a fire started in an **Aplington** livery barn and spread to every wood structure in the business district. Twenty buildings were destroyed with only the brick bank surviving. Guess what material was used in the rebuilding.

In 1913, the people of **Aplington** approved a bond issue for building a power plant to generate electricity. The powerhouse was built and the dynamos were installed. The supply was limited with electricity being supplied from 6:30 a.m. to 10 p.m. A flicking of the power plant's on-and-off switch at 9:45 p.m. warned the residents that, in 15 minutes, it was back to kerosene lamps.

Parkersburg and **Aplington** are one school district now, with the high school located in Parkersburg. The German ethnicity is still strong and there is a lot of pride in their high school. Four, active, National Football League players learned the fundamentals of the game playing for the Parkersburg/Aplington Falcons. The combined population of the two towns is only 3,000 people. Jared DeVries, Aaron Kampman, Brad Meester and Casey Wiegmann are solid contributors to their respective teams' successes. And they are good citizens—great representatives of our state.

Tom Teeple, a **Parkersburg** barber, had the privilege of coaching these rugged NFL players when they were little boys participating in fourth grade basketball. He said they are wonderful people. They remember where they came from; they stop and say hello when they are in town. Tom shares space in his shop with his wife Sue who is a hair stylist. A divider separates the two operations and keeps all the Saturday morning quarterbacks on the barber side as they rehash Falcon athletic endeavors. Since May 25, another subject has crowded out the sports talk. At about 5 p.m., an EF5 tornado struck and wiped out the southern one-third of the town. Six people were killed, 400 houses destroyed or damaged,

Rebuilding after the tornado, Parkersburg

Football field where the
Parkersburg/Aplington
greats played

Allison

Parkersburg High School under construction

the roof was blown off the high school
and the gymnasium was completely
demolished. There have been many talk
therapy session at Tom's Barbershop.

Tom and Sue's house was in the path
of the killer twister. When Tom heard the
train sound of the tornado shift into overdrive, he picked up Sue who has MS and
tried to carry her down to the basement.
A couple of steps down, Sue froze with
fear and Tom couldn't move her any further. He grabbed a blanket to cover her
and positioned himself on top. The storm
hit and he held on as his body floated up
like superman flying. The house above
completely disintegrated. They lost
everything except their lives. They were
ready to use the barbershop as temporary
shelter but the good people of East
Friesland Presbyterian Church adopted
them and provided an unoccupied parsonage for a temporary home. The pioneer
spirit of helping others in need has never
waned in Iowa as illustrated by this story
and others we heard in tornado and flood-
ravished areas. New Hartford, U.S.
Senator Charles Grassley's hometown,
was also hit by the same tornado with
similarly grave consequences.

290

Heery Woods State Park

Dick Vickers

Clarksville

It was the last week in September when we toured the area in south **Parkersburg** that had been hit by the tornado. It looked like a housing development with evidence of the storm disappearing. As I walked around, I saw an occasional, old house basement and some rubble but the smell in the air was that of new lumber and there was building activity everywhere. The scaffolding was up and the first courses of concrete blocks were being laid for a new high school. The adjacent football field was well groomed and being used for games. A new Kwik Star convenience store outpaced everyone in reconstruction and was open for business.

The first stages of the harvest had begun as we drove north into the center of **Butler County**. Large combines were cutting wide swathes through bean fields and transferring the beans to grain wagons or semi trucks. Traffic was getting hung up more often by farm equipment on the roads.

Large-scale farming operations are becoming more common today but there were also a few big operators in the mid-1800s. One was located in the heart of

Butler County. The Iowa Central Stock Farm was a 2,500-acre showplace with a beautiful house, barns full of pure-bred cows and some of the best standard-bred horses in the country. There was a deer park and the farm was a favorite resort for sightseeing, parties, picnics and other activities. A huge main barn had a large cupola and two small cupolas. The large cupola was used by the farm manager to observe the work of hired men in the fields. The barn (without the cupolas) and the house are still standing.

Allison, the county seat, also occupies a central location in **Butler County**. This central location was the critical factor in locating the seat because there are five towns with larger populations. Wilder Park, just east of town, offers complete camping facilities, Frisbee golf, fishing ponds, a playground, shelter houses and a link to the 12-mile Rolling Prairie Bike Trail.

We stopped at Norma Rae's Main Street Café for lunch. Light-colored sheet paneling covered the walls that supported a fabric wall hanging depicting Butler County's historical sites. Vinyl stack chairs and vinyl booths with wood grain

Formica tabletops completed the look. My ham and cheese on a croissant and Connie's French dip were satisfying.

The pretty Shell Rock River angles through the county, as does the Cedar River. We stopped to take a look at Heery Woods State Park that straddles the Shell Rock River near **Clarksville**. We drove through a grove of trees to campsites along the river's north side. In 1935, the WPA built a dam, shelter house and lodge that are still in use. Electrical hook-ups and showers are now available. A nature center and hands-on exhibits are available south of the river. There is also access to the Rolling Prairie Bike Trail.

We continued upriver to **Greene** where we called on Dick Vickers to get his view on living in the area. Dick's childhood years were spent traveling around the country while his father worked building the concrete, skyscraper elevators you see across Iowa. The family lived in a one-bedroom trailer that was pulled behind their car. They eventually settled in Mason City where his dad took a job as superintendent of Allied Mills. Dick attended several colleges and got married but did not avoid the draft. The

Allison

Butler County Courthouse, Allison

291

Greene

Bean harvest, Franklin County

Army selected him and sent him to Vietnam for 14 months where he served in the First Cavalry Artillery. He eventually graduated from the University of Iowa Law School. He moved to **Greene** to work in a Mason City attorney's branch office, which was later turned over to Dick. He and his wife Mary Ann, who put him through law school, have lived in Greene since 1974. They raised three children in the nurturing environment of good schools and recreational opportunities. Dick says, "This is just a nice, rural area. If we have a problem, we know the people we're dealing with. There is a comfort factor and you can be a lawyer with a ponytail in a small town."

Greene, a town of about 1,100, is home to the headquarters of the Iowa Northern Railway. Iowa investors bought the abandoned Rock Island tracks from Manly to Cedar Rapids so they could maintain service to elevators along that route. Another abandoned service in **Greene** was the generation of electricity at the dam's power plant. No more! A man has been buying up these water generating power sources and reactivating the generators. He sells the generated

Country Heritage B&B, Franklin County

Mother's Steak House, Latimer

Ackley

electricity to power companies.

Franklin County was our next destination in this rich agricultural region. We first stopped in **Hampton**, the county seat, and did some research at the chamber of commerce and the library. I followed this up by taking photos around the downtown area. It is a nice, clean town of 4,200 people with a very distinctive courthouse. It is quite a contrast to the first habitat of county records in the upper floor of a story and a half, log cabin. A year later, in 1857, a one-room frame building was constructed from home-sawn lumber to serve as the courthouse. In 1866, they moved up to a two-story, stone courthouse and, in 1890, they built the beautiful structure gracing the **Hampton** town square today.

In 1852, the first settlers found their way from Ohio to **Franklin County**. Progress in the county was made in typical, early-Iowa fashion until the 1860s when the Civil War took its toll. Out of a total population of 1,309, one hundred thirty men joined the Union cause. Many of these men were married; wives and children were left behind to manage new, undeveloped farms on the raw prairie.

The construction of homes, roads, bridges, stores and mills came to a virtual standstill. Forty-four of these men gave their lives, including James B. Reeve, the first permanent settler in the county. His son, Fernando, died in a Confederate prison and another son, Orson, survived to return to farm in the county. Why do we celebrate this horrible war? It should be remembered, but not glorified.

In the early 1890s, covered wagons passed through **Franklin County** heading east, not west. They were filled with refugees from South Dakota who had been starved out.

In the late 1890s, the notorious Cherry Sisters, who billed themselves as the "queens of comedy and song," climbed down off the train for a performance at Bailey's Hall in **Hampton**. This sad act put on their show without the usual wire screen to protect themselves from flying objects such as rotten vegetables and eggs. The people of Hampton should have been complimented that they weren't the type to behave in such a manner. However, people didn't attend their shows expecting a good performance. They came to laugh at and ridicule

them—the lowest form of humor.

After our county research, we drove about four miles west of **Hampton** on Highway 3 to the Country Heritage B&B and checked in. This house, built in 1921, appeared to be a Sears and Roebuck plan. Donnis Borcherding greeted us and showed us to our room. She said, for most of its years, the farm had been in her husband Rex's family. Their daughter Lacey manages the B&B and was busy getting the grounds ready for her wedding which was to take place in a couple of days. The original Sears and Roebuck house had been added on to, so there were four, nice-size guest rooms on the second level. Our room was spacious, attractive and adorned with two chandelier-type light fixtures (a first). We also had a balcony and a whirlpool tub and shower. We cleaned up, climbed back into the car and drove to Latimer for dinner/supper.

The restaurant, located in downtown **Latimer**, was named Mother's Steak House. It had a simple, clean, country atmosphere with worn, stack chairs and patterned tablecloths. Framed, old magazine ads were hanging on the walls above plybead, wainscot paneling. A charcoal

Butler County

293

Hampton

Hampton

Franklin County Courthouse, Hampton

Beeds Lake State Park, Franklin County

grill provided some pleasant aromas and the laugh track from a TV sitcom, also coming from the kitchen, provided some unpleasant sounds. The steaks were grilled to perfection, the salad bar was good and the waitress/owner was pleasant. All in all, a good dining experience.

We slept well that night and awoke to a beautiful sunrise. Lacey joined her mother in serving us breakfast. They both joined us for some conversation after breakfast. Connie entered into a dialog with the ladies discussing 4-H. Both of Donnis's daughters showed cattle and sheep at the county fair. Borcherdings still show animals, only now it is to tourists who haven't experienced farm life. During last year's harvest, they had a request from a Colorado couple to ride in their combine. They complied.

After packing up, we drove back to **Hampton** to meet with Duane Payne, a former **Franklin County** sheriff. Originally from South Dakota, Duane worked some jobs, served in the Air Force, married a nurse from Hampton and ended up in **Hampton** when his application for the assistant police chief job was accepted. He had previous law

Duane Payne

Lacey and Donnis Borcherding

Sunrise at the Country Heritage B&B

enforcement experience in an air police investigation unit and four years as a Mitchell, South Dakota police officer. When the **Franklin County** sheriff retired in 1973, Duane was drafted by a Republican and a Democrat to run for the office. His wife Lenora was related to most of the town so Duane had the odds with him in the race for sheriff. He won and was never seriously challenged in subsequent elections.

He hired a 340-pound deputy who could handle himself and began his career as **Franklin County's** top law enforcement officer. The first task the 28-year-old sheriff faced was condemning farm property for the construction of Interstate 35. It wasn't the type of police work he was trained to do so it was "learn as you go." Condemning land is always a struggle but Duane persisted day and night—drinking coffee and eating dough-nuts with the farmers. He gained 30 pounds but he got the job done and got to know many new people in the process.

When Duane ran for sheriff, Lenora immediately informed him she wasn't moving to the jailhouse. The system in many rural counties was having the jail in

the same building as the sheriff's quarters and the sheriff's wife was expected to feed the prisoners. That did not appeal to Lenora nor was Duane happy with some of the other unprofessional practices of county law enforcement. He and other sheriffs formed an association to upgrade standards and were successful in profes-sionalizing county police work.

His men became more professional but they didn't lose their sense of humor. One of his deputies would occasionally don a gorilla mask and drive up and down the Interstate and listen to truckers report on the CB about the ugly "County Mountie." Duane's closest call came when he went to serve papers on a men-tally ill man who had poisonous snakes for pets. The thought of snakes was bad enough but when he came out threatening Duane with a steel fence post, Duane thought it was all over. Then he heard the click of his deputy's gun behind him and the man, who was staring down its barrel, backed off. During his 28 years in office, Duane dealt with seven homicides, four bank robberies and everything the big counties deal with, but on a smaller scale. He had a 90 percent success rate in solv-

ing crimes. He believed in responding to every call and treating everyone alike.

In 1859, the first Franklin County Fair was held in downtown **Hampton**. The exhibitions were set up on the square and the courthouse was used to display fine art. The fair has grown to be one of the more impressive county fairs in Iowa. Grandstand shows include a PRCA rodeo, name entertainers and Figure 8 Races. The Franklin County Historical Museum is located on the fairgrounds and its Pleasant Hill Village and Grandpa's Farm come to life with work-ing exhibits during the fair. Homemade ice cream and sarsaparilla are the refresh-ments as you step back in time.

Beeds Lake State Park, located a cou-ple of miles from **Hampton**, was devel-oped on historical ground. In 1857, a dam and mill were built on this property by T. K. Hansury. William Beed bought the property in 1864 and operated the mill until 1903. The CCC built a 10-foot-long, limestone spillway in the 1930s. A special feature is a causeway across the lake that adds a third of a mile of shoreline that is great for fishing. Hikers and joggers like it, too. The spring-fed lake is also popular

Hampton

First Congregational United Church of Christ, Hampton

Quasdorf Museum, Dows

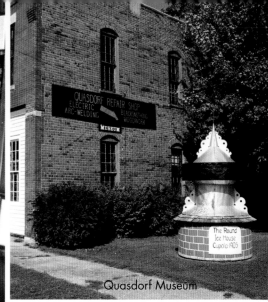

Quasdorf Museum

Lake Cornelia, Wright County

296

Belmond

for boating and swimming. There are pic-nic areas, trails and campgrounds with restrooms, hookups and showers.

In our transition to **Wright County**, we stopped in **Dows**, a town that strad-dles the county line and has a population of 675. The Mercantile Store and Fillmore Building, the Burlington Northern/Rock Island Depot and the Quasdorf Museum are all on the National Register of Historic Places. My favorite was the Quasdorf Museum—a black-smith, wagon and machine shop. As I walked in the garage-like door opening, I stepped on a worn, thick plank floor that bore gouges from horses and wagons from as far back as 1899. The Quasdorf family operated this shop continuously until 1990, at which time they turned it over to Dows Historical Society. It looks like the Historical Society simply left everything in its cluttered array—adding a guestbook, a wall display and a few notebooks explaining each area. There was a horseshoeing area, grinding wheel and forge area, machine area, a wheel and wagon area and there were belts overhead that transferred power to the machines. And the steady gaze of Frank Quasdorf

Dan Matheson

Wright County

himself was looking you in the eye from a life-size photo. I can't describe what a kick I got out of walking through this museum. I hope they never let any professional display artist come in and organize the clutter.

From time to time I have photographed and written about the co-ops/elevators that stand out in the prairie skyline. I decided it was time to stop and see if I could interview someone who runs one of these operations. The Dows Farmers Cooperative looked promising so I entered their office where I was greeted by a casually dressed man who asked if he could help me. My response was, "Are you the manager?" "Yes," he said and the dialog began as Dan Matheson, CEO and general manager, showed Connie and me to his office.

Dows Farmers Cooperative is one of the few co-ops left that is still owned by farmers. There have been many mergers and acquisitions. There are 400 to 500 farmers in the co-op with a Wright/Franklin/Hardin County base. From 25 to 30 employees serve patrons of the co-op. The main function of cooperatives is to buy and sell grain (corn, beans and oats).

Most of the grain is sold back to farmers after it is processed into feed. There are 100-railcar shipments to Texas and Arkansas. Ethanol plants and large feed mills are customers for corn. All the soybeans go to a local Cargill processor and the oil by-product goes to a biodiesel plant. They are also a retail outlet for fertilizer, seeds, chemicals and feed and are an in-house brokerage for commodities.

On October 14, 1966, a tornado, the equivalent of this year's Parkersburg tornado, ripped apart the town of **Belmond**. It destroyed or damaged 600 homes and 75 businesses. As in Parkersburg, there were six deaths. After this disaster, most residents remained and rebuilt and, in a short period of time, the population exceeded its pre-tornado number. I remember going through this town a few years after the ultimate storm and thinking, "What a neat town." We decided to take a look today. It appears that none of the post-tornado buildings in the business district are more than one story. Since my last visit, they have added a canopy over the sidewalks; it extends the full length of downtown on both sides of the street. Visually, it is one, long, monot-

onous, blue strip on posts with globe light fixtures. The look isn't great, but it protects people from the elements and a speaker system pipes in music or announcements. The latter is especially nice during street festivals. All in all, it is a quality, attractive community.

Driving from **Belmond** into the heart of **Wright County**, we passed Lake Cornelia Park, another nice little getaway with a natural lake and complete camping and picnicking facilities. There is also a 25-acre hunting area.

There were no limits on where you could hunt when the pioneers began streaming into **Wright County**. The hardships of pioneer life are well documented and I don't envy their struggle, but I do envy experiencing Iowa in its pristine state. The rivers were clear and full of fish. There was an abundance of prairie chickens and ducks. The woods produced wild fruits, such as plums, grapes, berries and crabapples. There were groves of hazelnut, walnut and butternut trees. There had to be joy in the hearts of the early settlers as they harvested these delicacies.

There was joy in the hearts of New

Dows Farm Cooperative

Dows Farm Cooperative

297

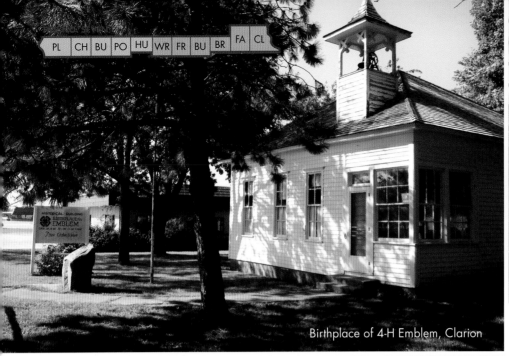

Birthplace of 4-H Emblem, Clarion

Karen Weld

Wright County Courthouse, Clarion

York City orphans when they were adopted by rural Midwesterners through an unusual placement system. A young, New York minister/social worker named Charles Loring Brace wanted to help the estimated 10,000 destitute children in the city. Brace believed a wholesome environment could reclaim the lives of these children and that rural America could provide such homes. The Children's Aid Society was formed and, in 1854, they began loading the children on trains that stopped in small towns where the passengers were offered for adoption. They were called orphan trains. There was great excitement in **Clarion** when a train with this special cargo arrived in 1892. Spectators and potential adoptive parents gathered at the opera house where the children were lined up for inspection. The women would talk to them and their farmer husbands would feel the young men's muscles. They were adopted out of love and sometimes for free labor. Many times, the match-up worked, but sometimes the adoptees were abused. The adoption agreement could be ended by either child or parent. Eventually the Children's Aid Society placed 100,000

298 Heartland Museum, Clarion

Heartland Museum

Wright County

children by way of the orphan trains.

When we arrived in **Clarion**, the first thing on our agenda was lunch. We chose the New Home Café just off the downtown square. It is a wonderful little restaurant with great sandwiches. My bacon-cheeseburger was as good as it gets and Connie had a delicious chicken sandwich. My side salad was very fresh with crisp lettuce, cucumber, onions and juicy tomato slices. I complimented Wayne Ehlers, the cook/owner, and he said the tomatoes were from a vine out back, which he later showed us. I asked if he went out and picked one especially for my salad. He smiled and replied that it was a day old; he had picked it yesterday.

As usual, we were eating a late lunch and there was only one other occupied booth. The conversation we were having with Wayne spread to booth occupant Willie Soesbe. We learned he had good reason to be eating late because he had worked late the previous night in his bar next door. As he described Little Willie's, we became intrigued. We finished our lunch and followed him over to the bar. Our intrigue morphed into fascination—what a cool place. The room stretched

from the street to the alley. A long bar was on the left as you walked in and there was a pool table and dartboard in the rear. There were tables and chairs throughout and Willie's many collections were nicely displayed on the walls. It had a clean, polished look. He said he used to book great blues acts like John Lee Hooker. I would have loved to experience that. Unfortunately, it was early afternoon and I couldn't even experience a beer. Connie and I will be back.

Generally, the Iowa countryside is uncluttered; it is one of the reasons I enjoy driving around the state. However, no county can top the effort by the citizens of Wright County when it comes to clean and they have a plaque to prove it. They earned the "Cleanest County in Iowa" award sponsored by *Our Iowa* magazine. Karen Weld of **Clarion** led the effort by laying out grids on a county plat map and contacting leaders in their respective squares. Everyone pitched in and you'd have been hard pressed to find even a scrap of paper in any ditch in **Wright County**. The judges didn't, so Iowa Secretary of Agriculture Bill Northey presented them with the plaque.

We gave Karen a call and she agreed to meet with us. She is a bright, articulate lady who covered a lot of ground during our visit. She has a degree in social welfare/human services from Buena Vista University. Her work experience includes writing, consulting, computer programming and co-managing the family farm. She volunteers through community service, youth work and the Clarion Church of Christ and United Methodist Church. It appeared to us that her greatest strength is organization and leadership. Her opinions on various subjects were well thought out and made sense to us.

Karen and her husband Jim live on a Century farm. She's an advocate of small town life—big is not necessarily better. She told us the International Teddy Bear Convention is held in **Clarion** every five years because of the warmth and comfort of the town where people open up their homes for lodging. An excellent teddy bear collection at the Heartland Museum also helps. We received a rundown on many more positive things in **Clarion**. She said, "I like the people and projects. All you have to say is, 'You know, what we ought to do . . .' and

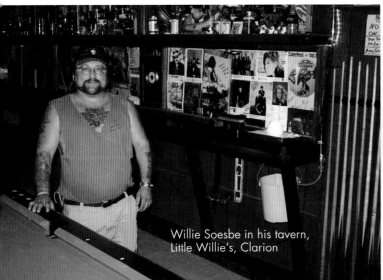

Willie Soesbe in his tavern, Little Willie's, Clarion

Waitress Kathy Fender and owner/cook Wayne Ehlers, New Home Cafe, Clarion

299

The trail at the bottom of the hill
divides Dakota City and Humboldt

Humboldt County Courthouse, Dakota City

Near Dakota City

Mill Farm Historical Village,
Dakota City

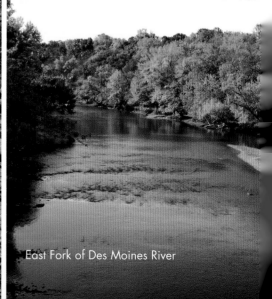

East Fork of Des Moines River

people are ready to pitch in and we do it. It's amazing! On Make a Difference Day, 1,500 showed up."

Clarion must be a world leader in volunteerism. The impressive Heartland Museum's displays and replicas were designed and built by volunteers and are presently maintained by volunteers. A volunteer let me in to take a look. These people are as talented as they are hard workers. I was overwhelmed by the professional quality of the exhibits.

Clarion's largest employer (300) has its roots in a **Wright County** cornfield. Ray Hagie never set out to produce the world's first, self-propelled sprayer. It grew out of a need of "above the crop" equipment for raising hybrid corn. Sixty years later, Hagie is an innovator and leader in sprayer manufacturing.

The harvest was all-inclusive as we continued west into **Humboldt County**. Looking out on the countryside, we viewed a sea of neutral colors punctuated by the farmsteads' trees that were still mostly green. Combining of bean fields was almost complete and some farmers had already retrofitted the combine heads for corn. Initial swathes

Hagie Manufacturing, Clarion

Dakota City

were being cut through the tall corn.

The east and west forks of the Des Moines River converge in south-central **Humboldt County**. A few miles north of the confluence are the towns of **Humboldt** and **Dakota City**. The beginning of each community had its roots in mills built on each fork of the Des Moines River. Settler activity began in the mid-1850s on the east fork and, in the 1870s, New York native Corydon Brown built a flourmill. He prospered and the brick, Italianate house he built next to the mill is now part of the Mill Farm Historical Village.

Dakota City grew on a hill near the mill—the high point between the river's forks. It was granted county seat status and it did not relinquish it. Today, it has one of the lowest populations (911) of any Iowa county seat.

On the west fork of the Des Moines River, a couple of miles straight west of **Dakota City**, the town of **Humboldt** was founded by the Reverend S. H. Taft. This man didn't just build a mill; he was involved in building all aspects of a community—houses, churches, schools and businesses. He was physically strong,

intelligent and had a commanding personality. He was a preacher, editor, writer, traveler, lecturer and farmer. In the early 1860s, Taft persuaded over 200 New York State residents to settle **Humboldt County** by arranging a deal with the railroad to bring anyone in his group to Iowa for two-thirds fare. With this kind of leadership, **Humboldt** prospered.

Taft's successes led him to take on another dream of starting a Harvard-like college in Humboldt. In 1870, he founded Humboldt College and served as its president until 1879 when exhaustion and mental strain forced him to give it up. It was a noble effort but **Humboldt County** was still a virtual wilderness with less than 2,500 people in the whole county and the majority of them were struggling to exist. The students who did attend during the college's short life received an excellent education and were successful in business and in their professions. It was reopened as a commercial college in 1895 and operated until 1916 when it was abandoned. The buildings were dismantled in 1926.

Another great **Humboldt County** man of a different persuasion was born to

German immigrants in 1877. Frank Gotch grew to be a muscular farm boy who loved to wrestle. He had no trouble defeating members of the neighborhood threshing crew so he decided to take on the professionals. (It wasn't rigged in those days.) He challenged a wrestler named "Farmer" Burns in an exhibition match and his superior strength was overcome by Burn's science-based technique. After the match, Burns announced to the crowd, "You have a future world champion in your midst." Burns became Gotch's trainer and, with new techniques, Gotch went on to great achievements. In 1911, Gotch established a training center in Humboldt's Riverside Park where he prepared for his defense of the World Heavyweight Championship. The challenger was the European champion, George Hackenschmidt. Gotch won and was willing to take on any other worthy claimant but there was no one in his class so bouts became fewer. He was credited with being the fastest, strongest, smartest, heavyweight wrestler of all time. *Des Moines Register* sportswriter Sec Taylor acclaimed him the greatest athlete in Iowa sports' history.

Mill Farm Historical Village

301

Humboldt

Rustix Restaurant, Humboldt

Abram Urbina and Bertha Galvan of Lomita's Restaurant, Humboldt

Humboldt

Legend has it that Eunice Grace Nicholl, an Irish Canadian, nearly married Frank Gotch. It was also rumored she wanted to marry a Reasoner boy and she didn't care which one. Whether the selection was random or preferred, Harry Ray won her hand. Harry Ray, who went by the name Ray was the lovable, humorous character of the boys and Eunice was a studious woman of quiet strength. Their son, Harry Truman Reasoner, combined the best of their talents and went on to become a world-renowned newscaster. The program *60 Minutes* was created in1968 with him in mind as host. Harry loved his boyhood years in **Humboldt** and always claimed Iowa as home. In 1972, he and Andy Rooney hosted an ABC special called *A Small Town in Iowa*. Rooney and a television crew spent ten days in **Humboldt** and Harry spent two days doing his on-camera work. Rooney later recalled, "I remember wondering if he might not have been happier in the long run if he had stayed there instead of leaving to become famous." Harry passed away August 6, 1991. He is buried beside his parents, sister and brother in Humboldt's Union Cemetery.

Spring Valley Golf Course

Humboldt

A biking/hiking trail located on a former railroad right-of-way is the only thing separating Humboldt and Dakota City. Efforts at consolidating the two cities go back to the turn of the century and they have all failed. However, for all practical purposes, they are one with shared amenities and economic opportunities. They combine in an excellent school district. **Humboldt** is home to 29 industries that employ 1,200 workers and the **Humboldt County** courthouse sits on a **Dakota City** hill overlooking both towns. The combined population of about 5,500 enjoys 15 beautiful parks, hiking/biking trails, a new aquatic center and the Des Moines River that is stocked each year with walleye fry.

There is an old tradition of harness racing and presently the **Humboldt** track is the number one training track in the state. There is a new tradition of drag racing that began in 1963 and draws fans from across the country to the Humboldt County Drag Strip. Celebrations range from the annual Polka Fest to the Kiwanis Christmasland and Hillside Spectacular. Both of these events draw people from across the country.

Our last stop in the twin towns was Lomita's Authentic Mexican Restaurant in **Humboldt**. We enjoyed an authentic Mexican lunch. I cannot recall eating in any Latino restaurant where the food wasn't good and the service superb. Owner Bertha Galvan and server Abram Urbina made sure this streak continued.

A friend of ours told us about a neat golf course near the town of **Livermore**. She called it "Iowagusta" because of the immaculately maintained grounds with a creek, ponds and beautiful flower beds (bringing to mind Augusta National in Georgia). We decided to see for ourselves and play nine holes at the Spring Valley Golf Course. It was a beautiful October day and the course lived up to its advanced billing, even though some of the flowerbeds were being cleared for winter. The course must have had a soothing effect on me because my normal erratic game morphed into playing par golf the last four holes. Connie was her usual steady self.

During our play, I struck up a conversation with a lady who was removing plants from one of the flowerbeds. I learned that her name was Jeanne Berte

and that she and her husband Gerald built the course. I asked her if she could take a break and talk to us when we finished the round. She complied. Her daughter-in-law Christie, who was working the pro shop and restaurant, also joined us.

The original nine-hole course was built on Jeanne and Gerald's farm in 1979. It didn't get a lot of play early on so they decided to go all out and develop a first-class course that would draw through word of mouth. They planted trees, developed ponds, added flowerbeds and a waterfall and the people came. In the late 1980s, it was rated "Iowa's best nine-hole golf course." Increased crowds prompted them to add nine more holes. On this layout, Gerald designed the course and he and friends built it using farm equipment. They outgrew the clubhouse and, in 1997, they built a new one. In 2000, Jeanne and Gerald turned the course over to their son Curt and his wife Christie. Curt and his four siblings spent many hours over the years working on the course and now Curt and Christie are passing that tradition to their three children. Gerald passed away in 2006. Jeanne continues to work with and enjoy Curt,

Jeanne and Christie Berte

Spring Valley Golf Course

303

Rutland Dam at Rose Mill Park on West Fork of Des Moines River

Rutland Dam

Pocahontas

304 Pocahontas County Courthouse, Pocahontas

Pocahontas

Christie and their family. You could feel the warm relationship as we talked to the two ladies. Jeanne grew up in a farm family of 13 children. She says, "I have never thought of moving from here. It is a great place to raise a family." Christie added, "I couldn't live in a city. It is quiet here and I know the majority of the people and it is comfortable raising children in a smaller community."

The nurturing environment of **Livermore** shaped Dallas Clark, former Hawkeye and present Indianapolis Colt football star. His athletic skills are exceptional and he has character to match. He is another fine representative of Iowa.

On our way to **Pocahontas County**, we stopped at the Rose Mill Park in **Rutland** where the Rutland Dam and Power Plant are located. As we disembarked from our landcruiser, we took a deep breath of the sweet, earthy smells of fall. Leaves crackled underfoot as we walked around gazing at one charming view after another. I love those old dam sites.

Entering **Pocahontas County**, we continued to witness the harvest at full bore. In this part of Iowa, the prime farm-

Pocahontas

land is occasionally interrupted by wet-lands. Fortunately, they haven't all been drained; they provide the environmental benefit of filtering water runoff.

Upon reaching the county seat town of **Pocahontas**, we were greeted by Pocahontas herself in the form of a 25-foot high, concrete statue. In 1851, when 50 new counties were being established, John Howell, a state senator from Jefferson County, suggested that one be named Pocahontas to honor the Indian Princess of Virginia. The town of **Rolfe** was named after her husband John Rolfe and **Varina** was named after her mother. (This was also the name of Pocahontas' home in England.) Deserving of the honor, Princess Pocahontas led a legendary life that included saving John Smith's life more than once, providing food for the starving settlers and promoting peace between Jamestown Colony and her people. Her only child, Thomas Rolfe, married an English woman and their descendants became some of the most respected families in the state of Virginia. She was revered in England where she died of small pox at age 21.

A site was chosen in the geographical center of the county and, in 1870, the town of **Pocahontas** was platted on the site. From 1885 to1893, there was accelerated growth, slowed only by a couple of grasshopper plagues. It was a bustling town in 1900 when the Rock Island Line laid tracks through town. The pleasures of early town life included social gatherings in front of the old court-house. It was the scene of dances, box suppers, school entertainment and church services. In 1900, the entertainment center moved to an opera house located on the second floor of a new downtown building. Movies and all types of enter-tainment passed through this venue.

The movies found a new home in 1939 when the new Rialto Theatre opened. It was a beautiful, art deco structure patterned after a theatre in Des Moines. The 300-seat auditorium was plush and air-conditioned. The sparkling, modern, art deco motif shone throughout the building and on the exterior façade and marquee. There was a cry room for fussy babies. The owners, Jack and Gladys Bouma, showed only the best movies. When they were forced to buy package deals that included inferior movies, they would not show the bad ones even though they had paid for them. The theatre closed its doors in 1985. For seven years, weather took is toll on this proud building before some community leaders decided to take action. It was esti-mated that it would take $235,000 to bring it back. A combination of dona-tions, grants, awards and 1,425 volunteer hours by 45 volunteers contributed to the successful completion of the renovation. The grand opening coincided with the 125th anniversary celebration of the town of **Pocahontas**.

Attending movies at the Rialto is just one of the small town perks that a trans-planted family from Denver, Colorado, enjoys. Leslie Petri and her husband Buddie Brooks, Denver natives, decided they had enough of the metropolitan scene so they began searching the United States for a small town that appealed to them. While searching on the Internet, they came across a yellow, Victorian house in **Pocahontas** that looked per-fect. By the time they arrived to inspect the house, it had sold. They tried to ply the house away from the new owners with cash incentives but were unsuccessful.

Leslie Petri

Ewe-Phoria Yarns, Pocahontas

305

Halderwood Farms B&B and restaurant/banquet room

Pocahontas

Halderwood Farms banquet room

306

Mark Pollock and Lee Halder assembling grain bins

Because they were in town, they checked it out and liked what they saw. They found another house and made the move.

Leslie had spent 14 years as an employment litigation lawyer in Denver. She experienced representing companies as well as employees. The cases became personal; she couldn't compartmentalize. She has replaced lawyering with a yarn retail and online business named Ewe-Phoria Yarns LLC. She also holds knitting classes and business overall is good. Her husband Buddie designs natural gas plants and was working on a contract job in Oklahoma City when we stopped by.

Two years ago when they arrived in **Pocahontas**, the first thing unloaded from the van were the children's bicycles. The children who were eight and eleven years old asked if they could go for a ride. "Sure!" Then they asked where they could ride. "Anywhere you want to!" They have been in love with the town ever since. Leslie says, "This is a very charming town. There is a lot here for the size. When we bought the house, the previous owners had to look for the keys because they never used them. The kids can go places on their own. The mayor

Linda Vander Zeyden

Pocahontas County

stopped in three days after we moved in and everyone waves. People offer to help." Leslie's parents and her brother have also made the Colorado to **Pocahontas** move.

The amenities enjoyed by the new residents include the usual, well-maintained ball fields, pools and parks. There are several state and county parks in the area and lakes are numerous. Fishing and hunting are good. The 33-mile Three Rivers Bike Trail is nearby.

Laurens, in the northwest corner of the county, was the home of Alvin Straight, a 73-year-old man who rode a lawnmower 240 miles to visit his brother in Wisconsin. David Lynch made a movie, *The Straight Story*, based on this trip. It starred Richard Farnsworth and Sissy Spacek and part of the filming took place in Laurens.

The Halderwood Farms B&B, a few miles west of **Pocahontas**, was our next destination. A four-guestroom cabin with a log façade on the front was our home for the night. Our room was paneled with rough-sawn cedar and the furnishings were traditional with a patriotic theme on the bedspread and wall hang-

ings. We also had access to a small sitting room with a television.

We drove to **Fonda** for dinner at the Backyard Grill Restaurant. It was located in a former bank building that retained some of the bank character with marble, dark wood trim and Craftsman-style light fixtures. The name Backyard Grill did not fit the building style nor did the pizza we ordered. It was good pizza, however.

If you read the sports pages in Iowa newspapers, the name Newell-Fonda probably looks familiar. Since 1991, Newell-Fonda has won four, State Class-A, boys' basketball titles in eight appearances. Kevin Larsen ('91), Jim Calkins ('91), Jason Sarchet ('99), Justin Lyman ('99) and Brandon Kies ('01) have earned McDonald's All-American honors. From 1997 to 2006, the football team had a 70-18, win-loss record and Top-Ten, Class-A ranking every week of that period. The girls' basketball team is no slouch either. They have appeared in five state tournaments and have reached the finals twice.

Back at the Halderwood Farms, we had a good night's sleep, woke up, washed up and joined Linda Vander Zeyden for breakfast. Linda and her hus-

band Lee Halder are a couple more people who enhance the renowned Iowa work ethic. They run a B&B, restaurant/banquet room, dance hall and grow crops on 1,250 acres of land. When we arrived, Lee and his helper Mark Pollock were building two, new grain bins. Lee is a mechanic and builder and a former helicopter pilot. He used to own two helicopters for spraying crops and, at Christmas time, he used one of the helicopters to deliver Santa to various stops in neighboring towns. Linda, a former high school math and physics teacher, handles the paper work and doesn't hesitate to drive any of the machinery. The 102-year-old barn they renovated for the restaurant and dance hall was built by Lee's grandfather and uncles.

The harvest was in full swing at the Halder farms and Linda answered a few questions about the process. The same combine is used for harvesting beans and corn. There are different heads for each crop so they try to finish the bean harvest before they start on the corn to avoid changing the heads more than once. The combine also has to be reset to chop corn stalks. When the harvest of a field is

Connie's presence in Backyard Grill restaurant creates the look of a Hopper painting

307

Cobblestone Ballroom where the big band greats played, Storm Lake

King's Pointe Waterpark Resort

complete, they go over the field with a disk ripper to open the soil to aeration. In the spring they go over it with a field cultivator at a slight angle so that there are no false grooves for the planter. These farming methods prevent wind and water erosion. Strips of grassy, uncultivated ground in areas where water runs also prevents erosion. Farmers who try to maximize crop production by planting in these areas pay the price of washouts and developing gullies.

The pioneering story changes a bit in **Buena Vista County**, the next parcel of land to the west. The entire area was almost a treeless tract. There was a small grove at the western end of Storm Lake that was quickly consumed by the early settlers. The few trees that lined the river valleys were not easily accessible to the prairie dwellers. The area surrounding Storm Lake in the southern half of the county was mostly swampland that was avoided by wagon trains. The only timber of any significance was along the Little Sioux River near the northern boundary of the county. Consequently, early growth centered on **Sioux Rapids**, which was located on the Little Sioux River. For

Harker House—the beautifully restored home of James Harker, Sr. (built in 1875), Storm Lake

308

Buddha statue at Buddhist Temple, Storm Lake

Buena Vista County Courthouse, Storm Lake

years it was the county's largest town and its seat. The Fort Dodge to Sioux City stagecoach runs stopped there, adding to its importance. The first mills were built in **Sioux Rapids**; Indians and trappers brought their furs to trade for supplies at local trading posts.

Out on the prairie, wood was more valuable than land so houses were built out of land. They were called sod houses and they looked like large gopher mounds with chimneys. They used wood sparingly to build a support frame and rafters over a dugout area a few feet deep. This was covered with sod cut from the prairie. It provided excellent insulation and weatherproofing. The door was hung with boards, skins or old quilts. Prairie grasses were used for fuel.

Abner Bell has been given credit as the first **Buena Vista County** settler because he was the only one to stay after the other early arrivals were driven away by blizzards. He was 32 years old, unmarried and a good shot. He never claimed any land but he supplied subsequent settlers with wild game and earned additional income selling pelts. In later years, he built a small shack and opened a store

that sold groceries and hunting supplies. He was unschooled, uncouth and unkempt with untrimmed hair and whiskers. He wore garments he made himself from animal skins; later when he bought ready-made clothes, he wore them until they were rags. Guess who was elected sheriff in the county's first government organization. Yup, it was Abner Bell. Bookwork was not critical in those days.

Abner hated Indians as did most of the settlers who followed. The cooperative relationship between pioneers and the Native Americans that is the history of most of Iowa ends here. The combination of broken promises and more war-like tribes added another hardship in the lives of the pioneers and Indians alike. The notorious Inkpaduta passed through with his renegades and terrorized the settlers as he continued his journey to Spirit Lake where the group's terrorist ways evolved into a massacre.

Sioux Rapids survived several votes to remain the county seat until 1877 when the courthouse burned to the ground. This provided an opening for a progressive little community on the north shore of Storm Lake. The town of

Storm Lake had formed a building association with plans to build a two-story city hall. After the fire they offered the county a ten-year lease on the building if they would relocate the county seat. A vote was taken and **Storm Lake** prevailed. The county seat was moved and has remained in Storm Lake.

The city by the lake has grown into a beautiful place to work and live. The recreational qualities of the lake have been enhanced by smart development along its shores. For starters, adjacent to the lake there is a five-mile hiking/biking trail that connects several attractive parks. Properties with old and new homes surround most of the lake. A fine resort complex has been built for use by visitors as well as locals. King's Pointe features a 100-room lodge with a restaurant, the best outdoor water slide in the Midwest, a family playground, a boat dock, a lighthouse and a beach. Tennis players, golfers, swimmers and fishermen find **Storm Lake** a wonderful retreat.

Tyson Fresh Meats (1,250 employees) and Sara Lee Foods (640 employees) are **Storm Lake's** largest employers. Tyson is a pork processing plant and Sara Lee is

Tyson Fresh Meats plant, Storm Lake

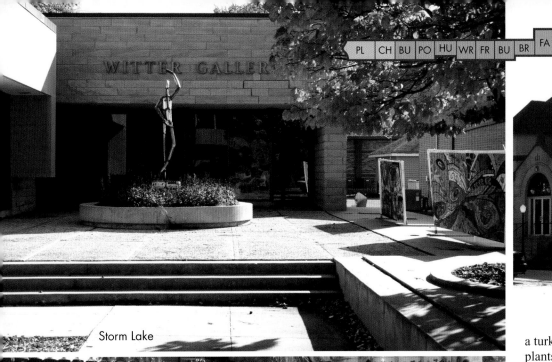

Storm Lake

Storm Lake

a turkey processing plant. Jobs at these plants have drawn a large number of Latinos from California and Mexico, thus dramatically changing the ethnic makeup of a previously all-white community. The transition wasn't without problems, but again Iowa natives and the newcomers made adjustments and both cultures have been enriched. The school district's student population is about 50 percent Latino and 10 percent Asian. The district is known throughout the state for its excellence in the fine arts.

We talked to Silvino Morales, a Mexican, who appreciates the quality of life in **Storm Lake**. Silvino owns Valentinas (named after his five-year-old daughter) Mexican Meat Market and Grocery. He was born in Mexico and moved to California as an adult. He began working in construction in California and then moved to Sioux City where he worked in a meat market/supermarket. He has owned his present store since 2005. He said he is working hard so his kids can go to college. I asked, "Buena Vista?" "Yes," he said. "Buena Vista." He said, "Storm Lake is a good community—it has Africans, Asians and

Silvino Morales and daughter Valentina

Buena Vista University

310

Dolores Cullen displays her artwork

Buena Vista University,
Storm Lake in background

Latinos." He is one of the 10 percent of Latinos who doesn't play soccer. He would rather ride horses. In Mexico, he was a charro (cowboy). This grocery store is a source for specialty meats, as well as regular Mexican brand foods. He said that business is good.

Word that we were writing a book reached *The Storm Lake Times*, a biweekly newspaper. We were invited to stop in and we are glad we did. The paper is locally owned and has the largest circulation in the county and the product has a nice, professional look to it. When we arrived, they were having a press run. The editor, Art Cullen, had slipped into a pair of striped, bib overalls so he could run the press. While he was trouble-shooting the whirling offset press, we talked to his wife Dolores—a photographer and artist. She said Art's brother John, the publisher, started the paper in 1990. They have total control. "The freedom of the press belongs to those who can run one." Another brother, James, edits *The Progressive Populist*, a national publication that is also published by John and printed in Storm Lake. Dolores took our photo and asked a few questions. We

don't know whether we made the cut.

We ate lunch at Plaza Mexico, a nicely appointed restaurant on the north side of **Storm Lake**. It was the typical, good food, good service Mexican restaurant.

Buena Vista University has its roots in the Fort Dodge Collegiate Institute that operated for six years before moving to Storm Lake in 1891. One of the reasons for the move was that, unlike Fort Dodge, Storm Lake had neither saloons nor the temptations of a big city. The college was given its name in grateful recognition of the interest taken by the people of **Buena Vista County**. The college struggled early on, but that did not discourage the Reverend George Herbert Fracker, professor of ancient languages. From 1891 to his retirement 39 years later, he was devoted to the welfare of the college. He mastered Latin, Greek, French and German. His students proclaimed in 1920, "To know Buena Vista is to know Dr. Fracker, and to know Dr. Fracker is an inspiration." The efforts of Dr. Fracker and other selfless faculty and a few civic-minded trustees managed to keep the college alive through a long era of financial crisis. Buena Vista survived

in spite of harsh economic times, wars and often indifference on the part of the Presbyterian Church.

Today's BVU students are glad the early college leaders stayed the course. It has grown to be the academically strong school the founders envisioned. It offers 45 majors, 30 minors and 15 pre-professional programs. The setting is a beautiful, well-maintained campus with several, new, striking buildings. The football stadium, where you can view the lake while taking in the action on the field, was named by *The Des Moines Register* as the best place in Iowa to watch a football game. BVU offers more than 75 academic, creative, cultural and faith-based student organizations. Each year, more than 300 student-athletes compete in 19 intercollegiate sports. They have a very successful NCAA Division III program and are a member of the Iowa Intercollegiate Athletic Conference. Highlights include: 24 Academic All-Americans, 220 All-Americans, 55 IIAC Championships, 11 Individual NCCA Division III National Champions and one NCCA Division III National Team Championship.

Before we left town we visited a

Art Cullen in his pressman mode

Storm Lake

311

Cherokee

Jim McKenna

SANFORD MUSEUM & PLANETARIUM

Cherokee

Buena Vista County

91-year-old Irishman named Jim McKenna. When we greeted him with a "How are you doing?" he replied, "I'm still perpendicular." We told him he looked good. He replied, "I'm sorry I don't have two bits." He added that every time he looks in the mirror while shaving, he thinks, "God, I'm getting old." Well, he is old but he really does look good.

Jim is a former Navy pilot who flew combat missions in the South Pacific during World War II. He married his wife Mary while they were both in the service. After the service he managed Fin & Feather Farms in Illinois, which he made profitable after its owner couldn't write off losses anymore due to a law change. Next he tried selling life insurance at which he says he was a total failure. When a potential client said, "I don't think so," he didn't argue. He folded his books and went home. He was more successful running the elevator of Mary's family and, when he sold it in 1954, he had enough money to buy a 200-acre farm. Mary was a town girl and she said to him, "I hope you don't start to smell like the old farmers I knew." He said he was a hog farmer. I asked how many hogs

312

CHEROKEE COUNTY COURT HOUSE

Cherokee

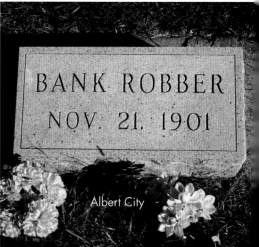

BANK ROBBER
NOV. 21. 1901

Albert City

Buena Vista County

he had. He said, "If you know how many pigs you have, you don't have enough." Three of his boys now run the farm that has grown to 960 acres plus 480 in Ottumwa. Jim and Mary had a total of eight children and they are a close family. Four years ago, Mary, a consummate volunteer, died after she had taken a nun to a dentist appointment. Jim and Mary had 59 great years together. He misses her.

It was the middle of October when we entered **Cherokee County**. I have always liked that name—it is a symphony of sounds in one word. The symphony played out in the countryside with the frenetic crescendo of the harvest reaching a high note. The beans were in the storage bins and the massive combines retrofitted with corn heads were consuming the corn. The concern that the heavy spring and early summer rains and flooding would cut the yield had vanished as *The Des Moines Register* was forecasting the second highest yield ever. The bounty was obvious as we drove by field after field of spectacular crops that were mature and ready to be harvested.

The word symphony is not only used as a metaphor in **Cherokee** because

this town of about 5,000 also has the real thing. It is believed that **Cherokee** is the smallest town in the United States that has a symphony orchestra and the Cherokee Symphony Orchestra probably has the best sounding name of any musical ensemble anywhere. Three concerts are given each season. There is a Pops Concert in the fall, a Mid-Winter Concert in February and a Young Artists' Concert in March or April. The orchestra was founded in 1956 by Merle Robinson of **Cherokee** and Delia Beth Thomson of **Cleghorn**. Lee Thorson, a cellist and instructor from **Rolfe**, has conducted the 60-member orchestra since 1981.

This sophisticated little town also has a successful jazz/blues festival that caresses the musical senses during the middle of winter. R. J. Baker started it about 15 years ago. Bands come from Kansas City, St. Louis, Des Moines and Minneapolis and fans come from Iowa and neighboring states. It's the first weekend in January with pub-crawls downtown and concerts at Western Iowa Tech.

Adding to the cultural mix is the Cherokee Community Theatre. They present full-scale productions, melodramas,

musicals, one-act plays and play readings. Each year more than 200 people volunteer to produce four shows.

The Sanford Museum and Planetarium features galleries that portray the struggles and triumphs of early settlers, the area's pre-history and nature exhibits. The planetarium—the oldest in the state—has monthly programs about the constellations and programs by appointment.

The western cowboy culture is alive and well with the annual PRCA Barnes Rodeo Spectacular held at the fairgrounds. Bob Barnes of **Cherokee** is a major, rodeo livestock provider and the most honored and experienced rodeo producer in the nation. He produces huge events such as the Last Chance Stampede in Montana and many state fairs—a total of about 40 events a year. The Barnes Rodeo stock trucks travel through 32 states and over 100,000 miles a year.

Outdoor recreation centers on the Little Sioux River that meanders through six northwest Iowa counties. Inkpaduta Canoe Trail runs from Spencer in Clay County to Smithland on the southern border of Woodbury County, thus bisecting **Cherokee County**. It is a leisurely

One man's museum, Marathon

Koser Spring Lake Park, Cherokee

Duane Mummert

ride with only a two-foot drop each mile. The scenery, areas of historical significance and good fishing add to the pleasure of the trip. Parks and towns along the way provide camping/lodging opportunities for those interested in a two- or three-day voyage. **Washta**, one of the river's towns, holds Iowa's record low temperature since they started keeping track. It was 47 degrees below zero on January 12, 1912.

I suppose the name Inkpaduta Canoe Trail was chosen because it follows the infamous Sioux chief's route north on his way to the Spirit Lake Massacre, but why honor this murderous renegade? Adding to the hardship of early settlers in **Cherokee County** were raids by Indians who were angry because of the whites' intrusion on their hunting grounds. Ikpuduta and his band of renegades were the most brutal. In 1862, a series of stockades with blockhouses was built by the U.S. government to end all Indian troubles in Iowa. One, Fort Cherokee, looked out over a community known as the Milford Colony.

The Milford Colony that settled the **Cherokee** area had its beginning in

The Grainery Lodge, Cherokee

314

Little Sioux River, Cherokee

Koser Spring Lake Park

Cherokee

Milford, Massachusetts. Dr. Dwight Russell and Dr. Slocum formed the Milford Emigration Company—an organized effort to establish a town in Iowa or the Dakotas. An advance party of two was sent to check an area where the Big Sioux and Missouri Rivers converged. They found the town of Sioux City was already underway and further exploration up the Big Sioux River revealed more settlement. This led to exploration up the Little Sioux River where they found an area of good soil, an abundance of pure water and timberlands. In 1856, the Milford Western Emigration Society was formed and the wheels were in motion for the move west to build the town that would become **Cherokee**. Many professional and business people joined them during the 1860s, believing it would become a railroad town. The Dubuque & Sioux City Railroad chose to cross the Little Sioux River a mile and a half from the settlement so, in 1870, the townspeople moved their dwellings, shops and the county courthouse to the new location. Rapid growth followed with the population approaching five digits by 1900.

We met another hardworking, enterprising Iowan when we arrived at The Grainery for our overnight stay. Duane Mummert has converted a farm granary into a lodge with four bedrooms, a recreation room with available cots, a kitchen, a dining room, a living room and a garage that can be used as a party room. He purchased the property 12 years ago and immediately evicted its residents. Raccoons, rats and pigeons were no longer welcome. After gutting it, he finished off the remaining occupants with 25 hours of pressure washing using five gallons of Clorox. The building began and is still in progress. You enter an alcove with a corn-burning stove that sits on a fieldstone platform with a fieldstone backdrop. Pulleys, flour/grain sacks and every imaginable, old farm tool are on display. On the first level, there is a garage, living room, dining room and kitchen—all nicely appointed with clear-finished pine, corrugated steel and recycled items. A porch wraps around two sides of the building. On the second level there is a suite with a king-size bed and deck and three other bedrooms that share a bath. On the third level, there is a recreation area with a pool table, a game table

and a TV with theatre seating. A Fairbanks scale motif is cleverly done for the bar. This area can also serve as a bunkroom for extra guests. The fourth level is a crow's nest with two bunks. Recycled materials are used throughout.

Duane's day job is director of Cherokee's Parks and Recreation Department and he is also a part-time remodeling contractor. The man does not rest. He says, "I guess I'm a workaholic." He doesn't do anything halfway. The planning and craftsmanship of his work are exceptional. He takes time for his children and they, in turn, help him on his projects. He says, "Cherokee is a small community where you get to know everybody. City amenities are close by in Sioux City and Sioux Falls."

After bringing our luggage in and visiting with Duane, we drove back to **Cherokee** for dinner/supper at a pub named the Gasthaus. Connie's hamburger and my bratwurst with kraut complemented our beers for an enjoyable, down-home, dining experience.

That night we had The Grainery to ourselves. We experienced the sights and sounds of the wild but our accommoda-

The Grainery Lodge

The Grainery Lodge

315

Cherokee Mental Health Institute

Remsen

tions were far from primitive. In fact, we had our own private theater where we watched the Obama and McCain debate.

The next morning there was frost on the car windows. The crisp, fall air had become cold. I started the car and turned on the seat warmers. Seat warmers! What babies we have become. We chose to eat breakfast at a plain eatery that had some Christian symbols for decorative motifs. As we were dining on bacon and eggs, a man sitting next to us said, "Some people say Obama is the anti-Christ." I replied, "No, he's a good, Christian man." "Well," he replied, "all politicians are liars." I replied, "They bend the truth because people won't vote for them if they tell it like it is." He said "That's because they are taking religion out of the schools." "Yah," I said, "maybe that's it."

After breakfast we went to visit the Cherokee Mental Health Institute. As with the three other Iowa Mental Health Institutes, this facility consists of majestic buildings on spacious, well-manicured grounds. This is not a coincidence—all four of Iowa's MHIs are linear Kirkbride hospitals. The Kirkbride resolution required that the hospital be in a rural set-

St. Mary's Catholic Church, Remsen

Denise Green gives us a tour of the Joseph A. Tallman Museum

Joseph A. Tallman Museum

ting (no less than two miles from a town) in the belief of the restorative powers of fresh air, sunshine, nature and the pastoral virtues of farming. The linear design required a central administration building with wards on either side. Cherokee MHI opened in 1902, the youngest of Iowa's four mental health institutes.

In the late 1940s, Iowa's four MHIs reached a peak population of 6,770 with 1,760 patients at **Cherokee**. A significant proportion of patients stayed for life. In 1954, the first effective treatment for the seriously mentally ill, Thorazine, was approved for use. Hospital populations began dropping and, today, there are only about 165 mentally ill patients in all four of Iowa's MHIs. Cherokee has about 50 and, as in the other hospitals, the vacated buildings are being put to other uses. The Civil Commitment Unit for Sex Offenders (CCUO) is located in Cherokee.

The Joseph A. Tallman Museum, with a collection of about 1,100 historical artifacts from the Cherokee MHI, is located in the tunnel area of the building complex. Denise Green, Public Service Supervisor II, gave us a tour. The artifacts show the history of mental health care in

Iowa. It was a special sensation to walk through the tunnels to view this unusual, interesting museum.

Continuing our trip, we entered **Plymouth County**, whose western border, the Big Sioux River, has a looping curve that gives the county the distinction of having the farthest western land in Iowa. The town of **Westfield** is located at the point of this loop. In the early days, Sioux City residents considered Westfield a rival. They are no longer concerned because they now outnumber them 85,000 to 200.

Settlers in **Plymouth County** who persevered were rewarded with prosperity and a good life but they were severely tested early on. In the 1850s there was an especially severe winter. At one point, the snow was an average of 30 inches deep with drifts in the ravines as deep as 60 feet. There were grasshopper scourges and prairie fires and the Sioux Indians did not welcome the settlers, to say the least. Their hostility was real and legendary. In 1862, there was a scare after a massacre in New Ulm, Minnesota, that there was a Sioux uprising; they were coming down the Big Sioux River, mur-

dering all along the way. Terror gripped the settlers and many were convinced they were coming down the Floyd River, also. The settlers fled in all directions fearing another Spirit Lake-like fate. A few days later, reliable sources reported there were no Sioux Indians within 100 miles of Iowa. The only man who dared to remain in his home in the Big Sioux River Valley was its first settler, the Honorable D. M. Mills.

Remsen, the first town we encountered as we drove into the county, was settled by Luxembourg immigrants. In Europe they were plagued by religious persecution, Prussian military conscription and limited economic opportunity. The first sight we saw was the steeple of St. Mary's Catholic Church protruding high above the trees—a testimony to the freedom of religion found in the United States. These hardworking, fun-loving immigrants retained other traditions that are evident today. The last Saturday in October they celebrate Octoberfest with polka bands; a beer garden; an arts and crafts show; and a large, family-style, Luxembourger meal served by citizens in traditional attire. Unfortunately, we hit

Wells Blue Bunny production plant, Le Mars

Wells Blue Bunny headquarters

town a week early—darn the luck!

John I. Blair never achieved the notoriety of a Vanderbilt or a J. J. Hill, but he was their peer as a tycoon of the railroading age. His name kept popping us as I read the histories of counties across the state. He left his name on Blairstown, New Jersey; Blair, Nebraska; Blairsburg, Iowa; and the **Cherokee County** towns of **Aurelia** and **Marcus** were named after his daughter and son. Legend has it that Le Mars was named after a group of ladies who accompanied Blair to what was then called St. Paul Junction. The ladies were asked to name the town and they submitted their own first initials—**L**ucy Underhilll, **E**lizabeth Parson, **M**ary Weare, **A**na Blair, **R**ebecca Smith and **S**arah Reynolds. The first official platting of **Le Mars** was supervised by John I. Blair in 1870.

The country sports of horseshoe pitching, wrestling and impromptu horse racing gave way to polo, cricket, fox hunting, and a more formal brand of horse racing during the Le Mars English era. The rough edges of the frontier were becoming smoother in the late 1870s when some well-connected English fami-

318

Plymouth County Courthouse, Le Mars

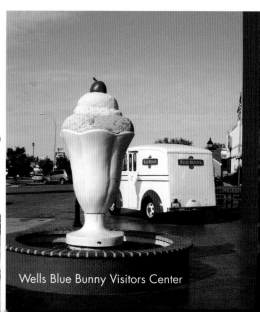

Wells Blue Bunny Visitors Center

Plymouth County Fairgrounds

lies gave it a look. One prominent type was established, upper class Englishmen who planned on developing large-scale stock farms. Another was the second sons of well-to-do farm families who were sent to learn farm management. They were called "pups." The English planted trees to lessen the monotony of the open prairie and supervised the breaking of tens of thousands of acres of prairie sod. They hired German immigrants to do the work. Most of the Englishmen moved on, but the German laborers stayed and developed and bought their own farms.

In the late 1800s, there was a growing dairy business in **Plymouth County**. By 1897, the Le Mars Creamery Association reported butter production of over 107,000 pounds annually, meaning the milk production was probably over 2,000,000 pounds. Years later, in 1913, Fred H. Wells started a milk route in **Le Mars** with one horse and one wagon. In 1925, he and his sons opened an ice cream manufacturing plant in **Le Mars**. The plant and Wells name were sold to Fairmont Ice Cream in 1928. In 1935, Fred and his sons wanted to get back into the business but they couldn't use their

name. They sponsored a contest to name the ice cream; the winner suggested Blue Bunny because of his son's fascination with blue bunnies in department store Easter displays. The Wells eventually got their name back and, in 1992, they began an aggressive campaign to expand nationally. Today, they have a 900,000-square-foot plant with a 12-story refrigeration facility. One thousand employees annually produce 75 million gallons of frozen treats with milk coming from large, Iowa dairy farms. A handsome new office building sits on a hill south of town and across the Floyd River Valley from the production plant. Wells Blue Bunny is the world's largest manufacturer of ice cream in one location, thus the claim of "Ice Cream Capitol of the World."

After eating lunch at VanderMeer Bakery, we stopped at the Wells Blue Bunny Visitors Center at the intersection of Highway 3 and Business Highway 75. I bought a chocolate, caramel, cashew cone that couldn't be improved upon—it was delicious. There is also a Hardees restaurant, museum, theater, exhibits and gift shop at this location.

Another museum worth visiting in

Le Mars is the Plymouth County Historical Museum. It is housed in a former school building and has five levels of exhibits. Domestic, agriculture and music rooms have been created in addition to other themed spaces and collections. The gym and auditorium of the 1925 school building have been restored.

From **Le Mars** we took a short jaunt down Highway 75 to **Merrill** where we called on Sara Jane Hauff. Her cousin Jane Prichard of Le Mars was there, also; they were quilting. Sara Jane was born in Des Moines and at age 11 moved to **Merrill**. She is a graduate of Westmar College (a good school that no longer exists) and she earned her master's degree from the University of Northern Colorado. After five years in California, she took a physical education teaching position at West High School in Sioux City where she taught for 31 years before retiring in 2004. She has a daughter who lives in Minneapolis; a son in Burbank, South Dakota; and a daughter who is the fifth generation to live in a house that Sara Jane's grandfather built in **Merrill**. Her husband, Ronald D. Osborne, lives in Des Moines. He is a retired Episcopalian

Le Mars

Terraced field in Plymouth County

Jane Prichard and
Sara Jane Hauff

priest who served as a chaplain at the University of Iowa for 25 years. Sara says she and Ronald visit each other frequently and their separate lives work for them. Her house is a pleasant, warmly decorated, 1920s, Craftsman-style bungalow.

Jane Prichard also has a master's degree from Northern Colorado. Hers is in special education, which she taught in **Le Mars** for about 30 years. She presently works as a tech in the physical therapy department at the Floyd Valley Hospital in Le Mars. She and her husband Bill are active members of the Mormon Church.

Sara Jane and Jane's grandparents stressed education. There was never any doubt that you would go to college. Their grandpa only had four years of formal education, but his informal education was ongoing. He loved inspirational sayings. The following was his favorite so he had it printed on cards, which he gave to his children and grandchildren: "Man is not educated unless he is morally educated as well as intellectually educated. Distinction is a beautiful thing, but morals and character are first and education second. The rest will take care of itself."

Sara Jane says, "This part of the state is unique unto itself with the Loess Hills. I love the slower pace of life with two large cities within an hour's drive." Jane added, "There are good, wholesome people living here."

There are plenty of attractions in **Plymouth County** for lovers of the outdoors. The 250-acre Hillview Recreation Area contains a mixture of open grasslands, reconstructed prairie, woodlands and wildlife habitat. It is a great place for camping, picnicking, fishing, swimming, hiking, horseback riding and cross-country skiing. A network of trails traverses the entire park. In a portion of the park, hunting is allowed from October 15 to December 15. You can hunt turkey in the 790-acre Five Ridge Prairie. Only foot traffic is allowed on this preserve. The county conservation board's first park, Big Sioux Park, provides fishing, canoeing and boating access to the Big Sioux River. The 33-acre park has undergone recent habitat transformation due to some major flooding. A Big Sioux River corridor is being established with donated and acquired land. These areas serve as public access to the river.

Big Sioux River (Iowa's western border)

SURF BALLROOM

CLAY COUNTY FAIRGROUNDS

Tier8

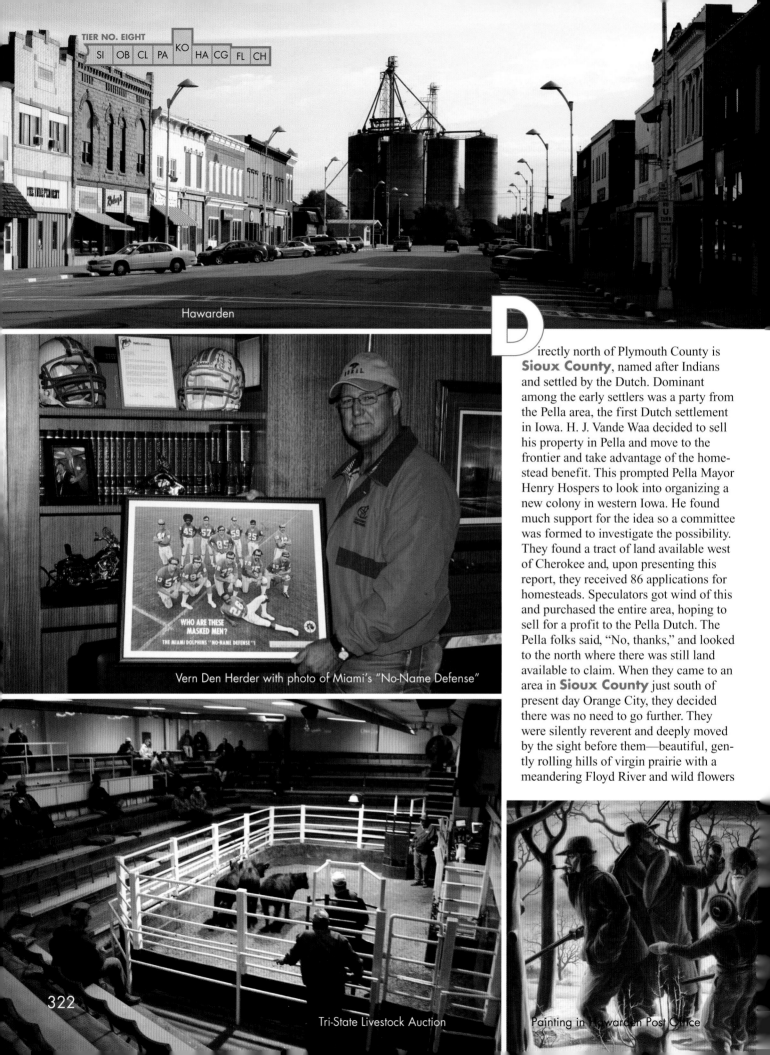

Hawarden

Vern Den Herder with photo of Miami's "No-Name Defense"

Tri-State Livestock Auction

Painting in Hawarden Post Office

Directly north of Plymouth County is **Sioux County**, named after Indians and settled by the Dutch. Dominant among the early settlers was a party from the Pella area, the first Dutch settlement in Iowa. H. J. Vande Waa decided to sell his property in Pella and move to the frontier and take advantage of the homestead benefit. This prompted Pella Mayor Henry Hospers to look into organizing a new colony in western Iowa. He found much support for the idea so a committee was formed to investigate the possibility. They found a tract of land available west of Cherokee and, upon presenting this report, they received 86 applications for homesteads. Speculators got wind of this and purchased the entire area, hoping to sell for a profit to the Pella Dutch. The Pella folks said, "No, thanks," and looked to the north where there was still land available to claim. When they came to an area in **Sioux County** just south of present day Orange City, they decided there was no need to go further. They were silently reverent and deeply moved by the sight before them—beautiful, gently rolling hills of virgin prairie with a meandering Floyd River and wild flowers

Sioux County

contributing to a pristine view. In the fall of 1869, seventy-five men (including three surveyors) loaded 18 wagons with provisions and made the trip to their future homes. After staking their claims, they returned to Pella and prepared for a permanent move the next spring. The "Mother" colony of Pella had given birth to a "Daughter" colony in Sioux County.

Hawarden, the first town we visited in **Sioux County**, had a different twist to its history. Calliope was the name of the town first located on this real estate. It was a stopping place on the stagecoach line between Sioux City and Sioux Falls. The Northwestern Railroad located its junction with Milwaukee Road about a mile south of Calliope and platted a town they named Hawarden. On the construction crews of the Northwestern Railroad were young Englishmen who were sent to America by wealthy parents who were unable to control the unruly behavior of their offspring. It was hoped the rough life of the frontier would teach them to become more responsible. It is believed the town was named after these young Englishmen's hometown of **Hawarden** in Flint County, Wales. A

rivalry developed between the communities of Calliope and Hawarden until Hawarden annexed Calliope in 1893. Presently, **Hawarden** is a progressive town of 2,500 people, some of whom find employment at American Identity, a manufacturer of baseball caps, or at Iowa Lamb Processing, Iowa's only sheep slaughterhouse.

We saw some sheep as we drove into the heart of the county, but mostly we saw cattle feedlots. We noticed there was an absence of abandoned farmsteads and the ones that were occupied were well maintained. There was a lot of activity with farm machinery, grain trucks and livestock trucks. Grain elevators loomed over the **Sioux Center** business district and there was a cattle sale in progress at the Tri-State Livestock Auction barn. The biotech firm of TransOva Genetics is located in Sioux Center. It is an embryo transfer business to replicate multiple calves from valuable beef and dairy cows. The ag industry in **Sioux County** is sophisticated and vibrant.

Vern Den Herder of **Sioux Center** is very proud of the area's agricultural prowess and he is also proud of being a

starting defensive end on the 1972 Miami Dolphins football team that went 17-0, the only NFL team to finish a season without a loss. When the New England Patriots took an undefeated record to the Super Bowl last year, he received calls from national and regional media to get his reaction. He didn't talk to them. He told us the calls were premature; they hadn't played in the Super Bowl yet. As it turned out, New England lost.

Vern grew up in **Sioux Center** where he starred in basketball and football. His rugged, six-foot-six frame and competitive play attracted scholarship offers from Division I schools. However, at the big schools, he would have had to choose one sport or the other. He chose to go to a Division III college, Central, where he could play both sports. He also wanted to be a true student/athlete where academics came first. He majored in chemistry with an eye on becoming a veterinarian. He said at Central the coaches had no problem with him coming late to practice in order to attend a late afternoon lab class. He played for legendary football coach Ron Schipper, one of the most successful coaches in NCAA history,

TransOva Genetics Research and Development Center

Campus Center Atrium, Dordt College, Sioux Center

Kathy Klein

regardless of division. Vern still holds a conference basketball rebound record. When the Miami dolphins chose him in the ninth round of the NFL draft, it was decision time. Vet school or football? He had been accepted at Iowa State's veterinarian school when he made the final cut with the Dolphins. His rookie season ended with a loss to Dallas in the Super Bowl. On the plane ride back, Coach Don Shula told him what he needed to do to be a starter and the hard-working Dutchman heeded the advice, thus earning a starting role on the following year's undefeated team. He led that team in quarterback sacks and was selected all-pro. They repeated as Super Bowl champs the next year. Vern played 12 seasons—all for the Dolphins.

When his football career was over, he and wife Diane (also a Central College chemistry major) decided they wanted to raise their family in **Sioux Center**. Even though he didn't have a farming background, it was to become his post-football career. It began with him taking a job working in his cousin's feedlot. This led to buying his own ground, building his own cattle feeding operation and

Central Reformed Church, Sioux Center

Windmill Park, Orange City

324

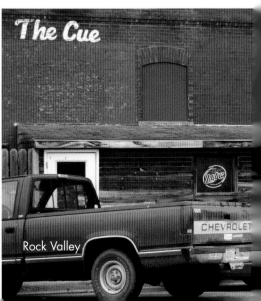

Rock Valley

Campus Center, Dordt College

eventually becoming a full-time crop farmer. Presently, he controls 600 acres and partners with another person to farm 200 more acres. Vern and Diane's two children live in town.

Before we left, Vern shared a couple of football stories with us. His Miami Dolphins defensive line coach, Mo Scarry, told of playing in the days when they first started wearing face guards. In one game, his opponent across the line grabbed his face guard and jerked him to the ground. They had not yet developed any rules on this so there was no penalty. He told the equipment manager to remove the guard. The first chance he got, he bit the guard-grabbing opponent as hard as he could. During a roast for Mo at his retirement party, Vern told him he had named his roping horse "Mo" in his honor. He added he didn't know which end reminded him the most of his old coach. Connie felt she should add to the story-telling so she told Vern that when I played, they still wore leather helmets. That is not true. Well, I wore them when I was in junior high, but I'm pretty sure we had plastic in high school.

As I walked around the Dordt College campus in **Sioux Center**, one of the first things to catch my eye was the Canadian flag flying along with the United States and Iowa flags. It is flown in honor of the 150 Canadians out of a student body of about 1,300. Another thing that distinguishes this attractive campus is the contemporary buildings—there is no Old Main. This school is not that old. It was organized in 1953 as Midwest Christian Junior College, mainly to educate qualified teachers for area Christian schools. Instruction began in 1955 with 35 students. One year later the name was changed to Dordt in honor of the Synod of Dordttrecht held in the Netherlands in 1618–1619. The first bachelor of arts degrees were awarded to the Class of 1965. The college grew rapidly to 1,200 students by 1978. Today, Dordt offers 36 majors and 60 programs of study and a masters program in education. The arts are emphasized. Free art exhibitions are open to the public at the Campus Center Art Gallery and there is a growing collection of outdoor sculptures. Each year the music department offers 35 public concerts and recitals with 300 musicians participating. The theatre department presents two main stage plays every year and student-directed productions at least once per year. Dordt has the typical Iowa college intercollegiate sports offerings, along with the not-so-typical hockey and lacrosse. The college is a member of NAIA Division II and competes in the Great Plains Athletic Conference. The teams are very competitive across the board and the athletic facilities are top of the line.

Dordt College grew out of a community of faith, a familiar story in varying degrees at Iowa's private colleges. At some of these colleges, the religious tie-ins have been de-emphasized or forgotten. Dordt is at the other end of the spectrum. With its relatively recent beginning, there is a freshness and openness about God's role in all aspects of life. While on campus, we talked to Kathy Klein, a financial aid assistant in the admissions office. Her life, growing up in rural **Sioux County**, exemplifies the character of the Dutch community and the Christian Reformed Church. She grew up on a farm between Orange City and Sioux Center. She went to a Christian grade school in **Sioux Center** and

Sioux Center

325

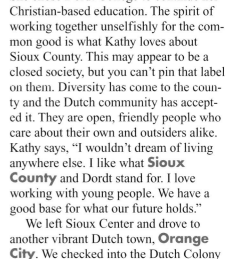

Zwemer Hall

Western Christian High School in **Hull**. She chose Dordt College to continue her Christian-based education. The spirit of working together unselfishly for the common good is what Kathy loves about Sioux County. This may appear to be a closed society, but you can't pin that label on them. Diversity has come to the county and the Dutch community has accepted it. They are open, friendly people who care about their own and outsiders alike. Kathy says, "I wouldn't dream of living anywhere else. I like what **Sioux County** and Dordt stand for. I love working with young people. We have a good base for what our future holds."

We left Sioux Center and drove to another vibrant Dutch town, **Orange City**. We checked into the Dutch Colony Inn, deposited our bags and headed for the Blue Mountain Restaurant. This restaurant was inspired by the Blue Mountains of Jamaica, a favorite getaway for Deb and Clayton Korver, the proprietors. They are travelers who have collected art and artifacts from around the world and have incorporated them into the décor of their restaurant. The art pieces are expertly blended with

Sioux County Courthouse, Orange City

Diamond Vogel Paints, Orange City

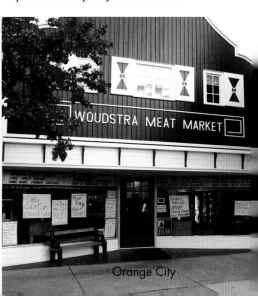

Orange City

Northwestern College, Orange City

Midwestern objects in a beautifully designed dining establishment that has a worthy menu of delicious food. I ordered a half rack of barbequed ribs and Connie chose a smoked brisket sandwich. It was a thoroughly enjoyable dining experience. Like Pella, **Orange City** exhibits its Dutch heritage by requiring Dutch facades on new buildings, including franchises. Their Tulip Festival rivals Pella's. Some of the natives will probably tell you it is better. It is a very clean city with the magnificent, Romanesque, Sioux County Courthouse contrasting with downtown Dutch architecture.

Dutch immigrant Andrew Vogel loved his new life in Iowa but he wasn't very impressed with the available paint. Using experience gained from working in his grandfather's paint shop in Holland, he began making his own paint in his garage. In 1926, he launched the Vogel Paint and Wax Company selling two paints he formulated—red for barns and white for houses. Quality sold and the company has grown to manufacture hundreds of hues and specialty paints. Now known as Diamond Vogel Paints, it is still family run. They have changed with the times and kept abreast of demands. A beautiful office, technical center and manufacturing facility are architecturally Dutch and Dutch-efficient.

Sioux County is blessed with another excellent liberal arts college based on the Christian tradition. Northwestern College, located in **Orange City**, has been around a little longer than Dordt College, but its four-year program began about the same time. The Reverend Seine Bolks provided the inspiration and Henry Hospers provided the land for the Northwestern Classical Academy, incorporated in 1882. Zwemer Hall, the first permanent building, was built in 1894; it is now the college's administrative center. In 1928, the academy added a junior college. The spring of 1961 marked the last graduating class of the academy and the first graduating class of a four-year college. They adopted a liberal arts program and were granted full accreditation by the North Central Association in 1970.

Education at Northwestern is Christ-centered. They believe college should prepare you to make a life, not just a living. Three-fourths of the faculty have Ph.D.s and there are no graduate assistants teaching classes. Course offerings are typical for an Iowa private school of 1,300-plus students. There is a balance of academics, clubs, the arts and sports—all educational. Varsity sports' accomplishments have given Northwestern regional and national recognition. In football they have won the NAIA National Championship twice. Men's basketball teams have duplicated that feat and the rest of the men's sports programs maintain comparable excellence. The Northwestern women's basketball team has won one NAIA National Championship. Competitors in all the women's sports consistently finish at the top in the Great Plains Athletic Conference and qualify for national competition. Athletic facilities include a 3,100-seat football stadium, a 2,200-seat gymnasium and a 2,700-square-foot weight/exercise room.

It was a cold, rainy day as we entered **O'Brien County** in late October. The big harvest machines had come to a halt—some were stranded out in the fields. The farmers don't like October rains; typically, it is a dry month. But

Northwestern College

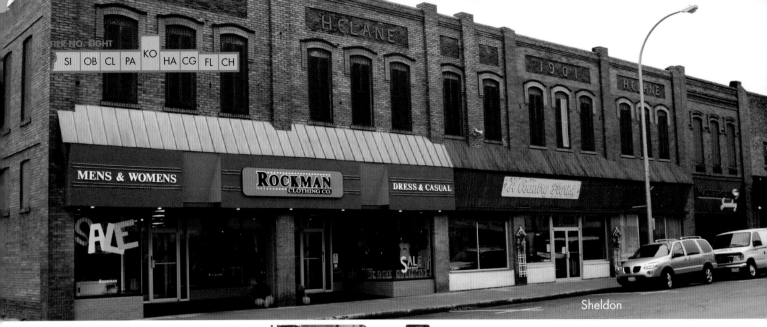

Sheldon

Sheldon

Sheldon

nothing is typical in this year's weather. The farmers will adjust and the bounty will be brought in even if the last loads will have to traverse frozen fields.

A county named O'Brien would probably signal a change in ethnic character from Sioux County where the Dutch dominate. There is a change but it is not to Irish domination. It is estimated that two-thirds of the early **O'Brien County** settlers came from other counties in Iowa, including Sioux County's Dutch. The Irish did settle in large numbers around **Sheldon**. The English settled in small numbers around **Archer**. Scandinavians occupied scattered, lightly populated settlements and the Germans gathered in more substantial colonies. Pioneer life on the open grass prairie was a non-discriminatory hardship for all.

The early structures were the shacks, log cabins and sod houses that I have previously described. Easterners who visited the settlements during those years would inquire, unthinkingly, "Why don't you have barns and houses and other conveniences like we do?" The answer was, "You are enjoying the fruits of labor of previous generations while we have to

Tom Schemper

AMPI Dairy, Sanborn

create all that we have. Our hope is that our descendants can build on our accomplishments to better their lives."

The first task for the early **O'Brien County** settlers was to break the prairie sod. Spring was the best time to turn the earth because the plants were green and growing rapidly, making it easier to plow. The vegetation would decay quickly and the soil would be mellow. The first plows were large and cumbersome. They had to be pulled by two to six oxen and the man with his hands on the plow handles had to know what he was doing or they would twist out of his grip. Later it was discovered that a smaller plow and a couple of horses worked better. The first crop planted was corn. As the soil was reworked, the persistent roots of the prairie grasses were vanquished and the land became more productive. Increased yields have been ongoing to the present day and scientists are developing ways to continue increasing yields into the future.

Sheldon, O'Brien County's largest town, is located on the border with Sioux County. The location was chosen by the Sioux City & St. Paul Railroad; surveyors platted the town in 1871. It was named after Israel Sheldon, a New Yorker and stockholder in the railroad company. Following the arrival of the first train in 1872 were carloads of lumber for construction of the town. The businesses built with wood lasted until 1888 when the obligatory, small town fire wiped them out. Solid, brick buildings sprang up from the ashes and many of them are still occupied by services and retailers.

Railroad service made **Sheldon** a hub of commercial activity in the early days and the whistle of trains passing through today has a nostalgic ring to it. Highways have replaced railroad tracks as primary surface transportation. When Highway 60 was made into a four-lane expressway, it by-passed the town creating concern for the survival of the downtown business district. Highway 18, an east/west route, continues to run through downtown and intersects with the north/south expressway on the west edge of town. The town leaders decided to take advantage of the improved highway transportation by creating Sheldon Crossing Business Park on Highway 18 near the Highway 60 by-pass. This proved to be a good move as many businesses have sprung up at this location. We observed that downtown businesses appear to be doing well, also. There are several classy-looking retail establishments and the old brick and stone buildings provide a charming atmosphere for the shoppers.

Sheldon is the home of Northwest Iowa Community College. In addition to having agreements for seamless transfers to four-year colleges, NCC has an arrangement with Briar Cliff University (in Sioux City) that allows students to earn four-year degrees without leaving the NCC campus. The third and fourth year academics are Briar Cliff courses delivered to NCC via the Iowa Communications Network.

Village Northwest Unlimited, a special community for special people, is located in **Sheldon**. A staff of 350 trained professionals works with persons, 17 years and older, who have developmental, physical or brain injury disabilities. At the Village, they lead a life of dignity and purpose in a Christian atmosphere. They are encouraged to participate in many activities, are given therapy and are taken to many events in **Sheldon** and surrounding towns. Individuals have oppor-

O'Brien County Implement, Sheldon

Little Sioux River valley, O'Brien County

Prairie Heritage Center, O'Brien County

Primghar

Ye Ohl Coffeee Shoppe, Archer

330

tunities to earn money at Northwest Enterprises and Futures Unlimited, a vocational division of the Village. Jobs such as sorting beverage containers, doing bulk mailings and newspaper inserting add up to about $1 million in contract work each year.

Dianne Schemper, a nurse at Northwest Village, is one of those Christian people who make life better for the Village residents. She and her husband Tom have three sons—one lives in Des Moines and the other two reside in California. The father of one of the Village residents likes to give his son a motorcycle ride when he visits (his son enjoys it also). He made a deal with Tom, whereby Tom could use his Harley if he provided storage for the machine between the father's visits. Tom said, "Sure." As a bonus for the Village resident, he gets more rides straddling the backseat of his dad's bike with Tom driving.

Tom and his brothers run O'Brien County Implement, Inc., a business started by their dad in 1948. In the early days, the dealership sold White and Oliver tractors. Those brands are no longer available, but there is still a need for parts.

Primghar

Tom has filled the niche to provide those parts and other hard-to-find farm implement parts. He fields calls from all over the United States, England and Australia. If he doesn't have the parts on hand, he knows how to tap into a network and find them. A guy in Michigan who needed parts for an old bailer called Tom. Tom found the parts in Wisconsin and Texas. The man's wife called to thank Tom for making her husband so happy. The dealership sells new and used farm machinery and industrial and commercial equipment. Agco, Buhler and New Holland are the brand names of the new products.

Tom is a graduate of the Reformed Bible College in Grand Rapids, Michigan, where he majored in Bible studies. These studies prepared him for missionary work. Rather than being a full-time missionary, he has chosen to serve on part-time, voluntary missions to various countries. He also does some prison ministry work. Of living in **Sheldon**, Tom says, "I like the quality of life—freedom to ride my motorcycle and hunt and the laid back character. Neighbors are really neighbors; we talk over the back fence."

We drove a few miles southeast of Sheldon, to **Archer**, for lunch. Ye Ohl Coffee Shoppe is located in a building that was originally a mercantile store and most recently used for construction equipment storage. Owner Don Wagenaar's boss and mentor Virgil Ohl gave him the building so he thought the least he could do was cleverly insert Ohl's name in the restaurant's name. The Wagenaar family of Don and his wife Dee and their four children and spouses contribute to the operation in varying degrees. It has a very pleasant, comfortable atmosphere and good food.

After lunch we drove to **Primghar**, the county seat of **O'Brien County**. With a population of 890, it is one of the smallest county seats, but it is located dead center in the county. I walked around the square photographing the courthouse and a couple of other buildings before continuing our trip.

We drove to the southeast corner of the county into the beautiful Little Sioux River valley. There was a rainy mist affecting our view negatively and positively. Spectacular photos of the breadth of the landscape were out, but I got some

nice, moody shots of the damp vegetation and meandering river.

After crossing the Little Sioux River, we drove to the Prairie Heritage Center located on a ridge overlooking the river valley. As we approached, we saw buffalo grazing in a fenced-in area next to the center's building. Inside the building, a stuffed buffalo dominated a display of other prairie animals and plants. The center provides education about the environment relating to the prairie and region; it also preserves the prairie heritage.

We continued our drive into **Peterson** of **Clay County** where we crossed the Little Sioux again. Wanata State Park is just south of Peterson on the Clay/Buena Vista County line. It is really pretty country with a nice mix of grassy areas and trees on the steep hillsides. Back up on the prairie, we motored toward **Spencer**. About six miles south of town, we pulled into Hannah Marie's Country Inn where we were to spend the night. Hannah Marie's daughter, Mary Nichols, greeted us and immediately began telling us about her family and giving some history of the Inn. Mary's mother Hannah Marie was a Swede who grew

331

Little Sioux River near Peterson

Mary Nichols

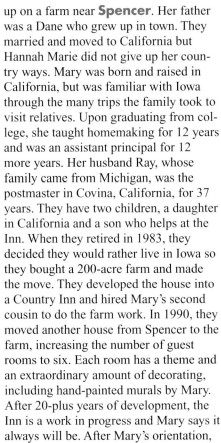

Hannah Marie Inn

up on a farm near **Spencer**. Her father was a Dane who grew up in town. They married and moved to California but Hannah Marie did not give up her country ways. Mary was born and raised in California, but was familiar with Iowa through the many trips the family took to visit relatives. Upon graduating from college, she taught homemaking for 12 years and was an assistant principal for 12 more years. Her husband Ray, whose family came from Michigan, was the postmaster in Covina, California, for 37 years. They have two children, a daughter in California and a son who helps at the Inn. When they retired in 1983, they decided they would rather live in Iowa so they bought a 200-acre farm and made the move. They developed the house into a Country Inn and hired Mary's second cousin to do the farm work. In 1990, they moved another house from Spencer to the farm, increasing the number of guest rooms to six. Each room has a theme and an extraordinary amount of decorating, including hand-painted murals by Mary. After 20-plus years of development, the Inn is a work in progress and Mary says it always will be. After Mary's orientation,

Hope Reformed Church, Spencer

332

Spencer Hospital

Prime Rib Restaurant, Spencer

Cornstalk bales, Clay County

we drove to **Spencer** for dinner at the Prime Rib Restaurant. We didn't try the prime rib, but I enjoyed a bacon-wrapped fillet and Connie said her chicken oscar was good. It is a large restaurant with an elegant, contemporary atmosphere.

When we returned to the Inn, we were treated to dessert. Connie chose French almond pastry with raspberry sauce and I had triple chocolate cheesecake, also with raspberry sauce. With full tummies, we entered the Northlands Hideaway Room, crawled into a queen-size feather bed and floated off to sleep. The gourmet food serving continued at breakfast. The first course was a baked apple puff pastry with whipped cream, brown sugar and nuts. Next, we were treated to Danish aebleskivers, which can best be described as light, fluffy donuts—shaped like balls and served with a knitting needle. The final course was Italian fritatta and buttermilk muffins containing cinnamon and walnuts. Everything was scrumptious.

The treeless prairie terrain covered most of **Clay County** when the earliest settlers arrived in 1856. Typically the first arrivals chose to settle in one of the few forested areas in the county near present-day **Peterson**. The beautiful Little Sioux River valley provided wood and wild life—the necessities of initial settlement. The dark, rich, loam prairie soil up to eight feet deep would await its cultivation until the pioneers got a foothold. There was poor drainage in many areas of the open grassland, creating many ponds and sloughs. Swarms of muskrats inhabited these waters. The pioneers trapped them in great numbers, using their pelts as cash to buy supplies. The hardships of blizzards, prairie fires, hostile Indians and locust plagues tested **Clay County** settlers as per other Northwest Iowa counties. Nostalgia for times past didn't just start with our generation. Believe it or not, when life became easier in the late 1800s, the settlers felt a tinge of sadness that the pioneer era was passing. No more breaking the sod, the prairie schooner wagon was no longer needed and the primitive, basic dwellings had been replaced. The elk, deer, buffalo and prairie chickens had either disappeared or were in small numbers. The abounding hospitality and the exchange of help was subsiding in easier times. The virgin land was gone—along with the hardships.

In 1866, the first settlers came to an area known as Spencer's Grove located at the confluence of the Ocheyedan River and Little Sioux River. A community grew rapidly with many businesses and a gristmill in place by 1871. Later that year, the county seat was moved from Peterson to **Spencer** and growth continued until an invasion of grasshoppers slowed settlement for a couple of years. In 1878, the railroad came and growth took off again. Many of the first residents were Civil War veterans. In 1890, the Spencer Improvement Club was organized which evolved into the Spencer Commercial Club in 1921; later it was renamed the Spencer Chamber of Commerce. No matter the name of the organization, its members spurred **Spencer's** development into a leading center of commerce. This leadership was severely challenged in June of 1931.

In 1931, the Great Depression was well underway, but **Spencer** somehow continued building civic projects, including the new steel and concrete, 5,000-seat grandstand for the county fair. The weather was hot and dry in the summer of '31. The temperature was a sweltering

Bogenrief Studios, Spencer

Bob Rose

Scharnberg Park, Clay County

97 degrees on June 27, when a little boy took an interest in the large fireworks display in the Otto A. Bjornstad Drugstore. No one is sure what happened next other than a lit sparkler was dropped on the fireworks display which resulted in an explosion that set downtown **Spencer** on fire. Conditions were perfect for a catastrophe. The heat, the drought and high winds fanned the flames that consumed two and a half blocks of business district establishments. More than 50 buildings were reduced to rubble but, unbelievably, no lives were lost.

The businesses that decided to stay relocated to temporary quarters and the rebuilding began. Within days of the fire, architectural firms from Iowa and Minnesota, as well as local architect W. D. Barton, began preparing drawings. They suggested a collaborative approach using a mix of art deco and mission revival styles for most of the new buildings. Their ideas were accepted, resulting in a large collection of art deco commercial buildings. Miami, Florida, is the only U.S. city with a larger art deco presence. In 2004, **Spencer's** downtown business district was placed on the National

334

Martin Arthur, executive director of Arts on Grand Gallery

Skate park, Spencer

Art Deco and Mission Revival commercial buildings, Spencer

Register of Historic Places.

Bob Rose is the present executive director of the Spencer Chamber of Commerce. The leadership in this historic civic organization has not waned. Spencer still has a traditional downtown with successful retailers in everything from clothing stores to jewelry stores. These retailers have seen a 25 percent increase in business since 2005. With a population of 11,000, it is the largest community within 100 miles.

Bob told us about a town benefactor couple named Irvin and Ruby Dvergesten. They moved from Minnesota to **Spencer** in 1930 and opened a women's clothing store. They had no children and the clothing store was their only business, but they invested wisely. In 2005, when they both died at an age over 100, they willed about $6 million to various city organizations, their church and Buena Vista University. This seed money stimulated many projects. Bob says, "The attitude of this community is so positive, that when there is a situation that requires attention, people step forward and solve it. It stems from the 1931 fire—the spirit of renewal and accomplishment.

Businesses didn't walk away. They stayed. There is a willingness to get behind it and stay with it."

The folks in **Spencer** have gotten behind the arts by forming the Spencer Alliance for a Creative Economy (SPACE). This organization was successful in getting Spencer designated as one of the first of eight Cultural Districts in the state of Iowa. A Cultural District is a well-recognized, mixed use, compact area of a community where there is a high concentration of cultural facilities. Included in Spencer's cultural scene are: the Bogenrief Studios, known nationally for their stained glass work and blown glass art; Arts on Grand, an exhibit gallery that offers workshops and educational programs, as well as a venue for jazz and other musical happenings; Spencer Community Theatre, a theatre group that puts on four main stage productions each year; the Spencer Municipal Band, a group of talented musicians who perform weekly summer concerts; Spencer Area Concert Association, promoters of concerts by professional performing artists; and the Parker Historical Museum, a collection of

Clay County historic artifacts displayed in a 1916 Arts and Crafts house.

It is not part of the Cultural District, but the Clay County Fair is a major entertainment event in Northwest Iowa. Small-time fairs and exhibitions were held in **Spencer** as early as 1879, but it was in 1918 that the Clay County Fair became a big-time event. It was the largest county fair in Iowa that year, drawing more than 30,000 people. The 1919 fair attendance climbed to 48,500 and it has gotten bigger and better year after year. Now it is known as the "World's Greatest County Fair" and draws over 300,000 visitors annually. Big name entertainment and many other stage and track events draw people to the grandstand. For the farmers, there is the nation's largest display of tractors and ag equipment. And all the business, livestock, food, crafts and other exhibits are well done.

Speaking of a little event evolving into a major obsession, there is the story of a cat name Dewey Readmore Books. On a cold January morning in 1988, **Spencer** librarian Vicki Myron found a little, rust-colored kitten in the library's after-hours book return. The staff adopted the kitten

Clay County Courthouse, Spencer

Spencer

335

Robert Emmet statue, Emmetsburg

Emmetsburg

Dave Carpenter

with the approval of the library trustees and the city council. The cat's antics for the next 19 years entertained library patrons (some just came to see the cat) and lifted the spirits of the community. Vicki Myron tells the cat's story in *Dewey: The Small-Town Library Cat Who Touched the World*. The book has made *The New York Times'* best-seller list and Meryl Streep is interested in playing Vicki in a proposed movie. Academy Award winning actress Meryl Streep! Vicki likes that.

We continued our drive through rich agricultural land into **Palo Alto County**. Several natural lakes dot the prairie terrain. There is Mud Lake in Clay County and Silver Lake in Palo Alto County and Lost Island Lake straddling the county line. Down the road, the town of **Emmetsburg** borders the southern shore of Five Island Lake.

The lakeshore was not the original site chosen by a colony of Irish settlers from Kane County, Illinois. In 1856, they chose a site on the west branch of the Des Moines River about two miles northwest of present-day **Emmetsburg**. They had come from a settled community and

Lost Island Lake, Clay/Palo Alto Counties

Clay County

knew little about hunting and trapping. When professional trappers came and camped near them, they observed and learned. The first lesson was the value of the abundant wildlife. The trappers harvested over $7,000 worth of pelts that winter. The colony of seven families was located close together in a compact little community for social convenience and protection. They became tough pioneers and were the nucleus of a settlement in central **Palo Alto County**.

A prairie fire destroyed the first attempt to build a small, log, Catholic church. In 1871, led by Father Linehan of Fort Dodge, the colony built a larger church. Father Smith, the church's first pastor, arrived while the church was still under construction. He was a fearless young man of strong faith. He led the effort to complete the church and organize his parish. There were only 39 Catholic families in **Palo Alto County**, but Father Smith's parish covered eight counties. He also attended to Southwest Minnesota and Eastern Dakota. He was tireless in his ministry on the desolate frontier plains. He was a kind and cheery friend and advisor to all the settlers, regardless of faith.

More people located in Old Emmetsburg, as it became known, and by 1874, there were about forty businesses, but all the buildings were small and poorly built. The residents sensed the location was temporary as the railroad had plans to build a depot about two miles southeast. Old Emmetsburg peaked in 1874, then disappeared and a new city on a hill by a lake took its place.

Emmetsburg's namesake, Robert Emmet, was an Irish nationalist rebel who led an abortive rebellion against British rule in 1803. He was captured, convicted of high treason, hanged and beheaded. Although his fight against the British was a complete failure, he became a heroic figure in Irish history. Thomas Moore (a Trinity College friend) wrote very popular ballads about him; Emmet's "Let no man write my epitaph" speech contributed to his legendary status. The bronze statue of him on the courthouse square is one of only four in the world. **Emmetsburg** is a sister city to Dublin and members of Irish government frequently join the Emmetsburg Irish in the celebration of St. Patrick's Day.

One of Iowa's newest casinos, the Wild Rose, is located in Emmetsburg so Connie had to check their slots. They were pretty tight. She lost all of her $10. The running score after eighteen casinos in $32.75 in the red. She has one more chance to hit the jackpot at the Diamond Jo Casino near **Northwood**.

We chose McNally's Bakery on the square for lunch. With Connie's gambling losses, all we could afford were sloppy Joe's and water. They were good, though, and so was the cookie we shared.

Driving a delivery truck for McNally's put bread on the table when Dave Carpenter launched his professional cartooning career. He is an **Emmetsburg** native—his great-grandfather, John Duffy, came from Ireland. After high school graduation, Dave went on to the University of South Dakota, where he earned a bachelor of arts degree in history and political science. In 1981, Dave took a correspondence course in cartooning. Upon completion of the course, he sent four speculative cartoons to *Golf Digest* and four more to *Skin Divers* magazine. *Skin Divers* magazine bought three, ran two and gave Dave $10 apiece.

Emmetsburg

McNally's Bakery, Emmetsburg

337

Five Island Lake, Emmetsburg

Palo Alto County Courthouse, Emmetsburg

His professional career was underway. He kept producing and sending ideas to magazines and newsletters. Rejects were given another chance in a system he developed to maximize the possibilities. These days he works full time converting funny thoughts into funny drawings with captions. Most of the ideas originate in his head; occasionally, he works with a couple of gag writers. His work appears in *Readers' Digest*, *Harvard Business Review*, *Wall Street Journal* and *Woman's World*—to name a few. I first saw Dave's cartoons in *Our Iowa* magazine. He loves **Emmetsburg**. He says, "It's very friendly. I know a lot of people. The costs are low and it is an easy-going life style. I wouldn't trade it for anything."

Recreational amenities begin with Five Island Lake. You can camp on the islands and use the lake for boating, water skiing, swimming and fishing. You can canoe and kayak on the Des Moines River, experiencing nature's wilderness. Additional lakes and sloughs provide wildlife habitat.

West Bend located in the southeast corner of **Palo Alto County** was the first settlement in the county. In 1855, the

Statue of Father Paul Dobberstein at the Grotto of the Redemption, West Bend

338

Grotto of the Redemption

Grotto of the Redemption

Emmetsburg

first settlers followed a trail made by wagons hauling supplies between Fort Dodge and Fort Ridgely. It was known as the Military Road and it led the pioneers to their new home that is now West Bend.

Little did the pioneers know that they were on hallowed ground where the world's largest grotto would be built. Father Paul Dobberstein spent a decade gathering rocks and precious stones from around the world before he began work on the Grotto of the Redemption. For the next 42 years, Father Dobberstein set the rocks and stones one by one in the walls and ceilings of the grotto structure creating a unique and inspiring shrine. Matt Szerensce, a parishioner, and Father Louis Greving, the next St. Peter and Paul priest, worked alongside Father Dobberstein and continued the project after his death.

The Grotto of the Redemption comprises nine separate grottos, each depicting a scene in the life of Jesus of Nazareth. The Trinity Grotto, the first one created, used mostly calcite rock from a cave near the Black Hills in South Dakota. The Stations of the Cross used Venetian mosaics imported from Italy.

White quartz is used to symbolize the purity of Christ's home in Nazareth. Sixty-five tons of petrified wood was used in the stable of Bethlehem. It goes on. With sacred music playing in the background, it is a moving experience to walk through the shrine.

Typically when we have overnight guests and on other special occasions, Connie serves a delicious, breakfast pastry called Butter Braid. It is an easy-to-prepare, frozen, braided pastry with a fruit filling. It has a freshly made quality and it satisfies my taste buds to a greater degree than any other pastry I have ever eaten. When I learned it was made in **West Bend**, I contacted the owners for an interview.

Ken and Marlene Banwart started out farming traditionally which led to truck farming which led to Farmers Market which led to selling pastries along with produce. The pastries sold very well, but it was tiring to get up and do the baking, then pick the vegetables from the truck patch. Ken suggested they mix the dough ahead of time and freeze it. Then they could take it out of the freezer the night before Farmers Market, let it rise

overnight and bake it in the morning. The popularity of the product encouraged them to start producing and marketing Butter Braid on a larger scale. In 1991, they set up a small production facility in their basement. Soon they had to retrofit the garage and, by 1992, they had moved into an available **West Bend** building. In 1997, they moved into a new building that they presently occupy. They added a warehouse in 2001. Five years ago, Country Maid, the company that produces Butter Braid, became employee-owned. Fifty-two employees continue to take pride in making the tasty pastry.

Ken and Marlene are humble, caring people who belong to the Apostolic Christian Church and live their faith. They have felt God's hand in their lives, their business, their family and community. In their faith, they look to the Bible for guidance. They are baptized as adults when they are ready to commit themselves to Christ. They don't drink, smoke or watch TV. They have no trained minister. Five members of the congregation are chosen to give sermons. They respect other religions. There is cooperation among Apostolic Christians, Methodists,

Marlene and Ken Banwart

339

Kossuth County

August Zahalten cabin in Ambrose A. Call State Park

Lutherans and Catholics in **West Bend**. Ken says, "There is a real respect for Sunday in West Bend. People work together when there is a need. It takes effort and they go out of their comfort zone." Marlene added, "And there is a nice group of young people coming up."

On our Iowa tour so far, we have experienced many Christian denominations, Jews, Muslims, Hindus and Buddhists. All the people we have met within these faiths were ambassadors of good will. Their faith works for them and they have a positive effect on society in general. It is unfortunate that there are radical leaders on the fringes who distort religion to further their agendas.

It was early November when we entered **Kossuth County**, the largest (area) in the state. It borders Minnesota on the north, thus disrupting the row of counties on Iowa's northern-most tier and causing a minor flaw in our tier-by-tier exploration of Iowa. There were many efforts to divide the county, but whenever it was brought to a vote, the more heavily populated southern half would oppose the move and nothing changed.

We have enjoyed a glorious week of

Ambrose A. Call State Park

Kossuth County HISTORICAL MUSEUM

Gides Law Firm

STOP

Algona

Kossuth County

Indian summer. That is such a nice term to describe sunny, warm, fall weather that comes after the first, winter-like cold snap. It is getting cold again, but Indian summers happen in November, too. High, westerly winds have stripped most of the leaves off the trees. The pin oaks stubbornly hang onto theirs and the grass is still green so the sights of fall haven't completely disappeared.

Barak Obama has just been elected the 44th president of the United States and the first black man elected! He gained his footing in Iowa by winning the Democratic caucus. This was significant because it was his first test and Iowa is an overwhelmingly white state. With the caucus win, his momentum grew and his resolve was tested through a tough primary fight and an even more contentious presidential campaign. John McCain gave the finest concession speech I have ever heard and Obama was just as gracious in his eloquent acceptance speech. I believe these are two great men who can work together and it is my prayer they will find other leaders who are willing to cooperate for the greater good.

As we approached **Algona**, the **Kossuth County** seat, I noticed a sign pointing to Ambrose A. Call State Park. This is a 138-acre, heavily wooded, hilly area near the east fork of the Des Moines River. There are two miles of trails for hiking and cross county skiing, 16 campsites and a picnic area with a log cabin-style lodge. There is also an 1855 log cabin built by August Zahalten, whose claim to fame is that he had the drop on the notorious Inkpaduta and threatened to shoot him. He didn't and Inpaduta went on to lead the Spirit Lake Massacre.

Ambrose A. Call and his brother Asa C. Call were the first settlers in this area where they built cabins of a similar style on a site near the park cabin. The Call brothers were the founders of **Algona**. When they stood on high ground where the courthouse now stands, observing the beauty of the location, Asa said, "I believe this is the place for our city." More settlers came and a community started developing. Many wagon trains consisted of a diverse group thrown together for mutual protection. This was personified in a six-wagon train that arrived in Algona. Two families were God-fearing people who became valuable assets to the community. Another family consisted of "poor pioneers" who kept moving from one frontier to the next hoping to have better luck at the next stop. Three men of the group were land speculators. Then on the other end of the spectrum, there was a gang of mixed family ties who liked their whiskey and weren't troubled with doing the right thing.

Joining the Calls as a community leader was William H. Ingham who loved to hunt and fish. He had a banking background in the East but his immediate plan in **Kossuth County** was to explore the wilderness. He accomplished this dream and then settled in to join the Calls in building the town of **Algona**. He had the distinction of being the only white man to kill a buffalo in Kossuth County. It happened near the town of **Titonka**. The town was named using an Indian word meaning "big cow" or "buffalo."

Gardner Cowles, the son of a Methodist minister, moved to **Algona** in 1885 to take the position of superintendent of schools. After the move, he met and married Florence Call, the daughter of **Algona** founder Ambrose A. Call. While serving as superintendent, Cowles

Kossuth County Courthouse, Algona

Kossuth County

1913 Louis Sullivan-designed building in the Jewel Box tradition—houses the Algona Chamber of Commerce (originally was a land and loan office)

bought half interest in *The Algona Republican*. Harvey Ingham, William Ingham's son, was the editor of a competing newspaper in which he wrote a front-page editorial accusing Cowles of neglecting the pupils to make a few dollars on a second-rate newspaper. Cowles left the newspaper and education field to go into business with his father-in-law, Ambrose A. Call, who had become a successful banker.

In 1903, Harvey Ingham approached Gardner Cowles (now a good friend) to buy *The Des Moines Register and Leader*. Harvey, the editor of the paper, was convincing and Gardner had the money to make the deal. The Cowles family moved to Des Moines and Gardner drew on his talents and work ethic to take a struggling daily, that was losing money, and make it a cornerstone of a publishing empire. The sons of Gardner and Florence Cowles (grandsons of Ambrose A. Call) took control of the Cowles Publishing Company in the 1930s and facilitated major growth. They expanded into the Minneapolis market in 1935. By 1941, with buyouts and mergers, they took command of the city's

342

Algona First United Methodist Church

Brian Schiltz

Algona

newspaper business, publishing the morning *Tribune* and the evening *Star*. In 1937, they launched *Look* magazine followed by several other publications. The company was profitable, well run and known for its journalistic integrity. Fifteen years after Gardner Cowles' death in 1946, journalism educators rated the Minneapolis and Des Moines' papers as the second and third, finest morning-evening newspapers published in America. By the time *The Des Moines Register* was sold in 1985, it had earned 13 Pulitzer prizes—second only to *The New York Times*.

In 1943, the Allies had turned the tide in World War II and were advancing on the Axis forces. The thousands of prisoners taken during the march to Berlin were overwhelming prison camps in England. The United States reacted by erecting 155 American base camps in record time. **Algona** was chosen as a base camp—no one knows why. In 1944, one hundred seventy-eight frame buildings were constructed on a site that is now the Algona Airport. The first arrivals were several hundred Italian prisoners who cleaned and readied the facilities. From April

1944 to February 1946, the camp was home to 10,000 German prisoners. A total of 34 branch camps were supervised from Algona. The prisoners hired out to work at various jobs. They were paid 80 cents per day in canteen coupons. Non-workers were allotted ten cents per day. Camp Algona POW Museum in downtown **Algona** features artifacts and information relating to the prison camp experience. It also honors the 2,500 **Kossuth County** residents who served their country in Europe and the Pacific.

Prisoner Eduard Kaib, an architect, was lonely and missing the happy holiday festivities of home in Germany. To combat his melancholy, he led a group of five fellow prisoners who worked long hours to create a nativity scene. The figures were made of concrete on a wire frame and finished with hand carving in plaster. Materials for the half-size scale figures were purchased by the prisoners with their own money. The scene is presently located in a special building on the Kossuth County Fairgrounds. It is open to the public during the month of December. Mr. Kaib and his family returned to the scene during Christmas of 1968.

Algona is a progressive town of about 6,000 people. Unemployment is very low, the amenities are of high quality and there is a comfortable pace to life. Brian Schiltz has lived in Algona all his life and loves it. He has traveled extensively but has yet to find a place that would lure him away from his hometown. He, along with his two brothers, own and run KOFAB, a small manufacturing company that produces USDA-approved stainless steel equipment for bakery, dairy, candy, meat, poultry and pharmaceutical processors. The products have a worldwide reach. Brian's dad, Don, founded the company in 1977. He passed away about a year and a half ago. Brother Gary is the fabrication plant manager, brother Bill is the project manager and Brian is the machine plant manager. Turnover is almost non-existent among the 43 employees. They have lost only one worker in the last eight years.

Brian started working for the company while in high school and joined them full time upon graduation. This totals up to 32 yeas of service. He and his wife Cindy have two daughters and a son. We noticed the wall behind his desk was covered

Algona

343

Algona Family Ymca

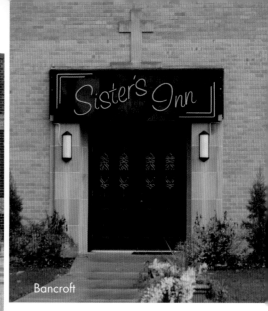

Bancroft

St. John the Bapist Catholic Church, Bancroft

Britt

with golf photos so we inquired about his association with the sport. Yes, he loves the game. His backyard won "golf yard of the month" in a John Deere contest and one of his daughters was a national NCAA Division III golf qualifier with the Wartburg College golf team.

Algona has a nice country club and the beautiful Spring Valley Golf Course in Livermore is handy. Brian was also quick to point out that Algona has a spectacular YMCA for year-around recreation. He says, "I love Iowa's ancestry, culture and hardworking people. It is home and I feel safe. People here are more realistic and live within their means, for the most part."

We drove north out of **Algona** and stopped briefly at Smith Lake, which was abandoned on this cold, rainy day. When the weather is nicer, you will find campers, fishermen, swimmers, picnickers and kids climbing all over the playground equipment. A new nature center has been built on the northwest shore.

Further north on Highway 169 is the baseball town of **Bancroft**. The town has claimed 20 state baseball championships in high school, American Legion,

344

Britt

amateur and semi-pro. They have produced two major leaguers: Joe (Lefty) Hatten, a pitcher for the Brooklyn Dodgers and Chicago Cubs from 1946 to 1952, and Denis Menke, a 13-year journeyman who played for Milwaukee, Atlanta, Houston and Cincinnati in the '60s and '70s. And, more importantly, it is home to the beautiful St. John the Baptist Catholic Church.

We left **Bancroft** and angled southeast on a zigzag route of north/south, east/west, Iowa country roads. We were traveling through the most expensive farmland in Iowa. Because of the rainy weather, there was no activity in the fields. Most of the corn crop had been harvested with corn coming out wet because of the late planting. This was expected and there will be added costs to dry the corn. Some warm, fall winds that aided the drying were too forceful and pushed over stalks causing a 25 per cent slow-down in combining. However, the yield was coming in at an average of 172 bushels an acre, as predicted. The process was just taking longer and costing more.

We crossed into **Hancock County**, named after the man whose signature is a dominant graphic on the United States of America Declaration of Independence. You will not find the arrogance of this signature symbolic of the county. In fact, it would be difficult to design a symbol that would reflect a county that is home to the National Hobo Convention and to the Duesenberg brothers, developers of the most luxurious auto of their time.

The town of **Britt** owes its beginning to the Chicago, Milwaukee and St. Paul Railroad's policy of have depots about ten miles apart when possible. On a rise of ground ten miles west of Garner, a depot was built in 1870. It was named after either a brakeman or chief engineer. The first half dozen years saw no development beyond the depot and a couple of shacks. Growth, typical of prairie town, began in 1876 as one business establishment after another formed a community. In 1900, the town became less typical when it held its first Hobo Convention. Originally the Tourist Union No. 63 held the Hobo Convention in Chicago. The union officers were persuaded by Britt promoters to move the celebration to **Britt**. Thirty-three years later, in 1933, the second convention was held in Britt featuring a parade, mulligan stew, a carnival and the crowning of King "Hairbreadth" Harry as the first hobo royalty. Polly Ellen Pep was the first Hobo queen, crowned in 1946. In 1974, four thousand people enjoyed a mulligan stew in which cinnamon was accidentally used instead of chili powder. When "Hardrock Kid" John Mislen passed away in Ogden on his way to the Hobo Convention, there were no relatives to claim his body. Britt gave him a funeral attended by 300 townspeople and hobos. "Steamtrain" Maury Graham delivered the eulogy and tossed red, bandanna handkerchiefs on the coffin—an old Hobo custom. Except for a period during World War II, the Hobo Day Convention has been an annual event. A photo of "Lady Sonshine" and "Tuck," the 2007 queen and king of the hobos, graces the cover of the 2008 convention flyer. They are wearing coffee cans cut in a crown shape and fur-trimmed capes over typical hobo duds. "Lady Sonshine" is the third member of the Hobo Gospel Trio to be honored as queen. A hobo king has to be a legitimate rail rider, either currently or in the past. Riding the rails is not a

Bancroft

Bancroft baseball park

Historic house, Britt

Evon Larson

requirement for the queen, but she must be familiar to the hobo community. The 2008 celebration lasted four days, including a multitude of events around the core hobo theme. In 1991, the only Hobo Museum in America opened in downtown **Britt**. Artifacts, photos, tramp art and convention videotapes tell the story. A quiet corner of Evergreen Cemetery was donated to the Hobo Foundation. It is the final resting place of "Hardrock Kid" and 13 more of his fraternity.

Britt won the Hobo Convention but lost the county seat fight. Sixty-two citizens signed a pledge to support a bond to build the courthouse. They also had a drawing of an elaborate, proposed courthouse building. The Garner people saw this proposal as a guide to what they would have to do to secure the county seat. They topped **Britt's** offer by actually raising the cash rather than a promise. The supervisors were given $30,000 and another $5,000 was set aside for courthouse grounds. A new courthouse that was built in 1899 is still in use today.

Bicycles made their debut in the 1890s. The early, high front wheel and small back wheel models made for some

Hancock County Courthouse, Garner

THE OLDE CREAMERY ANTIQUE SHOPPE

Garner

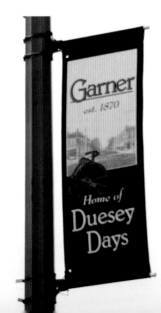

Garner
est. 1870

Home of
Duesey
Days

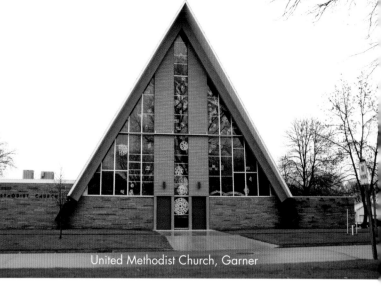
United Methodist Church, Garner

great, old-time photos, but when they evened the size of the wheels, the bike riding fad really took off. Bicycle shops sprang up and bicycle racing became as popular as horse racing.

Fred and August Duesenberg, self-taught engineers from Lemgo, Germany, settled in Garner and joined the bicycle craze by opening their own shop. It thrived but Fred and August had greater ambitions so, in 1913, they founded Duesenberg Automobile and Motor Company and began building sports cars.

Now that they were in the auto business, they decided to make the move to Indianapolis where they built their own racing motor and then the Duesenberg auto. These early autos were built by hand. In 1914, Eddie Rickenbacker drove a "Duesy" to a tenth place finish in the Indianapolis 500 and Duesenbergs won the 1924, 1925 and 1927 races. Jimmy Murphy, the first American to win the French Grand Prix, drove a Duesenberg. In 1921, Dusenberg passenger vehicles were manufactured but these expensive, extremely advanced automobiles could not find a market and only 667 were produced. Financial problems, buyouts and

renewed efforts to produce more luxury models continued through the 1920s and 1930s. At one point it was the ultimate luxury car owned by the nobility, rich and famous, including Clark Gable, Gary Cooper and the Duke of Windsor. If you own one today and it is in good condition, it would have a value of about $1 million. The slang word "doozy" meaning something extraordinary may have evolved from "Duesey." **Garner** commemorates the birth of the Duesenberg with Duesey Days held each July since 1980. The classic car show is the best fit for the celebration but there are many more fun events. There is a contest for Little Miss Duesey and Little Mr. Duesey and a parade of homemade floats accompanies their vehicle down the main thoroughfare. A craft show and 10K run add to the festivities and cow chip bingo is a major highlight. This is Iowa, you know. For the uninformed, cow chip bingo consists of a squared-off area in a pasture where a cow is turned loose to do its business. The owner of the square where the deposit is made wins the prize.

After doing some research at the Garner Public Library, we sat down and

visited with library employee Evon Larson. She and her husband Paul are Minnesota natives. A job for Paul as credit manager at IMT brought them to **Garner** about 30 years ago. IMT, a manufacturer of specialty trucks and truck bodies, employs about 360 people. Evon and Paul came from a larger town and have come to appreciate **Garner's** size (3,000) as ideal for raising a family. Organizations are the lifeblood of small towns but, Evon cautioned, "You can get overbooked." She began volunteering at her children's school, which led to part-time work at the public library. She gauges how well the economy is doing by the level of activity at the library. It is presently busier than normal. Evon and Paul have a son in Clear Lake and a daughter in Grimes. Paul is a marathon runner who has competed in 19 marathons. He is also a Norwegian and some day would love to run the marathon held in Tromsol, Norway. Evon said, "I didn't want to come to Iowa, to move far from family. But you bloom where you are planted. People come together here whether for benefits or crises."

It was a little after 5 p.m. when we left

Clear Lake State Park

Larch Pine Inn, Clear Lake

Darlene Sherwood

Last camper pulls out

Clear Lake State Park

Clear Lake

Garner. We were back on standard time so it was dark at five. Rain clouds shut out what little light we would have received from the constellations. I kept my eye on the highway's white line as we drove into **Cerro Gordo County**.

We found the Larch Pine Inn in **Clear Lake** with a minimum of looping. It is an elegant Victorian house that sits on a rise in an area of basically flat ground. Innkeeper Darlene Sherwood came to Clear Lake from Denver, Colorado, to help her daughter house hunt. Her daughter's husband, a physician, had just accepted a position in Britt. While in **Clear Lake**, Darlene stayed at the Larch Pine Inn and fell in love with the house. When she expressed this to the owner, she learned it was for sale. She bought it and continues to enjoy the house and the area. We also enjoyed the house but made no offer to buy it.

After checking in, we went out to dinner at the Half Moon Inn. It was a long, barracks-like building with a bar at one end and vinyl booths, stack chairs and tables in the dining area. We ordered the torsk special. Torsk in Norwegian means dried cod that has been brought back to

Clear Lake Arts Center

Surf Ballroom, Clear Lake

life. This torsk was cod but I have a suspicion it was never dried. One of the potato options was tater tots. Tater tots? I thought to myself, "Why not?" Tater tots and torsk, it was, and the only thing Norwegian about the meal was the guy eating it. I enjoyed it.

We awoke from a comfortable night at the Larch Pine Inn to a light dusting of snow—the first of the season. Darlene fixed us a tasty breakfast that fueled us through the morning as we toured Clear Lake. A light snow fell throughout the day but did not accumulate on the unfrozen ground.

The shore of **Clear Lake** was the chosen ground for Cerro Gordo County's first settlers. In 1851, the Joseph Hewitt and James Dickerson families set out from their homes in Clayton County in eastern Iowa with three wagons full of provisions. One night they camped near Buffalo Creek in Buchanan County. It was a pitch-black night with rain coming down in torrents. Flashes of lightning revealed that the creek had overflowed its bank and was rising. They were aroused by the fear of being washed downstream. Their horses evidently experienced the

same emotions because they were gone. This meant pushing the wagons through the mud to higher ground by hand. They succeeded in saving two wagons but time ran out and the third wagon with its provisions was swept away. Included in the lost provisions was a skiff that was to be used for crossing streams.

The two families pushed on until they arrived at **Clear Lake** where they gazed out on its crystal-clear water and decided this was it. They built their cabins and initially lived in isolation with the nearest inhabitants 60 miles away. They lived off the land by hunting and fishing and they went to Cedar Falls, Quasqueton or Independence once or twice a year to exchange furs for supplies. It was a couple of years before other families arrived.

Clear Lake is not crystal clear these days. Iowa is blessed with many streams, rivers and lakes but there is no large wilderness area of pristine, clear water. It is a developed land with easily accessible public areas of natural wonderlands that are susceptible to man's pollution. Our leaders realize this; conservation and restoration projects are in place and progress is being made on many fronts.

Funding, of course, is the key in restoration and sensible regulation prevents further damage. Dredging, limiting carp population, curbing runoff and restoring 500 acres to prairie and wetlands are measures being used to bring Clear Lake back to its former glory.

The town of **Clear Lake** has remained vibrant over the years. Its 8,000 people have been good hosts to tourists and celebrities and have been industrious workers in business and industry. There are many amenities for natives and visitors. There is swimming, boating and fishing on the lake. There are parks, golf courses, walking/biking trails, beaches and award-winning events and attractions. They have a wonderful Arts Center for the visual, performing and literary arts. Grant Wood spent the summer of 1941 in **Clear Lake**, using an abandoned railroad depot as his studio. He was there at the invitation of Park Rinard, a native of Clear Lake, who had become the Iowa icon's assistant. It was a typical summer with cottages around the lake filled with vacationers and young men and women cruising the streets and going to dances at the Surf Ballroom. In the

Zion Lutheran Church, Clear Lake

Clear Lake City Park

349

Downtown Mason City with First National Bank building in foreground

Music Man footbridge

Mason City

next few years, World War II removed the young men from the scene.

The Surf Ballroom in **Clear Lake** has been a premier dance hall since the heyday of the Big Bands. It was well known throughout Iowa as a great entertainment venue. An unfortunate tragedy in 1959 made the Surf famous throughout the United States and the rock and roll world. After performing at the Surf on February 2, 1959, the Big Bopper, Ritchie Valens and Buddy Holly were killed in an early morning plane crash on a frozen bean field. It was eulogized in Don McLean's famous song "American Pie" as "the day the music died." The bean field has become hallowed ground and the Surf Ballroom has kept the memories of those legendary performers alive. The annual February tribute to the classic rock and rollers draws pilgrims from around the country. The Surf is slated to be named one of the Rock and Roll Hall of Fame's "Landmark" award winners in February 2009. It is one of only four in the country to receive this award.

Cerro Gordo County's rich culture continues in Mason City, ten miles down the road from **Clear Lake**. Dale

Frank Lloyd Wright's Park Inn Hotel in the process of being restored

Frank Lloyd Wright-designed house

Dale and Barb Montang

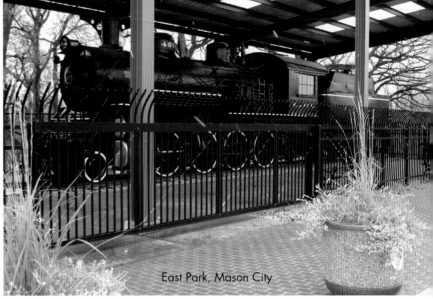

East Park, Mason City

and Barb Montang enthusiastically told us about the many attractions they enjoy in **Mason City**.

Young boys and men dream of having the job Dale had for 37 years. He drove trains; he was an engineer. Upon graduating from Moville High School, Dale took a position on the railroad working out of Perry. He was transferred to Preston, Minnesota, where he rode the trains as a fireman (assistant engineer). His wife Barb grew up in Preston and was teaching in Rochester when she met Dale through her brother. She and the fireman hit it off, got married and moved to **Mason City**. They raised three children in Mason City's nurturing environment.

At our urging, Dale told us about his engineering job. He worked for the Iowa Minnesota Railroad Line (IMRL) on freight trains that ran between East Dubuque, Illinois, to Sioux Falls and Rapid City, South Dakota. He would take a train from **Mason City** to Sioux Falls where he would stay over and bring a train back the next day. In one instance he was home and had to catch the train in Sioux Falls. Barb drove him to Albert Lea, Minnesota, to board a bus for Sioux

Falls. He took a "library" break at the station and while he was reading, the bus left the station. Not realizing it had departed, he waited a while before inquiring and learning that it was about 20 minutes down the road. A train sitting in Sioux Falls with no engineer would have been bad for his job security so he hailed a cab and directed the driver to catch that bus. The bus had a good head start but they caught up with it in Blue Earth. The meter ran up a nice tab for the cab driver before the mission was accomplished, but Dale climbed aboard his train on time and saved his job. After the story telling, Dale and Barb took us on a city tour.

I'm a fan of Prairie School architecture (I may have mentioned that before). **Mason City** has the largest concentration of the school's architecture outside of Oak Park, Illinois. I especially like the residential development of Rock Glen/Rock Crest on the banks of Willow Creek. It is the world's largest collection of prairie style homes in a natural setting and, true to the prairie philosophy, the designs are in harmony with the landscape. Frank Lloyd Wright made his Mason City contribution by designing the

Stockman House, City National Bank and the Park Inn Hotel. After decades of deterioration and vacancy, the hotel is being restored. The Stockman House has been preserved and is open seasonally for tours of the interior.

Meredith Willson's boyhood home, **Mason City**, was the inspiration for his hit musical, "The Music Man." The show first opened on Broadway in 1957 and became a hit with a three-year run at the Majestic Theatre, followed by another 1,375 performances at the Broadway Theatre. Numerous awards included nine Tony awards in 1957. Willson had many more accomplishments that you can learn about at The Music Man Square located next to his boyhood home. It's an exceptional museum that includes an indoor streetscape that replicates the Warner Brothers movie set for *The Music Man*.

In a 1934 bank robbery, the dastardly John Dillinger rudely disrupted the idyllic, wholesome, mid-American character of **Mason City**. He and his accomplice John Hamilton each sustained gunshot wounds while robbing the First National Bank. They got away with $52,000—far less that the $240,000 they expected.

Suzie Q Cafe, Mason City

Cerro Gordo County Courthouse, Mason City

351

TIER NO. EIGHT

| SI | OB | CL | PA | KO | HA | CG | FL | CH |

Holcim Cement Plant, Mason City

Shell Rock River, Rockford

Every year in March, there is a reenactment of the robbery.

The MacNider Art Museum has an impressive collection of American art that includes Native American pottery, Early American landscapes, contemporary abstracts, pottery and sculpture. Grant Wood, Thomas Hart Benton, Andy Warhol, Dale Chihuly and Alexander Calder are represented in the collection.

The MacNider name is attached to many public areas in **Mason City**. The benefactors, the MacNider family, were successful in business and industry. The huge cement plants north of town are part of their legacy. Cement is a finely ground powder composed of limestone and clay. When mixed with water, it becomes rock hard. There are abundant deposits of limestone and clay in the area.

In 1912, there was a **Mason City** brick and tile works that was one of the largest producers in the world, but that industry has disappeared. Today, Mason City has evolved into a service, retail and distribution center.

It was the middle of November when we crossed into **Floyd County**. The countryside had taken on a dormant look

352

Fossil and Prairie Park, Rockford

Beehive kilns at Fossil and Prairie Park

Floyd County

as we approached winter. The fields were mostly barren with a few stands of corn yet to be combined. The unseasonable, fall rain had continued into November, but the sun was shining on this day and a combine or two were out trying to complete the harvest. They were taking a chance with the soft ground and the muddy wheels of the machines left their tracks on the highways.

Our first **Floyd County** stop was at the Fossil and Prairie Park just west of **Rockford**. The abandoned clay pits from a once-booming brick and tile works exposed an abundant number of museum-quality fossils. The calcareous, ocean-bottom sediment that was deposited there never turned to hard stone. The fossils were preserved but not in stone. This is one of the few geological preserves where admission is free and collecting fossils for private use is allowed. I took the trail down to the historic beehive kilns used by the Rockford Brick and Tile Company. I did not look for fossils in the pits because the rain-soaked clay slopes would have greased a ride into the icy waters of the pond at the bottom.

The Shell Rock River was central to early **Rockford** history. Typical of Iowa river towns, a dam and mill were built in the 1850s and growth ensued. The railroad came in 1871 and the river came into play again—this time in a negative way. In December of 1871, a passenger train fell through a bridge into the icy water of the Shell Rock. Three of the crew were killed and two crew members were injured. The passengers escaped serious injury. The railroad replaced the bridge immediately and, in 1899, built an iron structure that stands today.

During World War II, the United States government paid farmers well to grow hemp. No, they weren't supplying pot to the troops. They were using it to make rope for the war effort. The slogan was, "Grow hemp—make rope—hang Hitler." There were many fields of the weed in **Floyd County**. One of the government's 42, hemp mills was located in **Rockford**.

A miller, who loved to hunt and trap, set up a camp near an Indian village of 150 wigwams on what is present day **Charles City**. That gave Joseph Kelly the distinction of being the first white settler in the area. When the Indians for-

mally released the land to the United States in 1850, Joseph entered a claim on the land where his camp sat. When he registered his claim at the Dubuque land office, the land agent questioned, "Man alive, do you know where that land is?" Kelly replied, "I believe I do." The agent said, "Well, it is worthless to you." Kelly responded, "No matter, it suits me." He went on to build a mill and prospered. **Charles City** was named after his son.

Agriculture was a struggle in the early days. Women growing gardens not only had to deal with weeds and insects, but they also had to ward off roaming farm animals. Hogs loved to root in the rows of growing produce. Corn was planted with a hoe and small grain was sown by hand. Pioneer farm equipment consisted of a few, meager implements that a settler could load in his wagon. As time passed, more laborsaving implements and machines were invented and developed. A major development occurred in **Charles City** with the establishment of the Hart-Parr Company in 1900.

Hart-Parr developed a gasoline traction engine and sales manager H. W. Williams decided a new name was need-

FOSSIL WASHING STATION

Transition time from fall display to Christmas decorations at Julie Miller's house, Rockford

353

Charles City

Floyd County Historical Museum, Charles City

ed for the product. He thought "tractor" would be easier to say than gasoline traction engine. **Charles City** thereby became the location of where the first "tractor" was built. Hart-Parr was bought by James Oliver and eventually became know as the Oliver Farm Equipment Company and later as Oliver Corporation. White Motor Corporation bought out Oliver in 1960. They did not survive the farm crisis in the 1980s and declared bankruptcy. Allied Products Corporation became the next owner and they gave up in 1993 and closed the plant. At its peak in the mid-1970s, the plant employed close to 3,000 workers. There is a fascinating collection of **Charles City**-built tractors in the Floyd County Historical Museum. Those early Hart-Parr tractors were massive, clumsy-looking machines.

A clean, progressive-looking Charles City business district came into view as we descended a small hill before crossing the Cedar River. It was lunchtime so we found the Uptown Café on the main drag to quell our hunger pangs. After dining in this pleasant little restaurant, we located a retail merchant and asked him if he

354   Mike Lidd

Pressing board in use since tailoring days

Charles City sculptures along Cedar River

would tell us a bit about himself and the town. Mike Lidd, of Lidd & Cordray Ltd. (men's and women's clothing), complied.

Mike's grandfather, John Lidd, and his brother Jim started a tailor shop in Audubon in 1889. Clothing was mostly custom made in those days. When it became practical, the business morphed into a retail clothing store. They moved to Shenandoah in 1906 and to their present location in 1923. Mike grew up working in the store and after attending the University of Iowa and working for five years at Donaldson's department store in Minneapolis, he returned to the family business. This is an attractive store with carefully chosen, moderately priced merchandise. He and his clerk were friendly, out-going people—the kind you enjoy dealing with when shopping. My discriminating wife ended up making a purchase. Mike's father Leo, who is 87 years old, still does the alterations.

Mike established himself as a marathon runner by competing in the Twin Cities Marathon in 2004. He later learned that he missed qualifying for the Boston Marathon by 90 seconds. Qualifying for Boston became his next

goal, which he achieved by running the Chicago Marathon in 3:18. To train for Boston involves a family commitment so he first obtained his wife Peggy's approval and received it. When the time came, he took the family along. His daughters Emily and Megan joined him in a pre-event called the Freedom Run, held the day before the Marathon. The run is two and a half miles and finishers are treated like they won the Olympics. Even though he had injured his knee five weeks before the race, he toughed it out and finished the Boston Marathon.

Mike told us about the many events that happen in **Charles City** and the county. Party in the Park is special and held every other Friday night during the summer. A band plays from 5 to 9 p.m. and it draws an average of about 1,500 people. The Fourth of July celebration goes on for about 4 or 5 days and draws large crowds. Mike says, "Charles City is a great place to work, play and live and a great community for raising a family."

With the loss of tractor manufacturing, **Charles City** has fought back by building three industrial parks with the latest one located adjacent to the new Avenue

of the Saints Highway. Speculative buildings erected in the first park greatly helped in drawing Winnebago Industries to the area. Winnebago has been hit by the present economic turndown but, if history is a guide, RV ownership will make a comeback and Winnebago's employment will rise again.

The arts are important to **Charles City** residents. There are outdoor sculptures throughout the city. The Mooney Collection of fine art prints by some of the greatest artists in history is a major treasure housed in a gallery at the city library. Rembrandt, Picasso, Matisse, Salvador Dali and Grant Wood are a sampling of the artists who produced the dry points, woodcuts, engravings, etchings, lithographs, aquatints and intaglios.

Arthur Mooney grew up in **Charles City** and studied photography under a local photographer. He moved on to art school in Minneapolis and then to New York City where he was employed by Eastman-Kodak. He rose to become one of the company's successful executives and began collecting fine art prints. In 1941, the entire print collection was bequeathed to Charles City.

Floyd County Courthouse, Charles City

Mary Ann Townsend, Director of Floyd County Historical Museum

Girlhood home of Carrie Chapman Catt, Floyd County

Sara Marquez waves
at us through the rain

Down a gravel road southeast of **Charles City** is a modest brick house that is listed in the National Register of Historic Places. It is the girlhood home of Carrie Chapman Catt, who led a successful campaign to win voting rights for women. At age 13, she questioned why her mother was not voting in the 1872 presidential election. Her sincere question was greeted with laughter and she never forgot that reaction. As an adult, she recalled that day as a turning point in her life. Upon the 1920 ratification of the Nineteenth Amendment to the U.S. Constitution, Carrie Chapman Catt founded the League of Women Voters. Her story is told in this neat, little farmhouse in **Floyd County**.

Another neat little attraction awaited us near **Nashua**—the Little Brown Church in the Vale. William Pitt, a young music teacher who was in love, stepped off a stagecoach in Bradford and took a walk into a nearby, wooded area where he drank in the serenity and charm of the scene. A vision of this natural beauty kept reappearing in his mind so he formulated it into a poem and set it to music in the song "The Little Brown Church in the

Little Brown Church in the Vale, Nashua

Chickasaw Wellness Complex and Logo Man sculpture

Chickasaw County Courthouse, New Hampton

Nashua Dam on the Cedar River

Vale." The hymn gathered dust in his desk drawer until he revisited the location of his inspiration and discovered a church was being built on the spot he had visualized in his hymn. Mr. Pitt's vocal class from the Bradford Academy sang the song in public for the first time at the church's dedication. He sold the song to a Chicago publisher for $25 and it eventually became popular while being sung at chatauquas and social events across the country. Presently, the Little Brown Church is popular for weddings and, since 1952, annual wedding reunions have been well attended.

Bradford appeared to have a future as it was **Chickasaw County's** first county seat. But its location in the extreme southwest corner of the county ensured that the seat would be moved. In 1857, it was transferred to Chickasaw Center; Bradford evolved into a pioneer village museum. Chickasaw Center was renamed **New Hampton** in honor of Hampton, New Hampshire, the hometown of early settler Osgood Gowan.

We had the opportunity to talk with two of New Hampton's boosters and civic volunteers who do their best to keep the town vibrant. Mike Kennedy, a native, enrolled at Notre Dame upon graduation from New Hampton High School. He earned a bachelor of arts degree in English. After taking some education courses at the University of Iowa, he took a teaching/coaching job at Newman High School in Mason City. Three years later, he married Linda Weiss and enrolled in the University of Iowa law school. When he graduated, he joined his father's law practice in **New Hampton**. In those initial years, he had some extra time so he ran for a seat in the Iowa legislature. He won and served two terms (four years) in the House of Representatives.

Linda grew up in Mason City where she graduated from St. Joseph High School (later renamed Newman). She earned a bachelor of arts degree in education from St. Theresa's College in Winona, Minnesota. She met Mike through her brother who was in Mike's English class. She has served as a first grade teacher, started a Winnie the Pooh pre-school and was Mike's secretary when he was in the House of Representatives. She has been the curriculum director in **New Hampton**

schools for the last 15 years.

Mike recalls growing up when the banks were locally owned; now there are four banks, but only one is locally owned. There were four or five doctors with individual practices; now they work for the hospital or the clinic. Times change; you gain something—you lose something. One gain is the beautiful new Chickasaw Wellness Complex (CWC) for year-around recreation. There is a new, all-weather track at the high school and a new bike/walking trail. Mike and Linda agree that when there is a need in the community, people come together.

Mike is a member of the "poor, unfortunate bastards club," a group of men who are or were in business with their fathers. One member came back after being a commander of 3,000 troops in the Philippines. His father wasn't impressed; he wouldn't give him the keys to the insurance business.

Mike is still an avid fan, to say the least, of Notre Dame football and he is passing that passion on to his grandchildren. Daughter Cara and her husband Jackson, who live in Des Moines, have three, active little boys who are frequent

Linda and Mike Kennedy

Pocket park and bike trailhead, New Hampton

357

New Hampton

Zip's Trucks, New Hampton

guests at the Kennedys. Their room has Notre Dame logos on everything—the carpet, the bedspread, the window treatment . . . Photos on the walls depict Notre Dame scenes, including a panoramic view of the stadium full of fans.

Celebrations in **New Hampton** are numerous. Heartland Days, held the second weekend in June, is the largest event. Many activities include a fireworks display and parade. Linda Kennedy was the 2008 parade grand marshal. Her little, "fighting Irish" grandsons rode with her. Two waved and one didn't.

New Hampton's central business district looks healthy and there are several successful industries in town. TriMark, an employee-owned tool and die company, employs 300 people. New Hampton Metal Fabrication is a leading manufacturer of concrete machinery and equipment. Progress Casting Group, Inc. has a new, 80,000-square-foot facility focused on the production of castings for Harley-Davidson. Zip's Trucks assembles tow trucks and Sparboe Foods has moved into the vacant Sara Lee plant. Soy Basics manufactures beanpod candles that are made from soybeans.

358

Connie and Diane Engelbrecht enjoy visting with Kerrys reps: Doug Skudas, Tim Prete and Tom Long

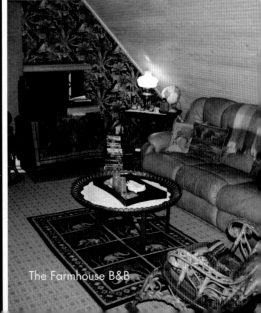

The Farmhouse B&B

Kerry's Fredericksburg plant

Several Rune stones found in Chickasaw County provide evidence that the adventursome Vikings may have set foot on Iowa soil a thousand years ago. Runes inscribed on the stones are icons of the Viking alphabet. Chickasaw resident, Orval Friedrich, has written two books and several articles on the subject.

Before we moved on to a B&B near **Fredericksburg**, we ate dinner at the Pinicon in New Hampton. It has recently been remodeled into a pub-like atmosphere. It was nice and their special of chicken parmigiana was tasty.

The Farm House Bed and Breakfast Inn is run by Dianna Engelbrecht and the farming operation is her husband Loren's responsibility. We had reserved a regular room but Dianna upgraded us to the Safari Suite on the third floor. It had a well-done theme with a sitting area, large whirlpool tub, king-size bed and balcony. All that luxury was short-lived because we got in late and left early the next day. That bed surely was comfortable, though.

The next morning we shared the breakfast table with three, young men who were in town on business. They were representatives of Kerry, an Irish compa-

ny that has 55 plants in North America. One of them is in **Fredericksburg**. The men were from Beloit, Wisconsin, where Kerry's North American headquarters is located. They explained what the company produces—something to do with creating fragrances and tastes that enhance food products.

Dianna and Loren both grew up on dairy farms. Loren informed us that Dianna was a Dairy Princess. No surprise there, she is still a very attractive lady. After working at non-farm jobs, Loren wanted to get back to farming. When he spotted this property, he told Dianna that if the farm ever came up for sale, he wanted to buy it. It did and they bought it in 1993. They worked for five years to bring it up to speed. Loren has a unique dairy operation. He buys pregnant cows, calves them out and, after milking them for about a month, he sells them to large dairies. He sells the calves to growers. He keeps many other animals on the farm for guests to enjoy—goats, chickens, peacocks, llamas, Jacob sheep, cats and a dog named HJ.

HJ is a hero dog. While watching television in the early hours on Easter

Sunday 2007, Loren developed an enormous pressure in his chest. The pain was so great that he couldn't move or call for help. HJ beat it to the bedroom and nudged Dianna until she awoke. Dianna sensed something was wrong and went to the parlor where Loren was in severe pain. HJ never left his master's side while paramedics worked to save his life. Loren had what is known as a "widow maker" heart attack. Without medical attention that night, he would not have survived until the next morning.

In addition to the B&B and farm, the hardworking Engelbrechts work a vineyard, winery, private dining room, gift/antique shop and summer dinner theatre. Dianna says, "I absolutely love my vineyard. I planted it and I tend it." Loren says, "I like my cows and the rural setting of **Fredericksburg**. I'm no city boy."

Dianna handled the city quite well before she retired from her professional job in 2004. She has a Ph.D. from the University of Northern Iowa. She was a principal at Hudson High School before returning to Northern Iowa to teach education leadership. She says she loved her work then and she loves her work now.

The Farmhouse B&B

New Hampton

Little Brown Church in the Vale, Nashua

Uptown Cafe, Charles City

360

Pinicon Restaurant Bar, New Hampton

Arthur Mooney art print collection, Charles City Library

BILY CLOCKS

ARNOLDS PARK

WALDORF COLLEGE

Tier 9

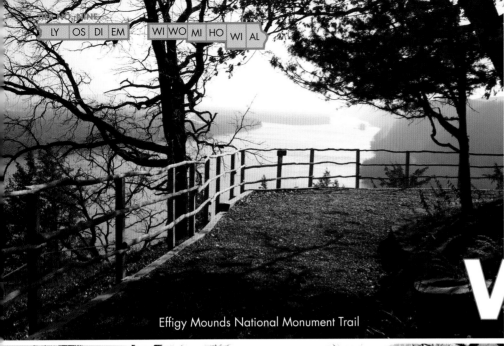

Effigy Mounds National Monument Trail

Lansing

View from Effigy Mounds National Monument

362   Coal power plant and fishermen share the Mississippi

We launched our trip through tier nine by starting at the Effigy Mounds National Monument. Woodland Indians built the mounds between 750 and 1,400 years ago. In the Upper Midwest, the mounds took the shapes of birds, turtles, lizards, bison and, most commonly, bears. The origin and meaning of the mounds remains a mystery. It is documented that there were more than 10,000 mounds in Northeast Iowa. Less than 1,000 have survived. In 1949, Effigy Mounds National Monument was established to preserve some of the remaining mounds.

The park is located along the Mississippi in northeastern Clayton County and southeastern **Allamakee County**. There is an interpretive visitors' center located near the county line and Yellow River, which divides the northern and southern areas of the park. I chose to hike up an "Iowa Mountain" in the northern area. It was a totally pleasurable way to spend a November, Indian summer day. I followed a well-marked path paved with wood chips and there were wood rail fences to keep me from tumbling down the hillside. It was sunny with a slight breeze rustling the fallen

Lansing

leaves. Determining the shape of the mounds was a bit tricky, while observing them from the side. These scenes were not as impressive as the spectacular views of the big river from the park's "mountain tops," but you can feel the presence of the early Indian culture's reverence of nature.

For present-day nature lovers, there is nearby Yellow River State Forest. One of Iowa's largest outdoor recreation areas, the preserve covers 8,500 acres of upland hardwoods and coniferous forests. This parcel is set aside for land stewardship, habitat development and protection, the production of wood products and outdoor recreation. The Paint Creek Unit has over 25 miles of hiking, bicycling and equestrian trails. In winter some trails are open to cross-country skiing. Except for campgrounds, the entire state forest is open for hunting. Two, cold water streams provide trout fishing. In the Paint Creek Unit, there are 176 campsites that are open year-round. They accommodate tents, trailers and RVs. Thirty-four of the sites are designated as equestrian. It is a perfect place to immerse yourself in nature.

Leaving this wonderful recreation area, we proceeded up the Great River Road continuing to enjoy magnificent scenery. The scene was blighted somewhat by trailer houses and shacks mounted on stilts along the banks of the river. They are summer getaways and I imagine there have been a few, freshly caught catfish fried in cornmeal on their stoves. I don't begrudge these pleasures, but the structures do disturb the view.

As we drove into **Lansing** on Highway X52, I heard a loud train whistle that sounded like a train was on my bumper. I quickly glanced over my hood to see if I had somehow jumped onto a railroad track. I hadn't, but I wouldn't have had to veer too far to the right to be on the track. It was virtually a third lane on the street. That is just part of the charm of this picturesque village of about 1,000 people. The town was named by a man from Lansing, Michigan, who built a shanty on the site in 1848 and contributed nothing to the town's growth after that. However, the name stuck. More enterprising settlers followed. It was incorporated in 1864; in 1899, the first pearl button factory was started, thus becoming another Mississippi town that harvested the river's clams to manufacture buttons.

Some rivers have mud bottoms and some have rock bottoms—the Mississippi must have had a clam bottom.

In 1851, Miss Harriet Hosmer, a talented young sculptor, debarked a Mississippi steamer that had stopped in **Lansing** to take on wood. She eyed a beautiful bluff overlooking the town and asked the boat's captain if she had time to climb it. He told her she could have all the time she wished. She hiked to the top and waved her handkerchief at the stewardesses. When she returned, a gentleman called the town fathers and requested the bluff be named after her. They agreed— she must have been very charming.

We drove to the top of Mount Hosmer. We saw deer along the road and, at the summit, we viewed an expanse of Mississippi backwaters, islands, bottomlands, marshes and the Lansing Bridge. We were looking at the Upper Mississippi River National Wildlife and Fish Refuge and it was awesome.

Waukon pioneer C. J. F. Newell grew up in Wayne County, New York. His father was a pioneer, hunter and trapper and his grandfather was a colonial captain in the Revolutionary War. He had the

Lansing

Mississippi backwater, Allamakee County

363

Yellow River Forest

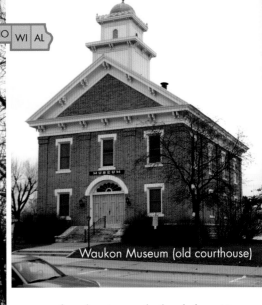

Waukon Museum (old courthouse)

Big Paint Creek, Yellow River Forest

genes for adventure so he headed west to Iowa in 1851. His destination was Garden Grove, near the Missouri line; however, on the way he was encouraged to look into **Allamakee County**. He was told it was a healthy section whose streams of sparkling spring waters were filled with trout. He followed their advice and bought an 80-acre parcel. He returned east for two years, then reappeared in Iowa with his wife and children. The county seat was located in **Waukon** and they were the first family to settle there. When a hut, first used as a courthouse, was replaced by a larger building, Newell purchased it, moved it and set up a blacksmith shop. The first essential business in a town's growth was in place and it was the county seat to boot.

As we continued our trip, we drove west on Highway 9 to Our Tara Inn, a B&B located halfway between **Lansing** and **Waukon**. Signe and Dan Buege own it and it was our next overnight stay. The accommodations were in a remodeled, 1896 barn that has been in Signe's family for the last forty years. Signe says, as a youngster, she stacked hay in the haymow and did a little cleaning up after

Ion Exchange,
Allamakee County

Howard Bright

Jane and Jens
Kallevang

Allamakee County Courthouse, Waukon

Signe Buege

the hay had been processed by the farm animals on the lower level. Years ago, two young lovers ran away and hid in this very barn for several days. When they emerged, their worried parents were thankful to see they were safe. However, the parents demanded their immediate marriage and the lovers were more than happy to comply. Connie and I would be classified as old lovers who enjoyed their stay in the barn with considerable more comfort and a clear conscience.

Before we turned in, we drove into **Waukon** where we met Jens and Jane Kallevang. Jens is a partner in a Waukon CPA firm that provides accounting, tax preparations, audits and estate work. Jane is a lab technician at the Winneshiek Medical Center in Decorah. They were high school sweethearts at Crestwood High School, a consolidated school that includes Jens' hometown of Cresco and Jane's hometown of Lime Springs. They have three daughters and two grand-daughters. They love the county's outdoor amenities of hunting, camping, fishing, canoeing, tubing, biking and cross country skiing. Within the county are the Mississippi, Upper Iowa and Yellow

Rivers, in addition to eight to ten premier trout streams. The Iowa tradition of helping your neighbor is alive and well here. Recently, $50,000 was raised for neighbor with a heart problem.

Jens said there are an increasing number of people moving from cities to **Allamakee County** to retire. Wooded, hilly land is competing with farmland in value for the new settlers. Summer homes are being built along the "Big River" and tourism is growing. Jane says, "We grew up in Northeast Iowa and we enjoy it. We like the outdoors and all the recreation." Jens added, "We like to camp and, when the kids were small, we used to go to the Mississippi for water skiing and tubing behind the boat."

Before we returned to the B&B, we drove to **Rossville** for dinner at The Old Rossville Store. It was a charming country restaurant with good food.

After our sound night's sleep, Signe served us a farmers' breakfast and we were off to explore more of Allamakee County. The next stop was the Ion Exchange, a native seed and plant nursery, located on the Yellow River near the Yellow River Forest. Howard Bright, a

lover of nature, wild flowers and spiritual learning, has built a life around these interests. He helped found the Ion Exchange, Inc. about 20 years ago. The purpose of the Exchange is to create natural beauty and to help and support others in creating their own beauty. He also helps others immerse themselves in the natural wonders of **Allamakee County** by providing lodging and activities at The Ion Inn and The Natural Gait Resort. There is a clever use of the word "gait" in the name with its multiple meanings of: a path/lane between hedges; a way of walking or running; and various foot movements of a horse. All meanings relate to the resort but there is much more. The Ion Inn sleeps up to 15 people and three Natural Gait cabins each sleep six to ten people. In addition there is a community lodge with six bedrooms attached to an indoor, horse-riding arena. There are numerous electric and primitive campsites. Activities include horseback riding, trout fishing and river fishing (including the big one), canoeing and kayaking, hiking and birding and simply kicking back to absorb the beauty of the "Iowa Mountains."

Old Rossville Store Restaurant

Waukon

Postville

St. Paul's Lutheran Church, Postville

SAINT
BRIDGET
CHURCH

St. Bridget's Catholic Church, Postville

We left this idyllic countryside and moved on to **Postville** where things have gotten a bit ugly, to say the least. In 1987, a group of Lubavitchers, an orthodox sect of Hasidic Jews, bought a vacant slaughterhouse and set up a Kosher meat-packing operation that grew to be the largest packing plant of its type in the country. The German/Norwegian, basically Lutheran community was not prepared for the invasion of these zealous, orthodox Jews. And the Jewish sect was moving into a community whose culture was totally foreign to them. The out-going, inclusive Iowans initially extended a welcome, but became confused at the response of the closed Jewish culture. There was a clash and Stephen Bloom, a journalism professor at the University of Iowa, wrote an excellent book doing his best to tell both sides of the story. The book's title is *Postville*.

Last May the Kosher packing house (Agriprocessors, Inc.) was raided and 390, alleged illegal immigrants were arrested. Since then, new workers were brought in and new workers left and the turmoil continued as accusations and denials filled the air.

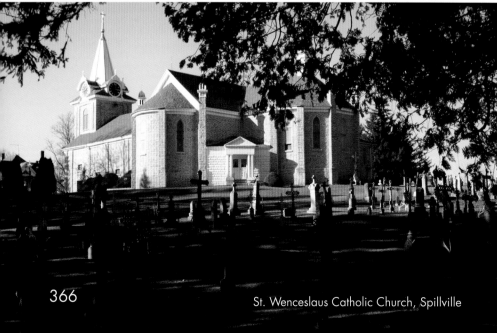

366

St. Wenceslaus Catholic Church, Spillville

Adrian Lofte

Agriprocessors, Inc., Postville

The victims of this mess are fortunate that 75-year-old priest Father Paul Ouderkirk came out of retirement to serve at St. Bridget's Catholic Church, where hundreds of Hispanic workers have sought refuge. He was listed by *Forward*, a national Jewish newspaper, as being among the most influential people in Judaism for his tireless efforts to administer to the needs of the conflict's casualties. Jews from across the country have donated tens of thousands of dollars to the church's humanitarian fund, which helps former workers.

It was quiet as we drove through town. A street decoration in the shape of a Jewish Menorah complemented the Christmas decorations. There is still hope in the community of **Postville**.

We drove back out into the countryside on Highway 52. When we reached **Ossian**, we took a left on a paved county road that morphed into gravel before we reached the farm of Adrian Lofte.

Adrian is a six-foot-six, Norwegian-German, diversified farmer who rotates his crops and lets his pigs run freely in an outside pen. He is contracted by Midwest Pride to raise the hogs naturally. This means straw bedding, no antibiotics and an open front building so they are free to go outside. The hogs are farrowed in pasture before they are brought to him. He has a few beef cows whose calves he sells at the Decorah Sales Commission where feeders bid on them. His farm consists of 120 acres of which 80 are tillable. In this hilly land, the fields are in strips to prevent erosion. He rotates four years of corn, one of oats and three of hay. He is the fifth generation to live on this farm. When Adrian's dad got married, he was living in a house where rooms had been added on to a log cabin. His dad thought his new bride deserved better, so he tore it down and built the house in which Adrian and his family presently live. His wife Mary Eileen, a graduate of the University of Northern Iowa, teaches fourth grade at DeSales Catholic Elementary School in **Ossian**. Adrian has an associate degree in farm management from Area 1 Community College in Calmar. He and Mary Eileen have three daughters; two are in college and the third is in eighth grade. Adrian says, "I like the work and the independence and it is nice to live in the country where it's peaceful and quiet. I enjoy knowing my country neighbors. I don't have to fight traffic. I sometimes have to battle the elements—or rather, adjust to them."

It was back to **Ossian** where we ate lunch at Shooters Bar and Grill and then on to the Bohemian town of **Spillville**. Spillville was first settled in 1854 by a German named Joseph Spielman who built a sawmill and later a gristmill. The name Spielville evolved into Spillville. Many who followed Spielman were from Bohemia and they gave the town its character. In 1860, the cornerstone for St. Wenceslaus Catholic Church was laid; in 1869 and 1870, a sanctuary, a tower and two wings were added. In 1876, the first pipe organ in the county was installed.

In the summer of 1893, the locals had the pleasure of hearing the great Czech composer, Antonin Dvorak, play the organ at daily Mass. Tired from a year's work as director of the New York Conservatory of Music, he longed for the companionship of his countrymen. He learned of **Spillville** through a resident and brought his family for a respite from city life. He did not compose "The New World Symphony" in Spillville, but he

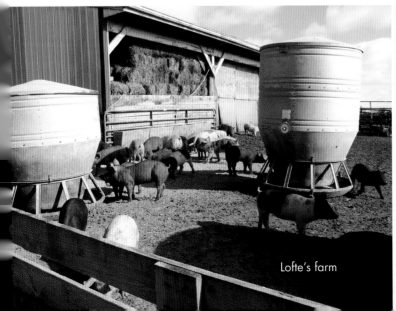
Lofte's farm

Spillville

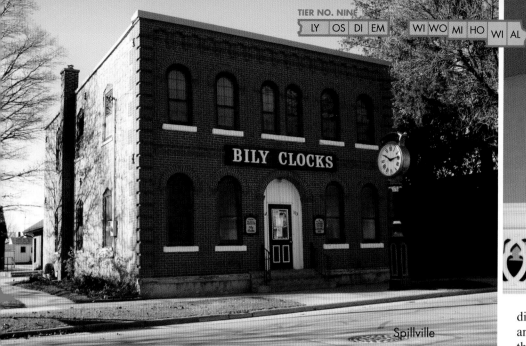

Spillville

Organ played by Dvorak in
St. Wenceslaus Catholic Church

did make some corrections while in Iowa
and it was performed for the first time
the following winter. During his stay, he
did compose "The American Quartet,
Opus 96" and it is believed he found
inspiration for "Humoresque" while fishing along the Turkey River.

The building the Dvorak family lived
in during their stay is now a museum that
houses a collection of Bily Clocks, as
well as Dvorak exhibits. Beginning in
1913, Frank and Joseph Bily began wiling away the long winter days and
evenings on the farm by carving ornate,
elaborate clocks. They made their living
by farming and the clock carving was a
hobby. Many of the clocks have themes
based on the Twelve Apostles, the
American pioneer, Charles Lindberg's
historic flight and other meaningful topics. They used many types of wood and
their craftsmanship was exceptional in
those creative pieces of art.

A unique fort was built at **Fort
Atkinson** located a few miles downriver from **Spillville**. It was built in 1842
to maintain order among various Indian
tribes displaced by settlers. Its purpose
was also to prevent settlers from trespass-

Washington Prairie Lutheran Church, Winneshiek County

368

Vesterheim (Western Home) Norwegian-American Museum, Decorah

Wild turkeys

The Inwood dance pavilion, Spillville.

ing on what was Indian land at the time.

Besides Spillville, **Winneshiek County** has several towns with strong ethnic character. Norwegians dominate **Decorah** and **Ridgeway**. **Castalia** and **Ossian** are German. Ossian was settled by Germans of different faiths— Catholics and Lutherans. They brought their old country prejudices with them. During much of the twentieth century, there were two high schools in this town of about 900 people. The most spirited competition was when they faced each other in sports. The public high school has since been consolidated with **Calmar**. The Catholic school no longer provides high school courses. And the generations have cleansed the prejudices.

Decorah traces its beginning to the settlement of the Day family in 1849. The matriarch of the family overruled the claim her husband had staked out in favor of a site beside running water. They built a log cabin and later they constructed the first commercial establishment—the original Winneshiek Hotel. The present Winneshiek Hotel sits on this spot. The spring has ceased to flow.

Water has played a prominent role in Decorah's history. At one time there were 13 dams scattered through **Decorah** for industrial use. They may have harnessed the Upper Iowa River but they didn't control it until the 1940s when they undertook a massive flood control project. It was a well-engineered plan that made it possible to develop the core of the city without the fear of ravishing floods.

In the 1850s, Norwegians began settling in **Winneshiek County** in large numbers. The Norse settlers possessed a cross-section of skills and intellect. They formed a dominant culture in Decorah and nearby rural areas. On the highest hill of the Washington Prairie faming community stands one of the most elegant, limestone country churches you will see anywhere. It was, and is, an inspiration to the Norwegians who work the land.

America's leading Norwegian language newspaper, *The Decorah Posten*, was published in **Decorah**. The Vesterheim Norwegian-American Museum in Decorah is the largest museum in the United States dedicated to one ethnic group. When Norwegian royalty come to the U.S., they most frequently visit Chicago, Minneapolis and Decorah.

During the last full weekend in July, **Decorah** shows its colors in Nordic Fest, a celebration of its heritage. There is ethnic music, dancing and food. Parades, 15K and 5K runs, Norse craft demonstrations, a 3-on-3 basketball tournament, a rock throwing contest and a lutefisk-eating contest are some of the events. I would imagine few people enter the lutefisk-eating contest. Lutefisk can best be described as fish jello—a taste not favored by many people.

In 1857, the Norwegian Evangelical Lutheran Church of America decided to found a college. In 1859, a Norwegian professorship was established at the Concordia College and Seminary in St. Louis, Missouri. The college and seminary were closed in 1861 at the outbreak of the Civil War. Professor Laur Larsen and his handful of students moved to a vacant parsonage at Halfway Creek, Wisconsin. In the summer of 1862, the school was transferred to **Decorah**. The first college "Main" building was dedicated in 1865. It was destroyed by fire in 1889 and its replacement caught fire in 1942. The present Main is a contemporary building with a central tower and no

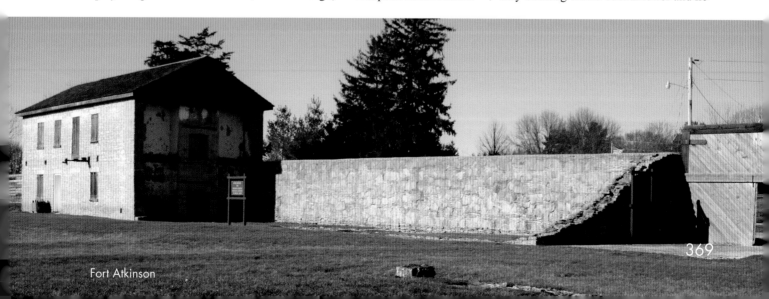

Fort Atkinson

Luther College, Decorah

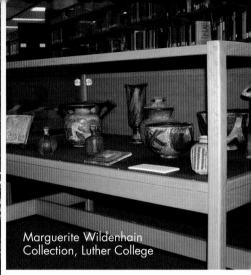

Marguerite Wildenhain
Collection, Luther College

wood in its construction. The original classical curriculum was changed in 1932 when Greek and Latin were dropped as requirements. After 75 years of men only, the college became coeducational in 1936. Today, Luther College is the second-largest private college in the state with an enrollment of about 2,500.

Luther was the first college founded by Norwegian Lutheran immigrants and it is loaded with tradition. It is closing in on 150 years of stressing academics and spiritual growth. In the interest of developing well-rounded students, the school has always supported striving for excellence in extra-curricular activities. Luther has never forgotten that it is a faith-based college of the Lutheran tradition. It takes an intellectual approach to exploring religion; students of other faiths are welcome and their beliefs are respected.

The Luther campus is alive with the sounds of seven choirs, three bands, three orchestras, two jazz bands and nearly 1,000 student musicians. Throw in other musical activities such as chamber groups, brass ensembles, opera workshops and you have one of the largest, undergraduate musical programs at a lib-

Dean Schwarz

370

Porter House Museum, Decorah

Dunning Springs, Decorah

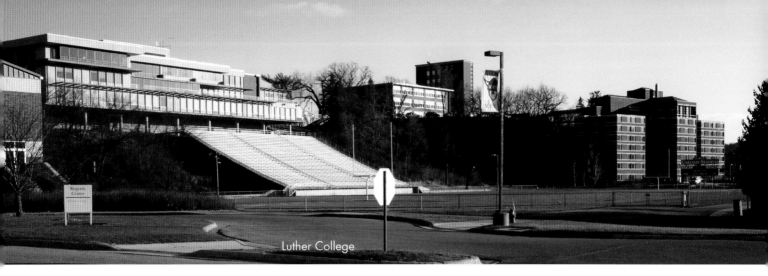
Luther College

eral arts college in the United States.

The emphasis on music is not at the expense of sports. Luther fields 19 intercollegiate athletic teams (ten for men and nine for women). About one-fifth of the students participate in varsity athletics. The following are a sampling of Luther athletic accomplishments over the last century: 61 NCAA Division III National Tournament appearances; 25 individual national champions; 43 Academic All-Americans; 26 NCAA Postgraduate Scholars (twenty-second among all NCAA institutions) and 186 Iowa Intercollegiate Athletic Conference championships.

A Methodist of English heritage was encouraged by his father to enroll at Luther College rather than the University of Iowa. That decision gave Luther the honor of schooling and employing a man who became a world-renowned musical legend. Weston Noble's conducting talents quickly drew the attention of the Luther music faculty. After service in the Army during World War II, where he saw action as a tank driver, he taught a couple of years in high school before Luther called. He was asked to serve as interim director of the band and choir. This evolved into a highly distinguished, 57-year career where Noble served as musical director of Luther College Concert Band from 1948 to 1973 and the Nordic Choir from 1948 to 2005. The 72-voice Nordic Choir is one of the most elite, a capella choirs in the United States. Noble has been guest conductor of more than 950 music festivals around the world. He is the only director to have led all-state choruses, bands and orchestras in all fifty states. Unique among his many awards is the Weston Noble Award for Lifetime Achievement in the choral arts; in 1998, he was the first recipient of an award named after him. When we visited the Luther campus, I inquired as to whether he might be in the area and was informed he was lending his services to sister institution, Wartburg College, while his friend Paul Torkelson took a one-year leave.

Northeast Iowa has become home to many professional fine artists. The picturesque towns in beautiful bluff country are part of the draw and the strong arts tradition of Luther College fills in what could be a cultural void. The artists participate in a self-guided, studio tour each October during the height of fall colors. Driving the country roads through this magnificent countryside with intermittent stops at working art studios, where you can view and purchase professional art, is a total pleasure.

On the art tour you notice there are some very good ceramic artists with exceptional pieces of pottery on display. They are protégés of Dean Schwarz who taught at Luther for 23 years and founded South Bear School in 1970. South Bear School is an innovative, summer arts school of instruction in pottery, painting and poetry. The facility for the school, and also the residence for Dean and his wife Geraldine, is a former, 65-room nursing home. They also operate a small book publishing company, South Bear Press, out of this establishment. The flagship book produced by South Bear Press is a 776-page, eyewitness anthology entitled *Marguerite Wildenhain and the Bauhaus*. Its 8 1/2- by 11-inch pages contain eyewitness accounts as well as 837 photos and illustrations. The Schwarzs spent more than ten years gathering material and editing this important account of a rich period of ceramic art and pottery.

Decorah

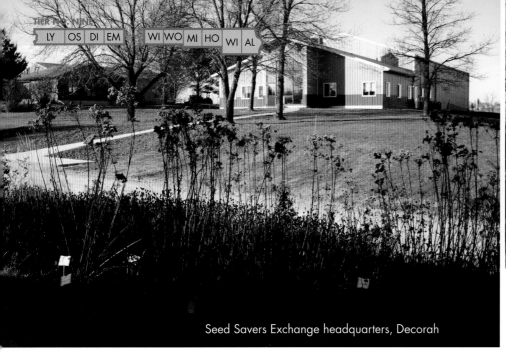

Seed Savers Exchange headquarters, Decorah

Diane Ott Whealy, co-founder of Seed Savers Exchange

Marguerite Wildenhain was a Bauhaus-trained master potter who had to flee Germany and then Holland because of her Jewish ethnicity. She found a home at Pond Farm, an art community in the hills of Northern California. Dean Schwarz sought out Marguerite (probably the greatest potter of her time or anytime) at Pond Farm in 1964. He studied under her that summer and returned two additional summers. The third year, he served as a teaching associate, getting paid in pottery. A friendship evolved and she developed a love for Luther College during workshops she presented at the college and South Bear School. She donated to Luther College a collection of her best pots, some rare books, a rock and mineral collection, drawings, personal papers and a collection of drawings, woodcuts and sculptures by Gerhard Marcks. They are displayed at the Preus Library.

Dean's work is in museums and universities throughout the world, including the Museum of Art and Culture (Wu Han, Hubei, China); University of Nottingham (Nottingham, England); Collection of King Olaf (Oslo, Norway); Pottery Museum (Mikawachi, Japan); Burg

Winneshiek County Courthouse, Decorah

Upper Iowa River, Winneshiek County

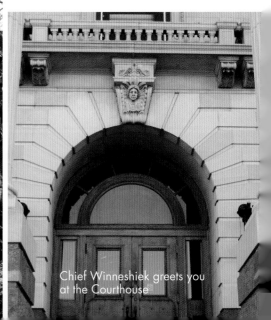

Chief Winneshiek greets you at the Courthouse

Winneshiek Hotel, Decorah

Calendar Corner of Upper Iowa River, Bluffton

Giebichenstein (Halle, Germany); and the White House Collection (Washington D.C.) (And in Carson and Connie Ode's private collection.) Presently Dean is collaborating with his talented son Gunnar in producing Schwarz pottery. Gunnar does the throwing and Dean does the decorating and glazing.

Dean and Geraldine raised five more children. There are some colorful stories of the children adapting to living on this unique piece of property. The six youngsters were ages four to fourteen when the family moved into the new home with 65 bedrooms. After first inspection, they began making plans for every room—there would be the Hot Wheels room, the basketball court, the gerbil room and so on. The gerbils were supposed to stay in their cages, but they were fun to take out and play with and, inevitably, some escaped. Their descendants may still be roaming the rafters.

Thirty acres of woods, grassy meadows, and two creeks coupled with sharing the grounds with summer art students sent the kids' imaginations into overdrive. Tree houses, climbing trees, swings of every type sprang up in unusual places.

Where the creeks came together, there was a fine swimming hole. Their son Jason wore his red swimsuit for three months straight. And Halloween—you can only imagine what the children did with the third floor attic.

We were pretty tired when we checked into **Decorah's** Winneshiek Hotel—an elegant, restored, 31-room hotel in the heart of the business district. These accommodations are second to none at any price. It is simply a beautiful place that Connie and I love. For dinner that evening we walked downstairs to Albert's, the hotel's restaurant, and chose a table with a view of the street. Christmas decorations were up and old Norwegian men were walking by with their flaps down. Winter is here.

The next morning we made one more stop at a Northeast Iowa, back-to-the-earth enterprise. The Seed Savers Exchange is a nonprofit organization of gardeners and plant collectors who save and share heirloom seeds brought to America by immigrants. Founded in 1975, the members have handed down an estimated one million samples of rare garden seeds. These heirloom varieties

are widely distributed to home gardeners, seed companies, farmers' markets and chefs. Their 890-acre headquarters is located just north of **Decorah**. They have a beautiful, post-and-beam visitors' center and several miles of hiking trails, gardens and animals of interest. They hold many events and celebrations throughout the year. Their 2008 catalog offers 647 total varieties, of which 15 are new and 181 are certified organic. It is a special, well-run organization that preserves the best of the past.

From the Seed Savers Exchange, we retraced our drive down Highway 52 to the Upper Iowa River valley where we took a right onto Pole Line Road. We drove alongside the river on our way to **Bluffton**, enjoying every minute of the scenery. The Upper Iowa is recognized as the premier recreational river in Iowa. It is also known nationally—it was nominated to be one of the first designated National Wild and Scenic Rivers with the Department of the Interior. Canoeists, kayakers, tubers and anglers love the Upper Iowa and its natural attributes of wildlife, cliffs, palisades, coldwater springs and waterfalls. The palisades at

Largest, capon-producing plant in America, Decorah

373

Cresco

Spiff Slifka and
Randy Mashek

Norman Borlaug statue, Beadle Park

Bluffton are so frequently photographed and published that this section of the river is referred to locally as "Calendar Corner."

We returned to Pole Line Road and continued our trip west, crossing the **Howard County** line just two miles east of **Cresco**. I think this makes Cresco the least centrally-located county seat in Iowa. We left the rugged bluff country and entered a rolling prairie landscape of rich farmland and wooded river valleys. It has its own beauty and the folks we talked to in Cresco think it is the greatest place in the world.

It is the job of Spiff Slifka and Randy Mashek to promote Cresco and **Howard County**. Spiff is the county tourism director and Randy is the executive director of Cresco Area Chamber of Commerce. You notice the surnames of these two have more complicated spellings than the Norwegians in Decorah whose names end in "son." The Czech Bohemians are in charge here. Spiff, however, is a Scandinavia who fell for a Bohemian and couldn't be happier. She was raised in North Dakota, attended college at North Dakota State and San Diego

Howard County Courthouse, Cresco

Cresco

Beadle Park, Cresco

State, moved to Los Angeles, moved back to San Diego, moved to Decorah and finally to **Cresco**. Randy is a Bohemian Cresco native and a graduate of Iowa State University, who moved to Chicago and then to Colorado. Fifteen years after leaving Cresco, he chose to return to the town he loved. They are a couple of vibrant, enthusiastic people who find it easy to sell the area. Connie and I love our home in Des Moines, but after talking to these two, we were about ready to look up a real estate agent. This urge has happened in many Iowa towns—we love this state. They covered a lot of ground in our chat; I've done my best to sum it up in the following report on **Cresco** and **Howard County**.

The headwaters of the Turkey River are in Howard County. When Marquette and Joliet came down the Wisconsin River, the river's current carried them across the Mississippi to the mouth of the Turkey River, making it the first river discovered in Iowa. Early settlers staked claims on its shores and followed it to the state's interior. In 1851, two settlers named Hiram Johnson and Daniel Carlin left their families in Clayton County,

planning to hit the Oregon Trail. When it took them several days to cover two counties, they decided continuing to Oregon wasn't such a great idea. They set up camp along the Turkey River, which evolved into a settlement, the first in **Howard County**. The town that resulted was named New Oregon. By the 1860s, it was a bustling frontier trade center of 850 people. However, a clever investor named Augustus Beadle, had a tract of land along a ridge about two miles north of the river that was ideal for the westward expansion of the railroad. Cresco is a Latin word meaning, "I grow," and grow it did when it was platted on the ridge of the railroad right-of-way. New Oregon's residents and many of its buildings moved to the new town on the tracks. **Cresco** is no longer on a railroad line, but it pays homage to its past with a restored Milwaukee Road FP7 diesel engine displayed in Beadle Park.

Also on display in Beadle Park is a bronze statue of Norman Borlaug. Borlaug, a Norwegian among the Czechs, was raised on a small, diversified farm south of **Cresco**. His education began in a one-room school and continued at

Cresco High School where his athletic accomplishments opened the door to attend the University of Minnesota. He wrestled for Minnesota while he studied forestry. In 1937, with a degree in forestry, he went to work for the U.S. Forest Service. Later he returned to Minnesota to earn a Ph.D. in plant pathology. In 1944, he began a sixteen-year stint of working to solve a series of wheat production problems in Mexico and to help train a generation of young Mexican scientists. The successful implementation of new wheat varieties and crop management spread to other Latin American countries and to Asia. It sparked what is known today as the "Green Revolution." It is said that Dr. Borlaug saved more lives than anyone who ever lived.

For his efforts he was awarded the Nobel Peace Prize (1970), Presidential Medal of Freedom (1977) and the Congressional Gold Medal (2007). He is one of only five people in the world to win all three prizes. After failing to convince the Nobel Committee that there should be a Nobel Prize for Agriculture, he created the World Food Prize in 1986 with General Foods Corporation as the

Cresco

TIER NO. NINE
LY OS DI EM WI WO MI HO WI AL

Plantpeddler, Cresco

Sue-Z-Q's restaurant, Cresco

Five admirals and Ellen Church

sponsor. In 1989, John Ruan II of Des Moines stepped in as sponsor when General Foods withdrew its support. Ruan believed the Prize is even more vital now to inspire a second Green Revolution. John served as chairman until 2003 when his son John Ruan III took the helm. The World Food Prize is awarded on or near World Food Day each year in the Iowa State Capitol building. A former library building in downtown Des Moines is being restored and remodeled to serve as a World Food Prize headquarters. The Norman Borlaug Harvest Fest is held annually in **Cresco** in September.

From saving lives with better agricultural practices to protecting our country with military might, **Cresco** nurtures strong leaders. No less than five Admirals walked the halls of Cresco High School and graduated from the Naval Academy. Vice Admiral Frank J. Lowry (1911) went on to lead part of the Atlantic patrol during World War I. Rear Admiral Michael J. Malanaphy (1917) went on to be flotilla commander of LCIs in the South Pacific during World War II. Rear Admiral Arthur T. Moen (1917) went on to be a commander over 300 ships and landing

CRESCO THEATRE

CRESCO

COMING
HIGH SCHOOL
MUSICAL III

PRAIRIES EDGE NATURE CENTER

Trail at Prairie's Edge Nature Center, Cresco

Cresco Country Club and Turkey River

vessels during World War II. Rear Admiral Wallis F. Petersen (1924) was commander of the USS Mustin when it rescued 337 survivors from the Hornet carrier during World War II. Rear Admiral George E. Peckham (1931) went on to serve in European, African and Philippine Liberation Theatres during World War II.

Another leader of note, this time of the female gender, was **Cresco** native Ellen Church. She was a humanitarian, war heroine and aviation pioneer. And she was the world's first airline stewardess. As a young nurse in San Francisco, she approached Boeing Air Transport, the parent company of United Airlines and proposed that stewardesses be added to flight crews. They thought it was a good idea; in 1930, she and seven other nurses, the "Sky Girls," began flying between Chicago and San Francisco. In her sales pitch she was quoted as saying, "If women were casually living and working in the air, wouldn't it help rid the public of any fear of the air?" As a captain in the Army Nurse Corps Air Evacuation Service, she earned the Air Medal by serving with distinction in North Africa,

Sicily, England and France. She combined imagination, persistence and personal warmth to meet life's challenges.

The last sentence of the previous paragraph is applicable to today's **Howard County** leaders. They are building on the past and living in the present. Enthusiastic youth work with old hands. The Cresco Opera House plays on this theme. It is billed as "a gem for all ages" and that it is, indeed. In 1914, construction began of a solid, well-designed opera house for live performances and movies. On February 13, 1915, there was a sellout crowd to watch the opening show, "High Jinks," by a New York touring company. The next night a five-reel, silent film, accompanied by an eight-member pit orchestra, was shown to a packed house. Today, the restored structure serves basically the same purpose with live performances and movies.

In **Howard County** you can buy your produce directly from farmers five days a week. They have a unique, countywide Farmers Market with towns taking turns hosting the affair.

Plantpeddler ships its young plant products well beyond the county to coun-

trywide distribution. The Cresco-based greenhouse can trace its roots back to an 1880 cypress and glass house where sweet corn, watermelon and muskmelon were given their start. The modern day Plantpeddler is a very large operation committed to developing, marketing and growing only the best genetics. Dominick's/Safeway in the Chicago area, Jewel/Osco and Hy-Vee are customers, as are greenhouses in Texas and Colorado and on the East Coast.

If you see a NASCAR driver or some other celebrity on the streets of **Cresco**, they are probably in town checking on a custom-made trailer built by Featherlite. The company has built some very luxurious living quarters on wheels. At their plant west of town, they also build horse trailers, stock trailers, car trailers, recreation trailers and utility trailers.

The annual Czech Days in **Protivin** are one of many celebrations in **Howard County** towns. Held each August, the festivities include softball tournaments, games, camping, dancing, eating and drinking. The beverage of choice for Czechs is beer and has been for a long time. In 1896, the **Protivin**

Cresco

TIER NO. NINE

| LY | OS | DI | EM | | WI | WO | MI | HO | WI | AL |

Lidtke Mill, Lime Springs

Wapsi-Great Western Line
bike trail, Riceville

town council had to deal with a contro-versial issue—drinking during Church. In those days the churchgoers would bring their tins and sip away during the ser-vices. It was a close vote of two for and two against the ordinance ordering all business places where intoxicating and temperance drinks were sold to be closed on Sunday after the third bell was rung until 12 o'clock noon. The mayor cast the tie-breaking vote for the ordinance.

After a nice lunch at Sue-Z-Q's diner on Highway 9 in Cresco, we took a little jaunt up to **Lime Springs** to check out the historic Lidtke Mill on the Upper Iowa River. It's a rustic gem! Then it was on to **Riceville**, a town of 900 that strad-dles the Howard-Mitchell County line. There are some nice recreational ameni-ties in and around Riceville with Lake Hendricks, the Wapsi-Great Western Line bike trail, a golf course, tennis courts and a softball field.

Beyond **Riceville** we continued our drive into the flat to rolling farmland of **Mitchell County**. The Little Cedar and the Cedar River traverse the county at angles, dividing it into thirds. The Cedar flows through a lovely valley that can be

Mitchell County Courthouse, Osage

378

Osage

Mitchell County Historical Society Museum, Osage

Osage

appreciated with a line in the water or cruising in a canoe over the gentle riffles and pools. The river is as beautiful as the surrounding farmland is rich.

Pioneers in **Mitchell County** came primarily from New England states, Norway, Sweden and Germany. They were allowed to stake a claim and later purchase it at $1.25 per acre. In 1856, when the land was actually sold, speculators from the East came to bid on the land with plans to sell later at a profit. They were not popular people. The auctioneers favored the settlers. Once the settler would submit a bid of $1.25 per acre on his claim, the auctioneer would ignore higher bids from a speculator. In some instances when a speculator tried to outbid a settler, the settlers would gang up on him and throw him into the river. However, the speculators bought a large piece of the county's unsettled land and it greatly delayed the county settlement.

Mills were built in great numbers across Iowa. Grain had to be ground, lumber sawed and wool weaved. The raw materials were abundantly available or produced and waterpower from the extensive network of rivers and streams was

available at virtually any location. In 1870, there were 502 flour/grist mills, 545 sawmills and 30 woolen mills, mostly operated by waterpower. In Mitchell County the count in 1874 was nine flourmills, six sawmills and one woolen mill.

The quality of milling operations varied. A story was told about an Iowa miller who had trouble getting his millstones within speaking distance of each other. On one occasion a boy brought back a sack of grist and told the miller his mother would like it ground finer. The miller responded, "I'm very busy and I can only promise to grind the corn so fine it won't grow." The boy replied, "That is all my mother expects, but she mixed up some of the last grist and it sprouted before she could get it in the skillet."

The town of **Mitchell** was the site of a flourmill built on the Cedar River in 1857. In 1925, a concrete power dam was built and stone from the old mill was used to build the powerhouse. Power production was resumed in 1998 after extensive repairs were made and new turbines were installed.

Mitchell County has a new twist in county seat fights. Mitchell was serving

as the seat when **Osage** and Charles City encouraged the Iowa legislature to give three tiers of sections (a three-mile wide strip) from northern Floyd County to **Mitchell County**. This made both Charles City and Osage closer to the center of their respective counties. When a judge made the decision to have Osage as the county seat, a number of Osage residents went out in the middle of the night and removed all county records and equipment from Mitchell and brought them to **Osage**. This was done so Mitchell couldn't contest the decision. Osage "stole" the county seat from Mitchell. A red brick building with two-story columns and a silver-topped cupola was built in 1862. It is still in use today. There have been two additions.

Highway 9 enters **Osage** as a main thoroughfare through the center of the city. We drove in from the east passing by stately, restored, turn-of-the-century homes fronted by elegant maple trees. Forward-thinking, early residents planted the trees that now give Osage the identity of the City of the Maples. We were a bit late for experiencing the beauty of the brilliant fall colors.

OSAGE STATE CHAMPIONS

| DAIRY FOODS 1973 EXPERIENCE THE ACTION 2007 | MEATS 1969, 1970, 1971 1973, 1976, 1977 1978, 1981 | FARM & BUSINESS MANAGEMENT 1977, 1978, 1979 1981, 1983, 1984 1989 | AG SALES 1993 1998 | AG MECHANICS 1999 2008 | AG ISSUES & PERCEPTIONS 1998 2000 | PARLIAMENTARY PROCEDURE 2004 2007 | WRESTLING STATE DUALS 1940 1989 1965 1992 1981 2001 2006 | BOYS BASKETBALL 1989 1995 | GIRLS BASKETBALL 1992 | CROSS COUNTRY 1970 |

FFA

ATHLETICS

First Lutheran Church, St. Ansgar

Pastor Mark Decker

Osage is a very clean, prosperous looking community. It is located in a good retail trade area surrounded by one of Iowa's richest agriculture regions. The past is kept alive at the Mitchell County Historical Society Museum housed in a distinctive building that was one of the central buildings of the Cedar Valley Seminary. Cedar Valley Memories displays rare, antique steam engines that are in running condition. Some are the only models known to exist. A 1914 Reeves 40-140 Cross Compound is the largest of all known steam engines and it is the only one in the world. It was designed to pull a 16-20 bottom plow. Cedar Valley Memories holds an annual show the second week in August with an array of early farm equipment and antique cars accompanying the machines.

Speaking of power, early Osage settler Benjamin C. Whitaker had plenty of it surging through his body. He came from Michigan where he reportedly quelled a railroad riot at White Pigeon, by decking a score of troublemakers with his fist. **Osage** folks believed the story when they saw him throw a man who outweighed him through a post office win-

Blue Belle Inn B&B

Our Savior's Lutheran Church, Osage

Solar home, Mitchell County

Cedar River, Mitchell County

dow. He was not a thug. He became the first treasurer/recorder of the county and he was the first man to bring a steam threshing machine to the area.

Osage continues to produce physically strong men who are good citizens. Osage High School is known as one of Iowa's top wrestling schools. They have produced 52 individual champions and have won three state team championships. The school's eleven runner-up finishes is a state record.

A boon to outdoor recreation was the creation of the Mitchell County Conservation Board in 1956. It was charged with purchasing lands for parks, fishing and hunting access and other recreational uses. They presently manage 2,000 acres of public lands including five county parks, 22 public hunting areas, two historic sites, one outdoor classroom and one hiking/biking/equestrian trail.

A fantasyland of rooms themed on children's books awaited us in **St. Ansgar** at the Blue Belle Inn B&B. Because we were the only guests on that Thursday, winter night, we were given our choice of rooms. We chose the Plum Creek room based on Laura Ingalls

Wilder's book *On the Banks of Plum Creek*. It was a spacious suite with a queen-size bed, whirlpool tub, fireplace and TV. The house is Queen Anne Victorian and the decor is a heavy mix of patterns and antique furniture. We enjoyed a fire and a little TV before we drifted off to sleep in more luxury than Laura Ingalls Wilder ever experienced.

Following breakfast the next morning, we had a chat with innkeeper Sherrie Hansen's husband Mark Decker. Mark is the pastor of Bethany Lutheran Church in Thompson, a congregation of about 500 members. He is a California native who traveled an interesting route to St. Ansgar. He was a golf pro for five years before he migrated to the Midwest to attend the Lutheran Seminary in St. Paul, Minnesota. His first assignment (his preference) was at an inner city, African-American congregation in Brooklyn, New York. He felt accepted and treated well but it wasn't a good match. After four and a half years, he turned the congregation over to an African-American pastor and returned to Minnesota for the position of youth pastor at St. Olaf Lutheran Church in Austin. Then it was

back to the Southwest for five years in Kingman, Arizona. The lure of the Midwest brought him back to take the position of pastor at Bethany Lutheran Church in Thompson.

Five years ago he married Sherrie, the innkeeper. He missed out on all the fun (work) of developing the Blue Belle Inn. Sherrie didn't miss out on any of it. She bought a run-down Victorian house in 1991 and, with the help of her handyman father, turned it into the elegant masterpiece it is today. Again we are talking about some hard-working Iowans. They have developed another house next door into added lodging. They serve lunch Monday through Saturday and dinner on Friday and Saturday nights in a main level tearoom. It is good place for a getaway in a quaint little town with a number of recreational activities. Mark says, "I have lived in several places. This is the smallest town I have lived in. It is much better living in a small town; many in my congregation have moved back."

St. Ansgar was named after the patron saint of Scandinavians who Christianized much of Denmark, Sweden and northern Germany between 830 and

Horizon cereal-making plant, St. Ansgar

Worth County Fairgrounds, Northwood

Flooding the ice skating rink, Northwood

Worth County Courthouse, Northwood

864. The Reverend Claus L. Clausen, a Dane and the first Scandinavian minister in America, was commissioned by the Lutheran Church of Norway to form congregations for Norwegian immigrants in Wisconsin, Iowa and Minnesota. In 1853, he founded the St. Ansgar First Lutheran Church and used it as a center for his mission to organize other congregations. From the mid-1850s to the late-1870s, he formed 21 comparable organizations in Iowa and Minnesota. Today, First Lutheran in St. Ansgar is the oldest, continuously active Lutheran congregation west of the Mississippi.

Lutheran churches are more common along the northern-most tier of counties of Iowa. Settlers' descendants from Scandinavia and northern Germany determine the base culture. We found that to be true as we motored into **Worth County**. The terrain is basically the same with the pretty Shell Rock River bisecting the county. English and Norwegians pioneers found a nice piece of ground above a crescent bend in the Shell Rock to build the town of **Northwood**. The railroad also liked the lay of the land and the town.

Sue's Corner Post restaurant, Northwood

Sue's Corner Post

Swensrud Park, Northwood

The requisite fire that cleansed most downtowns of their early frame buildings did half a job in **Northwood**. The south side survived in tact. Most of the current buildings on the north side were built during a building boom following the fire. On the south side, the last of the nineteenth century, wood-framed buildings were replaced in the mid-twentieth century with one-story, unadorned, modern structures. The entire downtown has been placed on the National Register of Historic Places.

The past of Northwood and **Worth County** is well documented with five museums located in **Northwood**. There is the Machine Museum, the Creamery Museum and the Log Cabin Museum located in a grouping on the west edge of town. Adjacent to the business district is the Worth County Historical Society Museum housed in a three-story brick building. Nearby is a historic country schoolhouse where Sidney Swensrud began his education. He went on to become president of Gulf Oil Company and founded the Swensrud Foundation that benefits the Northwood community. A neat little park, down the

hill from the business district in the crook of the crescent bend of the Shell Rock River, bears the Stensrud name. Another Northwood claim to fame is resident Hans Langseth's Guinness Book of World Record's longest beard.

Much of this information was gleaned from a conversation with Northwood Mayor Bob Perry. Bob, a native of the south side of Chicago, was drawn to the small-town Midwest to play football for Peru State College in Peru, Nebraska. He earned his master's degree at Wayne State, also in Nebraska. He came to **Northwood** to coach football and teach social studies. He coached for 33 years and taught for 40 years. After serving on the city council, he was elected mayor in 1999.

Bob loves his town and is always open to ideas that will benefit the community, but he was not prepared for a call he received from Steve Miller. Steve came from the Twin Cities to take a job as instructor at North Iowa Area Community College (NIACC) in Mason City. He and his wife Kim chose to live on a farm near Northwood. On the phone call, Steve asked, "Have you ever thought

about a casino in Northwood?" Bob was stunned. When he hung up, he told his assistant that it was the weirdest call he had ever received. Kim did an extensive job of lobbying the Iowa Racing and Gaming Commission and the casino became a reality. Bob was stunned again.

The spirit of **Northwood** continually impresses Bob. One proud occasion was when 300–400 volunteers out of a population of 2,000 came forward to help host an overnight for RAGBRAI (10,000-plus bike riders). Bob says, "I love Northwood for a lot of reasons. In the inner city of Chicago, my playground was streets and alleys. Iowa has been great—my three children had a real playground across the street."

Fun time celebrations and festivals around Worth County include: **Fertile** Fun Days, **Grafton** Turkey Days, Sundown Weekend in **Hanlontown**, **Manly** Railroad Ag Days and the Fourth of July celebration in **Northwood**.

Northwood has a healthy business climate with some small industries contributing to the economic health. ADA makes vinyl-covered steel apparatuses for confinement buildings and park benches.

Bob Perry

Northwood

383

A storm is threatening in Worth County

ACT fabricates exterior/interior acoustical components for a variety of vehicles. Northwood Foods processes boned hams for Hormel. And there is a classy, little microbrewery located in the historic Peoples Gas and Electric building downtown. Worth Brewing Company brews Pale Ale, Brown Ale and Slim Jim beers. Appetizers are served along with the beer in their elegant Tap Room.

We left **Northwood** and drove into a white sky with snow blowing across the road in feathery streams—an indication of potential blizzard conditions. It let up briefly and our hopes rose and then it started in again. As the flakes increased in size and number, I adjusted the car speed accordingly. Not everyone did. We didn't have far to go to the Iowa Welcome Center and the Diamond Jo Casino just off Interstate 35. How is that for an introduction to Iowa—a welcome center in the shape of a barn and across the street is a large casino full of slot machines and table games? I hope the barn is still more symbolic of the state.

It was Connie's last chance to hit the slot machine jackpot. After 18 casinos, the running score was $32.75 in arrears.

Iowa Welcome Center

Lake Mills school playground

Norwegian Immigrant Memorial, Lake Mills

384

TransLink, Inc. (a global logistics company with special equipment for loading wind turbines), Manly facility

The slots seemed to be tightening up as we moved north and they didn't give at all at Diamond Jo's. We had barely settled in out of the storm when Connie had lost the allotted $10. It was all over. After risking $10 at each of Iowa's 19 casinos, Connie ended up losing a total of $42.75.

The snow was letting up when we emerged from the casino and, by the time we arrived at **Lake Mills** in **Winnebago County**, the sun was shining. A clear blue sky was the backdrop for the American, Norwegian and Iowa flags that waved above a bronze memorial to Norse immigrants. The sun might have been shining, but when I opened my car door, a cold, bracing blast of air hit me in the face. However, to an old Norseman, it was invigorating and seemed appropriate as I walked over to observe the statuary of a Norwegian immigrant family. Mother, father, daughter and son are standing by a trunk with the son pointing the way. He is pointing to **Lake Mills**—a heavily Norwegian town of about 2,100 people.

There is no lake in **Lake Mills** but Rice Lake is nearby. It is shallow and not great for recreation. When the town was first settled, there was a lot of water in the low-lying areas and one could travel miles in a canoe through the wetlands. Most of that land has been drained and is now producing crops.

Early settler, C. D. Smith, convinced a miller in Bristol to move his mill to what is now **Lake Mills**. The town grew and Bristol disappeared. When C.D. sold or gave away lots, he stepped them off and said, "There, that's yours." That caused a few problems when the town was platted. In 1871, a fire consumed the mill, consequently causing a decrease in trade for the town's merchants. It was the same year as the Chicago fire, so it was said, "The cow that kicked the Chicago lantern must have switched its tail against Lake Mills." Life went on with saloons arriving in town before churches. In 1879, there were six saloons occupying the largest buildings on the main street. It was the early 1880s before churches were built.

When the Norwegian Lutherans came, church activities became more prevalent and saloon activity declined (but didn't disappear). Salem Lutheran Church in **Lake Mills** is the largest Lutheran church we have seen on our Iowa odyssey. It is symbolic of the fact that Lake Mills continues to be heavily populated by Norwegians.

When we drove into town we noticed an attractive manufacturing facility with a Larson logo flag waving between the American and Iowa flags. Oscar Larson in Albert Lea, Minnesota, founded Larson Manufacturing Company, a business that manufactures storm doors. He designed a storm door with interchangeable windows and screens that became very popular. When the company outgrew the Albert Lea facilities, it moved to **Lake Mills**. As the company continued to grow, a satellite plant was added in Brookings, South Dakota. Oscar's son Dale was sent to manage it. When Oscar passed away in 1968, Dale became president and CEO. He had settled in at Brookings, so the headquarters was moved to Brookings where it remains.

Larson's Iowa operations manager Brian Throne has his office in the **Lake Mills** facility. He took some time to visit with us. He is a Norwegian native (admits to some Irish) of Lake Mills who grew up on a farm. He loved farming but his opportunities were limited when his older

Salem Lutheran Church, Lake Mills

Lake Mills

385

LY OS DI EM   WI WO MI HO WI AL

Descending from Pilot Knob, Winnebago County

Brian Throne

Winnebago County Courthouse, Forest City

brother took over the family farm. Following high school, he attended North Iowa Area Community College and received a four-year degree in agriculture business from Buena Vista University. He worked in agriculture related businesses, was a sales rep for Pioneer and drove an over-the-road truck. This varied background prepared him for a job as production manager at Minnesota Corrugated Box for three and a half years before he took a similar position at a Pella plant in Carroll. After six months at Pella, the production manager job at Larson opened up and he was hired. Larson has since bought the Carroll Pella plant and it is now also under his supervision.

Brian couldn't be happier. He loves his job and is very complimentary of the company and its employees—from CEO Dale Larson across the board. Their quality product is the number one selling storm door in America. Brian's wife Debra is a native of nearby Thompson and works for NIACC as a tech prep coordinator. The Thrones have one son. Brian says, "I love the people in the area and both of our families live here. Tons of friends who went off to college have

386

Rhodes Mill, Fertile

Winnebago County

Larson Manufacturing Company, Lake Mills

returned to join some who never left. I feel so fortunate to have the opportunity to work at this job in my hometown."

It should be noted that **Lake Mills** was the boyhood home of one of Connie's favorite authors, Wallace Stegner. His most well-known and Pulitzer Prize-winning book is *Angle of Repose*.

Straight south of Lake Mills there are some isolated hills rising out of the prairie that the pioneers gave the name Pilot Knob because they were used as a guide for westward wagon trains. They were formed by deposits as glaciers leveled hills into prairie. The area was designated a state park in 1923 and, in 1930, the Civil Conservation Corps (CCC) built a limestone tower on its highest point. At 1,450 feet above sea level, it is one of the highest points in Iowa. From the top of the tower, you can see for 40 miles. The park includes Dead Man's Lake and man-made Pilot Knob Lake. The former is not for recreation but is a botanist's dream with its rare plant species. Fishing and boating opportunities are offered on Pilot Knob Lake as are camping, hunting, hiking and snowmobiling in the rest of the park. On this mid-December day, the park

was closed to cars. I took a little hike up a snowmobile trail, enjoying the solitude of a winter day—walking in the woods through white powder.

Forest City, a couple of miles west of Pilot Knob Park, claims to be the "largest small city" in the country. With a population of 4,400, it has a full-service YMCA; a four-year, liberal arts college; and the world's largest, motor home manufacturing facility.

In the mid-1950s, **Forest City** was in no condition to boast about anything. Industry was virtually non-existent, the farm economy was down and young people had no choice but to look elsewhere for work. A group of businessmen organized to deal with the malady. One member, John K. Hanson, took notice of hardtop camping trailers that were becoming popular in the West. He bought an Aljo trailer, manufactured by Modernistic Industries, Inc. He continued studying the industry and attended a dealer show in Indiana where he talked to manufacturers and picked up literature. This evolved into organizing a committee to raise capital by selling stock in Forest City Industries, Inc. That led them to sign an

agreement with Modernistic Industries, Inc. of Gardena, California, to build their popular Aljo trailers in Forest City.

After a rough start, five **Forest City** residents purchased the operation and John K. Hanson was named president. In 1960, the name was changed to Winnebago Industries. They began manufacturing their own furniture and other components designed specifically for its travel trailers. In 1966, the first motor home came off the assembly line. Through manufacturing innovations, they kept costs down making their product considerably less expensive than the competition's. The company expanded rapidly. In 1970, it was listed on the New York Stock Exchange and, in 1971, the stock appreciated 462 percent. Anyone who has followed the stock since knows it is an up and down ride with an industry that is sensitive to gas prices and other economic factors, but Winnebago has always come back strong.

There are 20-plus buildings on Winnebago's 200-acre production facility in **Forest City**. There is a total of 60 acres (two million square feet) under roof. It is the largest and most technologi-

Snowmobile trail

PILOT KNOB
STATE PARK

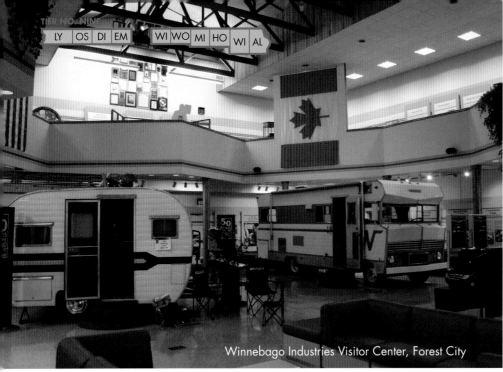

Winnebago Industries Visitor Center, Forest City

Sally's Cafe, where I ate my first graham cracker pie since I was a kid

Waldorf College (former Waldorf Hotel)

cally advanced, motor home manufacturing operation in the world. Every component of the end product is literally built from scratch in Forest City. Billets of aluminum, bulk dimension lumber and pellets or sheets of plastic are transformed into the Winnebagos you see cruising the highways and parked in campgrounds.

In the late 1890s, **Forest City's** business leaders decided the town needed a first-class hotel. They could not agree on where to build it so two hotels were built by the feuding factions. They were completed in 1900 and were very similar in scope and finery with steam heat, baths, electric lights, music and game rooms and European cuisine. They were very nice but they lost money competing with each other. In 1901, the Summit Hotel bought the Waldorf Hotel and closed it. Fourteen years later, the Summit burned to the ground. The Waldorf building stood vacant for two years. In 1903, a group of Lutheran churchmen, under the leadership of Reverend C. S. Salveson, bought the structure and opened Waldorf College, a Christian academy.

Waldorf College's beginning differs

Peg Taylor and Cindy Speltz display J. D. Speltz print in Speltz Studio of Wildlife

Mansion Museum, Forest City

Waldorf College Library, Forest City

from other Lutheran colleges in that it began as an academy and business college rather than a prep program primarily for future pastors. From the beginning, Waldorf has stressed service to others as the means to serve God and to achieve fulfilling lives. Since 1920, when Waldorf became a junior college, the curriculum has evolved to a liberal arts emphasis. In 1994, the college was accredited by the North Central Association of Colleges and Schools to offer its first bachelor of arts degrees. In 2001, Waldorf became a fully accredited bachelor's degree-granting college.

The original Waldorf Hotel building stands proudly on the northeast corner of the campus. Thirteen other well-equipped buildings are all within walking distance of each other. Courses in the sciences, business, communications, education, English, history, humanities, music, psychology, theatre arts and wellness are taught in average class sizes of 15. Hanson Fieldhouse is a complete physical education facility with a 1,200-seat gymnasium. It is connected to the Forest City YMCA, which is free to students.

Varsity competition is offered in 12 sports (six men and six women). They compete in the Midwest Collegiate Conference. With intramural options, there is no problem staying physically active. There are 35 clubs and organizations and many on-campus events. Athletic, communication, scholastic, musical and dramatic scholarships are available, as well as many other types of financial aid.

A couple more attractions in **Forest City** are the Mansion Museum and Heritage Park of North Iowa. The Mansion is the headquarters for the Winnebago Historical Society and it houses many historic collections and memorabilia. Heritage Park of North Iowa depicts farm history with buildings and machines. There are many active demonstrations including the big, steam-powered farm tractors.

We left Winnebago County and drove through the northern half of Kossuth County, a county that we covered in tier number eight. Our next stop was **Armstrong** on the eastern edge of **Emmet County**. (Yes, the county is named after the same Irish patriot as Emmetsburg.) Cruising through the busi-

ness district, we noticed a building identified as Speltz Studio of Wildlife. That piqued my interest so we stopped and I entered the store's retail area where prints of J. D. Speltz paintings and other items were for sale. In the next room Cindy Speltz (J.D.'s wife) and Peg Taylor were framing more of J.D.'s prints in a well-equipped shop. After graduating from the University of Northern Iowa, J. D. Speltz accepted a position in the Armstrong-Ringsted school district to teach and develop an art department. On his own time, he opened an art shop where he worked on commercial and private projects. That led to retiring from education to work full time at researching and executing new projects. He works in partnership with conservation groups and civic organizations using art to help raise funds. Over 500 groups have raised more than $2 million working with Speltz Studio of Wildlife.

Emmet County's earliest settler shared Speltz's love of nature and wildlife along the East Fork of the Des Moines River. However, Thomas Armstrong preferred hunting and trapping the animals rather than painting them. In the mid-

Emmet County

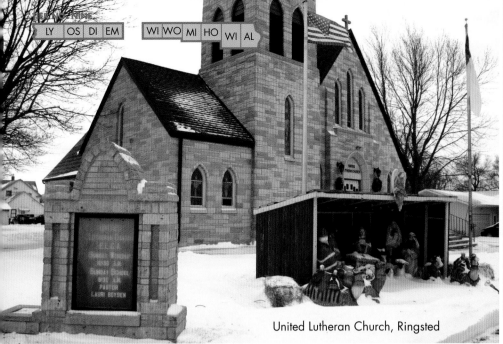

United Lutheran Church, Ringsted

Ringsted

Bud's Cafe, Estherville

1850s, he built a shanty in the woods and subsequently the woods became known as Armstrong's Grove. When settlement and a post office followed, the Armstrong name was adopted. Upon arrival of the railroad in 1892, the town of **Armstrong** was laid out and incorporated. Strong growth followed while the railroad worked its way west. Growth was curtailed when the line reached **Estherville** in 1899 and Estherville became a competing shipping point.

We continued our tour to **Ringsted**, a Danish settlement south of Armstrong. The Danish pioneers arrived in 1882 and soon formed a Lutheran congregation and built a church they named St. Ansgar, after the patron saint of Denmark. In 1893, the synod adopted a new more restrictive constitution and demanded member churches sign it. St. Ansgar refused and was ousted from the synod. Not every congregate agreed with this decision and a schism developed. A group of conservatives broke away and signed with the synod and the other group continued their more liberal ways, which included dancing. They formed a dance troupe named "The Happy

Estherville

Estherville

Emmet County Courthouse, Estherville

Dancing Danes." Consequently, the former group became known as the "Sad Danes" and the latter known as the "Happy Danes." We checked out the present Lutheran Church in **Ringsted** and noted it was named the United Lutheran Church. They must have settled their differences and I hope they are all "Happy Danes" whether they dance or not.

Estherville, the county seat of **Emmet County**, dates its beginning to 1858 when Robert E. Ridley acquired about 160 acres where the town now stands. He brought his family overland by ox team from Dubuque. When the town was platted, he named it after his wife Esther, the first white woman in town and the mother of the first white child. Fort Defiance was built on one city block by Company A, North Border Brigade, for protection of settlers against the Indians. In 1870, there was a heavy immigration of Scandinavians, Germans and Irish to **Estherville** and Emmet County. The northern Europeans fortunately had experience with severe winter weather such as the whiteout snowstorms they were about to face in Northwest Iowa. An old Anglo-Saxon term "blizzard," describing such storms was first put into print in 1870 by O. D. Bares, editor of the *Northern Vindicator*, an Estherville newspaper.

On a late Saturday afternoon, May 10, 1879, there was a clash of celestial bodies when a meteorite exploded into three large pieces just above the Earth about three miles north of **Estherville**. The resulting explosion in the sky appeared to be an Earth-ending scenario for the early residents of the county. The Earth didn't end but three large chunks from the meteorite buried themselves in the soft Iowa soil. The pieces (weighing 431 pounds, 151 pounds and 106 pounds) comprise the largest meteorite known to have fallen in North America. The largest piece, buried 14 feet deep, was dug up by a well digger and eventually ended up in a British museum. The second largest piece, buried four and a half feet deep, was acquired by the University of Minnesota. They in turn gave the Estherville Public Library a specimen that is now on display. A couple of trappers found the third piece of the meteorite buried about five feet deep and it was ultimately purchased by Charles N. Birge, a Keokuk attorney.

The Estherville Chamber of Commerce makes the claim, "Living is great at the top of the state." They have a point. Fort Defiance State Park is 191 acres of forested hills and trails leading down to School House Creek. There are picnicking and camping sites and an enclosed lodge is available for party rentals. Iowa Lakes Community College provides educational opportunities and cultural events. Next door is a wellness center with a pool, gym and exercise area. The Des Moines River Water Trail begins in **Emmet County**. This part of the state is peppered with lakes and sloughs including Iowa's Great Lakes in adjacent Dickinson County. Riverside Hills ski area offers downhill and cross-country skiing. A historic Carnegie library with a compatible, well-designed addition sits in the center of the downtown square. Celebrations include the Fourth of July Flight Breakfast at the Estherville Airport; Chuck Wagon Day with free hot dogs; Sweet Corn Days with free sweet corn, a parade, a car show and games; and Snow Globes Winter Festival.

A few miles northwest of Estherville, there is a farm that is a fine example of

Estherville Public Library

Estherville Foods, Inc.

391

Mark Guge

Defiance State Park trail

Kingman Place B&B, Spirit Lake

392

Kingman Place B&B deck on Spirit Lake

good land stewardship. The original Guge homestead was established in 1891 and fourth generation, family member Mark Guge has kept the family farming tradition alive. It promises to continue with his daughter Sara and her husband Mark More joining him as partners in running TwoRiver Cattle L.L.C., an 830-acre operation. Mark's wife Norma, the lead teller at NorthStar Bank in **Estherville**, enjoys lending a hand in the operation when time permits. Their other daughter Erin, who works out of her home in Ankeny, handles all the data input for TwoRiver Cattle L.L.C. Mark and Sara More's son Logan has it in his blood to become a sixth generation cattleman. He wore out a feed scoop before he was four years old. That might be a world record.

"Treat the land like a piece of borrowed equipment; return it in better shape than you received it," is the philosophy that Myron Guge, Mark's father, passed down to his family. Myron was practicing environmentally sound farming methods before there was the emphasis that is prominent today. The family rotates corn and soybeans on a terrace and contour system first put into place by Myron in

Karen Klassen

Defiance State Park lodge

the 1950s. The crop residues from both the corn and soybean crops are used to feed and bed the cow herd as well as the feeder cattle. In turn, nutrients from the feedlot are spread over the land to return fertility back to the crops. Myron realized early on that leaving residue on the field could reduce erosion. He experimented with conservation tillage before equipment was designed for that purpose.

Mark took to heart his father's philosophy and continues to pursue the environmental approach to farming, taking advantage of the latest information and equipment. There is no aspect of the operation that is not scrutinized by the environmental eye. In 1991, the Guge family began a rotational grazing method that has evolved into an eight-paddock system with one or two of the paddocks used for hay production. This results in less erosion and bare ground along a creek, few bare cow paths and more dense sod throughout the pastures. These and other environmental measures are the right way and a profitable way to farm.

Mark Guge submitted an application for the Environmental Stewardship Award presented by the National Cattlemen's

Beef Association. So far, they have won the Iowa and Region III awards. Region III includes Illinois, Iowa, Minnesota, Missouri and Wisconsin. The national winner will be announced at a national convention in Phoenix in January 2009. Mark has worked for the Iowa Cattlemen's Association and the Iowa Quality Beef Supply Cooperative. He presently works with other farmers in a marketing alliance. He has the contacts to accomplish his agriculture goals. We found him to be an articulate, personable man who is a credit to his profession. He says, "It is not that unusual for farmers to use the land properly." That is our sense after covering the state; land abuse is the exception; environmentally sound practices continue to be implemented.

Dickinson County begins on the other side of the road from the Guge farm. We drove into it with **Spirit Lake** as our destination. We arrived in town as it was getting dark and Christmas lights were shining especially brightly on this cold, clear night. We continued our drive around the lake until we came to Kingman Place B&B where we had reservations for the night. Innkeeper

Karen Klassen came to the door and gave us a warm welcome to an elegant, 138-year-old, Italianate house. It was the first house built on Spirit Lake; the builder was Alvorado Kingman, a military man who also served as treasurer and recorder for **Dickinson County**.

His brother Rosalvo Kingman brought his family to **Spirit Lake** in 1857 when there were only three other women living in the settlement. There was a fort for the protection of the settlers. Rosalvo moved his family into the old fort and built a roof and floors in the ten-foot space between the building and stockade, which he divided into rooms for a hotel. Business was good but not profitable because his customers' pockets were devoid of money.

Karen and husband Orvil live on Orvil's family farm near Mountain Lake, Minnesota. Mountain Lake is not on a lake or a mountain. They thought it would be nice to have a home on a lake. Karen and her daughter Delcy were driving down a Spirit Lake street when they noticed a "For Sale" sign on a lakeside property. Delcy said, "Let's take a look." When they drove through the trees and

Spirit Lake

393

Gardner Cabin and Memorial to Spirit Lake Massacre, Arnold's Park

Spirit Lake

the Kingman house was unveiled, they both flipped. A real estate agent was close by and quickly came over to give them the tour. It was perfect, it was purchased and, after some minor touchup, it was very tastefully furnished. Three bedrooms with full baths and queen-size feather beds are B&B guestrooms.

We slept well in our warm featherbed and Karen prepared a hearty, tasty breakfast the next morning. It was off to explore Iowa's Great Lakes Region—a major tourist attraction. The tourists were nowhere to be found on this mid-December day, but winter beauty was all around us. Walking through parks in the winter can be pleasurable—at least it is to me. The pure white snow crunching underfoot, the solitude and the pristine, clear water streams add up to a strong communication with nature.

In the early days of the lakes region, nature could be brutal. The historical reports of four feet of snow and drift-filled ravines are hard to fathom. In my lifetime I do not recall any four-foot snowfalls anywhere in the state. In 1858, hoards of blackbirds swooped down and ate enormous amounts of grain. There

Iowa Great Lakes Maritime Museum, Arnold's Park

Pearson Lakes Art Center

Dickinson County Courthouse, Spirit Lake

were too many to shoot and scarecrows were ineffective. About the only thing that worked was children standing on high platforms screaming, ringing cow-bells and drumming on tin pans until they were exhausted. From 1873 to 1877, grasshoppers annually consumed virtual-ly every plant in their path. They were so thick they blotted out the sun. Add prairie fires and floods and you can understand why growth in the late 1800s was slow.

Inkpaduta, a renegade Indian leader, had been working his way north along the Little Sioux River. He led a band of 50 to 150 reckless Sioux Indians who were bit-ter about being pushed out by the white man. The fact that a whiskey peddler and horse thief named Henry Lott killed sev-eral member of Inkpaduta's family didn't help. They raided settlements and terror-ized the inhabitants while stealing food and destroying property. They were despised by other Indians as well as the white man. The band arrived at Lake Okoboji during a harsh winter in 1856-1857. By late winter, supplies were run-ning low and tensions were running high as the Indians were unsuccessful in bar-tering with the settlers for food. On

March 8, frustration turned to violence and Inkpaduta's band went on a rampage killing 33 settlers and abducting four women. This horrible event is known as the Spirit Lake Massacre. Two of the cap-tives were released for a ransom. Inkpaduta eluded capture as he fled into the Dakotas and later moved to Canada, where he died in 1881.

Abbie Gardner, one the released cap-tives, married Cassville Sharp and raised two children. In 1891, Abbie returned to Arnold's Park and bought the cabin her father had built. She surrounded the cabin with latticework, added a gate and charged admission to see the site. One of Iowa's first tourist attractions was born. She also wrote a book entitled *History of the Spirit Lake Massacre*. Abbie Gardner Sharp died in Colfax in 1921.

It is ironic that **Arnold's Park**, the scene of so much misery in the mid-1800s, is now the heart of Iowa's fun cap-ital, the Lakes Region. Today, it is hard to find anyone who doesn't love living in Northwest Iowa. Over a million tourists love visiting the area during the summer. There are many attractions in addition to the beautiful lakes that provide the full

range of water activities.

Land-based recreation begins with a wonderful system of trails that wind their way around the lakes and through the countryside. There is a 14-mile, paved trail plus 60 miles of signed bike routes over low traffic county highways. Parks abound and there are sponsored nature hikes and bird-watching tours.

Faculty and students of Stephens College in Columbia, Missouri, have been producing summer theatre produc-tions at Okoboji Summer Theatre for 51 years. Nine shows include dramas, musi-cals and comedies. This talented troupe also performs special summer produc-tions for children at the Boji Bantam Children's Theatre.

Pearson Lakes Art Center is a year-round attraction featuring international, national and local exhibits. There are classes and workshops for all ages. An interactive gallery and a gift shop stocked with art items add to the mix.

Other attractions include: the Iowa Great Lakes Maritime Museum with its collection of photos and artifacts of the early golden days of boating; the Iowa Rock 'N Roll Hall of Fame Museum; the

West Okoboji Lake

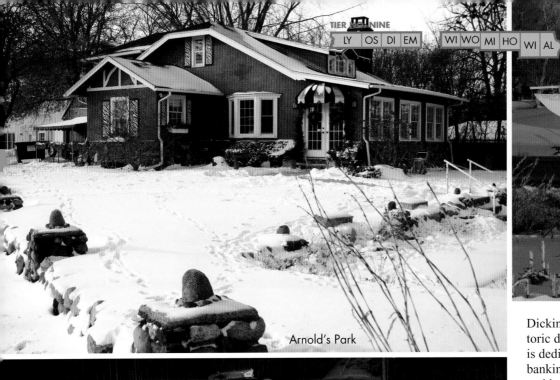

Arnold's Park

Sailboat for sale, Terill

Dickinson County Museum with its historic displays; the Higgins Museum that is dedicated to the history of the national banking industry; and, of course, the venerable Arnold's Park amusement park, home to a legendary, wood roller coaster, the '63 Ferris wheel and the area's fastest go-karts. There is colorful old town in **Arnold's Park** and resort-caliber golf courses, tennis courts, lodges and numerous restaurants. You won't get bored at Iowa's Great Lakes.

Tourism drives the economy of the Lakes Region, but is not the only industry. However, **Spirit Lake's** two largest employers are recreation-oriented. Polaris Industries employs 600 people manufacturing ATVs and Victory Motorcycles. Pure Fishing employs 520 people manufacturing fishing tackle, rods/reels and accessories. The latter was founded in 1937 by a 16-year-old boy who had a passion for fishing and the outdoors. When Berkley Bedell's young fingers tied a black thread around a tuft of whitetail hair, he planted the seed for a very successful manufacturing company. His business acumen matched his love of the outdoors and he developed a company

Sally and Guy Hoppe

Pure Fishing office and plant

Arnold's Park Old Town

that became a world leader in fishing tackle. The Berkley brand is still the flagship product of Pure Fishing.

Leaving tourism behind, we got back into the nuts and bolts of farming by visiting with Sally and Guy Hoppe who live near **Terill**. They each grew up on a farm, were high school sweethearts at Terill High School and married at a young age 43 years ago. Guy joined the Army National Guard, took his training at Fort Leonard Wood and returned to **Terill** and began driving a truck. His next job was manager of a co-op feed mill, which kept bread on the table for 15 years. Then, at the urging of a friend, Guy plunged into the crop-dusting business and hasn't looked back.

The spraying season starts in the spring going after thistles in pastures. In the summer, fungus on corn and white mold on beans are attacked from the air. In the fall the pastures get another going over. Sally drives a flag vehicle that provides a guide for Guy so that he doesn't overspray or skip part of a field. After each pass, she moves the vehicle 50 feet. GPS is now available but Guy feels more confident with the flag system. The wife

of another crop duster advised Sally to never say anything to the pilot. She abandoned that advice after a couple of years. She says, "Driving the flag vehicle is the only time I can tell him where to go."

In the winter Guy hauls grain with his 18-wheeler and does mechanical work. He used to overhaul pickups—one winter, he gave thirteen engines new life. He presently uses his mechanical skills for personal projects like building a kit plane and restoring vehicles. Sally and Guy appreciate their life in **Terill** and contribute what they can toward the betterment of the community. Sally says, "I love the seasons. It is pretty country. Texas in winter seems weird. I love the smell of the earth and seeing the stars." Guy says, "I like the fall. The harvest is coming in; it's like payday."

As we drove into **Osceola County** near **Harris**, we noticed some crews setting up new wind turbines. We had seen a lot of activity across the state involving this new source of energy. Oversize-load banners on trucks often meant the cargo was a wind turbine component. The northern tier of Iowa counties is heavily populated with the gleaming, white wind-

mills. Looking at them from a distance you can't appreciate how large they are. The towers range from 160 to 300 feet. When you add the rotor blades to a 300-foot tower, it is 442 feet from base to blade tip. As with any technology, improvements come quickly and a wind turbine is not expected to last more than 15 years due to obsolescence and parts wearing out. There is a whole new industry here and it has been good for the environment and the Iowa economy.

We talked to George Braaksma of **Sibley**, one of the pioneers in the wind power movement. George grew up a farm with seven sisters and one brother. He went to country school one year and he values it more than any year hence. He said that you worked at your own pace and the older kids helped the younger ones. (Educators should give this model some consideration.) He finished his formal schooling in **Sibley** but continued his self-education by reading a lot and asking questions. He loves to travel. In 1983, he spent 18 weeks in Australia where he worked and lived with different people in agriculture—a great experience and education.

Iowa Rock 'N Roll Hall of Fame

Erecting a wind turbine,
Osceola County

George Braaksma

A mid-1980s visit to a San Francisco cousin introduced him to wind power and he began reading everything he could on the subject. Back in Iowa, two men approached him to do wind studies. They brought five wind turbines from California and set them up on his farm. The towers looked like oil derricks—they were the Model T in the development of wind turbines. George climbed one of them every day noting problems with ice and sun and looking for ways to make them more efficient. When Iowa State University made its first wind study, George was asked to take part. There were many participants from overseas—he was the only farmer. As things progressed, larger companies with money got involved and it became a new game. George opted out of this competition but owns stock in Northern Alternative Energy, a company that bought his farm and has wind turbines in eight states. Now he has an arrangement with NAE to farm the land he sold to them and he still keeps a hand in the industry. He and his wife Margie live in an earth berm house with southern exposure windows. They have a son who is a senior in high school.

Osceola County Courthouse, Sibley

Sibley Public Library

Sibley

George and Margie Braaksma's eco-house

George still likes to travel and has added collecting tractors to his leisure pursuits. He says, "Iowa has the country's best values; that's what's critical. We have to keep them and fight for them."

Osceola County was named after the same legendary Seminole chief as the town of Osceola. His real name was Billy Powell and he was mostly white, but he courageously led a group of runaway slaves, Caucasians and Seminoles in resisting their movement from Florida to locations west of the Mississippi. The pioneers loved to talk about his exploits and about his romance with Creek Indian Princess Ouscaloosa. The facts were in question as the stories varied. Another story had Osceola married to a former slave girl who had worked for an aristocratic, southern family. At any rate, one more Iowa community was named after a man who never set foot in the state.

The borders, sections and quarter sections of **Osceola County** were platted in 1851. This did not set off a land rush because the lack of trees gave it a reputation as the "great American desert." There was also a fear of Indians, especially after the Spirit Lake Massacre a few miles to the east. In 1870, a lone wagon came slowly across the grassy plain driven by Captain E. Huff, a Civil War veteran. He brought enough lumber to build a shack on the banks of Otter Creek near a proposed railroad right-of-way. He chose not to winter there but it marked the beginning of a settler's attempt to tame the wilderness. The next spring he was joined by A. H. Lyman, who later became know as "Windy Jake." Lyman built a sod house.

Many, white-topped prairie schooners rolled across the plains during the early part of May. The tall, waving grasses obliterated the view of the oxen and lower wagons, giving the white tops the appearance of tall ships on a wind-swept sea— thus the name of prairie schooner.

In 1871, the Sioux City and St. Paul Railroad laid out the town site of **Sibley** and work began on a courthouse, schoolhouse, hotel and barn to shelter horses of hotel guests. The first train arrived on June 1, 1872, connecting **Osceola County** with the outside world. Sibley grew rapidly, becoming a trade center for a great new agricultural area. All trails led to **Sibley**. Large fleets of wagons hauled supplies from Sibley to points west and returned loaded with grain to ship on the railroad. At times there were 50 wagons waiting in line to be unloaded at the elevator. Sibley was an incredible boomtown during 1872.

It is not a boomtown anymore, but it is a solid community of close to 3,000 people. Agriculture is still the base augmented by healthy retail businesses, industrial plants and professional services. Good education and health care are emphasized. "Off, Off Broadway," a community theatre group that has the distinction of staging the first successful community dinner theater in the state, provides cultural activity. The first play was performed in 1973 at the Cedar Cabin Supper Club in **Ashton**. They've been packing them in ever since with two to three performances a year. There apparently is no shortage of actors in Osceola County because **Ocheyedan** has a group called the "Main Street Players" that puts on dramatic and comedic shows. Movies are shown in **Sibley's** historic Max Theatre and that's a lot more fun than going to the plex.

Another pastime that sounds like a lot

Exopack manufacturing plant, Sibley

TIER NO. NINE

LY OS DI EM   WI WO MI HO WI AL

Ashton Museum

Turn-of-the-century railroad, water tower and dam, Ashton

Lyon County school kids play King of the Snow Pile

400

B&L Vintage Brew and Sugar
Shack Restaurant, Rock Rapids

of fun is Sibley's annual Good Ole Summertime celebration. The name describes it. It is held the fourth week in June with four days of activities. It begins with a garden tour on Thursday. On Friday there is an art show of **Sibley** area talent that has featured artists from age 12 to 70. Saturday is packed with trike races, pony rides, 3-on-3 basketball and sand volleyball tournaments, an Ole Fashioned Bar-B-Que and Grand Ole parade. Ole Fashioned Gospel in the park wraps things up on Sunday.

The desert label of the mid-1800s is a total misnomer for **Osceola County**. For starters, the soil is Iowa-rich and there are plenty of recreation areas where you can commune with nature. The county's conservation board oversees a system of 40 parks, prairie preserves, wildlife management areas and refuges, as well as a recreational trail. There are 1,600 acres of land in the county conservation system. For those who like to get close to nature with a golf club in their hands, there is the Sibley Golf and Country Club—a pretty course named "Iowa's 9-Hole Course of the Year" in 1999.

There has been some dispute as to

Highest point in Iowa, near Sibley

Ashton

where Iowa's highest elevation is, but there is no doubt in which county it is located. For years it was believed to be the Ocheyedan Mound two miles south of **Ocheyedan**. Now a spot just north of Sibley has been designated as the highest point. There is no mound. It is quite flat and looked to me like the identifying, circular slab of concrete could have been placed anywhere in the area. It might even be under the nearby silo—that would be fitting. Another thought is they could have left the designation at the Ocheyedan Mound; it's more dramatic. The difference between 1,613 feet and 1,670 feet falls within a margin of error according to my calculations (not scientific, but from the heart).

On a Thursday night in mid-December we crossed our last county line into **Lyon County** in far northwest Iowa. The shade of darkness was coming down as we drove along Highway 9 toward **Rock Rapids**. A wintry night with sparkling Christmas decorations was the scene as we drove down Rock Rapid's main street. At the end of the business district we found the Four Seasons Motel and checked in. The motel had two sec-

tions—an older '40s-style section and across the street were newer units styled after a typical, modern motel. We stayed in the latter and it was very comfortable.

After checking in, we drove back toward downtown where we noted there was some commotion ahead. As we got closer, we could see a Christmas parade in progress. No one directed us off the street so we continued down our side as the parade came up the other side. We had a good view. Floats and vehicles were covered with lights made brighter with the dousing of the streetlights. It was nicely done except, with the street lights out, it was difficult to make out some of the figures. After the parade we found a parking spot near the B&L Restaurant.

We had read about B&L's Vintage Brew & Sugar Shack in *Our Iowa* magazine. Betty Medema of **Rock Rapids** had submitted them for "My Favorite Ma & Pa Restaurant" series. The initials stand for Beth and Lawrence Lupkes, the team that has been running it since 2005. They are another example of the Iowa work ethic. They both have full-time jobs in addition to the restaurant. Beth is the office manager at the Lyon County Law

Enforcement Center. Lawrence is a rural mail carrier. B&L's is open seven days a week from 7 a.m. to 8 p.m. except for Mondays, when it is open from 4 to 8 p.m. Beth and Lawrence serve the morning and evening patrons while hired help covers for them when they are at their day jobs. After closing, they prepare for the next day, including making pies and desserts. WOW!

We entered the restaurant on a busy night with just a couple of tables open. We chose one, sat down and looked around. The building was formerly a flower shop and some of the décor was kept for the restaurant. Their daughter had painted a mural on the wall next to our table. There was a lighted Christmas tree and there were Christmas lights in the lattice ceiling. The tables and chairs were a mixture of styles. It was a colorful and cozy atmosphere. We had plenty of time to observe the decor because no one seemed to notice we were there. We had read about how hard they worked so we were patient. Finally, I flagged down a waitress and she immediately apologized and the service began. After we had ordered, Beth and Lawrence made trips to

OCHEYEDAN MOUND
THE MOUND IS A KAME OF GLACIAL ORIGIN. KAMES ARE MOUNDS COMPOSED OF COMPLEXLY STRATIFIED SAND & GRAVEL DEPOSITED BY GLACIAL MELTWATER STREAMS WHERE THE STREAMS DECENDED INTO CRAVASSES IN THE ICE. THIS OCCURRED DURING THE FINAL STAGES OF ICE MELTING AND DISAPPEARANCE OF THE GLACIERS 12 TO 14 THOUSAND YEARS AGO.

Mural of cattle dealer Walt Jansma, Rock Rapids

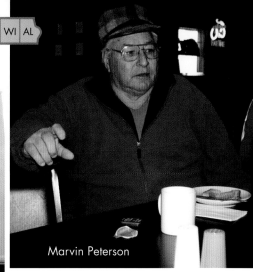

Marvin Peterson

our table and repeated the apologies. The food arrived and I enjoyed the tastiest, hot beef sandwich I had ever eaten and Connie was just as happy with her grilled pork chop dinner. We assured Beth and Lawrence that all was forgiven.

With our sustenance taken care of, we turned in for a good night's sleep at the Four Seasons. In the morning we chose the Sportsman's Lounge for breakfast. It was pure bar atmosphere with lots of black (including the ceiling) that set off the lighted beer signs. At about 7:30 a.m. in the morning, there were several regulars drinking coffee and eating breakfast. We tried to fit in and must have succeeded because a man sitting at the next table struck up a conversation. A thought crossed my mind that he could be our interviewee for **Lyon County**. When asked, he deferred to a man at the bar, who he said would be a great source.

Marvin Peterson picked up his coffee and toast with peanut butter and joined us at our table. He grew up on a diversified farm that was self-sufficient including doing their own butchering. He said, "We didn't have much money, but nobody ate better." His schooling ended when he

Island Park, Rock Rapids

"Ladies of the night" murals, Rock Rapids

Rock Rapids mural

completed eighth grade because his help was needed on the farm. He left the farm as a young man and took a job as a maintenance worker for the town of **Rock Rapids**. He stayed with the city, working his way up to become public works director. This was no small responsibility in a town that has 65 acres of parks, including a unique island park and a mini-zoo. The latter started back in 1935 with a resident displaying a bear. The bear is gone and hasn't been replaced, but it is still a fun place for children to observe a deer and her fawn, golden pheasants, roosters, bantam chickens, peacocks and more. There is no admission. It is supported by adults (resident and non-resident) who have fond memories of the zoo experience as children. After 38 years, Marvin recently retired.

Government work runs in the family with his wife Mary holding a job as deputy assessor for **Lyon County** and their son works for the city. Mary, who loves to save newspaper articles, is the historian for their church.

Marvin also has an interest in history. On his dad's farm there are the remains of an oval, quarter-mile track and no one knows its origin. It might be English, judging from the style of the house. (Indians' racetracks were perfect circles.) Marvin is also involved in researching the **Lyon County** fairgrounds track, which may be the oldest Iowa racetrack still in existence.

Marvin has no trouble occupying his time in retirement. While he was still working, he had a small acreage where he raised registered quarter horses. He raised them from colts and broke some and left it to the buyer to break others. This business is behind him so now he has more time for hunting and fishing. The Rock River is good for walleye, bass and catfish and he also loves to fish the Missouri River where you never know what might be on the line. When he dons his hunting gear, he goes after deer, geese and pheasants. He gave us a little insight on how the deer hunting seasons are managed by the DNR. The hunting begins in September with a youth season that lasts about two weeks. An archery season begins in October and lasts for over a month; there is a second season that lasts a couple of weeks. Muzzleloaders get their chance with one week in October

and two weeks at a later time. Hunters using shot guns with slugs get four days in December and one week at a later time. It all wraps up in January.

Hunting was more of a challenge in Northwest Iowa for an 1862 hunting party of educated gentlemen from the East Coast. Roy McGregor, George Clark and Thomas Lockhart found adventure beyond their expectations. Lockhart was killed by an Indian's arrow while he and McGregor were hunting elk along Little Rock Creek. McGregor rejoined Clark and the two continued to hunt and trap until Clark drowned in a spring flood. That was enough for McGregor; he returned to the East Coast.

Indians didn't want to leave this area even though they had relinquished all claims in 1851. This retarded immigration, making Lyon County the last county to be settled in Iowa. Fish and game and the water supply of the Rock River that sustained the Indians began attracting settlers in the 1860s. The end of the Civil War freed men and families and that added to the influx of **Lyon County** homesteaders.

Many years before the white man

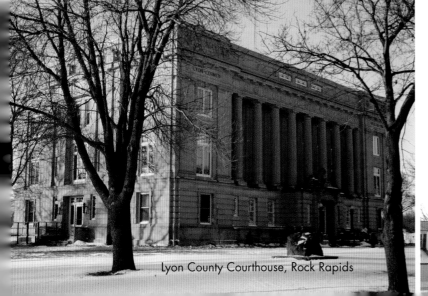

Lyon County Courthouse, Rock Rapids

United Methodist Church, Rock Rapids

403

Descending into the
Big Sioux River valley,
Iowa's western border

Ice fishing on Lake Pahoja,
Lyon County

arrived, there was a large Oneota Indian encampment known as Blood Run located on both sides of the Big Sioux River in **Lyon County** and South Dakota. It was a gathering spot for Indians from the western plains to trade and socialize with Indians from the east. Some 5,000 people lived there making it the largest Indian community in the Upper Midwest. They built hundreds of permanent circular lodges. Women made pottery, cooked meals, cleaned animal hides, worked gardens and processed grain. Men made bows and arrows, gathered wild plants and engraved red tablets. They raised corn, beans, squash and sunflowers. French fur trappers began arriving in 1700. They introduced white man's ways and brought with them diseases that the Indian immune system couldn't fight. By 1725, the traditional Oneota culture had all but disappeared.

Rock Rapids has an interesting industrial past. The first concrete blocks were manufactured here. Replicas of the block are on display at the Smithsonian in Washington, D.C. The first mechanical pinsetter for bowling was created by Alfred Olsen, and then perfected by his father Ole Olsen. H. C. Middlebrooke, a jeweler, patented two major improvements for banjos, one a new method for joining the head and neck and another for a new fret and peg system.

Rock Rapids has set itself apart from other small towns by becoming a city of murals. They are everywhere and quite well done. They depict everything from "ladies of the night" to patriotic scenes. One that caught my eye was a montage featuring Walt Jansma, who at one time was the largest, private cattle dealer in the country. I noted in the **Rock Rapids** visitors' guide there was an ad promoting the Rock Rapids Mural Society. Apparently, they are looking to paint the sides of a few more buildings.

Enough of Rock Rapids—it was time to drive further west. First, we swung up to the Tri-State Marker where Iowa, Minnesota and South Dakota come together—a pretty quiet place. We continued west to the Big Sioux River, crossed the bridge into South Dakota, made a U-turn and returned to Iowa. Looping a little further south, we stopped to look at Lake Pahoja where we saw some ice fishing activity. I noticed some cabins on a snowy slope that I'm sure attract occupants in warmer weather. We continued east to **George** where we had lunch at the Last Call Saloon. It was our last meal on our great ride through Iowa and it happened to be at the Last Call Saloon—how appropriate. The saloon was run by a couple of ladies and the patrons were farmers and blue-collar workers. The smoked brisket sandwich special, Wisconsin cheese soup and a glass of beer made a perfect trip finale.

You can't have any more fun than exploring Iowa—county by county.

Lyon County

Carson Ode

OUR HOME IS IN IOWA

A folk poem contributed by Shelby Mundt (author unknown)

Our home is in Iowa,
Westward toward the setting sun,
Just between two mighty rivers,
Where the crystal waters run.

It has towns and it has cities.
It has many noble streams.
It has nine and ninety counties
And we'll now repeat their names.

Lyon, Osceola, Dickinson
Where the Spirit Lake you see.
Emmet, Kossuth *and* **Winnebago.**
Worth *is near Lake Albert Lea.*

Mitchell, Howard, Winneshiek
And **Allamakee** *so fine*
Make eleven northern counties
On the Minnesota line.

Clayton, Dubuque, Jackson, Clinton
Together with **Scott** *and* **Muscatine,**
Lee, Louisa, *and* **Des Moines**
On the eastern side are seen.

Van Buren, Davis, Appanoose
Decatur, Ringgold, Wayne *we spy.*
Taylor, Page *and* **Fremont**
On the Missouri border lie.

Pottawattamie, Harrison, Mills,
Monona, Woodbury, Plymouth, Sioux
Are all the counties that surround
The border of our state well bound.

Next we name **O'Brien,**
Palo Alto, *too, and* **Clay,**
Hancock, Cerro Gordo, Floyd.
Now see **Chickasaw** *I pray.*

Fayette, Bremer, Butler, Franklin.
Next upon the map you see
Wright, Humboldt, Pocahontas
Buena Vista, Cherokee.

Ida, Sac, Calhoun *and* **Webster,**
Hamilton *with names are rare.*
Next are **Hardin, Grundy, Black Hawk,**
Then **Buchanan, Delaware.**

Jones, Linn, Benton, Tama,
Marshall, Story, Crawford, Carroll, Boone.
Let us not your patience weary.
We shall have them all too soon.

Cedar, Greene, Johnson, Iowa
And **Poweshiek** *by the same.*
Next are **Jasper, Polk** *and* **Dallas,**
Names of Presidential fame.

Guthrie, Audubon *and* **Shelby,**
Cass *and* **Madison, Adair,**
Warren, Marion *and* **Mahaska,**
Jefferson *and* **Keokuk** *are there.*

Wapello, Monroe, Washington,
Henry *we have missed.*
Lucas, Clarke, Union, Adams
And **Montgomery** *fill the list.*

BIBLIOGRAPHY

TIER NO. ONE

Des Moines, Iowa Historical Co. (1881), *History of Fremont County*, Reproduced by Unigraphic, Inc., Evansville, Ind., 1975.

Dicks, Joyce, *Wayne County Heritage Highlights - Sesquicentennial History*, Wayne County Historical Society, 1996.

Goehner, David, *The Graceland College Book of Knowledge*, Herald Publishing House, Independence, Mo., 1997.

Iowa Writers' Program of W.P.A. sponsored by Mabel Searl, *Page County History, Iowa*, Clarinda, Iowa, 1942.

Keokuk City Directory, R.L. Polk and Co., 1997.

Lempke, Ellen, *Poetically Speaking, Vol. 4*, Bedford, Iowa, 1985.

Lesan, Mrs. B. M., *Early History of Ringgold County 1844–1937*, Blair Publishing House, Lamoni, Iowa, 1937.

People of Appanoose County, *Appanoose County, Iowa*, Compiled by the Appanoose County Historical Society, Taylor Publishing Co., Dallas, 1986.

People of Fremont County, *Thumbprints in Time. Fremont County, Iowa - 1996*, Published by The Fremont County Heritage Book Committee, 1996.

Sloat, Ted, *Fort Madison - A Pictorial History*, G. Bradley Publishing, Inc., St. Louis, Mo., 1987.

Smith, H. Alan, "Space Station Schedule Picks up with Arrival of Shuttle," *Mount Ayr Record-News*, Mount Ayr, Iowa, Feb. 14, 2008.

Spurgeon, Gary (ed.), *Focusing on Davis County's Past*, Heritage House Publications, Marceline, Mo., 1995.

Taylor County Historical Society of Bedford, *Taylor County History*, Taylor Publishing Co. Dallas, 1981.

Terry, Jack R., *A Centennial History of Mount Ayr, Iowa, 1875–1975*, Jack R. Terry Publishing, Mount Ayr, Iowa, 1975.

TIER NO. TWO

Albia Chamber of Commerce, *Historial Sketchbook of Albia and Monroe County, 1859–1959*, Albia Newspaper, Albia, Iowa, 1959.

Allen, Mary, *Iron Sharpening Iron*, Johnson Machine Works, 2007.

Antrobus, Augustine M., *History of Des Moines County, Iowa, and Its People*, The S. J. Clarke Publishing Co., Chicago, 1915.

Baker, Chris D., *In Retrospect, An Illustrated History of Wapello County, Iowa*, The Donning Company, Virginia Beach, Va. , 1992.

Bied, Dan, *My Kind of Town - Burlington Memories, Etc.*, Doran and Ward Printing Co., Burlington, Iowa, June, 1988.

Biographical and Historical Record of Clarke County, Iowa, Lewis Publishing Co., Chicago, 1886.

Canon, Scott, "Maharishi's followers have integrated into small Iowa town," *The Kansas City Star*, Kansas City, Mo., September 27, 1999.

Centurama Publication Committee, *Corning Iowa Centurama, 1857–1957*, Free Press Publishing Co., Corning, Iowa, 1957.

Cook, Fred M., *SAC-GCC Counselor - Red Oak Edition*, Vol. 3, No. 10, Hastings, Nebr., December, 1952.

Coons, Daniel D., *Biography of Lebbeum Thaddeus Coons*, Salt Lake City, Utah, 1997.

Dietrich, Rob, and Dennis and Darlene Kingery, *Railroad Town*, Petznicks Printing Co., Creston, Iowa, 1981.

Graves, Clarence, *Who's Who in Iowa, Clarke County*, Iowa Press Association, Des Moines.

Hansen, Bob, *Around Burlington: the Good, the Bad and the Bold*, Des Moines County Historical Society, Craftsmen Press, Inc., Burlington, Iowa, 2004.

Henry County Bicentennial Commission, *Henry County History*, National ShareGraphics, Inc., Dallas, 1982.

Hickenlooper, Frank, *An Illusrated History of Monroe County, Iowa*, Walsworth Pub. Co, Inc., Marceline, Mo., 1896.

History-Civic Department of Corning Departmental Club, *Adams County History*, Corning, Iowa, 1984.

The History of Jefferson County, Iowa, Western Historical Company, Chicago, 1879.

Iowa Historical and Biographical Company in Des Moines, *History of Montgomery County, Iowa*, 1881.

Iowa Wesleyan College 2007–2008 Catalog, Mount Pleasant, Iowa, August, 2007.

Isley, Keith, *Images of the Past, Lucas County, Iowa*, Norval Lowe and Heritage House Publishing, Marceline, Mo., 1993.

Lucas County Genealogical Society, *Lucas County Heritage 2000*, Chariton, Iowa, 2000.

Mills County History Book Committee, *History of Mills County, Iowa*, Taylor Publishing Co., Dallas, 1985.

People of Union County, *Union County, Iowa*, Taylor Publishing Co., Dallas, 1981.

Pregracke, Chad with Jeff Barrow, *From the Bottom Up: One Man's Crusade to Clean America's Rivers*, National Geographic Society, Washington, D.C., 2007.

The Red Oak Express, *Red Oak at the Dawn of the Twentieth Century*, June, 1901.

Shaw, A.B. (ed.), *Corning and Adams County*, Corning:Fawkner Publishing Co., Corning, Iowa, 1889.

Spoon, Betty Jane, *Lucas, Iowa, 125 Years, 1968–1993*, Publishing House, Indianola, Iowa, 1993.

Springer, Arthur, *History of Louisa County, Iowa*, The S. J. Clarke Publishing Co., Chicago, 1912.

Taylor, James C., *Ottumwa - 100 Years a City*, Houchen Bindery Ltd., Utica/Omaha, Nebr., 1948.

Union County Historical Society, *Creston Centennial Celebration*, Creston News Advertiser and Petznicks Printing Co., Creston, Iowa, 1969.

Weaver, William O., *Hail to the Chief - True Tales of Old Wapello*, Louisa Publishing Co., Ltd., Wapello, Iowa, 1974.

Weltey, Susan Fulton, *A Fair Field* (Revised Becentennial Edition), Harlo Press, Detroit, 1975.

Widmer, Melba Rose, *Victorian Period Home Architecture - Mt. Pleasant*, Mt. Pleasant Beautiful Group, 1989.

Wortman, Allen, *Ghost Towns of Mills County Iowa*, Allen Wortman (pub.), Malvern, Iowa, 1975.

TIER NO. THREE

Adair County Historical Society, *Adair County, Iowa Sesquicentennial Edition, 1851–2001*, Bell Books, Rich Hill, Mo., 2002.

Atlantic Chamber of Commerce, *History of Atlantic, Iowa, 1868–1968*, Atlantic, Iowa, 1968.

Fisher, Kathy, *A History of Washington County, Iowa*, The Washington County Historical Society, Washington, Iowa, 1978.

Keo-Mah Genealogical Society and Mahaska County Historical Society, *The History of Mahaska County, Iowa*, Curtis Media Corporation, Dallas, 1984.

Keo-Mah Genealogical Society, Inc., *The Heritage of Mahaska County, Iowa, 2000*, Walsworth Pulishing Company, 1999.

Smith, Lloyd H., *Scenic Madison County, Iowa, Historic Significance*, Madison County Historical Society, Winterset, Iowa, 1961. Revised 1984 by Henry C. Miller.

Union Historical Company, *The History of Keokuk County, Iowa*, Des Moines, 1880.

Union Historical Company, *The History of Marion County, Iowa*, Birdsall, Williams & Co., Des Moines, 1881.

Union Historical Company, *The History of Warren County, Iowa*, Birdsall, Williams & Co., Des Moines, 1879.

Vogel, George A.W., *Greenfield, Iowa, One Hundred Fifty Years of History, 1856–2006*, News Printing Co. Newton, Iowa, 2006.

Warren County Genealogical Society, *The History of Warren County*, Curtis Media Corporation, Dallas, 1987.

Young, Lafe, *History of Cass County, Iowa*, Telegraph Steam Printing House, Atlantic, Iowa, 1877.

TIER NO. FOUR

Andrews, H. F., (ed.), *History of Audubon County, Iowa*, B.F. Bowen & Company, Inc., Indianapolis, 1915.

Audubon History Book Committee, *History of Audubon, Iowa, Centennial, 1878–1978*, Audubon, Iowa, 1978.

Clinton County Historical Society, *History of Clinton County, Iowa*, Clinton, Iowa, 1976.

Dinwiddie, James C., *History of Iowa County, Iowa*, The S. J. Clarke Publishing Company, Chicago, 1915.

Downer, Harry E., *History of Davenport and Scott County, Iowa, Volume 1*,

The S. J. Clarke Publishing Company, Chicago, 1910.

Guthrie Center High School Sophomore English Class, *A Glance into the Past*, Guthrie Center, Iowa, 1982.

Heckert, Connie K., *Lyons, 150 Years North of the Big Tree*, Lyons Business and Professional Association, Clinton, Iowa, 1985.

The History of Muscatine County, Iowa, Western Historical Company, Chicago, 1879.

Hurto, Larry Ray (ed.), *A History of Newton, Iowa*, Curtis Media Corporation, Dallas, 1992.

Lewis, H. W., *Picturesque Muscatine*, Muscatine, Iowa, 1901.

Lillie, Pauline, *Marengo, The County Seat, Marengo, The Town, A History*, Walsworth Publishing Co., Marceline, Mo., 1984.

Logan Centennial Committee, *Logan, Iowa Centennial, 1867–1967*, Logan, Iowa, 1967.

Long, Katherine and Melvin Erickson, *Clinton: A Pictorial History*, Quest Publishing, Rock Island, Ill., 1983.

Mansheim, Gerald, *Iowa City, an Illustrated History*, The Donning Company Publishers, Norfolk, Va., 1989.

Past and Present of Guthrie County, Iowa, The S. J. Clarke Publishing Company, Chicago, 1907.

Peterson, Leslie Perry, *The Bertrand Stores*, Friends of Boyer Chute & DeSoto NWR, Missouri Valley, Iowa, 2006.

Pratt, LeRoy G., *The Counties and Courthouses of Iowa*, Klipton Printing and Office Supply Company, Mason City, Iowa, 1977.

Quasquicenntenial Central Committee, *Quasquicenntenial Exira, Iowa, 1857–1982*, Exira, Iowa, 1982.

Shambaugh, Benjamin F., *Iowa City, A Contribution to the Early History of Iowa*, State Historical Society of Iowa, Iowa City, Iowa, 1893.

Souvenir Book Committee, *Adel Quasquicentennial, 1847–1972*, Adel, Iowa, 1972.

Starner, Everette (ed.), *100 Years in Shelby, Iowa, 1870–1970*, Shelby, Iowa, 1970.

Union Historical Company, *The History of Dallas County, Iowa*, Des Moines, 1879.

Union Historical Company, *The History of Poweshiek County, Iowa*, Birdsall, Williams & Co., Des Moines, 1880.

Weaver, James. B., *Past and Present of Jasper Country, Vol. 1*, B. F. Bowen & Company, Indianapolis, 1912.

Wundram, Bill and the Quad-City Times, *A Time We Remember*, Quad-City Times, Davenport, Iowa, October, 1999.

TIER NO. FIVE

Brewer, Luther A. and Barthinius L. Wick, *History of Linn County, Iowa*, The Pioneer Publishing Company, Chicago, 1911.

Chapman, Samuel D., *History of Tama County, Iowa*, Toledo Times Office, Toledo, Iowa, 1879.

Danek, Ernie, *Cedar Rapids, Tall Corn and High Technology*, Windsor Publications, Woodland Hills, Calif., 1980.

The Denison Newspapers, *A History of Crawford County, Iowa*, Richard Knowles, Curtis Media Corporation, Dallas, 1987.

"Gary Thompson—Still the Roland Rocket," (editorial staff), *Our Iowa*, Ames, Iowa, December/January 2009.

Historical Society Book Committee, *The History of Benton County, Iowa*, Taylor Publishing Company, Dallas, 1989.

The History of Jackson County, Iowa, Western Historical Company, Chicago, 1879.

The History of Jones County, Iowa, Western Historical Company, Chicago, 1879.

The History of Marshall County, Iowa, Western Historical Company, Chicago, 1878.

The History of Monona County, Iowa, National Publishing Company, Chicago, 1890.

Nachazel, LaRue Emerson, *Toledo, Iowa Celebrating 150 Years of Yesterdays*, Tama County Tracers Genealogical Society, Toledo, Iowa, 2003.

Nevada Community Historical Society, Inc., *Voices from the Past: The Story of Nevada, Iowa*, 2003.

Perez Jr., Juan, "Hindus celebrate tower's completion," *The Des Moines Register*, Des Moines, Iowa, June 8, 2008.

Setzler, Marilyn Schirck, *This Place Called Carroll County, Iowa*, The Donning Company Publishers, Virginia Beach, Va., 2002.

Stillman, Edwin B., *Past and Present of Greene County, Iowa*, The S. J. Clarke Publishing Company, Chicago, 1907.

Times-Republican, D. Michael Schlesinger (pub.) *Marshall Memories*,

Marshalltown, Iowa, 1992.

The Tama County News, *Tama, Illustrated*, September, 1901.

Union Historical Company, *The History of Boone County, Iowa*, Birdsall, Williams & Co., Des Moines, 1880.

TIER NO. SIX

Calhoun County Historical Society, *Calhoun County, Iowa*, Taylor Publishing Co., Dallas, 1982.

Doan, William Sayles, *A Book of Days*, The Messenger, Fort Dodge, Iowa, 1991.

Freese, Leslie T., *History and Government of Sac County*, The Odebolt Chronicle Print, Odebolt, Iowa, 1978.

Godbersen, Bruce L., *Our Heritage, A History of Ida County*, Midwest Industries, Inc., Ida Grove, Iowa, 1977.

Grundy Area Centennial, Incorporated, *Grundy Center - A Centennial Portrait 1977*, Walsworth, Marceline, Mo., 1977.

Grundy Center Historical Society, *Grundy County Remembers*, PenDragon Press, Bristow, Iowa, 1977.

Hardin County Historical Society, *History of Hardin County*, Taylor Publishing Co., Dallas, 1981.

Hart, William H., *History of Sac County, Iowa*, B. F. Bowen & Company, Inc., Indianapolis, 1914.

Hartman, John C., *History of Black Hawk County and Its People*, The S. J. Clarke Publishing Company, Chicago, 1915.

Lee, Jesse W., *History of Hamilton County*, The S. J. Clarke Publishing Company, Chicago, 1912.

Melendy, Peter (pub.), *Fifty Years: Historical Record of Cedar Falls, the Garden City of Iowa*, Cedar Falls, Iowa, 1893.

Nash, Russell W. (Project Director) and Dubuque Fine Arts Society, *Proceedings from Dubuque Beginnings*, Dubuque, Iowa, 1983.

Nass, Martin E., *The History of Hamilton County, Iowa, 1985*, Curtis Media Corporation, Dallas, 1986.

Nelson, Hannah, *An Era in the History of Stratford, Iowa and Community, 1840–1960*, Stratford Promotions Committee, Stratford, Iowa, 1970.

Nichols, I. A., *Pioneer Days of Iowa Falls*, Messenger Printing Company, Fort Dodge, Iowa, 1944.

O'Connor, Rose A., *Sioux City - A True Story of How It Grew*, The Public Library of Sioux City, Iowa, Sioux City, Iowa, 1932.

Odebolt History Book Committee, *Reflections, Sac City Quasquicentennial, 1855–1980*, The Odebolt Chronicle Print, Odebolt, Iowa, 1980.

RoadsideAmerica.com, *Battle Hill Museum of Natural History*, Battle Creek, Iowa, 2008.

Rockwell City Centennial History Committee, *Rockwell City's 100 Golden Years*, Golden Buckle Publishers, Inc., Rockwell City, Iowa, 1976.

Sorensen, Scott and B. Paul Chicoine, *Sioux City, A Pictorial History*, The Donning Company, Norfolk, Va., 1982.

Williams, Wm., *The History of Early Fort Dodge and Webster County*, Walterick Printing Co., Fort Dodge, Iowa, 1950.

Woodbury County Genealogical Society, *The History of Woodbury County, Iowa*, National ShareGraphics, Inc., Dallas, 1984.

Writers' Program (U.S.) Iowa, *Woodbury County History, Iowa*, Sioux City, Iowa, 1942.

Yates, Corrine (ed.) and Centennial Book Steering Committee, *The Holstein Centennial Book 1882–1982*, Miller Printing & Publishing, Odebolt, Iowa, 1982.

TIER NO. SEVEN

The Allison Centennial Committee, *History of Allison 1881–1981*, Butler County Tribune-Journal, Allison, Iowa, 1981.

Aplington 150th History Book Committee, *Aplington 1856–2006, 150 Years*, Aplington, Iowa, 2006.

Bowden, Fran and Marge Crandall, *150 Years of Making Memories*, West Union Sesquicentennial Committee, West Union, Iowa, 1999.

The Centennial Book Committee, *Storm Lake, Iowa Centennial: a Century of Progress 1873–1973*, Storm Lake, Iowa, 1973.

Cherokee Area Archives, Inc., *Biographical History of Cherokee County, Iowa*, W. S. Dunbar & Co., Chicago, 1889.

Cherokee Centennial Committee, *Cherokee Centennial, 1956–1956*, Cherokee, Iowa, 1956.

Crabbe, Carolyn (ed.), *Eagle Grove, Iowa 1881–1981*, Allen Printing Company, Clarion, Iowa, 1981.

DeGroote, Oliver H., *The History of the City of Humboldt*, The Humboldt

Centennial Committee, Humboldt, Iowa, 1963.

Doscher, Herman J. and Fran Bowden, *History of West Union, Iowa, 1829–1974*, West Union Quasquicentennial Committee, West Union, Iowa, 1974.

Flickinger, Robert E., *The Pioneer History of Pocahontas County, Iowa*, Fonda Times, Fonda, Iowa 1904.

Freeman, W. S., *History of Plymouth County, Iowa*, B. F. Bowen & Company, Inc., Indianapolis, Ind., 1917.

History of Fayette County, Iowa, The Western Historical Company, Chicago, 1878.

The Iowa Writers' Program of the Work Projects Administration in the State of Iowa, *Buena Vista County History, Iowa*, Storm Lake, Iowa, 1942.

Kilen, Mike, "Restauranteurs give tiny Elkader big-city flavor," *Des Moines Sunday Register*, Des Moines, Iowa, March 23, 2008.

Larson, Arthur, *LeMars - The Story of a Prairie Town*, LeMars Daily Sentinel, LeMars, Iowa, 1969.

The Parkersburg Historical Society, *Parkersburg Alumni Album (1892–2000)*, Ackley Publishing Company, Inc. Ackley, Iowa, 2000.

Powell, Harry, *The Elkader Story: A Narrative*, Elkader, Iowa.

The Storm Lake Centennial Committee, *Storm Lake Centennial Scrapbook*, Storm Lake, Iowa, 1973.

Stuart, I. L., *History of Franklin County, Iowa*, The S. J. Clarke Publishing Company, Chicago, 1914.

TIER NO. EIGHT

Britt Centennial Committee, *Recollections of Britt, Iowa, 1878–1978*, Graphic Publishing Co., Inc., Lake Mills, Iowa, 1978.

"Cowles Family Publishing Legacy" Drake University, Cowles Library <http://www.lib.drake.edu/heritage/GardnerCowlesFamily/Gardner Cowles.htm>, accessed on November 5, 2008.

Cowles, Florence Call, *Early Algona, The Story of Our Pioneers, 1854–1874*, The Register and Tribune Company, Des Moines, 1929.

Gallagher, Tim, "Memories of Perfection," *Sioux City Journal*, Sioux City, Iowa, Feb. 3, 2008.

The Garner Area Centennial Steering Committee, *Garner, Iowa, 1870–1970*, Garner, Iowa, 1970.

The Hancock County Genealogical Society, *Heritage of Hancock County, Iowa*, Curtis Media Corporation, Dallas, 1993.

Herker, Beth A., *White Clouds, Blue Waters*, Graphic Publishing Co., Inc., Lake Mills, Iowa, 1976.

Huston, Mary (ed.), *75 Years - Clay County Fair*, Spencer, Iowa, 1992.

Juhl, Paul C., *Grant Wood's Clear Lake Summer*, Brushy Creek Publishing, Iowa City, Iowa, 2007.

Kossuth County Bicentennial Commission, *History of Kossuth County Iowa, 1912–1976*, Graphic Publishing Co., Inc., Lake Mills, Iowa, 1976.

Leger, Tobi Ann Dummett, "It's Nice to See Cars On Main Street Again," *Our Iowa*, Ames, Iowa, October/November 2008.

McCarty, Dwight G., *History of Palo Alto County*, The Torch Press, Cedar Rapids, Iowa, 1910.

Nieuwenhuis, G. Nelson, *Siouxland: A History of Sioux County, Iowa*, Pluim Publishing Incorporated, Orange City, Iowa, 1983.

Peck, J. L. E., O. H. Montzheimer, William J. Miller, *Past and Present of O'Brien and Osceola Counties, Iowa*, B. F. Bowen & Company, Inc., Indianapolis, 1914.

Schmidt, Julie, *Conflagration, The Great Spencer Fire of 1931*, Spencer Alliance for a Creative Economy, Spencer, Iowa, 2006.

Sheldon Centennial Committee, *Sheldon Area Centennial, 1872–1972*, Sheldon, Iowa, 1972.

The Spencer Centennial Book Committee, *Centennial, Spencer, Iowa, 1871–1971*, Spencer, Iowa, 1971.

Umbarger, Duane R. and Ruth M., *Memories of Old Cerro Gordo: First Person and Contemporary Tales, 1850-1890*. Pioneer Museum and Historical Society of North Iowa, Mason City, Iowa, 1990.

Van Engelenhoven, E. (ed.), *The History of Orange City, Iowa, 1870–1970*, The Ad-Visor, Orange City, Iowa, 1970.

Wheeler, J. H., *History of Cerro Gordo County, Iowa*, The Lewis Publishing Company, Chicago-New York, 1910.

TIER NO. NINE

Allamakee County Heritage Book Commmittee, *The History of Allamakee County, Iowa, 1989*, Taylor Publishing Company, Dallas, 1990.

Bailey, Edwin C., *Past and Present of Winneshiek County, Iowa*, The S. J. Clarke Publishing Company, Chicago, 1913.

Bergan, Elaine Ness, *Footprints from the Past to the Present, The Story of Lake Mills, Iowa*, Stoyles Graphic Service, Lake Mills, Iowa, 1994.

Bulman, Barbara Hanson, *The Winnebago Story - Our First Quarter Century*, Winnebago Industries, Inc., Forest City, Iowa, 1983.

Commemorative Book Committee, *Spirit Lake Centennial, 1879–1979*, Spirit Lake Beacon Print, Spirit Lake, Iowa, 1979.

Davis, Robert H., *Decorah Visitor's Guide*, The Winneshiek County Historical Society, Decorah, Iowa, 1966.

Emmet County Historical Society, *History of Emmet County, Iowa*, Inter-Collegiate Press, Inc., Shawnee Mission, Kans., 1976.

Forest City Sesquicentennial Committee, *Forest City, Proud Past Bright Future*, Forest City, Iowa, 2005.

Hancock, Ellery M., *Past and Present of Alamakee County, Iowa*, The S. J. Clarke Publishing Company, Chicago, 1913.

Hanson, Cameron W. and Heather M. Hull (eds.), *Past Harvests, A History of Floyd County to 1996*, Floyd County Historical Society, Herff Jones, Inc., Marceline, Mo., 1996.

Howard County Historical Society, *The History of Howard County, Iowa*, Curtis Media Corporation, Dallas, 1989.

Iowa Writers' Program of W.P.A. sponsored by Jessie M. Parker, *Osceola County History, Iowa*, Sibley, Iowa, 1942.

Lee, Deemer, *Esther's Town*, Iowa State University Press, Ames, Iowa, 1980.

MacBridge, Thomas H., *History of Winnebago and Hancock Counties, Iowa*, Higginson Book Company, Salem, Maine, 1917.

Medema, Betty, "He's the Salt—She's the Pepper," *Our Iowa*, Ames, Iowa, December/January 2009.

Mitchell County Historical Society, *History of Mitchell County, Iowa, 1883*, The Klipto Printing Company, Mason City, Iowa, 1975.

Mitchell County Historical Society, *The Story of Mitchell County, 1851–1973*, The Klipto Printing Company, Mason City, Iowa, 1974.

Pecinovsky, Gerald G., *Protivin, The First One Hundred Years*, United States of America, 1994.

Pioneer Association of Lyon County, *History Reminiscence and Biography of Lyon County, Iowa*, Geo. A. Ogle & Co., Chicago, 1904–1905.

Smith, Paul and Lucy Jo Colby, *Rock Rapids, Iowa to 1922*, Lyon County Reporter, Rock Rapids, 1975.

Smith, R. A., *A History of Dickinson County, Iowa*, The Kenyon Printing & Mfg. Co., Des Moines, 1902.

Stahl, Myrl E. and Ellsworth Kisner (eds.), *Worth County Heritage 1853–1976*, The Klipto Printing Company, Mason City, Iowa, 1977.

Title Atlas Company, Inc. (compiled), *Atlas of Osceola County, Iowa*, Minneapolis, 1978.

Note: *Wikipedia* was accessed to help organize travel plans and was occasionally a source of information.
Barn quilt designs are from the Sac County barn quilt brochure.

Harvest Star
barn quilt